THE RADIANT MOUNTAIN

ALSO BY JOSEPH NAFT

Non-Fiction

The Sacred Art of Soul Making

Becoming You

Fiction

Restoring Our Soul

Agents of Peace

THE RADIANT MOUNTAIN

Presence to Go

JOSEPH NAFT

I.F. Publishing

I.F. PUBLISHING COMPANY
Baltimore, Maryland USA
info@ifpub.com

Copyright © 2013 by Joseph Naft

All rights reserved. No part of this publication may be reproduced, stored in or introduced into a retrieval system, or transmitted in any form, or by any means, electronic, mechanical, photocopying, recording, or otherwise, without the prior written permission of the copyright owner of this book.

ISBN: 978-0-9786109-3-7

Printed in the United States of America

CONTENTS

PREFACE • xv

Preface to Becoming You • xvii

1. Guiding Principles • 1

2. The Wonderful Gravity of Being • 3

3. Sacred Melody • 4

4. I Think I Am • 6

5. Spiritual Struggle • 8

6.0 Stages of Becoming Conscious • 10

6.1 Sensing Our Presence 12
6.2 Allowing All As Is 14
6.3 Opening to Conscious Energy. 16
6.4 Spaciousness, Peace, and Equanimity. 17
6.5 Perceiving Consciousness. 18
6.6 Inhabiting Consciousness 19
6.7 Concentrating Consciousness 21
6.8 Being Conscious 23
6.9 Beyond Consciousness 24

7.0 The Path of Right Living • 26

7.1 Care for Our Body. 28
7.2 Care for Our Family. 31
7.3 Professional Duties 32
7.4 Duty to Society and the Earth. 35
7.5 The Practice of Freedom 36
7.6 Conscience .40
7.7 Sensitive Presence. 43
7.8 Conscious Presence 46
7.9 Stabilizing Attention 48
7.10 Prayer 50
7.11 Faith and Love 53
7.12 Seeking God, The One. 55

8.0 The Path to Presence • 57

8.1 Body Sensation: Stronger 59
8.2 Body Sensation: More Frequent 61
8.3 Body Sensation: Wholeness. 64
8.4 Emotions as Emotions. 66
8.5 Thoughts as Thoughts 69
8.6 Letting Go .71
8.7 Inner Energy Flows 73
8.8 Emotional Presence 76
8.9 Cognitive Presence 78
8.10 Triune Presence 80
8.11 Conscious Presence 82
8.12 I Am Present. 84

9. Through Thick and Thin • 86

10.0 The Eightfold Path • 88

10.1 Right View 90
10.2 Right Intention 93
10.3 Right Speech 96
10.4 Right Action 99
10.5 Right Livelihood 101
10.6 Right Effort 105
10.7 Right Mindfulness 107
10.8 Right Concentration 110

11.0 The Way of Attention • 113

11.1 Scattered Attention 113
11.2 Passive Attention 115
11.3 Directed Attention 117
11.4 Focused Attention 120
11.5 Broad Attention 122
11.6 Receptive Attention 125
11.7 Participation: Being Attention 128
11.8 The Root of Attention 130
11.9 The Source of Attention 133

12.0 Stages of Freedom • 135

12.1 Illusory Freedom 138
12.2 Allure of Materiality 140
12.3 Wish for Freedom 143

12.4 Non-Dependence. 145
12.5 Transcending Personality 148
12.6 Illusion of Ego 151
12.7 Non-Separateness 156
12.8 Surrender. 159
12.9 The Sacred Partnership 162

13.0 Inner Body Development • 165

13.1 Body Contact. 165
13.2 Emotion Contact 168
13.3 Mind Contact. 170
13.4 Nourishing 172
13.5 Being. 175
13.6 Inhabiting 178
13.7 Persistence 180

14.0 The Path of Liberation • 183

14.1 Illusion of self 183
14.2 Cracks in the Illusion 186
14.3 Peace of Meditation 189
14.4 Coexistence 192
14.5 Exposing the Illusion 195
14.6 Freedom in Presence. 198
14.7 Be Your Attention 200
14.8 I Am 202
14.9 Complete Liberation 204

15.0 Obstacles on the Way • 207

15.1 Sense Desire 210
15.2 Aversion 215
15.3 Laziness 217
15.4 Hurry and Worry 220
15.5 Thoughts and Opinions 222
15.6 Greed 225
15.7 Envy 227
15.8 Fault-Finding. 228
15.9 Ego 230

16.0 Living in Presence • 233

16.1 Living in Six Senses 235
16.2 Sensing. 237
16.3 Living with Attention 239
16.4 Living in Consciousness 242
16.5 Living as I 244
16.6 Living in the Sacred Now 246
16.7 Living as the Sacred 248

17.0 Developing Will • 251

17.1 Habits: Self-Regulation 254
17.2 Keeping our Word 258
17.3 Responsibility 260
17.4 Attention 262
17.5 Frequency of Presence 264
17.6 Breadth of Presence 267

17.7 Duration of Presence. 269
17.8 Delving Deep 271
17.9 Equanimity and Non-Judging 274
17.10 Purifying Will. 276

18.0 Sacred Impulses • 279

18.1 Wish 281
18.2 Hope 283
18.3 Faith 285
18.4 Acceptance 287
18.5 Joy 289
18.6 Love 291
18.7 Wisdom 293
18.8 Participation 296

19.0 The Path of Purpose • 299

19.1 Suffering 302
19.2 Necessity. 305
19.3 Self-Improvement 307
19.4 Pleasure 311
19.5 Soul 313
19.6 Conscience. 316
19.7 Service. 318
19.8 Destiny. 321
19.9 The Divine Purpose 323

20.0 Spiritual Habits • 326

20.1 The Habit of Meditation 328

20.2 The Habit of Prayer 331
20.3 The Meta-Habit of Presence 334
20.4 The Habit of Letting Go 337
20.5 The Habit of Kindness 340
20.6 The Habit of Integrity 343
20.7 The Habit of Exploration 347

21.0 Presence in Daily Life • 349

21.1 Waiting Presence 352
21.2 Entertainment Presence 354
21.3 Task Presence 357
21.4 Listening Presence 359
21.5 Speaking Presence 361
21.6 Tool Presence 364
21.7 Walking Presence 366
21.8 Eating Presence 368
21.9 Presence of Mind 370
21.10 Presence is Mindfulness Plus 373

22.0 Growing a Spiritual Life • 376

22.1 Meditation 378
22.2 Soul Food 381
22.3 Prayer 384
22.4 Presence 386
22.5 Conscience 389
22.6 Doing and Non-Doing 391
22.7 Love 394
22.8 Contemplating the Source through Attention . 396

23.0 Learning to Be • 399

23.1 Not Judging Oneself: Acceptance 401
23.2 Not Judging Others: Acceptance. 403
23.3 Beyond Thinking. 405
23.4 Beyond Desire 408
23.5 The Wish to Be. 411
23.6 In Body, Mind, and Heart 413
23.7 Energy Management 416
23.8 Being Conscious 418
23.9 Affirming Presence. 421
23.10 Affirming the Higher 423
23.11 Flow. 426
23.12 Being in Love. 428

24.0 Who Am I? • 431

24.1 Am I My Body? 433
24.2 Am I My Thoughts? 436
24.3 Am I My Feelings?. 439
24.4 Am I Consciousness? 441
24.5 I am I 443

25.0 Developing Wisdom • 446

25.1 Regret 448
25.2 Self-Management 449
25.3 Deep Thinking 452
25.4 Natural Purity 455
25.5 Spiritual Efficacy 457

25.6 Asking 459
25.7 Conscience 461
25.8 Creative Wisdom 464

26.0 Opening our Heart • 466

26.1 Transcending Egoism 468
26.2 Love of Self 470
26.3 The Crucible of Relationship 473
26.4 Love of Nature 475
26.5 Love of Life 477
26.6 Love for All 480
26.7 Love of the Sacred 482

ABOUT THE AUTHOR • 487

PREFACE

A radiant mountain lies buried deep within us. Fulfillment in life, for those drawn to it, means uncovering and climbing that spiritual mountain as far as we can. This takes intelligence, agility, perseverance and a heart that heeds the call. We all have those and other valuable qualities, at least in potential. By exercising them we develop our soul and walk the path of spiritual transformation.

Participating in communal or individual worship, or in regular meditation can be a core foundation for our spiritual development. But what about the rest of the day or week? To turn more of our life to support our path toward the radiance, we need a spirituality on the go, a set of practices that build our soul without detracting from our appreciation of and engagement with our outer, material life. So in our daily life, in parallel with what do outwardly, we also practice presence, being, will, love, and more.

This book presents spiritual inner work exercises, each intended for a week-long effort. This is a second collection of such exercises. The first was published as *Becoming You: Cultivating Spiritual Presence*. One major difference between the two collections is that in the current volume all but a handful of the exercises are presented as part of a series, lasting anywhere from six to thirteen weeks. Each inner work series provides a context of steps that can lead toward greater depth along a particular aspect or dimension of the spirit. For a fully robust soul, we need a well-rounded spirituality, one that addresses all sides of our transformation. That is what I hope you will find in these pages, a way that enables you to live in presence while on the go in your life.

The preface to the earlier volume also applies to this volume, so it is reproduced next.

Joseph Naft
November, 2013

Preface to Becoming You

When a deeper reality begins to stir in our heart, we start looking for a way to open to it, to be embraced by it, to integrate it into our life, and to serve it. The inner landscape of the spirit, however, remains hidden from our perceptual capacities, untrained and undeveloped for that domain. But reason for hope lies within: we can adopt a way of life that awakens our latent soul, a way that addresses our deepest yearnings, a way that opens the sacred wellsprings of kindness and love. That is the way of intentional, intelligent, and heartfelt spiritual practice.

Without appropriate training and effective inner work, our spiritual aspirations do not approach fruition. And to develop the many facets of our soul, we need a variety of spiritual practices. In these pages you will find an extensive, detailed array of methods for cultivating spiritual presence, most of them applicable during our daily routines and each intended to be practiced intensively for a week.

One subset of these methods belongs to the wake-up bell category, in which we create triggers within our life to remind us to be present. Others prompt us to investigate and develop various spiritual qualities, deepen our perceptions, and expand our understanding. Through such week-long inner work, we gradually infuse the light of awareness and a sense of the sacred into every aspect of our lives. We further raise our possibilities for transformation when we incorporate these weekly practices into a comprehensive approach to spirituality, an approach that includes daily meditation, body awareness, presence, prayer, communal worship, and the like.

It is no easy matter to awaken. We habitually move through our days in a pre-programmed autopilot mode, in a cloud of thoughts and daydreams that obscures our contact with our surroundings and our self. In so doing, we accept to live half a life and create unnecessary difficulties for ourselves and others. To raise ourselves out of this situation, we turn to spiritual practice.

Even when attempting one of these weekly inner tasks, we often miss the intended moment. For example, say the task calls for us to eat consciously. After lunch we remember and suddenly realize that we just ate a meal without intentionally bringing awareness to the taste of the food. Depending on how strong our resolve was to engage in the week's inner work, that realization may cause us to feel something. At this point the whole process can careen off the rails. Though we may see that we neglected presence while eating, our next step is crucial.

Do we allow this moment of realization to turn against us by blaming ourselves, feeling self-pity, self-loathing, hopeless or discouraged by our forgetfulness and lack of presence? Much more profitable at that very moment of seeing our lack of awareness to redirect the energy thereby released to the immediate work of awakening and presence.

So... I see that I missed being present during the meal, as I had intended for this week. As soon as I see that, I begin to work at presence. The task did not awaken me during the meal, but it awakens me now. I have adapted the inner task to include not only eating consciously, but also to work at presence whenever I remember that I did not eat consciously.

This prevents a downward spiral into disheartenment. We do not try to hide from the fact of our lack of presence, indeed we take it to heart impartially. But we also use the resulting emotional energy and opportunity to further our practice in that moment. In this way, even our failures help us, transforming into presence and a reinvigorated sense of purpose, a strengthened resolve.

If we work seriously at one of these pursuits for a full week, it enters us, becoming part of our path, part of us, part of our repertoire of practice. Then long after the week has ended and we have moved on to other inner work, we may spontaneously rediscover opportunities for awakening that we established in prior weeks. We do not reject these simply because they come from earlier weeks. By all means, we step robustly into such moments with a renewal of our work of presence, heart, and service. Furthermore, we can quite profitably practice some of these tasks for much longer than a week, or intentionally return to them periodically over the years.

Because the multifaceted work of the soul is nonlinear, these weeklong inner endeavors are not organized by type or category. Instead they follow an arc of generally increasing subtlety as they cycle repeatedly through the many aspects of a balanced path, carrying us steadily deeper in our quest. Though we return to a method we have practiced before, our being has changed due to our efforts in the intervening time. So we come back to it with new understanding and the ability to carry it further than before. Nevertheless, you need not stick to the order presented and may find profit in skipping around within the book. Each theme stands both on its own and in relation to the all the others.

These weeklong exercises supplement our ongoing practices of regular periods of meditation, prayer, and the efforts of sensing our inner energy body and working toward presence during our daily routines. Meditation, prayer, sensing, and presence form the foundation of our path, with weekly inner tasks providing a focus, illuminating our outlook, broadening our perceptions, and leading us to discover new opportunities for practice.

As our inner work progresses, our days grow replete with spiritual practice. We train ourselves to practice in many ways and many situations. Slowly but, if we persevere, inevitably, our entire life transforms. We enter the beneficent, loving Reality that we seek.

THE RADIANT MOUNTAIN

1. Guiding Principles

Without principles we would wander rudderless through our life. Too often we forget whatever principles we do have and engage in the expedient, following the path of least resistance. This raises questions. What guides our myriad choices in life? Within the bounds of morality and societal norms, within the requirements of duty to our body, our family, and our society, and within the scope of our interests, we still enjoy an enormous range of choices and opportunities laid before us. So how do we choose what to do, what not to do, where to go, when, and with whom? Our principles, or lack thereof, fundamentally shape our choices and our life.

Our spiritual pursuit offers and requires a relatively clear principle to guide our choices. We can judge by asking ourselves questions like: does what I am about to do help me awaken, does it prevent me from awakening, or neither? Does what I am about to do serve others, damage others, or neither. And then we do what helps us awaken and/or serves others, we avoid what prevents us from awakening and/or damages others, and we make use of the neutral.

As a simple but important example, when we have a spare, not-fully-occupied moment, do we turn to our inner work, to the practice of body awareness through sensing, to the practice of presence? The opportunity to make this choice arises at many moments every day. Does the guiding principle embodied by our spiritual practice live in us strongly enough to penetrate our choice of what to do in these small, "spare" moments? Without the principle that values spiritual practice, or with a weak embodiment of it, these opportune moments flit by us unnoticed and squandered.

Similarly, do the principles of integrity, responsibility, kindness, and respect affect our actions? Unless such principles live in us, we miss the moment that calls for kindness and respect or we fail to act responsibly and with integrity.

To the extent they guide our choices, our principles intimately connect with our will and thus define us. We may see, particularly in difficult times, that our principles are our most important asset. If, to apply our principles however, we find we must try to remember them as we go about our day, then there is a gap between us and our principles. The closer and more central a principle is to us, the more it lives in us without any special effort to remember it. If there is a gap, we can narrow it by intentionally and frequently remembering and abiding by the principle. So if we practice kindness or presence, integrity or respect, then these principles grow in strength in us, effectively shaping who we are. We create ourselves by what we feed in us.

On the other hand, we do make choices, non-randomly. So something guides us. The question is what and does it need to be changed? Are our actual, effective values what we wish them to be? Our actual principles may be fractured and conflicting. But by supporting and attending to the ones of true value to us, we become ourselves.

For this week, examine how you make choices and decisions. What are your guiding principles? Do you apply them in your daily life? And to what extent does your spiritual pursuit itself guide your choices?

2. The Wonderful Gravity of Being

Where am I? We take this question not in the physical sense of our bodily location in space, but in the inner sense of "where am I centered now?" Usually our center is either someplace other than in our self or it is non-existent. Something or someone attracts our attention and we fly out of our self to that thing or person. Our center shifts outside of us and we abdicate our presence to its opposite, to absence from our self, to being at the mercy of each passing attraction, each ephemeral whim. Our body becomes an empty shell with no one at home.

Notice, for example, whether you are drained of energy when you go shopping at a large store or mall, or go to a museum or a fair. All that you see continually draws you out of yourself. How different might it be to stay centered and let the visual impressions come to you rather that you going out to lose yourself in them.

When your thoughts automatically range into past or future or to some other place, your center goes with them, out of the here and now, out of your presence which quickly evaporates along with your inner energies of sensation and consciousness. How different might it be to stay centered in yourself and let the thoughts and images pass through your awareness rather than you going out to disappear with them?

Sensing your body reminds you of where to be — here in this body. Though the deeper levels of the spirit lie beyond where and when, time and space, we would do very well indeed to live most of our time present in our body. Staying present within our body, being in our self creates in us the wonderful gravity of being.

Our developing inner body gives weight to our presence, though not in the sense of heaviness. Like a planet or a star, presence bends our inner space into a center of stability, a center that can maintain itself, our center of gravity. Being in yourself, being present creates a local sphere of influence that stabilizes your energies, your being. Then you can perceive, act, and interact from yourself. This being in yourself is not a matter of holding, of holding back, of holding together. It is a matter of opening into presence, opening into being here. Residing in your inner home, in your own stable center of gravity, you live each moment fully. And without holding them back, your energies no longer spill out wastefully — they just naturally gravitate to the center of your being.

For this week, live in your center of gravity, in the center of your being.

3. Sacred Melody

We all know that music has a remarkable power to affect our emotions. Sacred music, most often in the form of sung or chanted prayers, serves in every religion to move our heart toward the Divine. Such music partly accounts for the unreasonable efficacy of communal worship. But sacred music also proves profoundly effective in solitary and outwardly silent contemplative prayer.

To bring inner music to meditative prayer, we can inwardly and silently intone a sacred melody. The key is to use a melody that opens our heart and mind, and disposes us toward the Divine. This is, in part, a matter of training. We prepare by finding a melody that we have heard for many years, one we associate with prayer or religious ritual, one that moves us. If no such melody comes forward, we can explore more widely, even into classical or popular music, for a melody that touches our heart.

And then, when we reach the deepest part of our meditation, where we turn toward the Divine, we silently intone the melody in our mind-heart and allow it to suffuse and open our heart. We let the melody guide us into the sacred. As we continue to work in this way, the melody develops into a sure and swift representative of the sacred, having an immediate effect of drawing us upward, in joy, in love, and in meaning.

Repeated practice builds in us an association between the melody and the sacred. Eventually we can invoke the melody at any time, even when not in meditation or contemplative prayer, and it draws us upward. We ascend on melodious wings and the sacred descends into us. Higher energies and a purifying action on our will come down through the melody.

Having established the melody in meditation or contemplative prayer, use it from time to time during the day. But keep it special. Turn to it only in moments where you can give yourself to it completely. And, of course, engage it to turn a portion of your meditation into contemplative prayer, to help you reach deeper into your heart, deeper into the spirit.

We learn most sacred melodies with words. But the melody can stand apart from words. It may be even more powerful for us without words, because that leaves out all the associations we have with those words and it leaves out the language center of our brain. The sacred is well beyond language, well beyond thought. But a sacred melody, without words, can bypass our ordinary conceptual mind and put us directly into contact with the higher.

Work with only one or at most two melodies, so as to focus your training, focus the wordless meaning. Let the melody raise you up, into contact with the world of Divine light. With practice, the melody becomes a key to your heart, a key to the door of the sacred.

For this week, allow your sacred melody to enter and open your heart.

4. I Think I Am

We know ourselves most intimately through our thoughts. Our memories and concerns shape our thoughts, while current experience calls forth responses in the form of thoughts, often driven by or driving our emotions. Our thoughts mull over and ruminate, comment and plan, consider and choose, rehearse and recall. If we ask ourselves "who am I?" we may not have a sure answer. But our unexamined, operating definition of ourselves probably goes something like this: (1) "I am my thoughts."

A slightly more accurate definition would be: (2) "I am the one who thinks all the thoughts that flow through my mind." More accurate still is (3) "I am the one who is aware of thoughts flowing through my mind, some of which I intentionally think, but the vast majority of which arise automatically and conditionally by habit, association, and reaction, and without my intention."

Yet because we believe the first definition, or in our better moments the second, we give our thoughts a preeminent position in our inner world that allows them to masquerade as who we are, or very close to who we are. That is how we live: as flesh and blood thinking machines, with our true I either entirely absent, or identified with and entrapped by our everflowing stream of thoughts. But thoughts, most assuredly, are not us.

The easiest level to tease out of this illusion that we are our thoughts is consciousness. The term "stream of consciousness" usually really means the stream of thoughts as the content of consciousness. Of course consciousness has many other contents as well, such as all the other sensory experiences of our body-sense, vision, hearing, smell, and taste. To see our thoughts for what they are, we need to step outside their stream and stand in awareness itself, in consciousness, in the cognizant stillness that lies between and beneath thoughts, between and beneath all sensory experience.

Seen from the earth, clouds obscure the sky and substitute for it. But the sky can see that passing clouds do not change its own nature.

Meditation, in its quieter moments, opens us to the reality of the cognizant stillness of consciousness. At first it is not so easy to recognize because it seems so empty, like nothing at all, just a lack of content to experience. But pure consciousness, a very fine yet substantial inner energy, is the context, the container of experience. Its very independence of content makes it complete and whole.

In meditating, allow your body and your thoughts to relax. Notice the spaciousness between and beneath thoughts and sensations. Relax your grip on being your body or your thoughts, and move into that spacious awareness, into your body of consciousness. See your thoughts arising on their own and passing through your consciousness. See that you are not your thoughts.

While it is more true to define yourself as consciousness, even this stops short of the reality of your I, your will. There are in us the one who sees, the energy of consciousness that enables the seeing, and that which is seen, in this case our thoughts. We take a significant step toward liberation when we stop confusing the object, thoughts, with the subject, the one, the I that sees. To realize that we are not our thoughts, and that they do not necessarily speak for us, is to free ourselves of a heavy burden.

For this week, step out of your thought stream and into consciousness, and see that your thoughts are not you.

5. Spiritual Struggle

"...resist not evil..."[1]

Spiritual struggle, in many of its forms, serves to purify and develop our soul. There is first and foremost the necessary struggle with those habits that are obstacles or severe limitations on our inner work. Among the physical ones of these we can certainly include any use of tobacco, any non-medicinal or recreational use or abuse of drugs, excessive eating and excessive alcohol consumption. All these sap the inner strength, the energies we need for our work.

The destructive emotions, like anger, also fall into this category. Indulging in anger chews up our energies, damages our relationships, and leads to more anger. When we see anger arising in ourselves, we feel compassion for ourselves and, not wanting to harm ourselves by indulging it, we let it go.

Each of us needs always to look to see the ways we damage our possibilities and diminish our presence, and struggle with those ways. Not rejecting, but embracing and reclaiming the whole of ourselves, seeking to heal what needs healing.

And for the longer term, we struggle to be present more often, for longer, and more strongly. Another continuing struggle is the search to deepen our contact with the sacred.

Struggle itself, however, can become an obstacle in at least two ways. If we allow our spiritual struggle to devolve into an inner war, if we demonize what we are struggling against, we weaken ourselves. Spiritual struggle is not about defeating an inner enemy. That would just cut off a part of us. Rather we seek to transform our recalcitrant habits and destructive tendencies so that we can integrate all our parts, all our disparate and conflicting drives, desires and wishes, into the

---

1   Matthew 5:39

single whole of our unified being.

The second misappropriation of struggle arises from the fact that our motivations are mixed. We struggle with ourselves not only to develop spiritually, but also to feed our vanity, to think better of ourselves. This latter motivation, to remake ourselves in our own idealized image, serves our ego, subverts our struggle, and builds up our self-centered, self-aggrandizing illusory I. We seek not to reform, but to transform, to bring all our parts within the purview of our higher self, into service of the sacred. This also protects us from the kind of self-pitying, self-critical dejection that comes from failures of ego-serving struggles. When we fail in our spiritual struggle, we just get back up and go at it again, remembering that our purpose is to heal and reintegrate — not to defeat.

So what is the actual inner experience of struggle? First we notice the destructive or limiting impulse arising in us, in real time. We see how that impulse pulls on us, pulls us to do something we'd be better off not doing, or pulls us not to do something we'd be better off doing. Either way, the pull is definitely there, and sometimes powerful.

At this point, three possible paths open to us. First, we can succumb to the path of least resistance, indulge the impulse, and suffer the inevitable consequences, the negative impact on our inner work. No struggle here.

The second possibility is to fight the urge, to raise within ourselves an opposing force, an opposing intention to stop the destructive impulse. As noble and right as it seems, this strategy tends to backfire in several ways, even when successful. It causes the destructive impulse to grow even stronger in response to the fight. If the destructive impulse loses today, it most certainly will return to fight again another day. The fight splits our inner world between the two sides. While the tension between the two can temporarily create some energy, ultimately the split weakens us by perpetuating the inner division, the non-wholeness. And finally, the fight strengthens our ego, through the arrogance of victory or the self-criticism and self-pity of defeat.

The third possible response to a destructive impulse is to let it go compassionately. We inwardly relax in front of it. We let the destructive impulse be there, but we do not act on it. And we do not fight. We do not raise a loud and obvious No. We just see the impulse, see that it is part of us, choose not to act on it out of service to the sacred, let the impulse be there, relax with compassion toward this destructive part, give it room to dissipate, and let it wane until it vanishes, merged into our being. This seeing our destructive impulse and relaxing with compassion for it, compassion for ourself, reintegrates and heals us. This is the path toward wholeness.

For this week, notice a habit or tendency that limits your capacity for, or diverts you from, presence. Ask yourself whether you should struggle with it and how. And then work to stop or diminish that habit or tendency. Keep in mind the spiritual purpose of your struggle.

6.0 Stages of Becoming Conscious

Some may find the title of this inner work series, "Stages of Becoming Conscious," puzzling. Other than when sleeping in bed at night, aren't we already conscious? In the special way we shall use the term, the answer to this question is no: we rarely rise into the full experience of consciousness. In our better moments, we do rise to a step below full consciousness: sensitive awareness of the content of experience, in contact with our body, mind, and surroundings. Usually, however, we operate at a level below sensitive awareness, automatically, as if wearing blinders and responding to life in a robotic, programmed fashion. These three levels of living, the robotic, the sensitive, and the conscious, can be thought of as non-conscious, half-conscious, and fully conscious, respectively. A particular quality of inner energy characterizes each, namely the automatic energy, the sensitive energy, and the conscious energy.

The practice of full body awareness, of sensing our whole body, along with sensitive awareness of our thoughts and emotions, enables our transition from automatic, robotic living. This inner work series, "Stages of Becoming Conscious," addresses the next major transition, from sensitive awareness to being fully conscious.

The conscious energy forms the all-pervasive, underlying substrate of awareness, the pure, cognizant stillness that provides the context for all our experience. To enter the conscious energy is to emerge from time into timelessness, from body into spirit. The conscious energy marks a spiritual threshold, as the lowest of the sacred, higher energies. So while the conscious energy remains several steps removed from the Ultimate, it is nevertheless an important and necessary part of our path toward the Divine. To enter the conscious energy is to enter a high world and a gateway to the even higher, sacred worlds.

We will study the transition from sensitive awareness to being fully conscious in a nine-stage series of inner work practices, as follows:

1. Sensing Our Presence
2. Allowing All As Is
3. Opening to Conscious Energy
4. Spaciousness, Peace, and Equanimity
5. Perceiving Consciousness
6. Inhabiting Consciousness
7. Concentrating Consciousness
8. Being Conscious
9. Beyond Consciousness

In the coming weeks, we will take up each of these stages in turn, working to develop a new perception of consciousness and learning how to live in it. At first these should be practiced as a nine-part, formal, seated meditation. But later, as we gain the experience, the understanding, and the taste of it, we can also take these practices of consciousness into our ordinary, daily life.

By way of preparation, for this week, please return to the practice of full-body sensation, of being in direct perceptual, visceral contact with the whole of your body. You can practice this while seated in formal meditation and while going about your usual daily activities. Whole-body sensing sets the stage for all that will follow in this series on becoming conscious.

6.1 Sensing Our Presence
(Stages of Becoming Conscious: Part 1 of 9)

Our springboard to becoming conscious is full sensitive awareness. And full sensitive awareness begins with our body. A very important and readily available way to upgrade our awareness consists in sensing our body, or as a Thai Buddhist meditation master put it in 1936, we focus on "the inner sense of the form of the body."[2] As we work to establish our attention in this inner sense of our body, to develop our direct, unmediated, visceral perception of it, the sensitive energy gradually builds and collects in our body, drawn there by our attention. This energy of sensation enables us to be aware of our body. Furthermore, the sensitive energy forms the lower part of our

2   Ajaan Lee Dhammadharo, *The Craft of the Heart*, trans. by Thanissaro Bikkhu, (printed in 1982 for free distribution by: The Abbot, Wat Asokaram, Samut Prakaan 10280, Thailand), p. 114

soul. The practice of sensing our body can grow stronger and stronger, as well as more constant, and has many beneficial ramifications for our spiritual path, and for our ability to live well, to live a full, productive, and satisfying life.

We begin with placing and holding our attention in one of our hands or feet. Once we can feel the aliveness of the sensitive energy collecting there, we move on to sensing entire limbs, then torso and head, and eventually to sensing our whole body. We sense the total body, not just the surface, although we do not intentionally focus on particular internal organs so as not to interfere with their instinctive functioning.

Sensing the whole body helps make us whole inwardly as well and leads naturally toward the full experience of consciousness. That wholeness gives this method an advantage over methods that focus on a part of the body, such as breath awareness. However breath awareness, just because it is more tightly focused and because the breath is always moving, has its own advantages. Each method has a time, place, and purpose. For example, we might begin a period of meditation with focused breath awareness to calm our mind and collect our energies, and then move on toward sensing the whole body.

The sensitive energy also enables us to be in direct contact with our thoughts and emotions. Placing our attention on our thoughts we become aware of them as thoughts, we become aware of their meaning. Rather than allowing our thoughts to think us, we can think our thoughts. The former happens with the automatic energy and the latter with the sensitive energy. We can focus our thoughts on a problem or situation, thinking logically about it. We can visualize and think in images. Or we can simply be aware of our automatically self-generating associative stream of thoughts as thoughts. All this is due to the sensitive energy entering our thoughts. We combine this sensitive thought awareness with our practice of sensing our body and we become even more whole.

Further, we extend our sensitive awareness to being in

contact with our emotions as they arise and unfold. We notice how their feeling tone colors our awareness. We notice how the emotion manifests in our body, perhaps with tightness in our chest, a quickened breath, a particular expression on our face, or a changed posture. We notice how the emotion drives our thought patterns and vice versa. We have some choice, a modicum of control over our emotions. All this is due to the sensitive energy in our emotions.

With all three operating, with sensitive awareness of body, of thought, and of emotion, we move into a different level of wholeness and presence, a breadth of awareness that prepares us to open to the conscious energy, to being conscious. For this week, please practice whole body sensing, awareness of your thoughts as thoughts, and awareness of your emotions and their effects. We can call this practice sensing our presence.

6.2 Allowing All As Is
(Stages of Becoming Conscious: Part 2 of 9)

Having established ourselves, at least temporarily, in a state of sensing our presence, we move into a practice that can be described easily, yet profoundly affects the whole of our life, the whole of our spiritual path. That practice is letting go, non-doing, accepting, relaxing, not just our body, heart, and mind, but our very self.

In meditation, after sensing our presence, we do nothing. We just sit. We give up trying to shape or manipulate our inner experience to achieve some state. We do not even do non-doing. We just sit. For that time, we set down the burden of being who we think we are and doing what we want to do — or think we should do. When any thoughts arise, we let them come and we let them go. When emotions, physical sensations, sights, or sounds arise, we let them come and we let them go. We do not even intentionally observe or pay attention to what's going on. We just sit and do nothing. We do not try to be the one who is doing nothing. We do not be anything at all. We allow our life and experience to be as it is and as it changes, effortlessly. We release our grip.

Perhaps we grow tired, nearly falling asleep. So be it. We just sit, allowing the tiredness and sleepiness to be as they are, to unfold naturally. The fact that we have preceded the allowing practice with establishing a robust sense of our presence prevents the letting go from lapsing into an ordinary dreamy reverie. Something more is there. Eventually we find that, like all other things, the tiredness and sleepiness pass, leaving us alert and relaxed with our selfing selfness diminished — no experiencer, just experiencing. No one who is letting go, no one who is accepting, no one who is rejecting, just the ever-changing contents of the field of awareness.

This relaxed letting go allows our sensitive energies to settle into their place, to form the natural foundation for consciousness. The experience of our body, our mind, and our emotions flows vivid and rich. And our attitude of allowing it all to be as it is removes the hooks, the stickiness that usually sweeps us away with the stream of experience. The layer of sensitive energy stands smoothed and ready to receive and reveal consciousness.

The practice of letting go also trains us in a deeper way by preparing us for a different experience of who we truly are. It shows us we are not our thoughts, our body, our emotions, or our habitual patterns of acting and reacting.

For this week, in your meditation, after establishing a full sense of your presence, practice doing nothing, not becoming attached to the content of experience, not manipulating, and not even trying to observe or to be.

6.3 Opening to Conscious Energy
(Stages of Becoming Conscious: Part 3 of 9)

In a state of non-clinging, with a full sense of our presence, our inner stage is set for opening to consciousness, to the conscious energy. In fact consciousness is already here, we need only recognize and step back, into it. But for that, it helps to have some idea of what consciousness is. That idea can match up with our experience and expedite our learning the way into consciousness.

Consciousness is not the content of experience. We see a sight or notice a thought. These and all the other sensory impressions populate our awareness with a seamless layer of content, like the images on a movie, television, or computer screen. And we typically are so preoccupied with this ongoing flow our senses bring us, that the larger context of the screen itself escapes us. Sensory experience churns our sensitive energy and keeps us enthralled by the foreground content of awareness, by all that we see and hear, taste and smell, touch and think.

But when we sit quietly in meditation, our sensitive energy settles and everything slows down, even to the point of gaps opening between thoughts. Moving through those silent gaps, we enter consciousness, the backdrop of experience, the cognizant stillness, the knowing substrate, the pure awareness behind and beneath sensory impressions, behind and beneath our thoughts.

The practice of sitting still and closing our eyes, of relaxing and allowing, quiets our mind and reduces the flow of sensory perceptions, enabling us to see, to understand, to be in the consciousness that surrounds that flow, that surrounds us. By repeatedly opening to stillness in this way, we begin to acquire the subtle taste of the conscious energy.

Later, with practice, we discover the ability to open to

consciousness even in the midst of activity. But for this week, please practice opening to consciousness in the stillness of meditation.

6.4 Spaciousness, Peace, and Equanimity
(Stages of Becoming Conscious: Part 4 of 9)

In letting go and allowing all to be as it is, we develop equanimity and peace. In opening to the conscious energy, we touch the spacious stillness of consciousness. Thus, meditatively abiding in consciousness deepens our non-identification and ushers us into a world of spaciousness, peace, and equanimity. These are the hallmarks by which consciousness announces itself to us, especially in sitting meditation. But even in the midst of activity, once we have learned the way of sensing our presence and letting go into the cognizant stillness that surrounds us, we may enter consciousness. We can be in spaciousness, peace, and equanimity while we go about our daily doings.

Inner spaciousness derives from the vastness of consciousness without boundaries. Like being on a mountaintop, this big-sky mind enjoys an unobstructed view in every direction, an expansive perspective on the unalloyed background of all experience. With no boundaries between inside and outside, we enter an open and undivided field of awareness. Thoughts no longer bounce off the narrow walls of our mind to attract our attention, but instead dissipate into the distance, leaving us in quiet joy and contentment. In this unlimited inner space, we have no need or desire to stake out territory and call it mine.

Inner peace derives from the timeless quality of consciousness. In the vastness of pure consciousness, nothing happens. Consciousness is. Time disappears, replaced by the timeless wonder of eternity. In our practice of presence, however, where sensitive awareness is superimposed on consciousness, time and eternity coexist. Events happen, but in the context of timeless consciousness, eternity imparts its inherent flavor of peace throughout. We can just be, without feeling driven to do anything. However, if we so choose, we can do what we wish to do while inwardly staying in touch with the deep, still pool of peace that is consciousness.

Equanimity grows as we realize that consciousness is not centered in us, in any particular person or self: no exclusivity and no preferred viewpoint. No one can truthfully say "this is my consciousness" for consciousness has no center. This opens us to a particular type of unity with others, the unity of shared consciousness. In consciousness we learn to step beyond the narrow confines of self-centeredness. If I am not my personality and not my ego, then I can relax into equanimity and stop trying to impose my narrow will on life. I can stop desperately grasping at what I want and avoiding what I do not want.

So the qualities of spaciousness, peace, and equanimity exemplify some of the benefits and characteristics of consciousness. For this week, allow these qualities to guide you deeper into the experience of consciousness.

6.5 Perceiving Consciousness
(Stages of Becoming Conscious: Part 5 of 9)

As we grow familiar with the spaciousness, peace, and equanimity of consciousness, we come to recognize the taste of that still pool of cognizance that is the foundation of all our experience, the very medium of all perception. We start to be aware of consciousness itself, not just how it affects us. We notice the clear, almost viscous, mind-like substance of consciousness, more akin to space than to ordinary gases, liquids, or solids. We notice where it is: behind our thoughts, behind our ordinary sensory perceptions. We notice its all-pervasiveness, without boundaries, and without a center. We notice its unchanging sameness that is more than alive. We see that consciousness is always available: we need only make ourselves available to it. With all these remarkable qualities, it is little wonder that so many who enter pure consciousness mistake it for God.

Why does the perception of consciousness matter to us? First, consciousness gives us a foothold in a truly spiritual realm beyond space and time. Second, consciousness gives us a new level of inner freedom. Third, consciousness proves crucial to the integration of our will into a unified I, which allows us to be fully ourselves. The ability to perceive consciousness itself shows us the way more deeply into consciousness. We start to become able to work with consciousness itself directly. And by understanding consciousness we move toward the possibility of going beyond it, into the higher spiritual realms.

Like noticing the air or the space around us, we can turn our perceptive faculty toward the cognizant substrate of experience, toward the still pool of consciousness that surrounds us, inside and out. When meditative stillness flowers into spaciousness, peace, and equanimity, we can look to the conscious energy that supports that experience. We can notice the pristine, mind-like substance of our awareness in that moment. And in so doing, we touch and explore consciousness itself. The more we do that, the more we acquire the taste of consciousness, and the more we are able to open to consciousness in the midst of our day. As the fundamental energy of presence, the perception of conscious energy leads us directly toward a new, more vivid, warm-hearted, and satisfying life.

For this week, explore the taste of consciousness itself.

6.6 Inhabiting Consciousness
(Stages of Becoming Conscious: Part 6 of 9)

Inhabiting our life means intentionally and actively being the one who is living it, being the one who is present here and now, being the one who is experiencing the impressions our senses are bringing us now. We feel that "I am living, presencing, experiencing." Being the one who does what you do means more than being aware of what you are doing. It means having an immediate sense of agency, of being the agent, the decider, the chooser, the intender, the actor of our actions, and the liver of our life. It means being our attention.

This practice leads us to feel that "I am conscious." The intentional and ongoing act of being the one who is here attracts and entrains the conscious energy. Well-knowing by this stage the taste of consciousness, we can open to it not only in meditation but in the midst of our day. We open to it and occupy it. That cognizant stillness of consciousness is "where" we feel ourselves to be. It is at this level of the conscious energy that we can feel our I most distinctly.

When we practice inhabiting our body, we fill our whole body, our inner body of sensation, with our intention and attention, with our will-to-be. In the same way, the practice of inhabiting consciousness means filling consciousness with our intention, our will-to-be, our I. We occupy this whole place of pure awareness, this vast spaciousness, this context of all experience, even as the usual torrent of sensory perceptions continues unabated. We stay here, at home, in the peace of consciousness in the midst of the pleasant breezes and powerful storms of our life.

So we practice by inhabiting our life, by being the one who is doing what we are doing. Then we can notice the conscious energy and inhabit that as well. Thus we can live on two levels at once: in the level of sensitive energy, sensory impressions, and our physical and mental actions and occupations, where we can say "I experience," and in the level of pure awareness, presence, and consciousness, where we can say a wholehearted "I am."

We can first explore this practice most easily during sitting meditation sessions. Then we gradually move our practice of inhabiting consciousness into increasingly challenging situations: while going for a walk, while watching, while listening, while doing simple chores like washing dishes or sweeping.

For this week, practice inhabiting consciousness.

6.7 Concentrating Consciousness
(Stages of Becoming Conscious: Part 7 of 9)

Concentrating consciousness means accumulating the conscious energy in a particular individual or group. The group approach to concentrating consciousness generally seems easier to put into practice than the individual approach. However, because we are not often, perhaps once a week if we're very lucky, in the type of group situation that concentrates consciousness, we also can profit enormously from studying how to work at this on our own.

First, though, how can a group can concentrate consciousness? Communal prayer is the paradigm. The more each member of the community enters into the common prayer, the more support each receives from the others, and the more consciousness embraces them all. This positive feedback loop of simultaneous and proximate communal prayer offers profound help to all the participants, quickly bringing them into a deeper state of prayer than their own contribution would seem to justify.

That help derives from the shared purpose and shared focus, the confluence of separate wills into a common will, which gives the conscious energy a broad base of support among the worshippers, greatly multiplying the result. That broad base opens an umbrella of the stillness and peace of consciousness over the whole group. The same holds for meditation and other spiritually-oriented practices performed in a group. There is a type of spiritual magic at work here, reminiscent of Christ's saying: *For where two or three are gathered together in my name, there am I in the midst of them.*³ It seems magical because we are usually not directly aware of the workings of the conscious energy, even during communal spiritual practice. Nevertheless, the whole emerges as much more than the sum of the individual parts.

On our own, we can concentrate consciousness in many ways. The first grouping of these ways includes any practice in which we focus our attention on some object, inner or outer. Collecting, applying, and holding our attention draws the conscious energy into the effort and into our being.

A typical and effective example is the Buddhist practice of breath awareness with counting. Here's how. Place your attention on the sensations of your breathing, wherever you find them most prominent: the nostrils, the upper chest, or the abdomen. Do not change the breathing, just bring your attention to it and keep with it in a relaxed manner. Mentally count the breaths from one to ten, and then start over at one. The counting is secondary: keep your primary attention on the sensations of the breath. Between the continuous breath awareness and the counting, you are making a sufficient demand on your attention to leave little or none left over to stray into other thoughts. But if and when you do lose count, start over at one. When you can stay with the breath continuously for five or six cycles of ten, you can safely drop the counting and just be with the breath or move on to the rest of your exercise or meditation. You may find the nostrils most effective for this exercise, because its smaller area takes more focus to stay continuously attentive to it. The end result is a state of more consciousness.

Once we are aware of consciousness itself, we can draw more of it directly into our being by reaching out with our will, with our attention and intention, into the field of consciousness and willing the conscious energy into us. This is a subtle exercise, requiring as a prerequisite familiarity and contact with the

3   Matthew 18:20

formless substance of cognizant stillness, the endlessly adaptive, clear, and pliant stuff of consciousness itself. The effort is akin to pulling space itself into us. A strong presence can exert a gravitational attraction as it were on consciousness, making us even more conscious.

Finally, deep prayer creates consciousness in us. The high energies, beyond consciousness, that we open to in profound prayer, cascade into us, blending with our sensitive energy to create more of the conscious energy. This particular transformation of energies gives us the feeling that participating in this action is a key element of our role in life, our true role as human beings. The more we enter consciousness, the more the people around us can share in its peace.

For this week, practice concentrating consciousness.

6.8 Being Conscious
(Stages of Becoming Conscious: Part 8 of 9)

The principal distinction between this stage of Being Conscious and the earlier stages of Becoming Conscious consists in our being more established, more stable in consciousness, at least temporarily. Instead of needing to actively inhabit consciousness, we can just reside in it. We know it well enough and have enough facility with it to move into consciousness at will and stay in it for a time. And we do so.

Furthermore, we now realize a deeper reason that consciousness brings peace and equanimity, namely the changed perspective it affords. Recall flying in an airplane, gazing out the window at the towns and farms below. The everyday cares of life seem to lose their immediacy in that high perspective. So it is with consciousness: we see our life from a different perspective, one that raises us out of identification with all that goes on, outwardly and inwardly. We see external events, sensory perceptions, thoughts, and emotional reactions for what they are: only a part of the whole fabric of life. Our will, our I, freed from our usual urgent identifications, rests in awareness, in peace and equanimity. While some inner or outer events may still drag us for a time into identification with them, we are able to reestablish our stability and conscious perspective.

In being conscious, we are consciously conscious: we clearly know that we are conscious. Now when we enter consciousness, we not only enter a world of timeless peace, but we also know this peace as an inherent part of our endowment as human beings. Consciousness is no longer just a new quality of experience, but one more natural to us, though still and always new.

We recognize consciousness as spacious enough to embrace not only our self but all people and all life. That changes how we relate. The wholeness of consciousness reveals the wholeness of all life. Seeing that we share this one substance with other living beings shows our differences to be superficial. We feel less separate, closer to our self, to our near and dear ones, and even to strangers.

The core energy of presence is consciousness. When we can be conscious, we can be present, although the latter also involves our will, our I being the one who is present. Of course, if we reside in presence, this action alone brings consciousness with it. So we discover an intimate, symbiotic relationship between our I and the conscious energy.

For this week, practice resting in pure awareness, practice being conscious intermittently as you go about your day.

6.9 Beyond Consciousness
(Stages of Becoming Conscious: Part 9 of 9)

Familiarity and facility with the conscious energy brings a measure of freedom and peace. In its quiet way this causes a revolution in our inner life by releasing us from total dependence on and identification with the contents of our mind, with our thoughts and emotions and sensory impressions. This freedom feels like the attainment of a goal, perhaps *The Ultimate Goal*. But while it is a great and important stage on the way, it is not *The Ultimate Goal*. There are at least two levels of spiritual realities beyond consciousness.

The first is the World of Sacred Light. By sustained abiding in consciousness, it can become porous, allowing the high and blissful energy of the Sacred Light to trickle through to us, a trickle that can widen into a torrent. Knowing consciousness, we can begin to realize its limits and reach into a dimension beyond those limits, into the truly sacred. How to do this? We can only find the way on our own, by exploring our own inner world and groping with a pure heart beyond consciousness toward the Light. Contemplative prayer also offers a way into the Light. As we orient ourselves toward the Divine through prayer, we open to and are touched by the World of Sacred Light. And as we become able to open to that world and receive the creative energy of the Sacred Light, that energy works in us to create even more of the conscious energy in a positive feedback loop that directly contributes to the spiritual ecosystem of our planet — a profound act of service.

Ultimately, we seek beyond even the World of Sacred Light, to move toward the One, the Unity behind all diversity, the Sacred Source, the Prime Mover of all. We reach beyond all that we have encountered before, totally immersing ourselves in prayer and in surrender to the One to Whom we pray. Urgently and passionately, quietly and persistently we offer the whole of our self, the very core of our self in service to and in begged-for unity with that only and unique One. We return again and again, patiently and insistently presenting ourselves before the Truth, the Source of Love, knocking on the door that separates us from That. Though we do not know where that door is or how to reach it, we keep going nevertheless, making ourselves available to be found by that Great Heart of the

World.

So our practice in the Stages of Becoming Conscious leads us beyond consciousness, well beyond consciousness. For this week, reinvigorate your own inner work of seeking the way beyond consciousness. The deeper you go, the greater the level of your service thereby.

7.0 The Path of Right Living

How should I live my life? We all face this fundamental and ongoing question. Religions and spiritual paths offer at least partial answers or guidelines that leave most of the specifics to us. One such set of guidelines can be found in the comprehensive, simple, and powerful teaching of Right Living[4] presented by the Indian sage known as the Shivapuri Baba (1826-1963). The following is inspired by and adapted from that teaching.

Right Living means fulfilling our responsibilities in three broad areas: physical duty, being duty, and spiritual duty. Physical duty refers to our outer responsibilities. It means to act with intelligence, dexterity, and excellence for our body, for our family, for our profession, for society, and for the Earth. Being duty addresses our responsibility to develop our inner life, to develop a strong heart-mind-character-being, through wisdom, presence, and virtue. Spiritual duty consists of directly seeking God, seeking the One, the Truth that transcends both inner and outer.

4   Bennett, J. G. with Manandhar, Thakur Lal, *Long Pilgrimage: The Life and Teaching of Sri Govindananda Bharati, Known as The Shivapuri Baba* (London: Turnstone Books, 1965)

Living rightly brings satisfaction, serenity, and peace. Satisfaction derives from living our external life with intelligence, dexterity, and excellence. Serenity comes from attaining inner freedom and living by conscience. And peace comes from approaching and ultimately seeing God. Lack of progress toward any one of these limits the others. If our outer life is not right, it will keep calling us away from developing our inner life and from seeking God. If our inner life is not right, the ongoing inner turmoil will divert us from bringing the full powers of our intelligence to bear on our outer life and we will not have the inner stability to seek God. And if we do not seek God or the Truth, the lack of meaning will invade our external life in the world as well as our inner life.

The three duties also have positive synergies. The being duty of living by conscience supports our physical duties by making us honest and sensitive and enabling us to recognize excellence. The being duty of presence supports our physical duties by giving us the inner space to bring our intelligence to bear on our outer duties. Being duty gives us the inner strength and purity needed for our spiritual duty of seeking God. The intelligence, dexterity, and excellence we develop in our physical duty carry over into the domains of being duty and spiritual duty. And the attention, kindness, and peace we develop in seeking God make us better at our physical and being duties.

This teaching of Right Living with its three duties, physical, being, and spiritual, offers a complete path that encompasses all facets of life. It shows us how our whole life and all that we do can be an act of service and a part of our path. We can bring everything under the enlivening umbrella of Right Living. Serving well in all the domains brings a deep sense of fulfillment.

Over the coming weeks, we will practice twelve aspects of the three duties. The first four aspects will relate to physical duty, the second four to being duty, and the final four to spiritual duty, as follows:

Physical Duty
   1. Body
   2. Family
   3. Profession
   4. Society and the Earth

Being Duty
   5. Practice of Freedom
   6. Conscience
   7. Sensitive Presence
   8. Conscious Presence

Spiritual Duty
   9. Stabilizing Attention
   10. Prayer
   11. Faith and Love
   12. Seeking God, The One

These twelve aspects are not sequential stages, but rather simultaneous duties that we pursue in the normal course of our life. For this week, consider the breadth of Right Living and how you might apply it in your own life.

7.1 Care for Our Body
(The Path of Right Living: Aspect 1 of 12)

We need this body to enjoy our life, to serve by fulfilling our many responsibilities, and to create and approach our personal destiny. Caring for our body is obviously and absolutely required of us to maintain our life. So caring for our body is not a matter of egoism, though it can cross over into self-centeredness when our concern with our body unnecessarily overshadows all other concerns. Of course if we are ill or injured, then dealing with that must be our immediate priority. In our normal situation, however, we still act responsibly and with love toward our own body.

The guiding principle of Right Living with respect to our body is to give it what it needs and, in moderation, what it wants, and to avoid what is harmful to it. In practice this means proper nutrition, exercise, rest, health care, and recreation, including hobbies and avocations. It also means completely avoiding drugs of abuse, like marijuana and the rest: they sap the energies needed for our inner work and their mere possession is usually illegal. We refrain from using tobacco because it harms our body and also saps the energies needed for our inner work. If we drink alcohol, we do so socially and in moderation. We respect our body, this magnificent vehicle entrusted to us at birth. But we need not coddle it. Within its limits, we should not fear making demands on our body as necessary.

Care for our body also means care for its physical supports of food, clothing, shelter, transportation, and the rest. We maintain our home, keeping it clean and attractive. We keep our transportation vehicles in good working order. We take appropriate care of all the tools and objects of our life.

We care for our body and its physical supports with the three hallmarks of Right Living: intelligence, dexterity, and excellence. Using our intelligence in this case means being interested, noticing how our body responds to different kinds and amounts of food and other inputs, to different kinds and amounts of exertion and rest. We experiment and observe. We pay attention to the signals our body sends us about its state, so that we know when to stop eating, when to rest, when to move, and so on. We learn to understand our body, to be an intelligent steward guiding our bodily life thoughtfully and appropriately. The same applies to our home, tools, and other material objects of our life — we use and care for them intelligently.

To act with dexterity means to adapt creatively to our constantly changing situations and conditions. This requires being open to new and better ways of doing what we do, not always being stuck in our old physical habits. It also requires seeing each situation clearly, seeing its possibilities and limitations. And then we look for ways to make the best of it. The importance of dexterity is obvious in games, in sports, and in business. But much of our life can profit from valuing and developing our dexterity.

And we always pursue excellence in managing our bodily life by continuously seeking to improve what we do and how we do it. We act appropriately and well, neither too much nor too little. Excellence in bodily matters means aiming for perfection in what we do, as time allows. When we clean, we clean thoroughly. If we wash dishes, we make them sparkle. If we cook, we make it nutritious and delicious, even down to the presentation. When we shop, we shop wisely. Whatever we do, we aim to do it right and do it well.

Now the exigencies of life often prevent us from giving as much as we would like to a particular task. So be it. Of necessity, we settle for good enough. Furthermore, we can go too far by demanding perfection instead of pursuing excellence. Then nothing we do is ever good enough and we become too precious in our judgment. Yet pursuing excellence engages us fully in what we do and leaves us with a sense of satisfaction.

We recognize that caring for our body and its supports is a necessary, important, and valuable part of our path. In Right Living, we bring the whole of our life, including everything connected with caring for our body, into the fold of activities that we value. We integrate it all into our path, so that our spiritual path is not separate from our life, not just something we do when we meditate or attend communal worship.

For this week engage with intelligence, dexterity, and excellence in caring for your body and its supports.

7.2 Care for Our Family
(The Path of Right Living: Aspect 2 of 12)

Anyone who aspires to the spiritual path must pay very careful attention to their family life. You cannot be a saint on your meditation cushion if you are an ogre at the dinner table. Family life elicits our true character. Without the constraint of having outsiders witness our behavior, we face the temptation to indulge our destructive emotions like anger, selfishness, and jealousy when interacting with our immediate family.

Please consider these questions. How do you treat your family members? Do you always speak with kindness? Are you always respectful of everyone in your family? Are you aware of their current state? Are you solicitous and responsive to their needs and desires? Do you bring them joy? Do you support their endeavors and dreams? Do you support them in their difficult times? Can they count on you? Do you have their interests at heart? Are you reliable? Are you unquestionably faithful to your spouse? Do you share yourself, your heart and your time with your family? Do you contribute appropriately to the work of the household? Or do you shirk your chores? Do you make demands on your spouse? Or do you ask in a friendly and reasonable manner? Do you blame and complain? Do you train your children to do their own duties, both personal and for the household? And do you maintain contact with family members not living with you?

Strong and loving families are the foundation of a strong and loving society. A good marriage makes us more complete. And loving and caring for our children brings a unique and deep satisfaction, and a natural path to responsibility. If we can love our family and accept their imperfections, then we have a real chance to extend that circle of respect into the larger society.

The challenges of family life can play an important role

in our spiritual training and development. Family life chips away at our self-centeredness. It calls us to be attentive and aware. It requires us to be responsible and to keep our promises.

It pushes us to transcend our destructive emotions. Yet despite our best intentions, the inevitable friction of living in close quarters with others pushes us at times not to transcend our destructive emotions but to sink into reactivity. If we can find freedom in the midst of the demands of modern life, especially family life, then our freedom is strong indeed. This highlights the value of the work of non-identification, of letting go, which we shall study as aspect 5 of the Path of Right Living.

Again we bring intelligence, dexterity, and excellence into caring for our family. The application of intelligence here begins with awareness of the people in our family, with seeing their states and learning their patterns, with understanding them more and more. That intelligence feeds our dexterity in knowing how best to act in each situation. The value of creative dexterity shows itself especially in dealing with the continually changing needs, desires, and behaviors of our children. To be excellent in caring for our family means many things, but primary among them is to be loving and to act from love. Approaching family life with intelligence, dexterity, and excellence also enables us to honor our own needs while honoring the needs of each member of our family.

For this week, bring the Path of Right Living into caring for your family.

7.3 Professional Duties
(The Path of Right Living: Aspect 3 of 12)

No one is an island. We each fill our individual niche in this vast and remarkably elaborated civilization. By doing so, we live in a style far beyond what we could produce on our own. Filling our niche by using our talents to serve society is our duty, our professional duty, a duty that applies to all except children, the retired, and the severely disabled.

The staggering range of ways of fulfilling our professional duty leaves us with endless choices in what we do, what we produce, and how we serve. One great advantage of our complex civilization is the array of opportunities it offers us to find a profession that well suits us, one that accords with our temperament, abilities, and interests.

Whatever career choices we make, or feel constrained to make, the Path of Right Living addresses the quality we bring to performing our duties. It all begins with our attitude. Whether we love our work or not, whether we are paid well or not at all, whether our work is respected by society or not, we still have the option of engaging fully in our profession, of giving it our very best, of continuously improving what we do and our ability to do it. Our work matters. We all need each other's work and what it adds to the world's economy and well-being. If we approach our work with the understanding that it does matter, we not only produce a better result for society and for our family, but we also preempt all the debilitating boredom, regret, and resentment that comes from being inwardly unengaged in what we do.

Intelligence, supported by the knowledge we continually and intentionally acquire and the skills we persistently hone, is a key quality factor in discharging our professional duties. We approach our work with an alert and attentive mind, asking ourselves how we can work smarter. The more we bring our intelligence to bear, the more effective and efficient we become.

As computer pioneer Alan Kay said: "The best way to predict the future is to invent it." Intelligence enables us to anticipate the future, to see and make opportunities, to envision possibilities, and to understand the likely consequences of our choices. This operates both near term, as in planning our day, and long-term, as with goals and major decisions. With intelligence, we imagine the future and work to achieve it or prepare for it.

But because, in the immortal words of Yogi Berra, "it's tough to make predictions, especially about the future," we also need dexterity to adapt and make the best of the incessant change that characterizes all of life, including our professional life. Dexterity does not remain stuck in outmoded patterns. What worked last year in our professional life, may be less than optimal now, and will surely be archaic in the years to come. We need to embrace time, the gate of emergence, and respond creatively. Dexterity enables us to thrive amid the roiling seas of uncertainty.

And then there's the opportunity of quality, of truly giving our best to what we do. We earn our living by doing our job. A half-hearted approach leaves us disgruntled and flat. But by working with quality, at the end of the day, the glow of excellence crowns the results of our labor, and we go home with a sense of satisfaction, satisfying what society needs from us and satisfying our own need to be useful and productive, to serve well.

Outward service, performed with quality, prepares us for inner service by training us to accept and to give. Wholly engaging in our job or profession not only serves ourselves, our family, and society, but is also an integral part of our spiritual path. We need not make the false distinction between our working life and our spiritual pursuit. Work and spirit complement and complete each other. These two sides of life can go hand in hand, merging into the one life of service.

For this week, reexamine your attitude toward your work and reinvigorate your performance of your professional duties.

7.4 Duty to Society and the Earth
(The Path of Right Living: Aspect 4 of 12)

Last week we studied our professional duties and how we contribute to society through our job. But our responsibilities to society do not stop there. We are deeply indebted to society for the whole structure and infrastructure of our lives. For proof, we need only look around ourselves and consider how much of what we see and use we could produce on our own. This remarkable civilization provides so well for so many. We serve our own interests by serving society.

We would do well to take as our starting point the golden rule: to treat others as we would have them treat us, and not to treat others as we would not want them to treat us. That can be a very high standard. We act with civility, even when it's not easy. When driving in traffic, in a hurry, not feeling well, or confronted with a difficult or disliked person or situation, we can still be civil. With our neighbors, we can be friendly, considerate, and helpful. To our friends we can extend hospitality, consideration, and interest. With strangers, we can be courteous. With the less fortunate, we can be charitable. With the weaker, we can be protective. When we make a promise, we can keep our word. We can be respectful of our government as responsible citizens who vote, pay taxes, and abide by the laws. And beyond the baseline of the golden rule, we can each use our intelligence and creativity to further the development and well-being of society, even in small ways. If many do this, we multiply these small positive actions by billions to great effect.

Underlying the life infrastructure that is man-made, we depend even more fundamentally on the infrastructure provided by the Earth and all the life teeming on it. Our indebtedness and obligations to the Earth are unbounded. Because we are so many and have such a large collective impact, we are being forced to outgrow the adolescent and indiscriminate taking of all we can from the Earth. We are learning that we must temper our taking and also give back. This is not an easy transition for it goes directly against our individual and collective self-centeredness. But it is a necessary transition if our species is to survive and thrive.

Clearly we are each a part of society as whole. But in truth the society in which we live extends beyond the human to include the whole biosphere of the Earth, and indeed the whole Earth. A core, enabling aspect of our duty to society is to enlarge our perspective, to shift our identity from the solely individual, from being our family, from being our nation, to being the Earth. We are each a part of the unity that is the Earth. The life of the Earth is our life. We are each ourselves and we are the whole of humanity. We are each ourselves and we are the Earth, both simultaneously. The being and spiritual duties of the Path of Right Living help purify and strengthen us enough so that we can soften our personal boundaries and at least touch the reality of our identity with the greater whole, with the Earth, so that we can act as and for the Earth.

For this week, reexamine the impact of your role and actions on society and the Earth. Bring intelligence, dexterity, and excellence to fulfilling your duty to society and the Earth. And meditate on the widening circles of who you are. Be yourself, your family, your nation, humanity, the biosphere, and the Earth.

7.5 *The Practice of Freedom*
(The Path of Right Living: Aspect 5 of 12)

We now come to the first of the four being duties of the Path of Right Living, namely freedom, or non-identification. Taken to its ultimate, the practice of inner freedom or non-identification liberates us. Its importance for our happiness and spiritual development cannot be overstated. For example, in the Buddha's primary and famous teaching of the Four Noble Truths, non-identification enters as the third and crucial Truth, as the key to freedom.

To begin, we need to understand that we are not inwardly free, to understand what is meant by identification. It means allowing something to take our place. It means becoming that thing or that need. I cease to exist and in my stead there is only the wanting of the ice cream or the rumination over the insult I received. The ice cream or the insult become me, become the most important factor in my inner world at this moment. I abdicate my will to the object of identification and let that impulse rule my inner world. This is the opposite of freedom.

We need to understand it in practice, by directly seeing our own identifications in action, driving our inner life. The most common identification is with our thoughts, when our thoughts are thinking us. How does this work? Our brain responds to inner and outer stimuli by producing thoughts. That mode of thinking happens automatically throughout our life and without the need for any conscious intention or participation on our part. The thoughts just seem to arise on their own and think themselves. This is fine and normal. The trouble, and our identification, begins when we fall into that stream of automatically self-generating thoughts and get carried away by it. Daydreams and ruminations of all kinds can reach out and grab us and we just flow away with them. In this type of identification, the thoughts are thinking us.

The practice of freedom, of not identifying with thoughts can take several forms. First we can intentionally be aware of and think the thoughts that had grabbed us. We step right into the self-generating flow of thoughts, reasserting control with intention and with a higher level of awareness energy than the automatic by which they typically operate. Then we are thinking our thoughts rather than vice versa.

Second, we can allow our automatic, self-generating thoughts to arise and pass on their own, without us going with them. Mindfulness meditation trains us in this, trains us to be more globally, contextually aware, so that the thoughts are within our awareness rather than us being in the thoughts.

Third, we can remove our attention from the thoughts that have grabbed us and place it elsewhere. We can change our focus to awareness of our breathing, or awareness of our body, of being in our body. Or we can intentionally think about something else, something other than those identifying thoughts.

Fourth, if the identifying thoughts arise from some difficult situation, it may be necessary to take appropriate outward actions to alleviate or resolve the situation. All these approaches shift us from identification with our thoughts to not being identified.

And all those approaches apply just as well to any other type of identification. For example, if we are identified with an emotion like anger, we can intentionally feel the anger and all its components, which makes us more active and less identified with the anger, rather than being its passive host. Or we can simply be very aware of the anger and its physical components and let it rise, fall, and pass on its own. Or we can shift our attention away from the anger, for example into body awareness. We can go for a walk, be in our body, and let our emotional turmoil settle. Lastly, we may need to do something about the situation that is arousing our anger to enable the anger to subside. We need not let anger, or any other destructive emotion, take us over.

Identification can enter any of our realms, including the realm of performing our duties. We can be identified with our habitual ways of fulfilling our duties and react strongly against any interference or change. We can resent our duties. The practice of freedom or non-identification means not resenting having to work, having to do the endless little tasks it takes to keep our life together: paying our bills, sweeping the floor, polishing our shoes. We do not allow identification to take us over and prevent us from doing what's necessary and doing it well. We do not allow identification to impose a negative view of fulfilling our responsibilities. Perhaps we would rather be golfing or at the beach, but we need not let that preference invade and color our life in this moment. We just do what's necessary and leave the inner grumbling to itself.

If we ponder questions of identity, identification, freedom and non-identification, we might naturally ask: if freedom depends on no one being there to be identified, then who is present when I am present? The one who is present and free is at a deeper level than the pseudo selves that arise in identification. The one who is present and free resides at the level of the conscious energy: the vast and open stillness that is the foundation of awareness. At that level, our will is unified and whole. But in the lower energies, our will fractures into a mass of contradictory and competing urges. The selves of identification live in those lower energies.

We might also ask: if identification means abdicating my will to the object I am identified with, doesn't that mean there is no one to be my will in that moment, and isn't that the same as no one being there to be identified? If no one is there because I have abdicated my will and left the scene, isn't that the freedom from self, the no-self spoken about in so many spiritual teachings? Again this has to do with levels. The freedom we seek is freedom from the fractured, partial selves created by identification. My fractured will temporarily creates a self around the object of identification, a self that I mistakenly take to be the real me and thus identify with. At a higher level, in non-identification, these fractured selves reintegrate into our true Self, which is free. This true Self is the same as the no-self and selflessness spoken about in spiritual teachings. No-self and selflessness mean not being in one of our partial, identified selves.

Rather than becoming monastic, we seek freedom in the midst of ordinary life. It is natural and normal to enjoy our pleasures, be they sensory, emotional, or intellectual. But we need not identify with our pleasures. The difference between non-identification and identification is the difference between having our pleasures and our pleasures having us, between eating our food and our food eating us. Similarly with the inevitable pain and suffering that life brings us: we can have pain without the pain having us.

Ultimately, in the quiet peace within, we see identification as only an impulse, one that we can let arise and disappear on its own, without buying into it, without forming a temporary identity around the object of identification. We feel its pull and let it go. In essence, we let our supposed and temporary identity go. We see through the patterns. I am not the ice cream. I am not the insulted. I am not any thought. I am neither the desire for ice cream, nor the desire to avenge the insult. If I release into the vast openness within, the insult passes right through, with no fractured self there to be the insulted one. The desire for ice cream passes through, with no one necessarily acting on it.

For this week, notice the ways you succumb to identification and practice freedom, practice non-identification.

7.6 Conscience
(The Path of Right Living: Aspect 6 of 12)

To obey our conscience is our sacred duty, for conscience is how God speaks to us. That "still small voice" is the voice of conscience. If we cultivate our openness to it and abide by its promptings, our conscience serves as our individual compass to guide us through life. Conscience goes beyond what we learn from our parents, teachers, friends, society, and religion to a direct perception of the wisdom, creativity, and compassion at the heart of the world. Conscience is our channel of communication, our connection with the Divine.

And conscience is uniquely our own. One of the names

of God is The Unique. The Source of wisdom, creativity, and compassion also has the quality of uniqueness. The more we open to conscience, the more we open to The Unique, and the more we become our unique Self. That is why as people progress along the spiritual path they become more themselves, more unique.

But it is not always so easy. Our conscience, our inner sense of right and wrong tends to emerge at inopportune and inconvenient moments. Often our first impulse is to quash it, brush it aside, pretend we didn't hear it, and continue with a course of action that our conscience knows to be wrong. Every time we ignore our conscience, however, we bury this most precious part of us a little deeper. We can ask forgiveness for our misdeeds. But we must take care not to enter an action knowing beforehand that it is wrong and intending to ask forgiveness afterwards. That makes a mockery of conscience and forgiveness.

The practice of conscience arises in those unexpected moments of an intuitive perception of the rightness or wrongness of a choice we are about to make. The practice is to obey the promptings of conscience. But subtleties can and do enter. Our perception of right or wrong may not actually be from our conscience, but instead be from fear, anger, narrow-mindedness, over-eagerness, greed, lust, or some other identification. So we need to learn to discriminate conscience from the noise. We can apply basic sanity checks to the impulse. Will it harm anyone? Is it legal? Does it violate ordinary norms of society and morality? Does it make sense, common sense? But the surest way to learn is to see the results after we act. Do we later regret what we did or did not do? Extrapolating backwards by recalling the moment of choice, we may be able to see which impulse was the voice of conscience and which impulses were noise. In this way we gradually acquire the taste of conscience. And then by always acting in accord with it, we purify our heart.

The power of God to affect this world depends, at least in part, on our willingness to act on God's behalf, to live by conscience and do the right thing. This does not refer to those religious fundamentalists who attempt by force to impose their interpretation of religious codes on others. For guidance on what is right, the fundamentalist primarily looks outside, to holy script or to another person set up as an authority. Conscience looks within, deep within our self, to our own, direct connection with the very source of wisdom and love. And there conscience finds our guidance.

Conscience not only guides us about right and wrong in the moral sense, but also in a wider sense. It shows us how best to meet our responsibilities, how to fulfill our potential, which opportunities to create, which to take, and which to set aside, when to say yes and when to say no.

The success and value of democracy derives from its inherent fostering of freedom and conscience in its citizens. The right to vote, in governments where the citizens' votes really matter, draws us to look within ourselves for truth. Authoritarian governments push its citizens to abdicate responsibility. When someone else is making decisions for us, it diminishes the role of our individual conscience. Authoritarian parents need to let their maturing children make their own choices. Authoritarian spiritual teachers do their students a serious disservice by making life decisions for them, or even by advising them on such matters. To attain our full individuality, we need to make our own choices, and to do that well we need to cultivate conscience.

While outward freedom does support the development of inner freedom and conscience, the latter do not depend on outer freedom. People living in repressive societies and conditions certainly can become persons of conscience who are inwardly free. In extreme cases some are even helped toward conscience and inner freedom by the difficulty of their situation.

A clear conscience is a treasure and a prerequisite for a happy life. Our conscience is not something outside of ourselves. Rather, conscience is the voice of our own higher Self, calling us toward our true destiny, calling us to become our higher Self. A clear conscience is also an absolute requirement for approaching the Divine. Nothing can be hidden from the Light and we do not wish to be too ashamed to stand before It, too ashamed to accept Its Grace. A clear conscience removes the obstacles to deepening prayer. Yes, we can ask forgiveness and make amends for past misdeeds, but even more important is how we act going forward.

For this week, practice listening for and acting in accord with your conscience.

7.7 Sensitive Presence

(The Path of Right Living: Aspect 7 of 12)

Fulfilling the first six aspects of the Path of Right Living, with their emphasis on external action, will make us a mensch, a responsible and respectful person of integrity. The more people act in that way, the better off the world will be. But in the spiritual path we also aspire to become an enlightened or perfected person. And for that we also pursue the remaining 6 aspects, the first of which is sensitive presence.

Our physical body serves as a scaffold for our soul, for the building of our inner body. Body presence is thus a fundamental practice of spiritual development and offers many benefits as an important enabling factor and foundation for the whole of the Path of Right Living. When we practice body presence, we are working directly and tangibly on building our soul.

This tangible quality of body presence is the source of its power, giving us a vivid and relatively stable place in the present. Once we grow familiar with sensing, we clearly know the degree to which we are present in our body and we clearly know how to increase and enhance that presence. To practice body presence we simply direct our attention to our body and open to direct awareness of it. Sensation is the name we give to the form of sensitive energy that connects us with our bodily sensations.

If you sit quietly, holding your attention in your right hand in a relaxed manner, gradually the hand will become more alive, more sensitive. Comparing your experience in that moment of your right and left hands makes the difference more obvious. The right hand has more of the sensitive energy than the left, due to the attention you have given it. In the same way you can practice sensing the right foot, left foot, and left hand in succession, each for a minute or two. And then move on to entire limbs: each arm, each leg. And then begin sensing your body as whole. Building up the sensitive energy in your body, helps build your soul.

Sensitive presence, however, goes beyond body presence to include awareness of our thoughts and emotions. We can practice thought awareness by sitting quietly in meditation, stabilizing our awareness and attention by focusing. We might focus on body sensations, our breath, sounds, a repeated word or phrase, or some other object of meditation. Once we are inwardly settled, we can turn part of our attention to watching the thoughts and images passing through our mind and being aware of their meaning. This is one, but not the only, method of bringing the sensitive energy, sensitive presence into our thinking.

Another way occurs when we intentionally think about a subject or problem. Such intentional thinking is less common than we might suppose, since the great majority of our thoughts are not at all intentional, but rather self-generating, automatic associations reacting to inner or outer stimuli or just chaining off a previous thought or image. In meditation our thoughts may slow down and even cease temporarily, though we generally do not try to stop our thoughts directly, because they always come back. But we can work to bring more awareness to our thoughts, to see our thoughts and know their meaning. By doing so, we clearly see that they are not all "ours," they are not initiated by us, and we are not thinking them. Our associative thoughts are thinking themselves and only pretend to speak for us.

As for sensitive awareness of emotion, we find a wide range by looking in any given moment at how we feel right then. Often it may appear that we are not feeling at all. But some emotional state is always there, even in such cases of quiet emotions. The latter might be slight degrees of contentment, boredom, happiness, satisfaction or the like. Stronger emotions are more obvious, but also tend to submerge us in them, so that we are lost in the emotion without awareness of our state. We get so carried away with anger, fear, jealousy, greed, lust, frustration, excitement and other potent emotions that we have no sensitive presence, we are not aware of our emotion as an emotion, of fear as being fear or anger as being anger. We are just angry or afraid, having disappeared in the emotional storm.

So our practice is to be aware of our emotions and their qualities, to see them as emotions, to see that they are not us. Most emotions, like most thoughts, are self-generating in response to inner and outer events. We rarely choose to feel a certain way, but rather allow our feelings to be chosen for us. As a help in this, we can look at the effects of our emotions on our body and mind. Bodily tensions, postures, rate and depth of breathing, facial expressions, and tones of voice are affected by and reflective of our emotions. Similarly, our thoughts, in their content, tone, and attitude, often reflect underlying emotions. To be in touch with our emotions, we practice opening our awareness to this whole structure of how we are.

To be complete and whole, we practice sensitive contact with all three: body, thought, and emotion. Generally we begin with body presence, as it is the most tangible and offers a more stable foundation for opening to thought and emotion awareness. But the practice of all three together brings even more stability of presence. This is the necessary and ongoing fundamental approach to making our spiritual endeavor real. For this week, practice sensitive presence, both in sitting meditation and whenever you have some spare attention during your day.

7.8 Conscious Presence
(The Path of Right Living: Aspect 8 of 12)

Pure consciousness liberates us into the spacious freedom of the cognizant stillness within us. Consciousness is always there: vast, silent, and serene. But we allow the more superficial content of our senses to distract us, to mask the essential awareness underlying our sensory awareness. We pay attention to the sensory content displayed on the screen of our mind and lose contact with the screen itself. While sensitive presence forms the perfect foundation for consciousness, to be truly conscious means more than just being aware of all that our senses bring us. The energy of consciousness, the conscious energy, fuels our fundamental awareness behind all the sensory impressions, behind all the sights and sounds, body and thought, and all the rest.

Right now, as you read these words, open to the peaceful stillness within you, behind the seeing of the words, behind and between the thought-sounds playing in your mind. In that spacious stillness you can be, you are, you are yourself. The stillness need not be hidden by thoughts. Let the thoughts think themselves, while you let your attention settle into the silence beneath your thoughts, beneath your sensory awareness. Rest in the stillness, not entangled with your senses. Your eyes see, your ears hear, your thoughts think, and your emotions emote, while you remain here, within the cognizant silence of consciousness, taking it all in without it all taking you in.

This tranquil sea of silence is here within us. It gives relief, rest, and equanimity. It gives an expansive view of life. In it we readily widen our perceptions and our concern beyond the purely personal, beyond our ordinary self-centeredness. This sea of consciousness has no center, but rather a boundless, unimpeded spaciousness.

Yet because of its remarkable qualities, when we begin to recognize consciousness and experience it, we can easily fall into identifying with it, into believing that consciousness is what we are, that we have arrived at the ultimate level of ourselves and of reality. Indeed much of today's popular spiritual and new age teachings erroneously put forward the notion that our deepest nature is consciousness, even that God is consciousness. Those who have seen deeply enough, however, report otherwise. Even on the level of ordinary logic, we can readily understand that consciousness does not choose, that the one who chooses, the one who directs our attention is deeper than consciousness. The extraordinary freedom found in consciousness can seduce us into abandoning any further search, a condition known in Buddhism as a false enlightenment.

Nevertheless, to understand consciousness experientially and to live in consciousness, even temporarily, is to live in a very refined and marvelous state, one that marks a significant milestone on our path toward the Sacred. Consciousness, as it turns out, is the boundary between our ordinary worlds and the higher spiritual realms. We address the way beyond consciousness in the latter aspects of the Path of Right Living.

But even for conscious presence, consciousness does not tell the whole story. Conscious presence means more than the presence of consciousness, it means the presence of someone who is conscious, namely you, your I. The presence part of conscious presence refers to the action of your will. In conscious presence, we not only are here and now, we know we are here now, and we are the one who is here now. Thus the core of conscious presence consists of the presence of I, that I am here in this cognizant stillness, that I am here as my will-to-be, that I am in contact with all my sensory impressions, that I am the one who is doing what I am doing, that I am acting as my will to act, that I am at peace.

For this week, practice being conscious, inhabiting the spacious, cognizant stillness within you.

7.9 Stabilizing Attention
(The Path of Right Living: Aspect 9 of 12)

Of all the facets of spirituality, one of the most important is the development of our will. And the most accessible way to understand and strengthen our will consists in developing our power of attention. As we well know, the ability to focus and sustain our attention provides major benefits in our education, career, and throughout our daily life. But attention plays a crucial role in our inner work as well. All inwardly active forms of spiritual practice depend on attention.

Attention comes closer to who we really are than anything else in our ordinary inner world. We can truthfully say: I am my attention. Why is this so? Consider how active attention works in you. First you choose where to direct it and then you bring your attention, your self, into contact with the chosen object. This initiative is an act of will, an action in which your will interacts with your inner energies, in which your I, the one in you who chooses, brings your awareness energies to bear on the object. Next you hold your attention on the chosen object. This is a sustained act of will, a continuing choice to attend to something. Finally, when your attention choice lapses and you notice that your attention has strayed, you choose to direct your attention back to the object, and the cycle begins again. Throughout, attention is an act of will: your action, your choice, you. Your attention comes from you, as you, and intimately reflects who you are in this moment. Is anything closer to you than your attention? Where does your attention come from, if not from you? What is your attention, if not an embodiment of your will?

Our usual state, though, is one of passive attention, wherein we unintentionally allow our attention to wander onto whatever may attract us in any given moment. We do so by default, without choosing, and without particular awareness of how our attention is drawn or moves. We exercise little or no will in such a passive state. Our attention is scattered; we are scattered. Active attention, by contrast, is an act of will that requires us to initiate the action, monitor ourselves, notice where our attention is, and intentionally direct it moment by moment.

Any activity that requires active attention, including certain forms of meditation and prayer, develops this power in us. Take for example the attention a batter brings to the baseball flying toward him at ninety plus miles per hour, or the focus of a surgeon in a delicate operation, or you as you read, drive, converse, or engage in the myriad activities that demand your attention.

Because of its centrality in the spiritual path, we seek ways to collect and stabilize our attention, ways not to be scattered. When we practice sensitive presence, we are aware of our body, emotions, and thoughts. We bring our attention to these three areas of experience. Doing so persistently gradually forms in us what we can experience as an inner body, a sensation body inside our physical body. Attention plays a major role in this. We pay attention to our body, to our emotions, and to our thoughts. We inhabit our inner world, our inner body, by attending to it, by our attention keeping our awareness present here and now. By actively putting our attention into our whole body, into the sensation of our whole body, we inhabit our inner body. We are here because our attention is here. Our inner body in return offers a natural and appropriate venue in which to stabilize our attention. We keep our self here by keeping our attention based in our inner body. We practice this in sitting meditation and also as we go about our day.

In the latter mode, we widen the embrace of our attention to include both our inner body and the outward experience and activity engaging us at the moment. Our inner body serves as our home in the midst of activity. Time marches on, we go here and there, do this and that, and our sensory experience changes continuously. Through it all, our inner body offers a base of stability. True enough, our experience of our inner body also changes, but not as radically as everything else. So we can be here in our body, while also in our world. Rooting our attention in our body, while keeping open to our outer experience and engagement, carries us in presence through our day, and offers the possibility of a stable attention, a stable presence.

A key aspect of developing this inner stability is to notice and embrace the disrupting and distracting influences that weaken our focus, that lull us into passivity, into letting our attention stray haphazardly. Certainly there are times for that: in creative work, in recreation and relaxation, and in some forms of meditation and prayer. But ordinarily we want to stay here and now, based in our inner body. But our many disorganizing factors work against this. We consider these disrupting, distracting, dissipating, entropic factors as part of us and learn to work with them and around them. Our active choice to pay attention meets our passivity, while we stay in the middle to reconcile and unite the two within our being. And in that unity we find a way to stay present, to inhabit our inner body. Our attitude is neither totally active nor totally passive, but both and more. Just in that way, we are.

For this week, practice stabilizing your attention.

7.10 Prayer
(The Path of Right Living: Aspect 10 of 12)

The tent of prayer shelters us all, as we address the hidden force behind the veil of creation. Even if you do not believe in a Creator, you may still be inclined to prayer, because you know its efficacy, at least in changing your inner state. So in the worst case, we believe there is no God and we pray because it helps us find inner peace. In the best case we know God; we know there is Someone to Whom we pray. In truth, though, very few people know from their own direct experience that God exists. Much more common is an experience deeper than our ordinary awareness that shows the existence of a higher realm or realms, though not of God directly. And from such experiences springs the faith that, at the ultimate height, God does indeed exist, continuously creating this universe. For many others, faith is rooted in a childhood within the culture, doctrine, and ritual of their family religion. Wherever we stand on this wide spectrum of faith, from disbelief to direct certainty, from disregard to devotion, prayer welcomes us on our own terms with its warm embrace.

There are many levels of prayer — all of them valuable. Here we'll focus on how to move toward the deeper levels of prayer, toward the true worship that opens us to our connection with the Sacred. Please prepare by choosing a prayer, for example the Lord's Prayer or another formal prayer or a short phrase from your own religion, or one of your own creation. What matters is that the words of the prayer can touch your heart, that you know them by heart, and that they are capable of pulling you toward the Sacred.

Bring yourself into a calm, relaxed state. Begin repeating the prayer inwardly. As you do so, come into contact mentally and emotionally with the meaning of the prayer, with its thrust. Let the prayer both inform your heart on how to feel and guide your mind toward its purpose, toward your purpose in inwardly saying it. Gradually withdraw from actively repeating the prayer into receptively allowing the prayer to repeat itself in you, moving from inner forcefulness into effortlessness, form active prayer into contemplative worship. Remember the Sacred, Whom you address with this prayer. As you become less inwardly-active, invite the Sacred to enter you, to enter your prayer, to say the prayer in you, through you, as you. From your inmost inwardness, open to contact with the Sacred to Whom you pray and Whom you are inviting, imploring to say the prayer in you. After a time stop and be still. Make no effort at all to direct your inner state. Just be and let the prayer session soak into your being. This is a type of communion, sharing our inwardness with the Sacred.

As you practice this deepening prayer, you will see that this approach is open at both ends. We cannot fail at it, because any effort whatsoever to engage in such prayer has its own innate value. It is an act of will by which, in our own small way, we participate in the Great Will, in the Great Purpose of life. We also can never come to an end of such deepening prayer. There is always more service to be offered and further depths to be plumbed through prayer. For those precious moments in which we participate in the Great Purpose by way of prayer, we fulfill own purpose. Our heart and mind find a transcendent satisfaction, both personal and beyond the personal. For in prayer we serve the Sacred in one of the two major ways that human being are meant to serve, the other way being through outer service to other people and to all of life. True satisfaction comes from service, and the service of prayer is essential. It is not for nothing that in some religions communal worship sessions are called services.

In this practice of deepening prayer, we again see the three aspects of will. Our active will chooses to pray, begins and sustains the repetition, and engages in contact with the meaning and purpose of the prayer and its practice. Our receptive will moves us into the effortless and opening qualities of the practice. And the unifying, reconciling will enters on our invitation as the higher, Sacred will deriving from the Great Purpose Itself. The feeling of a sense of the Sacred, of holiness in prayer is the action of our reconciling, harmonizing, unifying will. Bearing within itself some of the qualities of actively praying and of receptively opening toward the Source, this third side of our will reconciles the other two, while serving as our connection with the Higher.

For this week, practice deepening prayer.

7.11 Faith and Love
(The Path of Right Living: Aspect 11 of 12)

We feel a very broad spectrum of emotions, from desperate and illusory desires, anxiety, and depression, to self-centered automatic reactions like anger, fear, jealousy, envy, and greed, to the non-destructive ordinary, sensitive emotions like friendliness, happiness, and sadness, to conscious emotions like kindness, joy, contentment, and equanimity, to the feelings that come to us from the Sacred such as hope, faith, compassion, and love. This list naturally divides into five categories of emotion: desperate and illusory, automatic, sensitive, conscious, and higher. Each category operates with a different and corresponding level of inner energy.

Emotions can cross categories. Take the example of anger. We can have a desperate flash of anger that then seethes and festers over time, feeding on itself, infecting our entire inner life, and disturbing our body chemistry. We can have automatic anger that reacts to unwanted events, such as a rude driver in traffic. We can feel sensitive anger in response to slights, insults and other affronts to us personally. And we can arouse conscious anger in response to evil actions. The higher an emotion is on this scale of energies, the less identified we are with it, the less control the emotion has over us, the more we are aware of the emotion as an emotion, and the more appropriate and real the emotion is. The lower categories of emotion arise unbidden and usually against some large portion of our fractured will, because the lower the dominant energy the more our will is fragmented.

In this aspect of the Path of Right Living, we turn toward the higher emotions, those that come to us from the Sacred. These spiritual feelings well up from deep within us, not necessarily in response to any external stimulus. But certain stimuli can and do evoke higher emotions. Worship rituals and some forms of music are designed to awaken faith and love in us. The sight of living beings in a state of suffering awakens compassion in us. Contact with nature can awaken connectedness and awe. We participate in the arising of these higher emotions by assenting to them, by our willingness to feel deeply and beyond our self-centeredness.

But also by our own inner work, such as the work of deepening prayer, higher emotions naturally well up from the core of our being. In deepening prayer, as we approach nearer to the Divine, we may touch the level of the higher, sacred emotions. In the practice of deepening prayer, we aim ourselves toward the Sacred Source. Along the way we come to the purifying light of a high spiritual world, not yet the Source Itself, but close to It. And in opening to that spiritual world, we open to the sacred emotions.

Faith and love are there, as welcoming and enlivening signposts that we are moving in the right direction, toward the Divine. These higher feelings cannot be manufactured or conjured by us. Faith comes to us as the certainty and confidence in the Sacred, as the Sacred touches us directly. The more we open ourselves to contact with the Sacred, the more our doubts dissolve into trust, and the more faith enters us. Love comes as the intuition of our unity with all, the non-separateness revealed in the descent of the Sacred into our heart. The more our contact with the Sacred, the more we realize the Source of all is One in all, the more we enter into Love.

The veil between us and that spiritual world of higher emotions is not so thick, and certainly not impenetrable. The purer and more devoted our seeking, the closer we come to the

Light and beyond. Indeed the Sought is the Seeker.
For this week, seek faith and love.

7.12 Seeking God, The One
(The Path of Right Living: Aspect 12 of 12)

The Shivapuri Baba taught that God is hidden by consciousness, that if we can remove consciousness, we shall see God. To remove the veil of consciousness means not only to go beyond our ordinary awareness, but even beyond the vast, cognizant and peaceful stillness underlying ordinary awareness. That stillness is consciousness. It seems to be the deepest experience available to us. And before we look to go beyond it, we need to steep ourselves in it, in the peace and silence of our background awareness. Quiet meditation can help in this, help us understand the transparent texture and spacious contours of consciousness.

Still, how can we go beyond that? How can we go beyond consciousness, this all pervasive awareness in which, in our more centered moments, we participate? This question can be a very fruitful entrée to contemplation and contemplative prayer. In such contemplation, we inwardly explore the question, not by thinking or ruminating about it, but by actually looking within ourselves for the direction leading outside the envelope of consciousness. It must be a direction of depth, but practically speaking, what or where is that? What lies behind, beneath our awareness of our ordinary awareness? The depth we seek transcends the categories of inner and outer. Persistently contemplating and creatively exploring all this, in humility and devotion, leads us closer to the Real, as we dive into our self and behind the field of consciousness.

Pursuing this exploration beyond consciousness, we first encounter the Sacred Light, a high world of great spiritual blessing and nourishment. Contact with the Light helps us enormously in many ways and is fully worthy of cultivation. But — this is not the Ultimate. Touching or entering the world of Sacred Light does not mean that our search is complete.

In seeking God, we seek the One Who continuously creates and sustains this universe and all the worlds, including the world of Sacred Light. So not only must we seek beyond consciousness, but also beyond the Light. This makes God sound remote from us. But that is mistaken. God is close, as close as our own will.

We can repeatedly align our inmost self, our will, with God's will and thereby come to participate directly in the One, or rather the One can come to participate in us, as us. Toward this, we make room in ourselves. We open, even more deeply than before: more deeply than opening to consciousness, more deeply than opening to the realm of Sacred Light. We open our very core, prostrating ourselves inwardly in abject surrender before the Ineffable One, both immanent and transcendent. We inwardly let go of all that we are and point every fiber of our being toward the Real. A sacred word or phrase can help as a focus, but only as a stepping stone toward total devotion, total surrender in that very moment, surrender of body, mind, and heart, surrender of our very self. Our lack of purity prevents us from entering the Sacred Presence. But the practice of surrender is the practice of purification.

Diving into the source of our will, into its unfathomable depths, we find that our source is the Source of All. When we love someone, say a person in our family, we are not separate from them. Their welfare is our own. We want for them what they want for themselves. Their pain is our pain. Their joy is our joy. Our self-centeredness disappears in this love. That love provides a foretaste of union with our Source.

The foregoing approach to seeking God can be called actively receptive or receptively active depending on the momentary emphasis. Yet there is another effective and traditional approach: that of pure receptivity, of letting go, of surrendering utterly, radically. After initially orienting our intention toward God, we sit and do nothing, or rather we sit and make no attempt to do or change anything. We leave all as it is. We just abide in being here, in awareness with no inwardly active movement, with no shaping of experience. We sit and be. Persisting in this, our inner state changes on its own. This non-doing, this surrendering to what is, as is, makes room for the higher will to enter us. In the perfection of non-doing lies the transcendence of egoism, of all that separates us from the Perfect One.

These two approaches complement each other. We can find great succor in either or in both, as our intuitive wishes guide us.

For this week, seek God.

8.0 The Path to Presence

The quality of our presence determines the quality of our life. The more present we are, the more profoundly we experience our life and the more effective we are, both on the surface and in the depths. To go from our fragmented, intermittently aware level of being, marked by self-generating associative thoughts and memories, reactive emotions, physical habits, and conflicting desires, to a level of being characterized by full, extended, and unified presence is an eminently worthwhile, major and, above all, practical undertaking. Practical in this sense means the persistent and frequent practice of presence in its three major building blocks — presence in body, in heart, and in mind.

Over the coming weeks, we will create an opportunity to engage in this enterprise of strengthening and deepening our presence, through a weekly series of twelve groups of practices aimed at developing presence:

1. Body Sensation: Stronger
2. Body Sensation: More Frequent
3. Body Sensation: Wholeness
4. Emotions as Emotions
5. Thoughts as Thoughts
6. Letting Go
7. Inner Energy Flows
8. Emotional Presence
9. Cognitive Presence
10. Triune Presence
11. Conscious Presence
12. I Am Present

    The basic dimension of this practice of presence, as noted above, involves presence in the body, in the heart, and in the mind. Another dimension concerns noticing, understanding, and raising the level of energy with which our body, heart, mind, and awareness are functioning. We will see the various energies in action within us. Such seeing matters to us because it confers understanding and purification of will, while supporting development of being.
    The two levels of energy which will concern us for most of this series are the automatic and the sensitive. In preparation for studying how these energies work in us, we can look this week at the action of the automatic energy in our body. For the most part, the automatic energy provides an essential service to us physically. It enables our body to carry out numerous learned actions and skills without our having to mentally direct each movement.
    We walk without having to decide which foot to move when and exactly where to put it. Our body automatically takes care of the details of walking, with only some high-level direc-

tional input from our mind. We speak without having to consider how to shape our mouth and tongue, how much tension to apply to our vocal chords, or how to breathe to make the sound of each phoneme. Our body automatically looks after all those details with only some high-level direction from our mind and heart on what words to say and what intonation to use.

This remarkable body of ours does so many things automatically and does them so well that our mind, our attention and intention, and our awareness need only participate peripherally in most of what we do. That is the beauty of the automatic energy: it enables a hierarchical style of control.

The other side of that coin, however, is that we succumb to the temptation to abdicate our life to the automatic energy. We let our life go on without much awareness and without much actual choosing on our part. Our physical actions go almost exclusively by learned patterns and habits. We sleep-walk through much of life, letting it all happen in its own preprogrammed way — automatically responding to stimuli. This automatic living is flat and dull. We live by rote, unengaged. To have any hope of improving matters, we first need to see the extent to which such unawareness characterizes our life.

For this week, notice the degree to which your body acts without your direct involvement.

8.1 Body Sensation: Stronger
(The Path to Presence: Aspect 1 of 12)

Self-awareness matures into an essential component of presence. But as soon as we begin to make serious efforts at self-awareness, we discover that awareness to be fleeting and unstable, despite our best intentions. Our attention all too readily falls away from self-awareness into whatever distractions pop up. For example, if you attempt to watch your mind, you soon find yourself slipping into and then washed away with the stream of thoughts. Try as you might, the siren song of that self-generating, associative flow of thoughts, so familiar and so intimately tied to you, pulls you out of your more centered self and into its less aware, automatic and more passive mode of living and experiencing. But there is hope, there is a way out of this conundrum. That way consists of increasing awareness of our body through the sensitive energy.

If you put your attention into your right hand and hold your attention there, your direct awareness of your right hand gradually grows stronger. Your hand may feel more alive, more substantial, more energetic, more there. Stay with this for a time. Then compare your experience of your right hand with your current experience of your left hand. See the contrast between the two: the left being relatively less alive, less substantial. This marks the presence of the sensitive energy in your right hand. We say that you are sensing your right hand and that it is full of sensation.

Now the great advantage of working with sensation is its relative stability. It does not evaporate immediately. It does not disappear as quickly as our attention might flit away. Because of that, sensation creates a wonderful basis for presence, a foundation for self-awareness that begins with our body and gradually grows to include heart, mind, self, and higher energies. Body sensation forms the very foundation of presence.

The more you practice sensing your body, the more sensation you have. This is only partly due to your growing familiarity with sensation. Even more importantly, the practice of sensing your body gradually develops an inner vessel, a container in which the sensitive energy accumulates. Little by little, the sensitive energy collects and stays with you. At unexpected moments during the day, body sensation spontaneously rises to the foreground of your awareness, awakening you toward presence, toward being here and now more fully. That inner vessel of sensation forms the foundation of our soul.

So our role consists of making repeated efforts to sense

our body. We start with sensing parts like hands or feet, then move on to larger parts like arms or legs, then we include torso and head. In sensing the torso, however, we do not try to sense particular inner organs so as not to interfere with their instinctive functioning, but rather we sense our torso as a whole. Also, we refrain from sensing in situations that crucially demand our full attention, like driving or chopping vegetables.

Making persistent efforts to sense our body pays enormous dividends. All levels of spiritual experience begin here and now. And sensing is the premier way into being here and now. And not only that — sensing trains our attention, more finely attunes us to the needs of our body, partially frees us from domination by our automatic thoughts and destructive emotions, expands our present moment, makes life much more vivid and rich, increases our confidence in the spirit by providing an ongoing experience of greater depth than ordinarily possible, and it creates a platform for higher spiritual energies to enter us. All these possibilities come to fruition through our efforts to sense.

For this week, practice sensing parts of your body and, in particular, staying with it to strengthen that sensation, to draw more of the sensitive energy there. If sensing comes to you spontaneously during the day, use the opportunity to strengthen that sensation by bringing your attention to it and staying with it.

8.2 Body Sensation: More Frequent
(The Path to Presence: Aspect 2 of 12)

In the spiritual practice of presence, a primary challenge facing us concerns how often during our normal day do we come back to presence. To meet that challenge, we first need a clear practice to come back to. For that, the relative concreteness of sensing, of bringing attention and awareness into our body, into the sensitive energy in our body, serves remarkably well. Far from being nebulous, we clearly know when we are in contact with sensation. If there is any doubt about whether we are sensing, then the answer is no. The sensing may not be strong and may be localized in a small region of our body, but we know whether our intention and attention are there, and having learned to perceive it, we know whether any sensitive energy is there.

The practice of sensing affords us a definite focus when we do remember to come back to presence. Without it, we may flounder. Something reminds us to return to inner work, but then what? Do we, at that point, start considering what and how to practice? Long before we reach any conclusion about that, we very likely will be swept away with other thoughts or by some external event. By preparing ahead of time, by knowing that we will practice sensing as often as we can remember to, we are ready when the moments come, and we turn that impulse of awakening directly into the inner work of sensing as soon as the impulse arises. These momentary impulses of awakening do come and our job is not to waste them by letting them evaporate ineffectually, missing the opportunity.

But beyond the issue of what practice to engage in when we do momentarily awaken looms the basic question of motivation, its strength and its depth. In the spiritual path, motivation is all important. The more we are motivated to practice, the more we do practice. Weak motivation means weak and less frequent practice. It means ignoring the opportunities that open whenever we remember the path. Strong motivation leads us to welcome those opportunities and act on them, again and again.

So how do we increase our motivation, our desire to practice? We build on what motivation we have through a positive feedback loop: the more we practice, the more we see and feel its value, which leads us to practice more. This holds for the moment-to-moment work of presence, as well as for meditation and prayer. We see that presence does not interfere with our life activities, but rather enhances them. How much richer is a conversation in which you are truly present, than one in which you are inwardly preoccupied, or busy formulating what you will say next, or passing judgment, or lost in your emotional reactions to what the others are saying? Feeling the vivid richness of life in presence motivates us to practice more.

An inverse feedback can also build our motivation. As our inner work continues, we may see more clearly that we ourselves are not all that we might wish to be. This lack, this shortfall can motivate us to be more, to practice presence more. For example, when a moment of awakening comes, rather than inwardly berating ourselves for not being present in the time immediately preceding that moment, we simply note our former lack and turn directly to the practice of presence, to sensing. By practicing more, we are more.

Perhaps the greatest motivator consists in understanding that our inner work serves a higher purpose. The transformation of energies that takes place in presence helps the other people in our life. Our behavior is different. We tend to be calmer, more attentive, less argumentative, friendlier, more caring, more engaged. And those qualities spread a positive contagion from person to person. The work of presence lays the foundation for our own deeper transformation. And it serves the sacred by producing higher energies. All of that confers a rightness to our inner work that gives it meaning.

As another, perhaps more practical and immediate motivator, we can harness our innate goal-seeking nature by counting how many times a day we return to the practice of sensing. Keep that count inwardly for a day or two. And then for the next day, set yourself a goal to maintain that number or even to increase it by a specific amount. The counting gives you a feedback mechanism, a quantitative measure that can help you adjust your inner effort. It also gives you a broader view of your life, linking together moments of presence across the whole day.

For this week, be alert to moments during your day when you remember about your inner work. And whenever you do remember, immediately turn to sensing your body: a hand or a foot, an arm or a leg, or your torso and head.

8.3 Body Sensation: Wholeness
(The Path to Presence: Aspect 3 of 12)

In contemplating what it might mean to develop our soul, we have precious little experience to guide us. But such experience does come in the practice of whole body sensation, which plays a fundamental role in the development of our inner body, our sensation body, the lower part of our soul. Over the past two weeks, we have practiced sensing parts of our body, bringing our attention to a hand or a foot, an arm or a leg, or our torso and head. The experience of the sensitive energy in our body, with its visceral reality, its staying power, and the way it anchors us to the present, offers a taste of what it could mean to develop our soul. Sensation brings the notion of soul out of the realm of imagination and into our direct perception. And by doing so, sensation focuses our inner work onto an effective practice with both short- and long-term value.

Sensing parts of our body is an essential beginning to this practice and could profitably be continued for months and even years until we become proficient with it. But its natural development moves toward sensing more of our body, toward creating a complete body of the sensitive energy. The difference here between part and whole is major, with whole body sensation bringing entirely new qualities not found in partial sensation. The latter does anchor us into the world of sensitive energy, which in itself is a welcome and significant step up from living in a primarily automatic fashion. Whole body sensation, however, creates a foundation that helps stabilize our contact with the conscious energy, with real presence. Conscious energy carries the quality of wholeness. And the wholeness of whole body sensation attracts and supports the wholeness of consciousness.

Partial sensation requires a focusing and division of attention that may leave little free attention for engaging in life activities. But whole body sensation can be sustained by the ongoing intention to be in our entire sensation body now. That leaves our attention undivided and free. Dividing our attention divides us, whereas whole attention makes us whole. Whole body sensation magnifies the wholeness of our attention and forms a strong base for it. Then if two or more objects require our attention simultaneously, they are both embraced within the broad reach of our unified attention. Instead of dividing, we expand.

For example, if I am in a conversation and practicing sensing my arm, I am dividing my attention between the arm and the conversation. I feel that I am withholding part of myself from the conversation, not fully participating. If instead I sense my whole body while in a conversation, my engagement in the conversation is enhanced. I listen more fully and speak from the whole of myself. I am no longer divided with part of me trying to practice inner work while the other part listens or speaks. I am more whole, more present, and more engaged. My inner work and my outer life merge. It becomes one complete and encompassing experience, not two partial ones: whole body sensing while conversing, not partial sensing alongside partially-engaged conversing. The other alternative of not practicing presence at all during a conversation leaves us splintered, at the mercy of our automatic thoughts and emotional reactions, hardly able to listen to the other person when our inner stage is so busy judging, reacting, and preparing what we will say next.

To come to whole body sensation, it helps to practice partial sensation first: an arm, a leg, both arms and both legs, and then the whole body. The practice of energy breathing, of drawing inner energies from the air around us, strengthens sensation throughout our body. That can be done intermittently throughout the day to refresh our sensation body. The end result: we experience ourselves to be more fully here.

Whole body sensation confers the strength of wholeness and a more stable organization of the energy of sensitive awareness. For this week, expand your practice of sensing parts of your body into the complete sensation of your whole body, your sensation body.

8.4 Emotions as Emotions
(The Path to Presence: Aspect 4 of 12)

Emotions drive us, for better or for worse. Emotions can drive us to distraction or to contact, to violence or to friendship, to self-centeredness or to service. The remarkable range of emotions, from the petty to the sublime, imparts richness to our life. All emotions share the common feature that they can and often do affect our behavior, inner and outer, as well as the quality of our experience. Emotions define our motivations and impose them on us. As such, every spiritual path addresses how to work with emotions.

In the way of presence, we begin with practicing awareness of emotions as emotions. Lack of such awareness relegates us more firmly into the grip of destructive emotions. We react emotionally to some event and we are just lost in the emotion, carried away by it. Our emotion controls us, at least inwardly, even if we do not react outwardly. Maybe someone angers us in a conversation and perhaps we choose to suppress it and not say anything. Nevertheless, the anger may seethe within. We feel angry. We may even know that we are angry. Yet the key fact is that the anger is the center of our world at that moment. We have no inner context within which to see the anger as anger, as an emotional state that arose and will pass. We collapse into the anger and have no presence, as the soul blood of our inner energies burns up. And so it goes with much of our emotional life.

One help in recognizing our emotions as emotions consists of noticing how they affect our physical body. We may experience a change in our heart rate or breathing, tightness in our chest, certain facial expressions, tones of voice, gestures, or postures. Each kind of emotion may have its own characteristic signature of physical effects. Stressful emotions also have more subtle effects on our physical health, effects not immediately noticeable. For now though, our practice is simply to see what we can see, to see our emotions in action, for example in our body.

Another help in recognizing emotions as emotions consists of noticing how they affect our thoughts. Repetitive and insistent patterns of thought can key us to their emotional driver. Thoughts can exhibit a tone that reflects the underlying emotion, just as our tone of voice often does. The tone of our inner thought-voice can manifest stressful or destructive emotions. So being aware of the qualities of our thoughts helps us recognize their emotional underpinnings.

Thankfully, the broad palette of our emotions is not all destructive. Far from it! Many emotions lift us up, both in the ordinary course of life and in our deepening spiritual practice. Awareness of emotions as emotions enables us to know which to nurture and which to let go. We allow and nurture the emotions that bring us closer to each other, to ourselves, to life, and to God. Much of our spiritual practice, such as meditation and prayer, nurtures those higher emotions.

We also allow the destructive emotions that create barriers, but we do not nurture them nor do we necessarily act from them. We allow, so as not to fight our emotions directly, which only energizes them. Any effort to suppress emotions backfires. Emotions are not illusory; they have a relative reality arising from causes within us. Suppressing emotions can, at best, only treat the symptoms, leaving their underlying causes untouched and ready to surface again and again. While we do not fight our destructive emotions, we also do not nurture them. We see and accept ourselves as we are, and our emotions they are, without layering on another level of emotional judgment and self-rejection. We see and accept and allow them to wane and disappear on their own. By opening our accepting and compassionate heart toward ourselves, including our destructive emotions, we heal their underlying causes.

Whether those causes lie in our personal history or elsewhere, they now take the shape of our identifications, our attachments, and our desires to have things be different than they are. We will address that in a later aspect of the path to presence.

For this week, please set yourself to notice your emotions as emotions, to realize in the midst of an emotion that it is an emotion that has you. If you watch television or movies you can see how the shows and commercials manipulate your emotions. If you drive, you can see how problems such as traffic and rude drivers activate your emotions. If you live with your family, you can see how the give-and-take of family life activates your emotions. In your favorite activities, in hearing a good joke, and in deep meditation, you can see and feel your joy.

Notice that this is not suggesting that we distance ourselves from our emotions. We feel and be in them, fully. We want to live fully, not impoverish our life by eliminating or stigmatizing our emotions. But we do want to heal the destructive and nurture the uplifting, without rejecting or even criticizing ourselves along the way. We open our heart and learn to love ourselves, emotions and all.

8.5 Thoughts as Thoughts
(The Path to Presence: Aspect 5 of 12)

Thoughts carry power: the power to create and the power to destroy, the power to understand and control much of our world, the power to guide us toward inner freedom and the power to keep us inwardly enslaved. For these and other reasons, our civilization worships the power of thought. Consequently our education revolves around enriching the content and developing the process of thought.

But in all of that, we miss the fact that the power and quality of thought depends on the quality or level of energy fueling the thoughts. The energy most commonly giving substance to our thoughts is the automatic energy. Our endless stream of self-generating, associative thoughts runs on automatic, without any intentional direction. One thought triggers another related thought, which triggers a third related to the second. Soon our thoughts have no apparent relationship with the first thought. And then some sensory perception pops into our awareness, the sound of a word, a sight, a pain, and our thoughts abruptly fly off in another direction altogether. This semi-chaotic mind goes on all day, every day.

In itself, our automatic stream of associative thoughts does no harm and even brings value. For example, that ongoing commentary on our life provides some comfort, something familiar, a touchstone amid the constant changes of our external world. But this is where our relationship with our associative thoughts passes into trouble, where power of thought exceeds its proper place.

The first problem is the extent to which we live in our thoughts. We listen to and occasionally participate in this ongoing mental commentary. And rather than just being about our life, our thoughts become our life. We allow our attention to be swept away in the stream of associative thoughts, veiling us from the simple and ordinary perceptions of living. For example, we often do not fully see the people around us because we are too busily engaged in our thoughts. We get lost in conversations because our thoughts distract us from listening. We sometimes walk with little awareness of our surroundings or our body, because we are in our thoughts. The thought stream substitutes for a more complete life.

The second problem is the extent to which we live as our thoughts. Their very familiarity lulls us into assuming that, in some fundamental sense, we are our thoughts, that what our thoughts think is what we believe, and that we are, or rather I am, the thinker of these thoughts. But even a little observation of our mind shows that these ever-present associative thoughts are thinking themselves, constructing themselves out of the material of our memory of experiences, information, and habitual patterns, coupled with those current sensory stimuli that are strong enough to break through our perceptual filters.

Out of this emerges our personality, a complex but fairly static pattern of thoughts, attitudes, memories, and responses. And that's who we believe we are.
When a thought comes into our mind, though unbidden and by association, we nevertheless believe that is what we think and even that we are that thought. But we did not think that thought. It thought itself. Thoughts masquerade as us. The thought stream substitutes for us, allowing us to live primarily on autopilot with minimal participation in our life. The thought "I," is not the I who we truly are. Live, in the moment, the challenge is to see our thoughts as just thoughts, and nothing more.

But if we are not our thoughts, not our emotions, not our personality, then who are we? The truest answer is that we are our will. And we shall explore that understanding in a later aspect of the path to presence.

For this week, notice your automatic, associative thoughts passing through your mind. The You who sees your thoughts is not just another thought, is not a function of your thoughts. Notice that your thoughts are not you, though they seduce you into believing that you are these self-generating thoughts chaining on in their own way. This is the ephemeral, insubstantial core on which our personality is based, the personality that we think we are, that substitutes for us. See your thoughts as just thoughts.

8.6 Letting Go
(The Path to Presence: Aspect 6 of 12)

The great insight of the Buddha some 2500 years ago revealed that the root of all our dissatisfaction and all our destructive tendencies lies in attachment, in identification, in clinging. From our personal study of how we relate to our thoughts and emotions, several truths begin to emerge. First, each emotion and each thought that takes center stage in our mind-heart purports to speak, or rather think or feel, for the whole of us. Second, we believe it. In that moment, we are that one thought or emotion. This process of collapsing our entire sense of ourselves into a single thought, or an emotion, or into a sensory perception such as a pain or a sight, or into one of our personality patterns is called *identification*. We become that thing. We identify ourselves as being that thought, emotion, sensation, or situation.

Third, this identification is false! For we are not any thought, emotion, sensation, or situation. Neither are we any collection of those nor any personality pattern. We are neither the weather nor the news we just received. All of this changes all the time. If we are anything real, then we cannot be one thought at one moment and some fear the next.

Fourth, because we believe ourselves to be each item of this endless stream of thoughts and the rest, our identity is fragmented and scattered. In this constantly changing inner multitude, we do not know who we are. The repeating patterns of our personality seem to promise unity and stability. But the promise falls short, because our personality contains so many conflicting patterns and is far from unified. We want to eat the cake and we want to lose weight and we cannot be certain which of these patterns we will be at the critical moment.

Our minds have constructed a virtual edifice we call "I" and "me." And this edifice does not hold up under scrutiny. Where is this me? Am I my body? But I can control my body to some extent. The I that can control is different from what it controls. So I am not my body. The only obvious and usual fall-back is to assume I am this virtual personality in my mind-heart. But we're always patching up the holes in that picture of ourselves. It does not really work. The virtual edifice of our personality turns out to be a haphazard collection of separate urges, desires, and mental and emotional habits. It lacks wholeness and unity. This is not who we are.

The further insight of the Buddha was that freedom from this conundrum comes through non-identification, through letting go of attachments, through not clinging to our desires and habits. This does not mean letting go of responsibilities or of caring. But it does mean seeing in the moment that our thoughts are not who we are, that our emotional reactions and desires are not who we are, that our situation is not who we are, and that our personality and its habitual patterns are not who we are. These are all just thoughts and emotions and sensory impressions. It is a mistake to promote them beyond what they are, or to promote our fragmented virtual "I" to being the real me. This personality of ours goes on without any intentional participation on our part.

To not identify, we look to see what does go on in us and we just let it be. We let it all pass without going with it. This is the beginning of liberation: to be in inner silence and peace, to see our inner processes without getting caught up in them, and to act outwardly as necessary.

The freedom is real. All the dissatisfied thoughts and emotions need not make us dissatisfied with our life, or even with our current experience. We can be and we can act, and we can use our personality and its many skills. Yet we are not bound by any of it. We are not bound by our past, by our conditioning, by our desires, or by our notions and assumptions about ourselves. This unboundedness is liberation.

The actual, in-the-moment work of liberation entails seeing ourselves becoming identified, entangled with some thought, emotion, or perception, and then just residing as the one who is seeing this, while letting the entangling thought, emotion, or perception pass by and fade on its own, without acting on it or reacting to it or assuming that it is us. This is the practice of liberation, of non-identification, of letting go, of non-clinging. It takes time and devotion, gradual refinement of our inner seeing, and much repetition. But it does lead us, little by little, toward inner freedom. And that inner freedom brings lasting joy and enables us to love and to be much more effective in our life and in our service to life.

For this week, please practice the in-the-moment work of liberation, non-identification, letting go, non-clinging, by seeing the entanglement and letting it pass.

8.7 Inner Energy Flows
(The Path to Presence: Aspect 7 of 12)

All that we do and all that we experience involves energy. And all of it depends on the quality and quantity of energy available. This applies just as much in our inner worlds as it does in the external, physical world. So our spiritual practice, our path to presence, our hope to become more real, and our ability to serve also hinge on energies.

That naturally raises some questions. What levels and qualities of energy are we able to perceive and contact? How well do we manage our inner energies? How adept are we at producing and harvesting more inner energy and of a higher quality? How well do we use the energies available to us? All these questions point to areas of spiritual development full of unlimited and unexpected possibilities.

As our inner work progresses our perceptions change. In particular our ability to perceive energies grows more subtle. With those perceptions comes the possibility of more insightful and skillful work with energies. There are three levels of energies of most immediate interest in our practice of presence. In our path these are known as the automatic, the sensitive, and the conscious energies. The next higher energy, known as the creative or as the sacred light, comes more into play in our deeper meditation and prayer.

In our practice of seeing emotions as emotions and thoughts as thoughts, we have become somewhat more familiar with the automatic energy and how it drives a certain level of thoughts and emotions: the self-generated, pre-programmed, associative and reactive ones. This automatic energy allows us to sleepwalk and daydream through life, while our fairly sophisticated auto-pilot manages things for us. That auto-pilot is so complex that it successfully poses, both to us and to others, as a real person. But it is only our automatic-energy-driven personality, the accumulated patterns of a lifetime of experience, memories, past choices, desires, and urges. Nevertheless, in our mind-heart the automatic energy performs essential functions such as forming memories from experience, making the connections between those memories, recalling memories and skills as needed, and the ability to read, speak and understand language. All that of course is most necessary. But this energy's spillover into automatic thoughts and emotions often results in negative thought and emotional patterns, or in fooling us into believing that we are these automatic personality patterns, or in masking the existence of deeper levels in us.

The same level of automatic energy drives useful and

vital activities in our body's instinctive and motor functions. Walking and talking, breathing and digesting, and many other processes use the automatic energy, whose flow is obviously very necessary for us. But here also, it spills over into patterns that are not so useful, such as habitual, unnecessary muscular tensions, fidgeting, overeating, drinking too much alcohol, and other physical addictions. Such bodily excesses burn up our energies and deprive our inner work of the energy it needs. So we need to manage our bodily excesses, manage our automatic energy.

In earlier aspects of the Path to Presence we studied the sensitive energy in our body. In coming weeks we will study it in our feeling and thinking. This is a crucial energy for our inner work, for its intentional use brings us a major step toward full presence and its accumulation gradually forms the lower part of our soul and grows our being. We can directly, with our attention and intention, cause this energy to flow into us from our surroundings. One such method, found in many traditions, is energy breathing: putting our attention into the air around us and intentionally and consciously breathing in the energy from the air. And we can stabilize it within our body by inhabiting the sensitive energy, by being in it on a frequent and continuing basis as we go about our lives. That takes a deep, vivid, and effective commitment to the path.

Our swirling thoughts and emotions, undirected movements of automatic and sensitive energies, distract us and thereby hide the still pool of consciousness beneath them. The conscious energy forms the context of our mind, the background of experience. In the emotions it often leads to peace, to equanimity. In the mind it enables seeing or direct knowing. When the cognizant stillness of meditation settles the automatic and sensitive energies that usually overlay the conscious energy, consciousness rises into the foreground of our experience. At such moments we are truly conscious.

The substance of our inner work, to a very great extent,

involves the flows and interactions of energies. For this week, please study these inner energies in yourself. Choose one or more specific aspects discussed in the foregoing and arrange your practice accordingly.

8.8 Emotional Presence
(The Path to Presence: Aspect 8 of 12)

In an earlier aspect of the Path to Presence, Emotions as Emotions, we studied our ordinary emotional life, how our emotions react to events, automatically and without our intention. In the aspect on Letting Go we practiced directly freeing ourselves from the grip of those of our automatic, non-intentional emotions that enslave us and darken our lives.

This week we will begin to practice bringing some intentionality into our emotions. Upon hearing that, you might immediately protest that intentionality would rob our emotions of spontaneity. But that would only happen if we tried to generate some particular emotion or tried to stop certain of our emotions, neither of which is our purpose in this. Rather we seek to feel more deeply, to raise the quality of our emotional life by bringing more refined energies to our emotions. This heightened emotional presence, by itself, can help lift us out of the muck of reactions and into spontaneous emotional connection with ourselves, with others, and with the Sacred.

When we practice sensitive presence in our body, we simply put our attention into a part or the whole of our body and hold our attention there. Gradually this awakens and attracts the sensitive energy into our body. To the sensitive energy in body awareness, we give the name sensation and call the practice sensing.

In a similar way, we can bring the sensitive energy into our feelings. We begin with sensing our body to establish a foundation of body presence. Then in addition, we put our attention into the area of our body where our emotions usually arise and act, namely the region that includes our chest and solar plexus. With a light and gentle touch, we hold our attention in the region of our feelings. We do not focus particularly on our heart or any other point, so as not to interfere with our body's instinctive functioning. We just keep a general awareness in that region, letting the sensitive energy of feeling collect there. We shall call this practice emotional presence.

One subtlety with emotional presence is that we are not only aiming toward awareness of the feeling region of our body, but more directly to have presence in our emotions themselves, in that part of us that generates emotions. So this is not a matter of sensing our chest and solar plexus, or of being aware of the physical sensations there. However, the latter method is used to great benefit in some Buddhist approaches to enable one to perceive the physical sensations associated with emotions. That helps free us from attachment to and identification with the emotion, by deconstructing its monolithic appearance, breaking the automatic, reactive emotion up into its physical, emotional, and thinking components.

We practice body presence by sensing our body with the sensitive energy, by being aware of our body from within our body. In the same way here, we practice emotional presence by feeling our emotions, or feeling our emotional part, with the sensitive energy. We feel our emotions, not from the outside as an observer, but from inside of them, feeling them from within. This intentional, sensitive presence in emotion brings us a big step forward from the automatic functioning of our emotions. We still feel, but our feelings are more real, more appropriately responsive to external situations, more subtle, more profound. Joy replaces pleasure. Even when there is no apparent emotion, we nevertheless feel sensitively in the center of emotion. In our chest and solar plexus region we practice emotional presence. We are not attempting to direct or dictate the content of our emotions, we are not attempting feel a particular emotion. But we are practicing presence in our emotional part. Just as sensing our body enhances our experience of our body, emotional presence changes the nature and quality of our emotions, giving us more of a feeling for our life.

For this week, practice emotional presence. Using your attention and intention, nurture the accumulation of the sensitive energy of emotion in the region of your chest and solar plexus, even in moments when there are no apparent emotions.

8.9 Cognitive Presence
(The Path to Presence: Aspect 9 of 12)

Cognitive presence means presence in our mind, in that part of us that cognizes or mentally registers perceptions and especially thoughts. We practice cognitive presence by putting our attention into our head and being there in our mind. Doing so attracts the sensitive energy of thought, the sensitive energy of cognition, into our mind. Just as the sensitive energy in our body enables us to be in contact with our body and its sensations, and the sensitive energy of emotion enables us to be in contact with our center of emotion and our emotions, so the sensitive energy of cognition enables us to be in contact with our mind and its contents.

But presence of mind means more than contact, because contact implies a division: something or someone who is in contact with something else, an observer and an observed. Body presence means inhabiting our body, being in our body, at one with it. Emotional presence means inhabiting our center of emotion, being in our chest and solar plexus region. And cognitive presence means inhabiting our mind, being in our mind, owning our mind. We are not standing back as an observer of our thoughts. We are right there in our mind — no division and no separation. But we are there intentionally and in sensitive awareness of our mind. Here I am in my head, in the place from which I cognize, know, think, and see.

This is a far cry from our typical mental state of being lost in thought, which operates on the automatic energy. In cognitive presence, such automatic associative thoughts may continue, but now you are present in them. The thought stream, whether associative or intentional, occurs within the mind you are occupying. Cognitive presence means being the one who is aware of and standing in the thought stream and, more generally, the one who is cognizing, knowing, and seeing.

The sensitive energy of cognition tends to raise the level our thoughts. Rather than arising by their typical automatic associations, our thoughts become more relevant to what we are doing, to our situation of the moment. We have less mental clamor and chaos. With cognitive presence we are more able to focus on a topic, more able to think clearly and logically, more able to see into the heart of matters. When automatic thoughts do arise, we are aware of them as thoughts and less likely to be swept away by them.

Cognitive presence is not about intentional thinking, but rather about intentional awareness in the context and contents of our mind. While this may include intentional thinking on a particular subject, it is not limited to that because you can be cognitively present in the absence of thoughts. You can be there, in your mind, knowing and cognizing without necessarily thinking.

The practice of cognitive presence works best when coupled with body or emotional presence. On its own, cognitive presence all-too-readily gets carried away in the stream of associative thoughts, opinions, daydreams, commentary, self-talk, attractions and repulsions. The sensitive energy of cognition thins out and scatters, leaving us adrift in our usual automatic mind. But when, along with cognitive presence, we simultaneously practice presence in our body or our center of emotion, we have a better chance at sustaining cognitive presence. Our body or emotional presence helps keep us from falling prey to the thought stream. Thoughts may come and go, but we stand anchored in body or heart and see our thoughts arising and passing. Here in mind and here in body, or here in mind and here in emotion, we are.

For this week, practice bringing your attention into your mind. Enter your mind. Inhabit it. Emerge from floating down your thought stream to anchor yourself in the present. Let the stream pass through you without passing with it. Become the context of your mind and aware of its contents. Be the one who cognizes, knows, thinks, and sees through your mind. Be the knowing, the cognizing, the seeing. Be your mind.

8.10 Triune Presence

(The Path to Presence: Aspect 10 of 12)

A stool, to be stable, requires at least three legs. So it is with presence. The act of simultaneously engaging all three presences of body, heart, and mind greatly multiplies our chances of maintaining our presence. The three interact and mutually support each other. When one of these presences weakens, the other two can reinvigorate it. With all three, we feel more solid; we stand firmly in the world of presence, of being here fully. So the first benefit of triune presence is the enhanced duration it enables.

Another major benefit lies in the breadth of triune presence. We become more fully human, anchored in our body with an alert, open, and adaptable mind and an appropriately sensitive heart. Our experience becomes more rounded, more balanced, and enriched. Clarity of mind is warmed by sensitivity of feeling, and both are grounded in the present moment of our body.

A third significant benefit is the intensity of triune presence, the vividness it imparts to our experience. The three presences of body, heart, and mind combine to form a stronger presence than one or two could. One reason lies in the degree and quality of attention needed to enter and maintain such presence. In meeting the challenge of being in all three, we raise the level of our inner work for those moments. But there is also a feedback from our awakened body, heart, and mind that supports the intensity of triune presence.

So how do we actually practice triune presence? In recent weeks we have worked at body presence, emotional presence, and cognitive presence. Now we can work on putting it all together.

We begin the practice of triune presence during formal, sitting meditation. After thoroughly relaxing our body, mind, and heart, we turn to sensing our body. First we sense parts of it: arms, legs, torso, and head. Then we move into sensing the whole of our body and staying with that wholeness. Once we feel grounded in whole body sensation, in body presence, we add to it.

We put some extra attention into our center of emotion, into the general region of our chest and solar plexus. We are there in our center of emotion, even if there are no particular emotions at the time. We are there in readiness to feel, in readiness to be our emotion, in readiness to respond with feeling. We stay with both, with whole body sensing and with attention to our emotional center. After having settled ourselves in both emotional and body presence, we add to that.

We place some extra attention into our head, into our mind, to establish ourselves in cognitive presence. We are in our whole mind, not just in our thoughts. We are there in our knowing, seeing, thinking, cognizing part. And then we stay with all three: sensing our whole body, emotional presence, and cognitive presence. Toward the end of the meditation period, we let all that go and allow the effort and energy to soak into our being.

We also wish to live our ordinary daily life in full presence. So we can practice entering triune presence at any time during our day when we have enough spare attention for it. As with the sitting meditation version of this practice, we begin with sensing our body, the whole of it. Then we add emotional or cognitive presence. And finally we add the third. With practice, you may be able to come into all three at once. So when you find moments during your day that do not require your full attention to whatever you are doing, you can try entering triune presence and staying with it. Ultimately you may find that triune presence does not detract from your engagement in your life activity. On the contrary, triune presence may add to your attention, so that you can do whatever you are doing more fully. But, of course we maintain the caveat that critical situations (e.g., driving, chopping vegetables) deserve our full attention without inner efforts of presence.

For this week, practice triune presence. Even if you are only able to enter such presence for brief moments, those moments repeated offer a taste of new possibilities, a new way of living.

8.11 Conscious Presence
(The Path to Presence: Aspect 11 of 12)

Having worked on sensitive presence in our body, in our emotions, and in our mind, and in all three together, we may wonder what if anything comes next for presence. Is there more? Indeed there is — much more. The sensitive energy allows us contact with the content of experience, with our body, heart, and mind. The next higher energy, the conscious energy, offers us an entirely new perspective, a vast and timeless perspective. The triune, sensitive presence in body, heart, and mind provides the needed foundation on which an opening into the conscious energy, into consciousness, can persist for more than a few moments.

First, let us note the various qualities of consciousness

as it manifests in body, heart, and mind. Conscious energy in the body brings awareness of wholeness, focused unity of action, and complete coordination. Conscious physical actions flow with effortless perfection, like an athlete in the zone. But even the simplest actions, like reaching for something at the dinner table or like walking, can be conscious.

Conscious energy in our mind brings cognitive presence beyond just thinking. That state opens into the timeless stillness of consciousness, into cognitive stillness. It yields a higher, unifying perspective, the ability to see, to see objectively and impartially, to see our life as a whole.

Conscious energy in our center of emotion opens into our basic layer of peace and equanimity. That peace at heart carries us into the wonder of life. Joy naturally flows out of this, as does every other constructive emotion appropriate to a given situation.

These qualities of real consciousness offer us guidance on how to enter it, how to step into that higher perspective. From contact with our thoughts, we open to the silent, cognitive awareness surrounding thought. From contact with our center of emotion, we open to the peace and equanimity underlying all emotion. From sensing our whole body, we enter wholeness and unity of body action. What we do, we do with our whole body, with every part of our body participating, playing its appropriate role.

Building on the foundation of triune, sensitive presence in body, heart, and mind, we allow all three to come under the umbrella of consciousness. The conscious energy subsumes sensation, feeling, and cognition, unifying the three into the wholeness of our being. The hallmark of the conscious energy in all its forms is that through it we can be. Simply and directly, in this moment, we are. We are whole and here.

For this week, please practice entering the stillness, the peace, the wholeness of consciousness. Try it first in sitting meditation and, as you are able, during your ordinary activities.

8.12 I Am Present
(The Path to Presence: Aspect 12 of 12)

The stool of presence may be stable with its three legs of presence in body, presence in heart, and presence of mind, but that situation is not complete. The purpose of a stool is for someone to sit on it. That someone is You, your I, your I Am, the agent of your life, the one who is present in your body, heart, and mind. It would be more accurate to say that the stool is not one of presence, but rather a stool of awareness — unless there is someone sitting on it. There can be awareness of body, of heart, and of mind. But without You there as the one who is aware, the one who is present, it is simply like a robot with sensors.

The core of presence is the one who is present, the one who inhabits your body from within, the one who feels your emotions, the one who cognizes through your mind, the one who lives your life and does what you do. Ordinarily we take this one for granted. We assume that we are always here as the one who experiences and lives our life. But even a cursory investigation reveals that sensory awareness, thoughts, and actions typically go on by themselves without "You." This is particularly obvious in our automatic thoughts, which think themselves by association, without us thinking them or directing them or even necessarily being aware of them. Such awareness often comes after the fact, when we notice that a whole train of thoughts has arisen on its own and passed through our mind.

So this final aspect of the Path to Presence involves the practice of being the one who experiences and lives our life, the practice of being here at home in our center. Be the one who sees through your eyes, the one who is aware of your thoughts, aware of your mind, aware of your center of emotion. Inhabit your body. Inhabit your feeling. In habit your mind.

Claim it all as your own. Instead of letting so many of your words and actions happen on their own in a stimulus-response cycle and without your participation, say what you say and do what you do. Engage and be who you are.

The subtlety is that who we are, our I, is will. And will does not exist in the same way that material objects or even energies exist. Will cannot be touched or seen or weighed or experienced. Indeed, it is will that does the touching, the seeing, the weighing, and the experiencing. Just as our physical eye cannot see itself, will looks, but not back at itself. Will acts but is not acted upon. But we can enter our will, our I, by being it, by being the actor, the agent, the seer, the decider, the director of our attention.

There are two levels in this. At the level of the conscious energy, we can be our I directly. We have a sense of wholeness and agency, a sense that I am the agent of my life, that I am the decider, the chooser, the experiencer — here in this moment. We feel ourselves to be the one who is here. We will our self to be and we are. But ... this is not our actual I. We could call this our True Self[5]. And we would do very well to live in our True Self, more and more.

To get a taste of this, just ask yourself "Am I here?" And then *you* answer with full intention and with the whole of yourself: "Yes, I am here." As you do so, be here, be the one who is saying this, thinking this. This is you, your True Self, sitting in the seat of presence.

There is, however, a deeper level of I, one which we do not enter directly, but rather one to which we can open, one which we can allow to enter us. The difference between True Self and I is where it begins. With True Self, we may feel ourselves to be our own source, to be our own individual self, separate from other people, from other selves. The transition to I occurs when we, as our True Self, open inwardly to the source

---

5   See J. G. Bennett, *Deeper Man* (Santa Fe: Bennett Books, 1978), pp. 108-112

just behind our True Self. We open our very core to let our own higher will flow into and through us, as us. That is our I, but is not so separate from other I's. We recognize our I as fully our own, as who we really are, yet also as not just our own, but as connected at its root, at our root, with something vastly greater than us.

For this week, practice being your True Self, and even opening to your I. Be the one who lives your life, who makes your choices, who does what you do, and who experiences your experience. Rather than leave the seat of presence empty, inhabit your own center and complete your presence.

9. Through Thick and Thin

If we only practice our inner work when all is well in our personal world, or when it's convenient, we miss far too many opportunities. Life brings unexpected and unwanted difficulties, as well as expected and wanted engagements. External demands on our attention may leave us little inner bandwidth to spare. Or perhaps we have had a disappointment and are slightly depressed. Maybe we are ill, didn't sleep well, ate too much or too little, had an argument, received an insult, rushing because we are late, overloaded with busyness, tasks, information, and errands — in short, living in this twenty-first century world. In any given moment, we can and too often do take one of these many apparent impediments as a reason not to practice, as a reason to forgo the work of presence, or not to meditate. Moreover, there are always difficulties and distractions in the way of inner work. Even in our quiet moments, our thoughts and emotions can draw us into identification and away from the opportunity of presence.

So the great imperative, the secret to making our way

along the spiritual path, the basic enabling factor of the inward service of presence and prayer, is to keep at our practice come what may, to be wary of and not to accept the myriad excuses our mind offers up. Naturally, our presence practice may be stronger in some moments and weaker in others. But in the midst of difficulties or distractions, even weak practice is far better than no presence at all. Weak practice in difficult moments can be even more valuable than strong practice in quiet moments. Persisting with inner work in less-than-optimal conditions strengthens our will, sharpens our intention, awakens our determination, and reinforces our commitment.

Indeed the impediments to practice challenge us to rise to meet them. By repeatedly facing up to the challenge of practicing presence in seemingly inopportune moments, we raise the level of our inner work. Venturing to awaken in the midst of the sometimes roiling waters of our life spurs us to try harder, to practice more intelligently and more heartfully, to create presence where it is most needed.

Now none of this implies that all practice is solely a matter of effort and directed attention. We can very simply open to being present in demanding situations. Even without spare attention, we can to some degree open to our own presence. It need not be an either-or choice between inner work and external engagement. That is the secret of spiritual practice in ordinary life. We can simultaneously be both present inwardly and engaged outwardly, in parallel and mutually supportive processes. We enter our life wholeheartedly, embracing and thereby transforming the would-be obstacles. That way we maintain a conscious, though perhaps tenuous, connection to a deeper world.

And the more we practice the more presence comes back to remind us in our absence. So for today, and for every day this coming week, practice presence through thick and thin. Whenever during your day, you remember about the inner work of presence, come back into yourself right in that moment, sense your body, feel your emotions, know your mind, and be here. Nothing else, inner or outer, need stop you from that, because presence need not interfere with whatever else you need or want to do.

10.0 The Eightfold Path

Some 2500 years ago, the Buddha and his disciples elucidated what is known as *The Noble Eightfold Path*, which prescribes a way toward freedom. This venerable teaching, in various interpretations, has been at the core of the Buddhist way ever since.

For the non-Buddhist as well, the Eightfold Path offers enormous value in unlocking our hidden potentials. While the Buddha neither asserted nor denied the existence of God, we can clearly see that the Eightfold Path brings one closer to God. And while this particular teaching does not explicitly address love and compassion, clearly those qualities were taught by the Buddha in other contexts and are developed in following the Eightfold Path. In the coming weeks, rather than rehash what has been taught and written at length about the Eightfold Path, we will revisit each of its eight aspects with a new perspective.

The English translations traditionally given to the names of the elements of the Eightfold Path are:

1. Right View
2. Right Intention
3. Right Speech
4. Right Action
5. Right Livelihood
6. Right Effort

7. Right Mindfulness
8. Right Concentration

Now these eight aspects, though typically listed in that order, are not meant to be taken in a linear, sequential fashion. Rather we practice them in parallel, in an eightfold mutually supportive synergy. Each aspect interacts with all the others in creating a complete and robust path toward freedom, wisdom, and compassion.

By way of preparation in this introductory week, we note that these eight titles all begin the word "Right." How do we know what is "Right" in Right View, Right Intention, and the rest? It means much more than just correct. Consider other descriptors of the meaning of "Right," such as appropriate, proper, skillful, intelligent, and compassionate. In doing so, we see that it is not enough simply to study, either books or with a teacher. To truly follow this path, one must also develop one's own insight, one's own vision, intuition, and creativity, and one's own taste for the truth. The path cannot be learned by rote, nor by simply following some set of moral prescriptions, such as the ones usually included under Right Action.

How do we know what's right? Something in us does know and we call that something conscience. It does not lie. But we can mistakenly construe our own self-centered urges for the promptings of conscience. And those same urges can cause us to misinterpret, ignore, or bury the actual indications of our conscience. To acquire the taste of conscience, we pay attention to our feelings, our intuitions of what is right and what is not. We test that against common sense and ordinary morality. If what our conscience appears to be telling us passes that sanity test, then we may go with it, which brings us to the further test of evaluating the results of going with it. Through this trial and error process, we learn to hear the promptings of our conscience and distinguish it from our self-centered or fanciful impulses.

As a complement to conscience for guidance on our path, we need something else that the Buddha recommended — investigation. In this context investigation means looking into our own experience, looking into the inner workings of our mind, feelings, body, and awareness, and seeing how various actions, inner and outer, affect our inner life. Investigation brings to light many situations and processes, about which conscience can then guide us. For example, certain teachers and teachings may not be appropriately adapted to our current state, skills, quirks, and possibilities. But our conscience is always in touch, if only we can be in touch with it.

A third factor complementing both conscience and investigation in discovering our way is exploration. We bring our creative flair to our inner work, to our meditation, presence, and prayer. We look carefully and deeply and try new approaches, not necessarily ones we have been taught. Not everything can be taught nor put into words, particularly the deeper realms and more subtle aspects of spirituality. Through exploration we push beyond our inner envelope and into uncharted inner territory. Investigation and intuition of conscience guide our exploration toward the Light.

We will look at conscience again when we come to Aspect 4, Right Action. For this week, investigate and explore your inner experience to notice your intuitions of what is right. See how you respond to those sometimes inconvenient promptings.

10.1 Right View
(The Eightfold Path: Aspect 1)

Our personal world view directly shapes not only our actions, but also our perceptions. Whatever does not fit, we either do not perceive or our mind reinterprets to accord with our view. Thus our world view can be both limiting and self-reinforcing. An open-minded world view, though, can be expansive and self-transforming.

From the standpoint of the spiritual path, the single most harmful but commonly-held concept about reality is that we are separate from each other and from the world around us. This illusory sense of a separate self, known as ego, occupies us nearly full-time with its care and feeding, dominating our life and our relationships. But through spiritual practice our ego grows porous and we begin to see through its illusion. This is almost the definition of liberation: freedom from the false self that occupies our core. In the process, our world view changes toward openness and connectedness.

One way to notice our ego in action is to see how we consider ourselves to be special. We may harbor an attitude that we are better and more important than other people, or some other people. Or we may feel the opposite, that we are worse than others, less important. But the truth that we are equally children of the one Creator, shows that we are equally special, miraculous, and important, or to put it more directly, we are all just ordinary people. So the Right View in this regard holds that each of us is ordinary and equal, neither more nor less than a human being.

Many other useful concepts can shape a wholesome view of the world. The notion of karma — as you sow, so shall you reap — tempers our actions. An understanding of the hierarchy of the spiritual worlds and energies gives us a map of the path and our inner life. Recognition of the role of identification as the root of our inner slavishness offers us hope of releasing many self-imposed burdens. The understanding that through our inner work we serve not only ourselves, but the world around us, as well as the Sacred, places our spiritual efforts in their proper context and gives us new motivation.

Now all such deep truths that can form and transform our world view begin as mere intellectual concepts that we hear about. But a full cup has no room for the new. By being open-minded and non-dogmatic in our assumptions about life, we allow new concepts actually to enter us for consideration. By applying ourselves to the practices of the path, true concepts develop from ideas into direct perceptions. Knowledge grows into understanding based in experience. And new understanding changes our world view, thereby transforming us and our life.

Our world view also depends on what world we live in. In the world of automatic energy, where our actions and reactions go solely by habit and our thoughts by association, where we live on autopilot, nothing brings true satisfaction. Our contact with life lacks immediacy and everything, including ourselves, is subject to decay and dissolution in time. Our self-centeredness dictates our actions and experience, inner and outer. That includes building up and defending an inherently empty edifice of an independent self, while in reality we live passively dependent on external events to motivate us. Thus we see the world as all about me, yet essentially unsatisfying and temporary. This is typically where we are when something breaks through to draw us onto the path toward liberation.

And so we begin our climb into the next higher world, characterized by the sensitive energy and actual, direct contact with ourselves and our surroundings. Much of practical spirituality concerns just that: learning to live in the here and now. This changes our world view: life is more vivid and satisfying, but still about me and subject to time.

Beyond that, in our lifetime of spiritual practice, we move toward even higher worlds, of the peace, equanimity and spaciousness of the conscious energy, of the sacred and creative Light, of the unity of Love beyond individuality, and finally the Ultimate. And while we engage in this gradual cultivation of our soul, we also recognize that all of that, the whole depth of the spirit, is available here and now. So we have these twin sides to our view of the spiritual path: one of progressive development over a lifetime of practice and the other of immediate connection with all the worlds. Both are true and together they inform a view of the path balanced between the temporal and the eternal.

Another aspect of Right View concerns the centrality of will, in life and especially in spiritual practice. All eight limbs of the Eightfold Path concern will, as shall see in studying them. Typically we only consider energies in our practice, particularly the energy of consciousness that enables us truly to be conscious, to be mindful and present. But will is at least equal to energies in importance. The facets of will include but are not limited to intention, attention, choice and decision, determination and commitment, responsibility, conscience, love, acceptance, and surrender. If we are anything at all, we are our will. Yet will is impossible to see directly, because will is the one who sees.

So these elements of truth — the hierarchy of energies and worlds, will, karma, identification, liberation and the rest — combine in us to form a Right View of the world and of the path. Through our practice that view develops and deepens, as its truth enters us experientially and viscerally. This Right View gives us a viable map, showing where we are, where we are going, and how to travel.

For this week, notice your own world view and how it shapes your life.

10.2 Right Intention
(The Eightfold Path: Aspect 2)

Broadly speaking, the way of Right Intention has two major sets of features: first, to have a coherent and effective intention, and second, to have that intention be "Right." We'll begin our discussion with the second, that our intention be "Right." In the context of the Eightfold Path, the intentions alluded to by the word "Right" include the intentions to follow the path, to do the practices, to serve, and not to cause harm. But the primary emphasis is on following the path. Ordinarily we may have many wholesome intentions such as to care for ourselves and our family, to develop our skills and talents, to serve society through our employment and through kindness, to engage in creative and productive endeavors, and to enjoy our life. The intention to follow the path does not preclude any of that. We can live full lives while devotedly pursuing our inner work.

Right Intention depends on our understanding of the path and its practices and on our ability to actually do those practices. Our knowledge of the path develops by learning from teachers, from spiritual friends, and through reading. As with Right View, knowledge transforms into understanding through our experience of working with the practices. Our ability to do the practices grows through practice, which changes our perceptions, sharpens our attention, accumulates our energies, and defragments our will. This process continues throughout our path as our understanding deepens and our perceptions refine. All the while our intention to practice provides the essential impetus to keep us going and to apply our full intelligence and creativity to our inner work.

Along the way, plateaus come. Perhaps the practices bring us great satisfaction, even joy, and we are content and tempted to settle for maintaining our current level of practice. But if our intention includes full liberation and maximizing our potential for service, we persist in refining our efforts and in our experimentation to find what's possible, necessary, and appropriate for us at each new period and at any particular moment. Now there are teachers who tell us to relax into the natural unfolding of our path and life, to realize that we have already arrived. And certainly there is truth in that. At the same time, however, we pursue our practice indefatigably, not toward some distant goal, but to enter into this very moment more deeply, more durably, and more lovingly. All this is driven by our intention. Lack of intention means lack of inner work. So we respect and nurture our intention to practice. And that intention can grow into determination and commitment.

The intention to practice creates a kind of self-imposed inner pressure. This is necessary if we are not to stagnate on those spiritual plateaus. However, this inner pressure must be appropriately modulated, tuned. It should not be so overly dogmatic or desperately, inflexibly muscular that it causes us stress. Rather, we stay relaxed, inwardly and outwardly. At the same time, however, our intention to practice should not be so lax that we become inwardly lazy toward our inner work. We remain relaxed but diligent. This whole dynamic changes over time, as we open more and more to the Sacred and to liberation. The Reality Itself draws us, attracts us, effortlessly boosting our intention to practice, which moves from being solely active to being more receptive and responsive. The path shifts into being something we wish for with all our heart, rather than something we impose on ourselves. Instead of needing discipline to meditate regularly, we look forward in joyous anticipation to our periods of meditation. Similarly, the Sacred draws us more profoundly into the practices of presence and of prayer. At that stage our heart is really in it.

Intention is an aspect of will. In the practice of presence this manifests as the intention or will to be, to be present, to be here now, to be aware of our inner and outer perceptions, to be aware of our body and our surroundings and our self. In prayer, we have the receptive intention or will to open ourselves to the Higher. In acting with excellence in life, our will manifests in a third mode, neither active nor receptive, but a synergy of the two and more. These three modes of will, active, receptive, and synergic, in various levels and permutations, enter all that we do.

Indeed, we are our will, the one who sees what we see and does what we do. We can practice living as intention, being the one who lives our life, being the center from which our actions and our attention emanate. The typical alternative consists of living half-aware, while abdicating our center to let our life follow a haphazard, reactive course.

You may wonder how to reconcile the feeling of being the one who sees what you see and does what you do, being the agent of your life, with the Buddhist teaching of no separate self. The reconciliation has to do with levels. If we are just inwardly scattered, there can be no letting go of separateness, for we are caught by everything. So we need to have a self to open, we need to develop the inner collectedness that comes with being the one who lives our life. Then ultimately, in every religion, we work toward opening ourselves to our oneness with the Sacred and in doing so overcome our separateness.

Here are some examples of how to put this inner work of intention into practice. In watching TV, be the watcher. In walking, be the walker. In speaking, be the speaker. In listening, be the listener. In thinking, be the thinker.

In reluctantly doing a necessary chore that part of you does not want to do, choose to do it, choose to engage in it fully. While doing the chore, make the ongoing choice to do it, to be there doing it, to be the one doing it. Choose to do what you are doing.

For this week, notice your intentions. What does Right Intention mean to you, in your life, in your inner work, in practice?

10.3 Right Speech
(The Eightfold Path: Aspect 3)

The uniquely human power of speech may be the single most important factor biologically distinguishing our species. The use of that power merits its own aspect of the Eightfold Path, called Right Speech. This concerns what we say and how we say it, or more broadly, what we communicate and how we communicate it. These, in turn, depend on the intention and awareness behind our communication.

To be right in a moral sense, our speech needs to be helpful, appropriate, and true, non-harming, not divisive, not abusive, and not negative gossip. Listening to our conscience, our intuition of rightness, can guide us in knowing what to say and what not to say. Beyond questions of morality, which concern intentions, we need to understand in advance the likely effects of our words apart from the intentions behind them. Too often those effects work at cross-purposes to what we intended.

By continually seeking to improve our ability to communicate, to bring excellence into our speech, the practice of Right Speech passes from the required realm of morality into the realm of being-work. Excellence in speech includes a broad vocabulary used incisively and the appropriate emotional tone, supported by facial expressions and body language, which all combine to communicate our intended meaning. Words matter, enough to warrant taking the trouble to speak well and with quality. This practice affects the quality of our being, because speaking with excellence requires attention, intention, and presence.

Too often, particularly in intimate, family relationships, we speak from a destructive, emotional reaction, with anger being a common example. Speaking angrily to someone near to us poisons our ongoing relationship. On the other hand, repressing our anger, trying to stuff it down and not feel it, poisons our own psyche just as a surely as speaking angrily does. So we seek the middle ground by inwardly noticing and accepting how we feel, actually feeling it, and crucially not identifying with it. There may be anger coursing through us, but that does not mean that we must be angry. We need not become the anger and we need not dump our destructive emotions on the people around us. Instead, we see the anger, allow it, but realize that it will surely pass. It is just a feeling. It is not who I am. Then, if necessary and appropriate, we may choose to speak about the situation with the others involved. But if we are not identified, not clinging to the anger, we can speak in a constructive manner that leaves room for the other person to engage with us, without reacting.

Many of us love to talk, but fewer give equal importance to listening. Right Speech includes right listening, being interested in other people and what they have to say. In right listening we are simply quiet inside and attentive to the speaker, not inwardly criticizing, and not preparing what we will say next. Those who talk too much miss opportunities to know and enjoy the people around them as anything more than an audience. Those who talk too little, whatever the reason for their reticence, miss the opportunity to make themselves known, to fully engage in the give and take of conversation. Right Speech means finding the balance between speaking and listening. It means not being so identified with our own private world that we leave no room to listen to others, no opening for others to enter our field of care.

Right Speech also means conscious speech, being fully present when we speak and when we listen. While speaking we can practice the inner work of being aware of the sound of our voice, its emotional tone, the physical sensations in our throat, mouth, and chest, the meaning and effect of our words, and our facial expressions and gestures. This can be summed up as the practice of presence in body, in heart, and in mind, while speaking and while listening. Add to this an awareness of how our listeners are responding to what we are saying and we have the fullness of conscious speech.

Finally, there is freedom. Particularly in friendly circumstances, we relax and let the creative and spontaneous enter what we say and how we hear, which often manifests as simple joy and a sense of humor.

So the inner work of Right Speech means speaking in a way that does not offend our conscience, speaking with excellence, not speaking from a state of identification with reactive emotions, making room for others by listening, and being fully present in speaking and in listening.

For this week, be there when you speak and when you listen, and practice Right Speech.

10.4 Right Action
(The Eightfold Path: Aspect 4)

What we actually do in this world defines us, both individually and collectively. One of the great revelations implicit in the Bible shows that the Creator both cares about and acts in human history. To make that relevant to our personal path, we simply realize that the Sacred Spirit can act through us, particularly if we are free enough of egoism to respond to the deeper promptings. But that communication channel is noisy and thus easily corrupted by self-centered illusions. So we need some basic, clarifying ground rules of what not to do. And for that we adopt the moral norms of our society, tempered by the Golden Rule and its variants: "do to others what you would like to be done to you" and "do not do to others what they would not like to be done to them."

If we engage in some form of spiritual inner work on an ongoing basis, we may feel that the issue of being moral in our actions is somehow behind us. We may think: *of course I am already moral; my real challenge is being present*. But throughout our life, questions of right and wrong continue to appear in both large and small ways. And this is a challenge to presence, a challenge of paying attention to what we do, to ensure that all our actions pass the test of morality. This becomes particularly clear if we broaden the domain of morality to include doing right not only by other people and human society, but also by plants, animals, and the Earth as a whole. Then we see that moral issues confront us at every turn, challenging our attentiveness, our judgment, and our purity. Life situations abound in conundrums of our own conflicting values.

Our development along the line of resolving those conflicts can be summed up in the word *conscience*, the voice of the Sacred within us. We can aspire to be a person of conscience by not attempting to sweep our questionable actions under the rug of unawareness. Our conscience sees all.

There are very deep spiritual reasons for living in such a way as to have a clear conscience. We do this out of love and connectedness. We do it for the inner freedom it affords us. And also because to become worthy of entering the highest abodes of the Sacred, purity of will is an absolute requirement. At that level we encounter a barrier through which self-centered agendas cannot pass. Only a moral person with a clear conscience and a pure heart can have any real hope of becoming a vehicle for the Sacred. Given the many exigencies of life, this high standard of purity may seem an impossible goal. Yet it needs to be the foundation of our choices and our aspiration, to which we bring the best of our presence, attentiveness, heartfulness, judgment, and willingness to learn from mistakes.

But there is more to conscience and Right Action than what we should not do. The positive side, what we should do, can be an even greater challenge, because of the bewildering array of possibilities continually opening to us. How do we find a pattern of action for a life that offers us personal fulfillment? Innumerable questions arise about how we will choose to live. We can begin by following the basic guideline of doing the right and responsible thing. Further, again, we can seek guidance in our own feeling, intuition, judgment, and willingness to learn from mistakes.

There is, though, another overarching path toward Right Action: the path of excellence. What we do, we do with excellence. We seek perfection, but without demanding it, without making it into a constricting and impossible burden. We can aspire to excellence in anything we do. Take the mundane example of walking. It is possible to walk with excellence. We walk with the appropriate purpose and intention, with the degree of physical effort and speed that corresponds to that purpose, with awareness of ourselves and our surroundings, with presence in our body, heart, and mind. Between our active inner impulse that drives the walking and our receptive awareness of our body and surroundings, we find the balance of synergy. The walking goes on, while inwardly we are free, at peace, and in the moment.

This kind of approach to excellence can be applied in any activity, from washing dishes to playing a musical instrument, from speaking or writing to watching, listening, or thinking. We look at the activity to discover what excellence could mean for that particular situation. Through trial and error, attention and judgment, we refine and improve what we do and how we do it. Seeking rightness of action through excellence directly feeds into creating a satisfying life for ourselves and supports our spiritual inner work. More than that, acts of excellence raise the quality of the world and thus become acts of service. So even something as seemingly mundane as excellence in walking emanates a quality that we all need.

Finally, in the pantheon of Right Action, we must include service, both inner and outer. With the guidance of our conscience, we serve as we can our family, our society, our planet. And by our inner work, our prayer, presence, and meditation, and our inner attitude of kindness, we also emanate a quality that serves the transformation of the world.

For this week, raise the quality, the rightness of your actions.

10.5 Right Livelihood
(The Eightfold Path: Aspect 5)

In considering the meaning of Right Livelihood, the point of view of spiritual practice divides the question into the two great domains of what we do and how we do it. The first issue in this regard concerns how we find our particular niche in life. Much has been written and a whole industry exists to help us answer that uniquely individual question through aptitude and interest testing, career counseling and coaching, internships and job placement services, and so on. Navigating the task of choosing or changing careers also requires that we pay attention to our feeling, intuition, and judgment regarding how well it suits us and how well it will fulfill our responsibility to support ourselves, our family, and our society. To our great good fortune, we live in a highly elaborated society, which affords so many possibilities and career choices that we can tailor to our own unique nature.

To all of that we can add the condition that what we do for a living must not go against our conscience. The difficulty lies in the gray areas. If we are continually needing to justify and rationalize to ourselves why what we do is ethically and morally acceptable, then our unsettled conscience is telling us to beware. Staying in an ethically-challenged career forces us to harden our heart and ignore our conscience, effectively blocking our spiritual path and chaining us to the material world.

Turning from the question of what we do to how we do it brings us squarely in front of opportunities to spiritualize our livelihood by our inner work, opportunities which fall into three areas: presence, excellence, and service. The practice of presence in the workplace need not detract from our performance on our job. On the contrary, presence can improve our performance by making us more alert, more interested in our work, more appropriate and less reactive in our emotions, more forthright in our dealings with coworkers, vendors, and customers, more aware of our creative impulses, more perceptive of opportunities for improvement, firm when it's called for and supple when that's needed, better at dealing with the subtleties of our job and the relationships it entails, and more able to do our job despite any reluctance we may feel. Presence also improves our memory because the more alert we are in a situation, the better we remember it later. All this adds up to a powerful practical argument for working at presence as we work at our job. But dwarfing all that is our true reason for practicing presence: its enormous benefits to our spiritual path and its inherent service of transforming higher spiritual energies and defragmenting our will.

The main exception where the practice of presence could detract from our job performance is if our job is a life-critical one, demanding our full attention. For example, we want our surgeon totally focused on our surgery and our bus driver just driving the bus. By the demands they place on attention, such jobs carry their own inherent benefits for the spiritual pursuit.

As with Right Action, the practice of excellence plays a fundamental role in Right Livelihood. To strive for excellence in what we do for a living serves us well, both inwardly and outwardly. The challenge of excellence calls us to pay careful attention to detail and to the bigger picture, to opportunities for improving both what we do and our ability to do it, to creative possibilities, to our own inner state and how it affects the quality and productivity of our work, and to keeping what we do aligned with the actual purpose of our work. The effort of excellence benefits us broadly, for a job done well brings satisfaction, which spills over into the rest of our life in positive ways. A half-hearted effort at work leaves us half-hearted in other areas of our life. Dealing with the obstacles we encounter to fulfill our job responsibilities, not minimally but to the best of our abilities, aligns us with our conscience, strengthens our will, and increases our being. To work with excellence requires discovering what excellence means in the context of our particular line of work. Thus the effort of continuously improving what we do and how we do it, engages our body, our heart, and our mind. So the practice of excellence and the practice of presence support and enhance each other.

Jobs that pay offer some service to society in exchange for the value society places on that job. The better we do our job, the better we serve. Holding to this reality of service as the ultimate reason for our employment places our livelihood outside the domain of self-serving egoism. We do what we do to serve. And the primary personal benefit of serving, even more important than the financial compensation it brings, consists of the meaning it imparts to our life. In serving we fulfill our role in society, adding the measure of our own abilities and efforts to the general good. We have a deep-seated need, based in conscience, to be useful, to do something that matters. Performing our job meets that need, because in doing so we give back to society. But the material blessings we receive from society and from this Earth far exceed our personal capacity to give back. So we are humbled by all we receive and we feel the obligation to serve.

Fortunately, our spiritual inner work offers us another, uniquely human way to serve society and the Earth by serving the sacred, through the transformation of spiritual energies, through the purification from egoism, and by living in accord with conscience. Right Livelihood also supports that inner service, because accepting that we answer to others, whether a supervisor or a customer, helps purify us of egoism and prepares us for opening to the higher will of the sacred spirit in our periods of prayer.

So earning our place in the world and earning it well directly ties our livelihood not only to our own well-being, but also to that of our family, our society, the Earth, and the Sacred. For this week, reinvigorate your approach to making your livelihood right.

10.6 Right Effort
(The Eightfold Path: Aspect 6)

The notion of Right Effort strikes us first as requiring strength of will, like the effort of lifting a heavy weight. Perhaps the qualifier of "right" brings to mind an intelligent effort, working smart. And certainly both aspects play a role in Right Effort. But there is much more to it. What is an inner effort? What does it mean to work smart in the domain of spiritual practice? This is not only a matter of the necessary proficiency in techniques, but also of understanding the classes of efforts, which we may call active, receptive, and synergic. Experience teaches us the appropriate conditions for each and how to find a right balance among them.

Across the many spiritual and religious paths, the fundamental examples of active inner efforts concern our attention: directing it and maintaining it. Active inner efforts have the feel of ordinary effort, like lifting that weight or an extended period of physical labor. We focus our attention, we form our intention, and we carry it out. The practice of sensing our body and the practice of presence are both primarily active efforts. In the former we hold our attention in our body to awaken and stabilize the energy of body awareness, sensation. In practicing presence, we actively inhabit our life, we will ourselves to be here, to be. We make an initial effort in choosing and beginning a particular practice in a particular moment. And then we make the ongoing effort of continuously maintaining that practice for more than a few seconds, or repeating it regularly. Such active efforts build up enduring pathways in our will, which we experience as determination, commitment, and increasing ability. The steady accumulation of active efforts makes subsequent efforts a little easier and a little stronger.

Receptive efforts do not have the same effortful feel, because they entail letting go, allowing, and opening. But consider letting go of anger in a situation where you notice it just starting to arise in you. You believe in it. You believe you are it. You feel justified in it. To let go of that anger regardless can be a very difficult, wrenching choice, an act of will, an effort of de-identification. This is the core of mindfulness and mindfulness meditation: to let our attention go wide, to notice all that is arising in us, whether thoughts, emotions or sensations, to let them arise and to let them pass without going with them, without becoming enmeshed in that content of awareness, but rather to stay in awareness itself. This is the effort of non-effort, of just being. It brings us into the spacious peace of consciousness.

We can be receptively open to body sensations, by relaxing into body awareness. The energy of sensation then awakens on its own. Acceptance of ourselves, of others, of our situation, comes through a receptive attitude. And total acceptance leads to what is known in Buddhism as a precursor of enlightenment, namely equanimity. In receptivity, we also have the surrender at the heart of certain deep forms of prayer. We open ourselves inwardly to the Sacred, to allow It to act on us, in us, as us. Our job in this is simply to dispose ourselves toward the Higher with love.

Synergic efforts combine elements of active and receptive efforts with a third type, an embracing, harmonizing and enabling attitude that creates a new unity of practice. This is, for example, the effortless effort of just doing what we are doing. We are active in our presence of doing what it is we're doing and receptive in our awareness of it, in allowing it to happen through us. The result is the doing of non-doing, described so well in the Tao Te Ching. The activity we engage in goes just right, when we let it flow. We do not interfere to improve on the perfection of what we are doing, but neither are we passive in it. We are simultaneously active, open, and riding the wave of synergy.

Synergy also enters deep meditation and prayer. We

inwardly reach up toward the Higher, extending our will in love into the Sacred, begging to enter there, begging the One to enter us. At the same time we inwardly step aside to make room for the Sacred. Knowing full well that we cannot control the action of the Higher, we nevertheless do everything in our power to be an attractive receptacle for It, to be simple, direct, and urgent in our need. We strengthen our presence by standing in our will-to-be. We simultaneously open to the higher will and let it come down through us to bolster our will-to-be. A potent energy flows into our being. This welcoming of the higher will into our own will-to-be connects our individual being with the great being of All.

Right Effort also addresses the question of level of effort. The amount of effort makes a difference. But levels of effort are not just a matter of quantity or intensity, but more importantly a matter of which world, which level of reality we address with our effort. We can make efforts not to fall into obsessive states, to see our autopilot mechanisms, our automatic associative thoughts and reactive emotions, to enter sensitive contact with our body, heart, and mind, to inhabit the spacious peace of consciousness, to connect with the world of Sacred Light, to taste and appreciate the unity of Love, and to worship and serve the Ultimate. Right Effort means addressing all these levels with our inner work and finding a workable balance among them.

For this week, reinvigorate your spiritual practice efforts and make them right.

10.7 Right Mindfulness
(The Eightfold Path: Aspect 7)

The practice of mindfulness, in its many manifestations, lies at the core not only of Buddhism but of every major spiritual path that leads to transformation. One might object to this claim by pointing to devotional ways which do not explicitly teach mindfulness. But even prayer, at least in its deeper forms, depends on the kind of well-developed awareness that results from mindfulness, not because that awareness necessarily enters into the prayer directly, but because the broad, non-judgmental awareness of mindfulness purifies our heart. And the deeper stages of prayer absolutely depend on purity of heart.

What is mindfulness? We can start by saying that it is awareness of perceptual awareness. In mindfulness we are aware of whatever perceptions, be they mental, emotional, or sensory, are at the forefront of our mind. This notion of being aware of whatever we are aware of is not a tautology. Rather there are two levels of awareness involved in mindfulness, operating with the sensitive and conscious energies respectively. The first is the perceptual awareness of content: a sight, a sound, a thought, an itch, a feeling. The second is awareness of that perceptual awareness, a sort of meta-awareness of the whole field of perceptual, content awareness: consciousness aware of sensitivity. Mindfulness means being the context, being the broad awareness, not just its content of perceptions.

In addition to its energy/awareness component, the other major enabler of mindfulness is a particular attitude of will. The attitude of mindfulness consists of impartial openness, allowing, non-judging and non-identifying. In mindfulness practice, we do not seek to shape the content of our experience. We just see the content of our mind and allow it all to arise and to pass, while we remain rooted in impartial awareness. This attitude is known as equanimity.

Two things should be pointed out here. First, to adopt the attitude of equanimity is not so easy. Just consider the challenge of letting anger subside once it has arisen in you. Our typical approach is to feed the anger with our thoughts and even to act on it. In mindfulness, we see all that and let it go. The second point to make is that equanimity does not mean a passive attitude toward our life. Indeed equanimity toward and non-identification with the contents of our mind and heart leaves us freer to act in an energetic, creative, and responsible fashion.

For maximum efficacy, mindfulness must be practiced in two broad ways: in daily periods of formal meditation and in our ordinary life activities. These forms mutually support each other. The more we develop our meditation, the more it spills over into a mindful life. And the more we practice mindfulness in our daily rounds, the stronger our meditation.

Mindfulness meditation typically begins with some type of focusing or concentration of attention, for example on the sensations arising from the process of breathing. The practice of concentration, of directed attention, will be discussed in next week's aspect of the Eightfold Path, so we will leave the subject for now. After focusing our attention and becoming established in a concentrated mind, we open to mindfulness meditation proper. Instead of holding our attention on a single object, such as the breath, we widen our attention to the whole field of awareness. We notice whatever is most prominent in that field, for example, a sound, a thought, a feeling, or a physical sensation, and we let that perception subside on its own. Then again we notice whatever is most prominent, follow it, and let it pass. In this way we do not allow ourselves to be carried away by a particular train of thoughts or sensations. We remain in the noticing, in the seeing, not lost in the streaming objects of our perceptions. Whatever arises in our body, mind, and heart is OK. We just notice it and let it pass, without comment, without judgment, and without interpretation. If there are comments or judgments or interpretations, we notice those and let them pass as well.

Mindfulness leads toward peace, purification, and liberation, because by allowing everything to arise in our mind and letting it be, we retrain ourselves not to be identified, not to believe we are these perceptual objects. The subtlety of mindfulness practice is to see with an open, accepting mind, to see with impartial objectivity. We neither grasp at nor reject what we see. We just see. And in doing so, all the many urges and desires and fears that would formerly grab our attention and our energy gradually lose their power over us. For that, though, we need to practice mindfulness in our daily life and in meditation sessions.

To live in mindful presence, we need to remember to be mindful and we need an anchor. The most common anchors for mindfulness are the physical sensations associated with breathing and the more general physical sensations of our whole body. Intentionally basing our mindfulness in one of those anchors boosts our chances of staying mindful for more than a few seconds. Keeping the physical sensations in our awareness, we broaden out to include whatever else might be prominent in our perceptions, and we become aware of those perceptions as perceptions, thoughts as thoughts, just as we do in our sitting meditation practice of mindfulness.

The great power of living mindfully transforms us, gradually and organically. So by staying with the practice mindfulness for the long-term, our heart opens to joy, to peace and equanimity, to compassion and love.

For this week, practice being and living in mindfulness.

10.8 Right Concentration
(The Eightfold Path: Aspect 8)

Mindfulness and concentration form the two wings that make our spiritual practice fly. Mindfulness brings freedom, wisdom, and compassion, while concentration develops stability and depth. We need them both. Without concentration, mindfulness evaporates all too easily. Without mindfulness, concentration remains sterile.

Concentration refers first to the practice of focusing and holding the spotlight of attention on a single object of perception, most commonly on the sensations associated with breathing or on the repetition of some phrase. We train ourselves to direct and hold our attention, while staying relaxed. This affects both our will and our energies. Attention is one of the powers of our will. Through attention we will our awareness toward a particular direction. Energies are the medium of awareness. So our will, as attention, entrains our energies, as awareness. The net effect is that the longer we are able to hold our attention, the more our inner energies collect and stabilize. A session of concentrating on awareness of our breathing, of our body, or on a sacred phrase, leaves us centered and at peace.

There are stages or levels of depth in our practice of concentration. We begin at the stage of momentary concentration, where we can stay on target only for a brief time, measured in seconds, before our attention wanders off. The continuing effort of refocusing our attention whenever it lapses gradually opens us to the conscious energy, which offers a timeless stability leading to the next stage of concentration. That second stage brings the power to stay focused, while staying relaxed, for longer periods, measured in minutes. The second stage is the crucial one for mindfulness to be effective; it enables us to see what's going on in us over more than a few seconds, to watch the unfolding and changing of our thoughts, emotions, and sensations. So in any session of meditation, we begin with some type of concentration practice, focusing our mind, our attention. Once we establish the relatively stable attention of the second stage, we can leave the concentration practice and proceed with the other parts of the meditation.

A good example of a concentration practice, this one from Zen, consists of paying attention to the physical sensations associated with breathing, while counting our breaths one to ten, and then starting again at one. The primary focus of attention is on the sensations, while the counting goes on in the background of our mind. At the start, we notice where our perception of breathing is strongest: at our upper lip and nostrils, in our chest, or in our abdomen. Then we choose to focus all our attention at that place for the duration of this part of the meditation. We do not intentionally change our manner of breathing. We just let our body breathe itself normally, while we sense the process. The counting follows the breath, not the other way around. When our attention strays off our breath, even for a moment, we begin the counting again at one. If we find ourselves counting eleven, twelve, thirteen, we know we have lost the exercise and again begin at one. When we can get through several sets of ten breaths without a break in our attention, we have reached the beginning of the second stage of concentration. At that point we can either continue the breath counting to increase our concentration further or we can shift to other parts of the meditation practice, such as the wide awareness of mindfulness.

Further stages of concentration practice can open us to the ocean of peace and stillness, the pure experience of the conscious energy. Beyond that we may find the cascading energies of the Sacred Light. And beyond that we may rest in complete equanimity and unity. These deep states of concentration profoundly affect our soul, nourishing us with a very high food. One difficulty is that these states are so blissful that we can easily become attached to them. And then our inner work becomes a chase after high states rather than the search for freedom, completion, and the ability to serve. So while there is great value in working toward the deeper states of concentration, we also work toward the full and liberating mindfulness in daily life. And for the latter, we need only the second stage of concentration: stabilized attention.

Concentration practice strengthens our will-to-be and mindfulness practice opens us to the whole of experience. Together they give us a more stable presence. Concentration practice also sharpens our major tool for spiritual inner work, our attention. And by sharpening our attention the practice sharpens us, for in a very real sense we are our attention.

Strong attention enables us to practice energy breathing effectively to nourish our soul. If we so choose, a strong attention along with its stable energies can carry us into the subtleties of prayer, particularly contemplative prayer in which we focus our entire being on the Divine. The more we focus on the Divine, the more the Divine focuses on us.

This completes our survey of the Eightfold Path, which culminates in mindfulness and concentration. For this week, practice focusing your attention, focusing yourself.

11.0 The Way of Attention

11.1 Scattered Attention
(The Way of Attention: Part 1 of 9)

In any given moment our attention defines us. What we attend to is what we perceive. And the sum of our perceptions is our life, in this and in every moment. So our attention determines our life, simply and directly. This holds even more so for our inner life. If our attention takes in a particular thought or emotion, notices it, then the effect of that thought or emotion can be much different than if it goes unnoticed, unattended. Attention steers our awareness, when we so choose. Attention and choice are intimately connected, with each act of attention being a choice. And both are aspects of our will, of who we really are. The use of the word "I" rings truest when we say "I pay attention" or "I choose."

Because attention is the most fundamental and invaluable tool for our spiritual practice, we will study attention and how to develop it, in a 9-part series on the Way of Attention:

1. Scattered Attention

2. Passive Attention
3. Directed Attention
4. Focused Attention
5. Broad Attention
6. Receptive Attention
7. Participation
8. The Root of Attention
9. The Source of Attention

We begin with noticing what our attention does as it is now, how it flits around, drawn by everything, how scattered it is in our ordinary condition. Like the distracting ding from our computer announcing a new email, or like the ringtone of our phone, each new thought, each new sound, each new sight takes us. Perhaps only momentarily, but there it is nevertheless, soon to be followed by yet another diversion. Our experience in this state of scattered attention is a long series of detours. Even when we are, for the most part, focused on something, say some task, we still fall prey to intermittent distractions. We fidget, scratch an itch, or follow some stray, irrelevant thought or an impulse to move on to the next thing before finishing the current one. Every such intrusion finds a willing and distractible partner in us, a scattered partner.

How scattered we are varies; there are degrees. The more frequently we fall into distraction and the longer we stay distracted, the more scattered we are. Notice though, that this assumes that we have something to be distracted from. But we do at times fall into aimless states where we are completely unmoored, buffeted about in the stream of experience, without even a tenuous hold on some activity, task, interest, or direction. At such times we are totally scattered. Every successive thing takes us zigzagging among the waves and currents of experience.

This is not a deficit of attention, but rather a failure to make use of, to control our attention. Scattered attention is like a live wire on the loose: always looking for something to connect with. And connect it does, with an endless series of inner and outer objects of attention. This unregulated nature of scattered attention shows both the problem and a path toward resolution. The first step consists in seeing whether and to what degree there is a problem, whether our attention needs improvement.

So for this week, notice your attention. Notice how stable it is. Does it stay engaged in one place or does it flit here and there? Or both? Notice how often you are in the flitting, scattered state of inattention. Notice, in your most focused states, whether your attention escapes intermittently. Is your attention elsewhere or are you doing what you are doing?

11.2 Passive Attention

(The Way of Attention: Part 2 of 9)

In contrast to the scattered condition, where our attention hops erratically among the various objects presenting themselves to our awareness, in the passive state our attention stays more or less put, captivated by what's in front of us. We just let ourselves, our mind and feelings, be played by the spectacle, without bothering to stay alert to it. This is passive attention: focused, perhaps, but only by default, not intentionally directed. We are absent, having fallen headlong into that one thing that attracts us now.

Imagine sitting in a lecture on some complex subject. You are stuck there with no escape. But rather than make the inner effort to carefully follow each sentence, each concept, their meanings and how they fit with the overall theme of the presentation, you just sit there hearing the lecture but not really taking it in. You hear without listening and see without noticing. Later, you may not remember anything said by the lecturer. This is passive attention.

In such cases, your attention may be taken by your thoughts and daydreams, your emotional reactions, your boredom, which screen you not only from the outer event, but from yourself. Being absorbed in your thoughts and reactions does not mean you are in contact with yourself, only with a superficial layer. Buried under that, out of touch, lies the one who sees, chooses, and acts.

Passive attention only yields absence, no presence. In this state, no one is at home to experience our life, to receive our sensory impressions, our thoughts and emotions, and to choose our actions and responses. Instead, it all comes in and gets processed by the automatic mechanisms of our habits and propensities, our conditioning and personality. Passively, we are only half alive.

You absent-mindedly enter a room in your home and don't know why. You know that a mere moment before, you had a reason for going to that room, but now that you are there, you cannot recall it. Passive attention brought you here.

You find yourself driving in a particular direction, by habit. Then you remember where you are going and realize that you are driving in the wrong direction. Passive attention brought you here.

You are watching television, though you know you have other things you need to do. Yet you sit there in a half-daze, mesmerized, zombified, procrastinating. Passive attention holds you here.

Contrast all that with a different approach to a concert or play, movie or TV. Again you let yourself, your mind and feelings, be played by the spectacle. But not just. Perhaps your emotions engage and you become fascinated. So you stay alert, you send your attention out, as it were, to meet the event halfway. You are there with it, drinking it in. This attention is not passive, but rather receptive and maybe in part active.

A period of passivity may leave you feeling drained, empty, and somehow cheated. A receptive period is more likely to leave you feeling relaxed and refreshed. But mitigating factors can arise. If you have been working hard and find yourself physically and/or mentally depleted, then a period of passivity, such as zoning out in front of the TV, may be just what you need to recoup your energies. The problem comes when passivity changes from a need to an indulgence. When needed, passivity regenerates. When indulged, passivity enervates.

One constructive role that passive attention plays in spiritual practice and meditation is in relaxation. Attention needs energy. At times, the depletion of our inner energies precludes a more active attention. Passivity allows our energies to settle and combine, an important and beneficial action. Further than that, in meditation the do-nothing approach of passive attention can gradually transform into the non-doing of receptive attention. You may be sitting, doing nothing, just letting go into relaxation. Perhaps a deep fatigue wells up and you feel bone-tired and nearly asleep. Yet if you stick with it, the fog of fatigue may slowly evaporate, your awareness collects and regenerates, and you become alert and awake, effortlessly.

For this week, notice the ways and situations in which your attention is passive. Notice how this feels inwardly and its results.

11.3 Directed Attention
(The Way of Attention: Part 3 of 9)

Because attention plays a central role in who we are, it also plays a crucial role in our spiritual practice. In the first two parts of this series, we observed the as-is condition of our attention, particularly its errant manifestations of being scattered or passive. In the remaining parts of this series, we explore the practical aspects of developing our attention. And the first of those consists of exercising attention by directing it, exercising our ability to direct our attention.

Now we frequently do direct our attention. Otherwise we could not hold a job, nor could we have made it through school. But our ability to direct attention needs to go much further for spiritual purposes than it typically does for material purposes like jobs, schooling, or driving. A finely-honed and stable attention serves as our all-purpose tool across the spectrum of spiritual practices. For that reason, some spiritual exercises are designed specifically to develop attention.

The exercise of directing our attention can be seen an iterative process of seven steps. First we **choose** a suitable object to which we will direct attention. Some classical examples include the sensations of breathing, the sensations of parts or the whole of our body, our thought stream, a repeated inner phrase, a repeated chant, a ritual, a flower, a statue, or a painting. So we choose something to be the exclusive focus of our attention for the limited period of the exercise.

Second, we **aim** our attention toward the chosen object, inner or outer. Attention tends to waver. Aiming herds our attention toward the intended object. This intentional aiming distinguishes directed attention from other forms of attention, such as scattered, passive, or non-directed practices.

The third step is **contact**: once our attention is aimed directly at the object, it contacts the object. We have an unmediated contact between attention and the object, between us and the object. Unmediated means, for example, that no thought intervenes, that we are not merely thinking about the object. Rather, this contact gives us direct sensory perception of the object, be it a thought or a flower.

In the fourth aspect, we **maintain** the contact between our attention and the object. This takes a clear, ongoing intention to stay in contact. It also takes an ongoing meta-awareness of whether our attention is still in contact with the object and of each small movement of our attention away from the object. That continuing awareness of the quality of the contact informs and feeds our effort to keep our attention on our chosen object.

Fifth, we have the inevitable but unintended **lapse** of our attention. It wanders off the chosen object. This happens all by itself, despite our best efforts to maintain our attention on the object. Our energy or intention wane and something distracts us. We forget what we are about and unintentionally stray off in a different direction.

Sixth, we **notice** that our attention has wandered off the object. Our job here is to notice quickly, not to let too much time pass between the lapse of attention and realizing that it has lapsed.

Seventh, we immediately choose to **begin again** with the first step of reinforcing our choice of object. The key here is not to waste time and energy on self-recriminations or frustrations about having lost the thread, but rather to begin again right away.

This seven-step process does not define or limit the style of directed attention. The many forms of directed attention fall across the dimensions from active to receptive and from narrowly focused to broadly aware. For example, in prayer we might direct our attention to be receptively focused toward the Divine. In the mindfulness practice of choiceless awareness, we direct our attention broadly toward the entire field of our awareness, simultaneously active and receptive. In the practice of concentration, we actively and narrowly focus our attention. Active listening and active seeing combine both active and receptive elements. All these and other modes of directed attention can be iteratively practiced in that seven-step process: choose, aim, contact, maintain, lapse, notice, and begin again.

In the coming weeks we will practice several forms of directed attention. For this week, please notice when and how you direct your attention. Practice directing your attention and see whether the seven-step process described above actually fits.

11.4 Focused Attention
(The Way of Attention: Part 4 of 9)

The exercise and training of attention actually exercises and trains our self, for we are our attention. If attention is scattered, we are scattered. If attention is strong, we are strong. If attention is refined and subtle, we are refined and subtle. And the first mode of directed attention we need to develop is **focused attention**. This means actively directing our awareness and perceptions onto an intended object and keeping our attention there. From the endless variety of practices for focusing attention, the following examples have both immediate and long-term benefits for our spiritual journey.

The first practice concerns a type of conscious breathing, done in sitting meditation, in which we focus on a very narrow aspect of experience: the physical sensations of breathing at the nostrils. Place and hold your attention on the sensations associated with the air going in and out of your nostrils. To help you stay focused, mentally count the breaths 1 to 10, and then begin again from 1, while keeping your attention mainly on the actual sensations of the breath at and around your nostrils and upper lip. When you lose the count, simply start again at 1. Your attention should be primarily on the sensations of breathing and only secondarily on the supporting practice of counting: the breath in the foreground of attention and the counting in the background.

Do not alter the natural, physical patterns and rhythms of your breathing. Only alter your attention and awareness through continuing contact with the breath. The count and the words are ancillary and can be dropped when steadiness of attention to the breath has been achieved. Because you are focusing on such a small area and the sensations tend to be fairly subtle, this demanding practice can quickly and profoundly steady your attention and calm your mind.

A second practice involves sensing our hand or foot. Place and hold all of your attention in your right hand. Become aware of the hand directly, not by thinking of the hand or by looking at it, but by inwardly opening to the immediate perception of your hand, from within the hand. Keep your attention in your right hand, in a relaxed way. When you notice your attention wandering, gently bring it back to the hand.

After some time your right hand may seem more substantial, more alive, vibrant, warm, even tingling. This marks the accumulation of the sensitive energy in the hand. To establish the "taste" of sensation, notice the difference at that moment between your perception of your right hand and of your left hand. One hand is full of sensitive energy brought there by your attention. The other is empty. You are sensing your right hand. Leaving that aside, sense your right foot, then your left foot, and then your left hand. In addition to training your attention, with practice you will be able to contact the sensitive energy in your hands or feet quickly and at will.

A third practice involves whole-body sensing, at first in a quiet time set aside solely for that. After relaxing, sense each limb in turn, then both arms at once, then both legs at once, and then all four at once. Finally, add your torso and head. Without trying to sense particular internal organs, so as not to interfere with their instinctive operation, bring your attention into your torso and head, allowing the sensitive energy to arise and collect there, joining the sensitive energy in your limbs.

At this point we shift from sensing parts of our body to sensing the whole body. With your attention spread throughout your body, open to and engage with a complete sensation, with your aliveness as a whole. Keep your attention in continuing contact with your entire body, through the sensitive energy. Whenever your attention wanders, gently and simply bring it back to your body. With practice, you will become able to engage in whole-body sensing directly, without starting piecemeal with each limb.

A fourth practice concerns attention on the sensations of our body in movement. One approach entails being fully in our body, aware of our physical sensations, whenever we walk. Begin with sensing your feet as you walk. Then extend your attention and awareness to include more of each leg and, ultimately, the sensation of the whole of your body, as you walk.

Now these four practices all develop our attention through focused contact with the sensitive energy in our body. Sensing enlivens us, making life more vivid. And the vibrant aliveness of the sensitive energy attracts and helps stabilize our attention. This energy gives our attention a home, a refuge from its incessant wandering. Because sensitive energy is the stuff of perception, using it as our focus begins to train our attention in the subtleties of our inner world. Furthermore, awareness of the accumulating sensitive energy initiates us into the possibility of creating our soul.

For this week, practice focusing your attention on the sensitive energy in your body. Actively exercise your attention to improve your ability to focus.

11.5 Broad Attention
(The Way of Attention: Part 5 of 9)

In Part 4 of this series on the Way of Attention, we worked on improving our ability to focus our attention on a limited domain of experience, namely our body and the perceptual energy of sensation associated with it. Now we widen the lens of attention to include the whole of our experience in this moment.

Attention across the entirety of current experience is known as mindfulness or choiceless awareness. Choiceless in this context means not choosing to focus on one particular object within our awareness to the exclusion of other objects. Instead, we allow the stream of consciousness to proceed as it will, while we maintain attention to all of it. Some parts of that stream will be more prominent than others, which calls for a fluid attention to the succession of prominent sensory objects. Those may be something external to us, like a computer screen or our lunch, or something internal like a thought or emotion, or something intermediate like the sensations of our body. But broad attention means also opening our attention sideways to the rest. Not only do we see what's front and center for us, but we also attend to the entire contents of awareness. The most vivid objects of attention need not block our awareness of all the rest. We take off our blinders and see the whole panoply surrounding us, inside and out.

You might rightfully question whether and how the broad attention of mindfulness or choiceless awareness differs from our ordinary state. The distinctions lie in our not being carried away with the stream of consciousness and in our awareness not collapsing into some narrow domain. We stand, as it were, on the bank of the stream of objects of awareness, seeing it all pass without losing ourselves in it. We recognize each thought as a thought, rather than just being lost in the thought and having the thought think us. We feel our emotions as emotions, rather than just being lost in anger when anger arises in us. We do not drown in the stream. It does not take us over. We are not identified with the contents of awareness. We just cognize them with a wide and all-inclusive attention.

The difficulty with this type of broad attention is that it evaporates all too readily. After surfing the stream, we fall in. We may start off mindful, but very soon we find ourselves buffeted about at the whim of whatever enters our awareness. To resolve this conundrum we return to focusing attention in our body. Awareness of the sensitive energy in our body offers stability, a platform from which we can open to the broad attention of mindfulness without being so easily swept away. Rooted in body sensation as the continuing and intentional backdrop of attention and awareness, we apply choiceless awareness to the never-ending stream of objects in the foreground of awareness. We perceive it all, as it is. We notice the succession of prominent objects of awareness. We see a person, then we see our emotional reaction to that person, then we see our thoughts about that person, then we hear that person speaking, then we see ourselves replying, and so on. All the while, though, we are rooted in body awareness, in the energy of sensation, which gives us a place to stand, a place to be. And from seeing the most prominent, in-our-face objects in the foreground of our attention while intentionally sensing our body in the background, we also broaden our attention sideways to include all the rest of our immediate environment, internal and external. This is not a matter of dividing our attention between foreground, background, and the rest, but rather of opening an all-embracing attention to the whole of this present moment.

Thus broad attention entails simple and direct perceptions of where we are, what's inside us, and what's around us, of our total, immediate situation. Reflective consideration is not part of this practice, because such thoughts tend to insert themselves between us and what we perceive, coloring and masking our perceptions thereby. Instead, we treat our thoughts themselves as objects of attention. When our typical ongoing mental commentary, our judging mind, rises to prominence in our awareness, we just turn our attention to that stream of thoughts and recognize them as thoughts. While we do cognize the meaning of our passing thoughts, we also see the process of thoughts coming and going. Noticing the flow of our associating thoughts, helps keep us here and now rather than washed away with the stream, especially if we maintain some ongoing attention to our body sensation. The same holds for all the other, non-thought contents of the stream of awareness.

In practicing broad attention, we are simultaneously active and receptive. We actively direct our attention toward the whole array of our perceptions in this moment, while we receptively open our attention to embrace the wide range of the present. In the spacious context of broad awareness, our yammering thoughts and reactive emotions diminish in relative importance. We become less prone to collapsing our world into a small knot of self-centered thoughts and emotions.

And whenever we find ourselves rootless and drifting, we begin again. We start with re-establishing attention to the sensitive energy in our body and then broaden out from there, moment to moment.

For this week, practice broad attention. Sense your body and open your attention to the whole of experience in each moment.

11.6 Receptive Attention
(The Way of Attention: Part 6 of 9)

With the practice of receptive attention, we turn to a very different side of spirituality, a side that complements and also depends on the active modes of attention we have pursued in the earlier parts of this series. Those active practices build a strong, fluid, and subtle attention, which we now put to use in receptivity.

For example, we practice being receptive to other people by listening. We pay attention to the person and allow what they say and how they are to enter us. We get who they are in this moment without judgment. We also practice being receptive to ourselves by accepting our limitations and weaknesses, while working to improve. Such receptivity to ourselves and others makes our connections real and puts us on the road to love.

The spiritual paradigm of receptive attention also concerns receptivity directly to the spirit. Initially this means opening to the silence, the stillness deep within us, beneath our thoughts and emotions, beneath all our sensory perceptions, beneath all our efforts and aspirations. We open our attention to the ground of awareness, the pure consciousness, the cognizant stillness, the context prior to all contents. For this, we sit in quiet meditation, attending to the stream of awareness, without attempting to block the stream, or stop it, or grab hold of particular items in it, and without allowing them to grab our attention. We just sit in simplicity. When thoughts come, we let them come and we let them go as they will, while we sit and watch with an open, receptive attention. Gradually our thoughts slow down. We notice the gaps between our thoughts and we attend to those gaps. With our attention we see into those empty spaces. We enter those gaps and open to the stillness there. We receive that warm silence and allow our whole being to soak in it. We recognize the simple, unadorned conscious awareness between and beneath our thoughts, between and beneath our emotions and sensory perceptions.

We become pure perception without an object to perceive. In this cognizant stillness, the strings of thought, the ribbons of emotion, and the tapestries of sensory perception no longer mesmerize us. First and foremost we are aware. That pure awareness moves from the background of experience to the foreground. We are receptive, receptively attentive. And the first new level that arises in that receptivity is consciousness. We luxuriate in consciousness itself, open, contented, and free.

There is an interplay between directed and non-directed receptivity. Non-directed receptivity, non-doing, leads organically into the silence, the cognizant stillness. As we relax, our thoughts and emotions also relax, to the point of growing indistinct, disconnected, and transparent. The cognizant stillness of consciousness then naturally shines through our inner quiescence. Once we have acquired the taste of this, however, a new possibility opens to us. We can direct our receptivity into the stillness. We touch and even enter the stillness at will, without waiting for the natural unfolding of non-directed receptivity.

A similar situation occurs with the world just beyond consciousness, the world of Sacred Light. In the state of stillness, non-directed receptivity gradually loosens consciousness itself. Our awareness grows porous and the Light begins to shine through. The first sign of this comes as an unmistakable cascade of energy descending into us as we begin to open to the Light. Staying receptive, even in the face of those energies, can gradually open us to the realm of the creative Light itself. Again though, once we have acquired the taste, we may also discover the possibility of directing our receptivity into the Sacred Light at will.

Beyond that, however, the distinction between directed and non-directed receptivity tends to blur as, in heartfelt yearning, we approach the threefold Unity at the root of creation. Here we may direct our attention beyond all that is, but the grace that descends from that Unity comes not at our will, but at the will of the Higher.

Directed receptivity puts us at the center, directing our receptive attention, choosing what we will be receptive to. The issue here is who occupies our center, an issue we shall explore in the upcoming parts of this series. Non-directed receptivity, however, bypasses that question by bypassing our center. Non-directed receptive attention has no center. We just let our experience take its own course. But this is different than passive attention, which has no particular intention behind it, or at most an intention to allow oneself to be played upon as in daydreaming or in being entertained. Receptive attention, even the non-directed form, does have an intention behind it, an intention to open to, to receive from what is higher than us. Receptive attention to the Higher naturally loosens us up, relaxes the grip of self-centeredness, and opens us to an unexpectedly vibrant inner life.

For this week, practice receptive attention.

11.7 Participation: Being Attention
(The Way of Attention: Part 7 of 9)

Participating in our life means shifting from seeing to being, from witnessing to engaging, from sensing our body to inhabiting it, from being aware of our situation to occupying it intentionally, from paying attention to being attention. The inner practice of participation entails joining the stream of attention to be attention itself, to feel and experience: "I am my attention."

Attention entrains our awareness, whether narrowly focused or broadly open. We participate by being right here in awareness, inserting ourselves through and as attention. We do not just watch our life as if we were an outside observer, a semi-objective witness. Rather we jump headlong into the midst of it. We feel what we're feeling. We think what we're thinking. We see what we're seeing. We hear what we're hearing and we touch what we're touching. We are not lived by our life. We live it. We experience it unreservedly. We revel in living. Engagement means more than awareness.

Notice that participation is always intentional and not to be confused with being lost in our life, nor with being identified with its particulars. We become our attention, but we do not collapse into our thoughts, or emotions, or pains, or anything else. We live and experience all of it, but nothing takes us. Neither our thoughts, nor our reactions, nor our sensory perceptions cause us to contract. We neither turn away from the distasteful, get lost in the desirous, nor fall flat in the neutral. We just continue being attention.

Perhaps the easiest way to acquire the taste of participation consists of being in our physical movements. When you pick up the phone, be in that picking up motion. When you move your arm, be in that movement. Not just aware of your arm moving but being in your arm as it moves. When you walk, be in your legs as they move, in your arms as they swing. Be here in your walking body.

Many of our movements, however, can and do go quite well by habit, without our participation. We need not be in every step as we walk. Our body knows quite well how to walk on its own, thank you. So we allow what is best done automatically to go by rote. But we profit by participating in our experience as we walk. Without being in each particular aspect of walking, we can nevertheless inhabit our body and mind and senses globally. We can be whole and in that wholeness as we walk, not merely a thought-filled and distracted mind being carried along.

Of course, the same opportunity exists without moving. When we sit, we can be there sitting, inhabiting our body, mind and senses as we sit. When we think, we can be there in our thoughts, aware of their meaning and direction, fully engaged in thinking. When we eat, we can be there tasting our food. When we speak, we can be there in awareness of the sound of our voice and the meaning of our words.

Participation also has forms that go beyond the personal, into for example a shared attention, as with a team, a class, or an audience. It may seem ordinary enough, but something magical emerges through shared attention: something more than the sum of the participants. A team whose members are not the greatest individual players, may nevertheless emerge victorious due to their teamwork. A concert may rise into an event qualitatively different than the same musicians playing the same music before an inattentive audience. Communal prayer or group meditation can take us much deeper than we can go on our own. An inspiring speaker depends on the audience for inspiration, and together they may reach new heights. All these examples depend on the shared attention of a group, on a common direction. Intention is not enough. Actual participation through attention enables a collection of individuals to become, for those moments, a group, to form a singular wholeness.

Still higher forms of participation await us. When we give our attention to another person, without judgment, and we enter that attention to be with that person, we touch our shared sameness, our common humanity. Similarly with an animal we may touch our common life. These are harbingers of participating in love.

In deep prayer, when we become the prayer, when we enter it as our attention, unreservedly and whole-heartedly, we participate in the work of the Sacred. This comes first by participating in the silence. We put our attention into the stillness beyond thought, beyond sensory experience. And we enter that stillness through and as our attention. Established in stillness, we engage our body, mind, and heart to put our attention beyond the stillness, into the Sacred Light and enter there, through and as attention.

For this week, please practice participating in your life.

11.8 The Root of Attention
(The Way of Attention: Part 8 of 9)

In all of the approaches to attention that we have practiced in the previous parts of this series, the arrow of attention points toward whatever we are attending to, be it inward, such as our thoughts or energies or the silence, or outward such as what our senses bring. Notice, though, that the arrow has had no anchor, no clear starting point or foundation. We cannot base our attention in our thinking mind or in our emotions, in our sensory experience or in our energies, because attention is in its essence will. Part of the reason our attention tends to wander is precisely this lack of a foundation or root. So now we shall turn to being the anchor of our attention, being its starting point. We will practice being the director of our attention, the one who chooses where to point the beam of attention.

We cultivate the experience of having our attention emanate from us, from I. We cultivate the experience of being that I at the root of our attention. When we look at something, we might ask ourselves: *"who is looking?"* And that question can elicit us, our I, to step forward, to be the one who is looking. The core of this practice is not the question, though. It is, simply and directly, to be the one who is looking, to experience that I am the root from which this looking begins. To come into our I in any situation, we may ask ourselves *"who is doing what I'm doing?"* I am. And in particular for this part of the Way of Attention, we practice being the one who directs our attention, from whom our attention emanates, and experiencing being that one.

As the director of our attention we shift from being to doing, from engaging to owning, from occupying our life to being the one who shapes it, from being our attention to being the one who directs it, the one who does what we do. Whatever we do, we are the one who does it. Rather than our actions proceeding on their own by habit, we take our rightful place as the one who directs and does these actions. Rather than our experience happening on its own without someone witnessing it, we arrive as the one who sees and hears and feels, as the one who experiences our experience. When you walk, walk. Be the walker. Be the one who intends your movement. Be the one who moves. When you read, be the one who reads. When you speak, be the one who speaks.

The thought of I is merely a thought. It can, however, be backed by the force of our true I, our full intention, though it rarely is. When you ask yourself *"who is looking?"* or *"who is doing what I'm doing?"* or *"who am I,"* the valid response is no mere thought, but rather the core of your presence. And although your I may be focused on one particular object, it is never partial. It always represents and speaks for the whole of you, your body, mind, and heart.

The stages in the relationship between our experience,

our I, and the Sacred can be looked at as follows. We begin at the stage of just reacting. What actually happens in the world around us gets overshadowed, even overwhelmed by our reactions to it. We live in and through our reactions and hardly see the actual world. Life serves up events that trigger our exaggerated highs and lows, our dramas.

At the second stage, the intensity of our identifications and attachments moderates enough for us to find a balance between what we see and our reactions to what we see. This ordinary mode of life still enslaves us to our reactions, which drive and motivate our actions. But it also allows us some direct experience in between our reactions.

At the third stage, the burden of reactions lifts from our shoulders and our experience just happens, vividly. We find the clarity and peace that enables us just to see, just to experience, without inserting our reactions, but also without our I, without being the one who experiences. This is the practice the Buddha called clear comprehension. We see things as they are, just so, or in today's vernacular, it is what it is. There is no separation between the seer and the seen. There is just the seeing.

At the fourth stage, which is the work of this part of the series on the Way of Attention, we become the true seer, the one who sees what we see, the one who experiences what we experience, the one who does what we do. We become I. This action of being I unifies the whole of ourselves, our body, mind, and heart, in the embrace of our I. Being I not only entrains our energies, but also creates a vessel that organizes and maintains them. For that, however, we must extend the sojourn of our I, we must be I longer and often. This is not just a matter of dogged perseverance to remember and to be, but even more a matter of coming to appreciate the surprising, wonderful, and transformative power of this simple act of being I. And, paradoxically, even as I, there is no separation between the seer and the seen. We do not set up our I as separate, but rather as the core from which we touch the world. I is not ego, centered but not self-centered.

In the next part of this series, we will explore the fifth stage of this relationship between our experience, our I, and the Sacred. For this week, please practice being the root and director of your attention. Ask yourself questions such as *who is doing what I'm doing* or *who is looking*? Then be your I. Be the center from which your attention arises. This is not so mysterious. Once you recognize this basic experience, it is easy to do for a moment. Our work for this week lies in extending the duration of our presence as I and in making it more frequent.

11.9 The Source of Attention
(The Way of Attention: Part 9 of 9)

In becoming the Root of Attention, we become ourselves, our I, the one who sees what see and does what we do, the one who directs our attention. But roots have a purpose beyond stability: we need to open to the waters of the spirit. That sacred nourishment can enter us through the channel of attention. Our I, the director and root of attention, is not attention's ultimate origin.

To approach that origin, we defer to the Source by surrendering our place at our center. From being our own source, we let go to become a channel. We open beyond our I to just seeing, to allowing the higher, the Sacred, to see through us, as us.

This is the fifth stage in the relationship between our experience, our I, and the Sacred. Though it looks superficially similar to the third stage, it is very different. Recall that in the third stage we are just seeing, with no separation between the seer and the seen. In that stage, there is no one who is experiencing what we experience; there is just the experiencing. But in this fifth stage, the Sacred is the One Who is experiencing through us. We enter a cooperative synergy with the Sacred.

The fourth stage, being our I, being the root and director of attention, plays a crucial role. We need to become fully ourselves, fully individual, fully present, so that there is someone in us who can surrender to the Source, so that we can deliver a strong, worthy, and effective vessel, our individuality, into serving the Source.

If we open our attention on its inmost side, it can act as a lens to focus the rays of higher will into and through us. When we are there at the inmost side of our attention, we are in our I, which acts as our lens to focus our attention. By intentionally stepping aside to leave our inmost center open, we allow that lens to continue functioning, but now in a higher and more subtle way, with its inner cap removed. This inwardly open attention becomes a channel for joy, love and purification, for pure experience, and for a cascade of the energies of the Sacred Light. But most importantly, this takes us a step closer to re-connecting with the Will of the Sacred, to becoming fully and continually responsible to the treasure entrusted to us at birth. That sacred trust calls us to become ourselves, to open ourselves, and to serve thereby.

The actual practice toward the source of attention involves a simple but subtle act. We notice as we look out into the world, that our attention is open and receptive on the outside, on the side in contact with the world, in contact with our senses. Then we notice that on its inmost side our attention appears to be closed. But it seems closed because we are standing in the gap of its inner opening, blocking that opening. Often it is our ego, our self-centered attitude standing in that gap. And much of our inner work involves seeing and letting go of that egoism. We can, however, be in our I, centered but not self-centered, yet standing in that gap on the inmost side of attention, being ourselves and directing our attention. So the step required is for our I, for us, to step out of that center, out of that gap, and let attention be open on the inside as well as the outside. And then it, our will, becomes a channel for the higher to flow through us. Prayer and silent meditation can help. But it is that act of inner opening that transforms our situation, at least temporarily.

This opening not only allows the energies of the Sacred Light to flow into and through us, it also carries an emotional component. A mixture of joy, devotion, exaltation, and love comes to us. These are not prerequisites for the opening, but come as a result, as an indicator of the rightness, reality, and purifying nature of the action.

With our ordinary self, our ego, and our small-minded motivations temporarily set aside, we enter a partnership with the Source. This is the domain of conscience, whose promptings become clear. We become transparent and responsive to our conscience. Nothing stands between us and our Source, between us and doing the right thing, between us and being the Reality.

For this week, please practice opening to the Source of attention. Explore what this might mean and how to actually do it. Return to this exploration again and again.

12.0 Stages of Freedom

Life pulls us in two, apparently opposing, directions: outward and inward. Outward into the material world, into this remarkable, intriguing, complex and beautiful universe, planet, and town that we inhabit, with all its people, buildings, machines, animals, plants, rivers, sky, fields, forests, mountains, oceans, and our own body. Outward into the world of necessity, of earning our living, of caring for ourselves and our family. Outward into the world of opportunity, of understanding this great universe, of understanding people, of creating, of consuming.

And inward into this unknown muddle of our inner life, into the intuition that calls us, that some deep, important secret, the Real Truth, lies hidden from us, obscured by our mind, yet accessible only from within. Inward into the nonstop thinking, emoting, perceiving, doing, attituding, judging machine that is our mind, that is our master, that is who we believe we are.

So here is our ongoing challenge: how to fully drink in what the outer has to offer, how to organize the inner and unlock its secrets, and how to honor and serve both, without being completely subject to our changing outer circumstances or enslaved by our chattering, emoting mind.

Outer freedoms, political and economic, matter to us all. Yet even the wealthy and powerful cannot banish all unpleasantness from their own lives. Utter fulfillment cannot be found in the outer alone. Something is missing: we are incomplete. To find our completion, we need inner freedom. The more inwardly free we are, the more peace, fulfillment, and love we experience. Even in the most dire of circumstances, some people find a way to maintain their humanity and their dignity.

Spiritual teachers have long called us to inner freedom. They have variously termed it liberation, death and resurrection, enlightenment, union, or perfection. And they have laid out specific steps along the path to that freedom. Over the coming weeks, we will explore the meaning and practice of inner freedom through a nine-part representation of its stages:

1. Illusory Freedom
2. Allure of Materiality
3. Wish for Freedom
4. Non-Dependence
5. Transcending Personality
6. Illusion of Ego
7. Non-Separateness

8. Surrender
9. The Divine Partnership

These stages of freedom primarily revolve around the purification and refinement of our will, but also depend on the development of our being, on our ableness to be, on inner order, on our inner unity. The more we are, the more clearly we can see. The path to inner freedom depends on seeing how we are not free and seeing the associated possibility of becoming free. We ascend the ladder of freedom in stages, with each rung leading us toward the ultimate freedom.

Each new stage of freedom opens to us gradually. At first, we receive glimpses of the new freedom. Sometimes those glimpses go unrecognized by us. At other times, the glimpses arrive so dramatically as to jar us from our usual mode of existence. These temporary tastes of freedom quickly pass, leaving us however with confidence in our direction, in our inner work, and renewed vigor for it. After a time, the glimpses of the new freedom come more frequently. We accept the new mode of living as right and normal for us, even if temporary. Then we may enter extended sojourns in the new freedom. Our state rises into it, but in time we descend to our previous level. And eventually, we come to live the new freedom, our new station, and we rarely fall back into our old modes of thralldom.

Our inner work adapts as we go. Even if we use only one method of meditation, prayer, or presence for our entire life, our relationship with that method changes, we enter it more deeply. Those who use a variety of methods find themselves needing one or another from their repertoire at different times of their life. Either way, a map of the stages can help us stay on the path. Even without knowing exactly where we are on that map, it helps orient us in the direction of increasing freedom.

For this week, please consider your own situation. Where do you stand with respect to inner freedom? How free are you, inwardly? In what ways are you not free? What would it mean to be free?

12.1 Illusory Freedom
(Stages of Freedom: Part 1 of 9)

"... the truth will set you free" John 8:32

To have any chance of inner freedom, we first need to see and understand that we are not free. We will not make any effort to develop a quality that we think we already possess. Indeed, our usual mode of living offers us a pseudo-freedom. But that false freedom is not our own freedom. It is the freedom of our incessant thoughts, commentary, and judgments, the freedom of our reactive emotions, the freedom of actions driven by our mostly self-indulgent urges and drives, the freedom of living in the most superficial layers of our being. All these aspects of our psyche pretend to speak and act for the whole of us, for who we really are. We are so accustomed to this situation that it lulls us and fools us into believing that all that is who we are. And if all that is who we are and all that is free, then we must be free. Right?

Scratch the surface, though, with even a little introspective observation and we see that we live in an inner fog made up of all those associative thoughts and emotional reactions, of our self-centered urges, drives, and identifications. This mental/emotional fog distracts us, is never quiet, leaves us no peace, and obscures our own reality. Perhaps the greatest benefit of meditation is that it creates space for our mind and heart to settle down and lets us enter the peace and consciousness that bring us closer to our Self, closer to true freedom.

As it is, everything takes me. Every conversation, every activity takes me out of myself, leaves me fractured and devoid of being. Put the cake in front of me and it disappears down my throat, with hardly a taste. Have I eaten the cake or has the cake eaten me? Someone insults me. Anger immediately wells up, coursing through me, generating vindictive thoughts. Is it a true representation to say that I am angry or is the anger angry, having invaded me and taken control? Someone slights me. Self-doubt and insecurity suddenly infect my mind and heart. Someone praises me. The confirmation of my great worth arouses an inner preening.

In the typical aftermath, my mind and heart perseverate on such events. In these and in so many other ways, I am a slave to what happens around me and in me. A stimulus comes into my senses and the response is automatic, predictable, and lacking in freedom. It is not I who respond, but rather the conditioned, pre-programmed, pre-determined working of my personality, this hodgepodge of memories, tendencies, habits and addictions that passes for who I am. Looked at in this way, it becomes clear that it is my personality that is free, not me. In fact, I am subject to my personality's repertoire of responses.

Freedom would mean reversing this situation, so that my personality would serve my true wishes, choices emanating from my center, from me. But that's how it appears to be already. My personality says "I" all the time, claiming to be me, and I even believe it. But it is not true. The thought "I" is not who I am. No matter how many times a day my thoughts say "I'll do this" or "I will do that," the thought of I only represents the machinery of my personality, not my inwardly free center, my unified will.

Actually seeing this lack of inner freedom in ourselves can come as a painful shock. It goes against our entire belief system of who and what we are. And having seen it clearly in one instance, we start to see it in many others. We may begin to feel, correctly, that we lack freedom in nearly all we do. Worse, we may feel, incorrectly, that there is no way out, that our situation is utterly hopeless. But there is hope, magnificent hope. That hope lies in spiritual practice, in inner work, and is attested to by our many great predecessors on the path. It does, however, mean work, wisely conducted, persistent, devoted, and compassionate inner work: first to see and then to set aside our inner slavery and enter the silent presence in us where our true freedom awaits.

Our mind and heart follow their own conditioned processes. The first step to freedom is to see this, to see these pre-programmed patterns of action and reaction, of thought and emotion. The collection of these automated patterns is what passes for us, what we unquestioningly assume we are. My personality may be unique to me, but its freedom is not my freedom. Seeing our situation clearly and accepting the truth of it can set us on the path to freedom. This does not happen all at once, but gradually, bit by bit over a period of years as we come to see and understand our actions, inner and outer.

For this week, notice your own illusion of freedom.

12.2 Allure of Materiality
(Stages of Freedom: Part 2 of 9)

The basic fact of our existence is that we have these physical bodies. This fact imposes a whole host of constraints on us, from the effort we must put forward to feed, clothe, and care for our body, to family obligations, to limitations on the kinds of experiences we can have and on what we can do. So from the outset we are wedded to this material world.

While this physical reality does limit our freedom, or at least defines its parameters, our usual attitude toward the material world limits us even more severely. We take the material as the only reality and shun the possibility of inner freedom, of a higher spiritual reality in the here and now. Those who seek the spiritual have somehow come to recognize its existence, perhaps through some higher experience, or perhaps through seeing that nothing in the material world can give us complete and lasting satisfaction. Indeed, the latter realization informs the first of the Buddha's Four Noble Truths and is the first milestone in the Sufi representation of the path.

But the depth of our realization of that Truth can vary over time. The fact of our physical body and all the limitations it imposes on us do not disappear just because we have begun to suspect or even see the reality of the spiritual. We have to continue dealing with the material world regardless of any inner freedom we might achieve. So the question comes to transforming our relationship with the material, to love, accept, and honor it, without looking solely to the physical world for our life's fulfillment. We seek a way to live not only in the physical world, but also in the inner world of our mind-heart and in the spiritual world beyond our mind-heart. Spiritual practice is about becoming able to live in these three worlds simultaneously.[6]

As it is, however, we are matter bound, body and soul. We are mesmerized by this physical world and believe it to be our only reality. We look for meaning and fulfillment through it. We believe our net worth defines our self-worth, that our resume and portfolio define who we are. Even if some event or insight has jarred us out of the absoluteness of that view and we have begun our inner work in earnest, we still mostly believe in the material. Perhaps 80% or 90%, our goals and interests are material. You might argue that many people find fulfillment through their life's work in the material world. But that fulfillment comes from what they give to the material world, not what they take from it.

None of this is to say that material wealth or material goals block a person's access to the spiritual, just as material poverty does not enable that access. The issue concerns what we identify with, our attachments. We have to earn our living, but our identification with the material results of our earnings

[6]   Gurdjieff, G. I., *Life Is Real Only Then When I Am* (New York: E. P. Dutton, 1978) p.170

or lack thereof, with our status in society, does stand between us and the sacred. This Earth with its natural splendor, all the life on it, and all the wonderful things that humans create, is amazing and beautiful. We can and should love, respect, enjoy, and care for all this, but not expect to be satisfied with however much we personally take from the abundance. We seek the spiritual wealth that is enabled by freedom from identification.

Many of the things in the material world offer important support to our spiritual search. Some art, architecture, music, drama, ritual, and literature, for example, can bring us to a moment of inner silence, awaken our longing for the sacred, and open our hearts and minds to the Real. But most of it only keeps us on the surface of materiality, filling our boredom, emptiness, and ennui with entertainment and distraction.

At the root of our desires and attachments to the material lies our inner emptiness. We cannot fill our emptiness with things from the material world, not only because of the inherent incompatibility and differences between that world and inner worlds, but also because the emptiness itself is illusory, is a false emptiness. Our ego manufactures this emptiness and, in fact, is the emptiness. Within an indivisible continuum, our ego erects a false boundary that defines it. Our ego sets itself up as separate from everything and thus as needing to be filled and able to take from outside itself. But as soon as the ego steps aside or dissolves, even temporarily, we find ourselves reconnected and full, full of life, full of the spirit, full of an utter and deep contentment, no longer needing or wanting to take. With ego, there can be no fullness; without ego, there is only fullness.

For this week, please notice how you are affected by material things, your relationship with the material world, and the many aspects of its allure. Can you enjoy your food, your entertainment, your things, and the beauty of nature and yet remain inwardly free? If something goes missing or breaks, do you break with it? If your net worth drops, does your heart also drop? When wrinkles or gray hair appear in the mirror, do you inwardly rail against time? Do you resent the weather when it doesn't suit you? Do you view other people in material terms, their wealth, their beauty, or lack thereof? When you notice something attractive and expensive beyond your reach, does it sadden you that you don't have it? Look and see.

12.3 Wish for Freedom
(Stages of Freedom: Part 3 of 9)

Seeing that the freedom we thought we had is illusory, seeing that nothing is perfect in the material realm, and seeing that everything fades in itself and in the value we place on it leaves us empty and disillusioned, with a gap where our desires and identifications used to be. Out of that heartfelt gap there arises a true feeling, a longing for completion, a passion for the Real. This feeling is central to every spiritual path: the Buddhist Pali term, for example, is sanvega. Through this gap our inner fire shines, sometimes brightly and sometimes weakly, but always warmly. And once that inner fire lights up, it can never be extinguished, for it is not our fire, but comes to us from the Sacred. We are the keepers of that flame. Our wish for freedom, our passion for the Real is how the spirit calls us.

Freedom, love, and the spirit draw us, while our wish and our passion propel us along the Way. In response, we practice presence and prayer, kindness, responsibility, and service. We practice more and more. And as we do, we see more, we soak in the welcoming silence, the gap at our core. The more we touch that stillness, the more the spirit touches us. In the process, our wish to be and our passion for the Real deepen. This virtuous circle of passion enlivening practice, which further awakens our passion, sustains our path. Seen in this light, we understand and respect the centrality of our wish for freedom and we nurture that yearning by responding to it through our inner work.

Everything depends on the purity and depth of our need, the need that draws us into the Sacred. Our perceptions of the wish for freedom come through our emotions. We feel the need. We feel the passion. We feel the hunger. It drives our interests toward the Sacred. We find ourselves wanting to know more, to understand more, to be more. If we look with our thinking mind for that wish, for what's driving our interest and actions, we cannot see it. It is not mental. It's emotional. Our mind may agree and have its own rationale for why we practice. But our heart is the channel for this drive: we simply feel that we must.

Personal crises and failures remind us of our vulnerability and our thirst for something that never decays, never fails or disappoints, something permanent. That one and only something is the Sacred. Thus, crises and failures can open opportunities to renew our wish for inner freedom. But because those roots lie in wanting to escape the unwanted, this can only take us part of the way. The further we travel the path, the more the goal, the Sacred draws us into Itself. As glimpses beyond the veil, or even just intimations of the Real, are granted to us, our attraction to and need for the Sacred deepens. The Great Heart of the World embraces us, enlivens our wish, and promises fulfillment.

This wish for freedom, for reconnecting with the Sacred, has a different character than most of our other wishes. If we wish for some material thing, we can have a clear image of what we wish for. If we wish for some material quality, like health or wealth or success, we can have a fairly clear representation of that. But when we wish for freedom, any mental representation of our goal ultimately hides it from us. The true wish for inner freedom can only be non-conceptual, because what we seek transcends the bounds of our mind. This applies even in religions that employ sacred images, which can indeed take us part of the way. But the reality of Christ far surpasses any conception we might have of Him.

For this week, be aware of and respond to your own wish for freedom, your own passion for the Real. Our heart is mixed: many disparate feelings compete for the center of our stage. But we can support and strengthen our wish to be by recognizing it, by accepting it, and by our persistent inner work, both on our own and in the company of others. And like our inner work, our wish operates in and for the present, not for some imagined future freedom. We wish now and allow our wish to infuse our practice here and now.

12.4 Non-Dependence
(Stages of Freedom: Part 4 of 9)

We depend on the world outside us in a multitude of ways. Most obviously, we depend on nature and on other people for our material well-being. Our vast and complex world ecosystem and world economy fulfill our material needs and many of our material desires. This necessary dependence comes with having a body. We cannot get around it.

But we also suffer another and unnecessary type of dependence. Our inner experience is almost completely subject to outer situations and events. We live in an inner world of emotional reactions, physical attractions and repulsions, likes and dislikes, physical habits, and all kinds of grasping and clinging. So our spiritual work at this stage consists in becoming able to be inwardly free in front of our automatic reactions, habits, likes and dislikes. Notice that to be free "in front of" is fundamentally different than being free "of." The latter would mean not having reactions, habits, likes or dislikes — a dull existence indeed. To be free in front of means being able to choose whether to act on, whether to indulge whatever emotional reaction, habit, like, or dislike happens to arise in us.

One approach entails resisting, going against our likes

and dislikes. Such efforts generate an energy useful for our inner work, while showing us the truth of our conditioning, our slavery to our likes and dislikes. As long as these set patterns control what we do and how we feel, we remain dependent, not free at this level.

Perhaps you hate tomatoes. So you set yourself to eat tomatoes. Perhaps you dislike a particular person. So you set yourself to spend a little time with that person, honestly and openheartedly. Perhaps you like chocolate. So you set yourself not to eat chocolate for a time. Perhaps you have a habit of chewing gum. So you stop for a while. Each of us has our own set of habits, likes and dislikes. So we experiment with this practice, with how and when to apply it in our own particular case.

The point isn't to learn to like what we dislike. It's perfectly fine to hate tomatoes. Nor is the point to learn to dislike what we like. We are not after a Spartan lifestyle of always denying ourselves pleasures. The point is freedom, to be able to eat tomatoes or not chew gum, to be able to choose what we do despite our ingrained habits, or our likes and dislikes.

Going against our reactions, likes and dislikes is easy in theory, but difficult in practice, especially with powerful reactions and strongly ingrained likes and dislikes. The first requirement consists of having a clear intention to choose a certain course whenever a particular reaction, like or dislike arises. But that intention may not be enough. It needs an ally, a supporting technique.

Whenever we attempt to stop or change one of our patterns, that pattern resists the change. The resulting tension builds up an energy in us. Usually that energy will overwhelm our intention to change the pattern, even temporarily. And if we are able change the pattern in that instance, the repressed energy will typically come out in some other undesirable way. For example, we may successfully resist eating a piece of cake today, only to succumb to eating two pieces tomorrow. Or we may resist yelling at someone this morning only to honk our way through traffic in the afternoon. This work of freedom requires vigilance, intelligence, and persistence.

To supplement our intention to change a particular behavior, we add a method of dealing with the energy released in the process. Whenever we experience the impulse to do the action we have chosen to stop, or the impulse not to do the action we have chosen to do, we put the resulting energy to positive use: we send it into sensing our body. We can sense an arm or a leg, or our whole body. We use the impulse of the reaction, like, or dislike, as a reminder to sense our body.

Say you have a habit of eating cake and you set yourself not to eat cake for the next month. Of course, the urge to eat cake will come to you repeatedly. When it does, rather than mentally arguing with that urge, you begin sensing your body. With some practice, this will take the energy from the urge and channel it into sensing, into more presence, into a benefit for your soul. It also moves your focus, your attention away from the urge and into something productive. And this method does all this without repressing the urge. You feel and experience the urge to eat cake. But you do not act on it, nor do you give it more energy by engaging in an internal debate on whether to act on it. You just see the urge and let it go by sensing your body instead. Each such effort earns you another drop of freedom, makes you a little less dependent, and puts you more in contact with your body and thereby with presence.

Throughout, we need to remember that our practice is not about permanently changing our personality. It is about raising our level of being, about becoming inwardly free. Going against our habits is only one of the methods in our repertoire of spiritual practice. Forgetting this, we can easily lapse into a rigid, inflexible approach to life. Our personality may change as a byproduct of our inner work, but we do not want to be sidetracked into making personality change our goal. That is a never-ending process that tends to strengthen our ego, the one who wants to improve our personality. And as our inner work deepens, instead of resisting, we will open to the whole roiling catastrophe of our inner life and bring to it the healing embrace of our love and acceptance, a process that restores us to unity.

Nevertheless, there are some destructive habits or addictions that block our progress on the path. Some are physical like smoking, excessive drinking, drug abuse, and the like. We are also prone to destructive emotional addictions, like the extremes of chronic anger, jealousy, greed, and self-importance. Such destructive habits do need to be changed. Engaging professional help or groups like Alcoholics Anonymous can expedite that change. We will not find true peace and freedom while damaging our body and subverting our mind with destructive habits.

For this week, please take a step toward non-dependence and freedom by resisting a habit, like or dislike. When the targeted impulse arises, let its energy and the energy released in resisting it go into sensing your body. Carefully choose which habit, like, or dislike to resist, selecting one that will not exceed your strength but still present a challenge, even if a mild one.

12.5 Transcending Personality
(Stages of Freedom: Part 5 of 9)

Even after we increase our non-dependence, our measure of freedom in front of our likes, dislikes, and habits, we still suffer from a mistaken identity that enslaves us. We believe in our thoughts and particularly in our patterns of thought and emotion, our opinions and attitudes, our modes of speaking and acting. We believe our thoughts are driven by a thinker, our emotions by an emoter, and our actions by an actor. We believe we are that thinker, emoter, and actor, that we are the one who holds our various opinions and adopts our various attitudes.

But the great majority of the time our thoughts think themselves, our emotions emote, our opinions opine, our attitudes react in a fixed way, and our actions go by predisposed patterns. There is no one behind all this, driving our conditioned and automatic functioning. Like the robot-controlled cars of the future, it all just happens on its own. The whole intricate dance of these self-generating patterns of thought, emotion, and action creates an illusion of a person that we believe we are. We call that illusion personality. And we believe we have a personality, when in truth our personality has us.

The first clue we might notice is that our personality lacks unity. Its various patterns sometimes even conflict with each other. We want to eat the cake and lose weight. We want to have plenty of money, but not have to work for it. We want to watch TV and read and be out and about — all at the same time. We wish our space was not such a mess, but we begrudge the time to straighten it up. We want that expensive trinket, but we do not want to spend that much on it. Such inner conflicts force choices on us, choices that deny parts of our self.

Those inner conflicts help perpetuate our personality by energizing both sides of each conflict and drawing our I into that quicksand. Even without conflict, our personality perpetuates itself masterfully. The events of our life are transformed into dramas of inflated importance, dramas that are the very substance of our personality. Our successes and our failures, our joys and our pains all play prominent roles in the pantheon of our personal history, the building blocks of our self-referential world view, our personality. Everything we do and everything that happens to us passes through the filter of our personality and is incorporated into it, even our spiritual search. Because of this, our personality seems all encompassing, seems to be all of what and who we are. But that is the illusion.

Our personality hates silence. In the gaps between thoughts and between emotional reactions, personality vanishes. There are two reasons for this. First, the stuff of our personality consists precisely of those automatic, associative thoughts and reactive emotions. In their absence, our personality just fades out. Second, the silence reveals the conscious energy, which transcends personality.

In transcending our personality, we come toward the possibility of a right relationship with it, of our personality serving a higher purpose under the direction of our I, our true self. Yet this does not mean a separation between our I and our personality. We seek unity. If we attempt to stand back at a distance, viewing the machinations of our personality as if it were not part of us, we exacerbate a catastrophic split in our inner life, setting one part of us above and against another. This only serves to weaken the whole, multiplying and deepening our inner conflicts.

Instead, we seek unity by seeing all the automatic and reactive functioning of our mind and heart, by accepting and welcoming all of it as part of our makeup, and by clearly understanding that no automatic thought, no reactive emotion can speak for our totality. We begin to see that the automatic functioning of our mind and heart is akin to the automatic functioning of our body and its inner organs. Our mind ruminates just as our digestive system digests. Our emotions react just as our hand jerks back from a hot surface. It all just happens in response to inner and outer circumstances. Just as we have a body with its own limited intelligence, we also have a mind and heart with their own limited intelligence. In the midst of it all, we are. Our will and our awareness penetrate and unify all our parts into the wholeness that we are. In this way, our personality transcends itself by joining our greater unity.

The field in which this can occur is just that pure consciousness, the conscious energy that reveals itself in inner silence. Behind our thoughts and emotions, we abide in consciousness. This cognitive stillness embraces all our parts, body, mind, heart, and personality, and enables our I to connect it all into a unified whole. The clear seeing that consciousness enables sees all and includes all and makes room for our I, for the one who sees, to take its rightful place at our core. In our inner stillness, we find the freedom that transcends our personality.

For this week, look at yourself, your patterns of thinking, feeling, and acting. Notice your personality for what it is: this collection of patterns that pretends to be you. Be the one who sees all this from the place of non-judgmental stillness within you. In that state of seeing, no thought or emotional reaction can successfully pretend to be you. You see thoughts as just thoughts and reactive emotions as just reactive emotions. Yet you embrace it all, bringing it within the purview of your greater Self. This is the freedom that transcends personality.

12.6 Illusion of Ego
(Stages of Freedom: Part 6 of 9)

What in us blocks our connection with the spiritual depths? If heaven is real, why am I not in contact with it? All religions and paths address this central question, under a variety of names, the most common today in the West being "ego." The term ego, in this context, alludes to our deeply ingrained self-referential, self-seeking disposition, our well-hidden and highly adaptable attitude that life revolves around me and mine. Ego cuts us off from other people, from Nature, from God, from our authentic self, from our true responsibility, and from fulfilling our destiny. Our ego is the great usurper. It focuses on our local independence, falsely presuming it to be a global independence. The ego convinces us that we are truly separate beings with ultimately separate will, having no inherent connection with other people or with God.

Our ego installs us at the center of the universe, separate from all and enslaved by time. Dwelling on our past history, our conditioning, our grudges, our manufactured identity, our personality, or on our future hopes, dreams, fears, anxieties, desires, and pressures, ego creates a constant torrent of mental structures, each of which proclaim "This is me." In childhood we become so involved and enamored with the growing arsenal of our ego, that we unquestioningly assume it is who we are. That insidious assumption constitutes the ego's iron grip on us.

This ego, this false pretender, whenever it arises grabs the seat of honor at the core of our being. It purports to speak for the whole of us, even though our various parts lack integration. It adopts the voice and desires of whatever part of us pushes itself temporarily to the top of the heap. So for example, our ego, under the influence of one part of us, "decides" to do something, but later under the influence of another part, we find ourselves doing just the opposite. I may think "I am going to quit smoking tomorrow." But tomorrow my hand, not caring what my mind thought yesterday, reaches for a cigarette. The pretender to the throne does not bear the royal seal, does not have the power it ascribes to itself.

Why is it that the ego, or separate self, produces such a major difficulty in the spiritual path, indeed THE major difficulty? The answer can be found in the subtlety of the place occupied by ego and I. That place is not readily visible, even to our inner eye. It lies in the realm of Will, more interior than all our thought, emotion, and sensory experience, more interior than our awareness or consciousness itself, more interior than our mind. Ego and I reside in the place of who we are, that in us which chooses and decides, or abdicates choosing and deciding. A thought that says, "I will …," masquerades as the source of decision. When this does represent an actual decision, the true source is will itself. Our will, however, usurped by the self-centered ego, an aberration of will, enters into a wrong and self-referential mode of working. Our true I, our true will, does not act by force, but rather by the cooperative assent of our various parts. The uncooperative ego can thus come and stand in the place of the I, hiding and splitting off our authentic I from the rest of us. Under the influence of ego, we believe ourselves to be our own source. It turns out that, although we are indeed our own source, that very source is the Source of All.

Religions and paths portray the nature of our egoism and how to deal with it in one of two quite distinct modes. Usually, and to our misfortune, the ways reify and solidify ego into a something, an enemy, which must be overcome, which must die, which inherently resides in our tainted nature, which must be purified. True enough. One cannot argue with the accumulated wisdom of great religions. For our modern culture, though, the notion that our ego must die seems frightening. More importantly, the notion that we harbor inherent spiritual taints gets interpreted by our self-bashing, insecure psychology to mean that we are bad, or at least inadequate — something that we in the West are often trained to believe from childhood on. We believe we are not good enough. So we don the knowledge of being corrupt to our core as a mantle of supposed wisdom, and flock to those that teach it. Then the religious teaching about egoism simply gets co-opted by the self-denigrating side of our ego, eagerly adopted and accepted as yet another weakness. We hang our heads and beat our breasts and feel the better (or worse) for it. Unfortunately, all this only strengthens our egoism and leads us into an endless cycle, akin to a dog chasing its tail.

Casting our ego as the enemy in an inner holy war and winning that battle is an exceedingly difficult proposition, primarily because the ego proves to be a most subtle adversary. In fact, the ego will even join the battle against itself. It will take it on and say "this is wonderful, I'm going to battle against ego, I will become free, I will be wonderful, I will be better than I am now, and I will be better than other people, because I will be a highly evolved spiritual being." The ego joins our forces. As an enemy, it infiltrates our lines, wearing our own uniform, its soldiers and officers indistinguishable from ours. How does one fight a battle against such a devious and resourceful enemy? For most of us, it comes to nothing but another heap of suffering as we merely fight ourselves in the name of spirituality and sink more deeply than ever into the morass of self-centeredness. Only the rarest of souls find a way through this conundrum.

An alternative, but also traditional view casts ego in an entirely different perspective, not as an enemy, but as an illusion, and invites us to see our ego for what it is: an empty, ephemeral sham, a hall of mirrors, a self-referential and insubstantial web. The rise of Buddhism in the West is, in no small part, due to this kinder yet no less incisive and perhaps more tractable formulation of the problem of egoism.

Our belief in our ego, or separate self, is to a large extent learned from society. All the people around us labor under a self-centered perspective on life, which naturally devolves to impressionable children. Repeatedly shining the light of awareness directly on this sense of separateness gradually disperses it. But if we look carefully for our ego, for this separate self that we think we are, we shall not find it.

Am I my body? I can control my body, I can be aware of my body, and my awareness is greater than my body. So I am probably not my body.

Am I my feelings? I can be aware of my feelings and have some rudimentary influence on them, so I am probably not my feelings.

Am I my thoughts? My thoughts claim the title of I, thinking "I think," "I am hungry." But that "I" is just a thought, having no more substance than any other thought. It fools me though, this thought "I." I believe in it. I believe it refers to something real and substantial, to the real me. But if I look at it clearly, I see it as only a thought with no real referent. At best, I may have a vague idea that I am some combination of my thoughts, feelings, and body. Again it proves empty to the insightful observer.

Am I my knowledge and experience, my habits and

desires, my style — in short, my personality? But I can see all this at work in myself. And clearly, the one who sees seems closer to me than this whole complex of acquired patterns and inherited predispositions that I call my personality. So no, I am not my personality. I need my personality because only through it can I function in life, but I also need to remember that this personality is not who I am.

How about my awareness? Am I my awareness? Two problems here. First, I have some control over what I am aware of. So there must be something deeper. Second, the deeper I go into awareness, the less it is centered in me, so how can that be me as a separate entity, as an ego?

How about my attention? How about that in me that decides, my will? This is the subtlest of all. Yet again, the deeper I look into my will, the less it is centered in me, and the more it opens beyond me.

So wherever we look, we do not find this self, this separate person that takes our name, this self-important actor on the stage of our life. The more carefully and persistently we look, the more this once-compelling ego, this self disappears. Or perhaps we see that it never existed to begin with. Gradually, our belief in our ego assumes a porous quality, which rather than cutting us off from others, merely clouds our relationships intermittently. This separate self never was. Our devotion to it shrivels and we are left to truly be ourselves, to play our unique role in the larger story of our common life. When moments come in which we fall back into that trance of selfness, we feel uncomfortable, like in a shoe that no longer fits, and we let it go.

Our ego, this illusory pattern, however, endures with remarkable resilience and persistence. Complete freedom from ego comes only at a very high station of spiritual development, something to which we may aspire and work for with diligence. The best approach lies somewhere between the two outlined above. Seeing and letting go can only work insofar as we are able to see. The depth and subtlety of our seeing must increase. For this, efforts of various kinds are necessary. These efforts may include grappling with some of the propensities of our separate self. Doing so can illumine the tentacles of egoism, while creating energy for seeing more. Only we must not have the idea that such struggles will, by themselves, reform our recalcitrant self-centeredness. A project of reform by force is doomed to fail. Efforts at reform can only be useful to the extent that they help us to see. Sensing the energy body and working at presence also help us see. And seeing, it is said, leads to liberation: liberation from the illusion of the ego and into the freedom of interconnectedness.

For this week, do what you can to see your own ego at work and also to see its absence. The paradox is that the more you look and the more deeply you look, the less ego there is to see.

12.7 Non-Separateness
(Stages of Freedom: Part 7 of 9)

As the illusion of ego evaporates, so do the walls of our inner life. As our egocentric attitude goes, so does the distinction between self and other. We open to our inherent unity with all life. One ancient way we might experience this is in nature. The trees, the sky, the ocean, the mountain, the landscape, wherever we happen to find ourselves in the natural world, our consciousness fills with our surroundings. The beauty, the reality, and the comfort, welcome us back into our natural home. We drop our defenses. We are just here, along with everything else, in the seamless whole. Our awareness merges with nature's own awareness into one big cognizant continuum. We are of a piece with Nature, no longer setting our self apart. Fear, grasping, and exploitation fall away. For many, the practice of non-separateness comes most effortlessly in Nature. We slip into the simple ease of the one being of Nature, a being that includes and embraces us.

With people, the practice of non-separateness arouses our resistance. We seem so separate. And that separateness has layers: material, emotional, mental, being, and will. The material aspects of separateness have to do with the fact that you are in your body and I am in mine. Differences in race, sex, and social class divide us at this superficial level. At the emotional layer of separateness, you have your desires and I have mine. Anger, hatred, jealousy, envy, greed, and the like confirm and deepen our separateness from each other. At the mental layer of separateness, our world view, attitudes, and agendas are built on the illusion of separateness, both individual and collective. Differences in nationality, politics, and religion divide us at this mental level. Then we have the separateness of being arising from the fact that you are there and I am here. What happens to you does not happen to me, and vice versa. Finally, we encounter the separateness of will: you are not me and I am not you. You do not choose what I do, and I do not choose what you do.

These layers of separateness also apply within ourselves. At first, we are identified with our body, our emotions, our attitudes. Then we notice them and consider all of that to be separate from who we are. We might think of our body or our personality as something to do battle against. At a later stage, we reunite everything into a new wholeness. As we overcome the layers of separateness within us, we can also overcome our separateness from other people.

Some people are blessed with a naturally compassionate disposition which recognizes our non-separateness. Those of us who are not so blessed need a way beyond separateness. First, we can recognize that though separateness holds true at all but the highest levels, so does non-separateness. At the level of our body, certainly we have clear separateness: your body, my body. But we also have non-separateness in the forms of similarity and interdependence. Our bodies all function almost identically. We share the air and we all must eat. And we need each other to maintain our life. One makes ploughs, another raises wheat, and a third bakes bread.

At the level of our emotions and thoughts, we have separateness in the sense that your emotions and thoughts are private to you, as are mine to me. But we also have non-separateness in the similarities between your emotions and mine, between your thoughts and mine. We all share the same basic human motivations and modes of reacting. We know joy and we know anger in each other, because we know them in ourselves. This fellow-feeling is a source of compassion.

At the level of our being, or more particularly our consciousness, we have the separateness of our experiencing: you experience your life and I experience mine. But something deeper also operates at this level, namely sameness. Our basic consciousness is one and the same in all of us. There is one, indivisible, all-embracing energy of consciousness. Our body-mind-heart enables us to experience consciousness individually. We may share an experience, for example, as part of a crowd attending some entertainment. That common experience brings a kind of unity among the crowd, albeit a limited unity based on shared sensory perceptions, but nevertheless a unity that hints at the truer unity.

If we look carefully into our consciousness, going beneath its sensory contents, to see with pure consciousness, then we come into our shared being. When another person looks or experiences, they do so with the very same fundamental consciousness that is in you. Listening helps open us to this reality. This is not merely a similarity of awareness, but rather one and the same awareness: the silent, pre-sensory consciousness that we all share. We all swim in the one ocean of consciousness.

At the level of our will, we have the separateness of our intentions, choices, decisions, and understanding. Obviously, your choices are different than mine and we may well be in conflict. But in some situations, such as being a member of a team or organization, we share intentions with others. Again, that shared intention brings a kind of unity among the team or organization, albeit a limited unity based on shared choices and intentions, but nevertheless a unity that also hints at the truer unity.

If we look deeper, beyond our particular choices and decisions, to that in us which chooses and decides, we get closer to our unity in will. The same fundamental will flows through all of us. Its Source is One. And although will appears divided at our level, it is inherently indivisible and sacred. This is the deepest mystery of all on the spiritual path, but also the most important. One approach to this mystery is to follow our attention back toward where it comes from, back toward its Source. The closer we come to that Source, the less separate we are.

For this week, look at how you habitually consider yourself separate from others and practice seeing beyond our separateness toward unity.

12.8 Surrender
(Stages of Freedom: Part 8 of 9)

Surrendering to the Sacred takes us right into the central reality of the spiritual pursuit. Although the ultimate step may come in a particular moment, surrendering is a process, a long process of practice and purification. Along the way we engage in relaxing, accepting, letting go, and opening.

The word "surrender," however, can be off-putting, intimidating, and even frightening. But spiritual surrender is not a matter of capitulating to an enemy after a battle. Rather, at each step we simply let go of the lower to enter a more direct relationship with the higher.

The process of surrendering can be represented in the following steps:

1. Relaxing tensions: physical, emotional, mental, and interpersonal
2. Accepting our life as it is, but also free to seek to change our circumstances
3. Accepting to learn about spiritual practice from others
4. Accepting our self as we are, but also free to seek to change
5. Accepting that spiritual practice is our lifeline, even in our darkest moments
6. Opening to the inner peace of cognizant stillness; letting go of personality
7. Opening to the Sacred Light beyond consciousness; letting yourself be drawn toward it; taking the plunge; letting go of being
8. Utterly giving yourself, your innermost core, over to the Highest One and discovering that, at root, you are an emanation of That; letting go of doing

This process is not linear. We may be working on any or all of these steps in any given time period. The practice of relaxing our body, heart, and mind, both in meditation and in everyday life, paves the way for all the other steps. Coming to accept our life, even while working to change our circumstances if we so choose, leaves intact the inner resources we need for our spiritual pursuit. Accepting to learn spiritual practices from others can be humbling and thus helps free us from any inflated self-image we might harbor. Like accepting our life as it is, accepting ourselves as we are, even while seeking to change in necessary ways, conserves our energies for reaching toward the spirit, rather than continually draining our energies in self-reproach. Once our feet are firmly planted on the spiritual path, we discover in our darkest moments that the path and the spirit offer an essential lifeline, a true, unwavering, and loving friend. And all of those steps prepare us for the deeper work remaining.

Leaving aside our thoughts and reactive emotions to enter the silence of inner peace, the cognizant stillness of consciousness, allows us temporarily to surrender our identification with our personality. Abiding in the inner temple of peace, we drop our need to buy into or assert some self-image that we mistakenly believe. In that stillness, we are, simply and directly. We experience just being, just awareness, just the crystal purity of consciousness.

Remarkably, that wonderful peace of consciousness is only the beginning of the truly spiritual realms. Beyond consciousness — yes, there is a domain beyond consciousness — we may touch the world of Sacred Light. Toward that we open our heart and soul, we surrender for those moments any other need or desire, even the need to be ourselves, our separate selves. Wholly focused on the Higher, we plunge beyond consciousness and toward the Sacred, entering the depths of prayer, through the depths of our being. Dropping behind our thoughts and emotions, behind our consciousness, back through our own core, ever closer to where our self would be, we discover our higher Self in a cascade of higher energies.

And finally, utterly, giving over our independence of action to the One Actor, the Creative Will of the World, the ever-present Source of All, surrendering our uniqueness to the Great Unique One. For this prayer can help. The sacred words, sounds, and images of prayer can guide us beyond words, sounds, and images, toward the Ultimate. And in surrendering we reconnect with the Whole, becoming a particle of the Unity.

Now all of this is not merely some imaginative language, but points toward an actual reality. For this week, practice surrendering the lesser to enter that greater reality.
And in the process, you will deepen your freedom.

12.9 The Sacred Partnership
(Stages of Freedom: Part 9 of 9)

Those who reach the ultimate degree of spirituality are variously said to have communed with the Saints, entered the Kingdom of Heaven, attained union with the Divine, found perfect submission to Allah, reached nirvana, achieved liberation, or become a friend of the Friend. This last description of the goal as friendship with the Sacred particularly appeals to our sensibilities today. Between two friends there is both unity and independence. The unity is a unity of purpose and devotion. The independence, rather than detracting from the unity, actually enhances it by both parties bringing their strengths to the collaboration.

The most perfect service is the freely given. We need not presume that union with God means a robot-like submission of losing our individuality and taking orders. On the contrary, just as any wise owner of a complex enterprise wants intelligent, creative, self-motivated associates with initiative, these qualities also matter deeply in serving the Sacred. But that service also requires that we "know" what to do and that we are able to do it. We develop the ability for spiritual action through our path of inner work. The question of "knowing" what to do, however, comes down to perception of purpose and communication with the Sacred. The primary channel for that communication is our conscience.

As long as we have a physical body, though, the impulses from the Higher must pass through our mind, heart, and personality. No matter how pure and devoted a person we are, this material-world filter still operates to some degree. Though inner peace helps, the promptings of conscience always tend to get garbled. This is where our personal intelligence and wisdom enter, to ask the hard questions and apply the light-of-day tests of sanity, reality, compassion, and ordinary morality. And if what our conscience appears to be telling us passes all those tests, then it is truly calling us to respond appropriately to those promptings, to do the right thing.

The most expedient way for the creative Force behind the universe to act in our world is through us human beings. If the Sacred is not to violate its own laws of Nature, then It must act through the uncertainties inherent in Nature. Within us, those uncertainties manifest in the partially random vagaries of our emerging thoughts and perceptions, thus opening a possible channel for the higher will. So an obvious method of communicating the higher will to us is through our conscience, our perception of right and wrong. To align our actions, inner and outer, with that Force, we pay attention to conscience. It speaks to us as our intuition of right and wrong. When we know or feel what is right and we know or feel what is wrong, we can bind ourselves to that knowing or feeling. And more often than not, if we look inward, that knowing or feeling becomes clear.

This is our point of freedom, the inner freedom we have gained through our inner work. We are free with respect to our personality and its self-centered motivations, free to be responsible. If we are at peace, not driven by our mass of conflicting desires and attitudes, we have less resistance to hearing our conscience and acting on it. Conscience does not force its edicts upon us. We are free to respond or not, to comply or not. But if we do respond or comply, we take our place in our growing partnership with the Sacred. We become our conscience. True responsibility and true service begin here.

This great and beautiful universe must have a Purpose. The Divine Will of the Creator embodies that Purpose. Though we cannot know that Purpose in the way we know human purposes, we can cooperate with It, thereby giving purpose to our life. That is why we engage in spiritual practice and why we seek partnership with the Sacred through the medium of conscience.

But conscience is not the whole story of that partnership. If it were, then the partnership would only be intermittent, as the episodic promptings of conscience seem to be. We also need a more continuous way of partnership. For that we look to the role of presence itself. If we can be present, fully present, we have clarity of awareness, peace in our heart, no identification with our thoughts or emotions, and no room for ego to usurp our actions. These are the perfect conditions for presence as partnership with the Divine. Can it be that in pure presence we become God's eyes and ears, God's body and soul on this Earth? In our moments of non-doing, of allowing our experience to be as it is, of simply willing ourselves to be, that will-to-be is not just our own, but comes through us from the higher unity, from the Source, from the One Sacred Will. We enter an intimate partnership with the Sacred, a unity of the partners. The more perfect our presence, the more perfect the unity, both within ourselves and with the Higher. No longer merely personal, presence becomes an expression and manifestation of the Sacred partnership.

In prayer we deepen this effect by letting go of self-centeredness and opening our inmost center to the Higher. We delve within, seeking the Sacred behind and beyond all. Into and through our very core, we seek the Partner.

Yet another aspect of participating in the partnership emerges through our practices. In spiritual practice, our inner work of meditation, prayer, and presence, we transform energies. We raise lower energies to a higher quality and we receive higher energies from above. That intentional and conscious process of transforming energies also serves our role in the Sacred Partnership, for those energies are desperately needed for the spiritual ecosystem of the world. Walk into a room where a group of people are meditating or praying together and you may immediately notice the atmosphere of peace and presence and its calming, awakening effects on you. The energies being transformed spread out, with positive effects on other people. The stronger and deeper the practice, the more effective it is.

Each moment of our own individual practice makes this constructive contribution, serving our soul, humanity, the Earth, and the Sacred.

For this week, deepen your own partnership with the Sacred.

13.0 Inner Body Development

13.1 Body Contact
(Aspect 1 of 7)

We know from experience that when our spiritual practice depends on maintaining our attention on particular thoughts or feelings, it quickly goes off the rails. Distractions and disturbances channel our interest away from the practice, away from presence. All this reflects the amorphous and disordered state of our soul. We need a place to stand in our inner world. We need an inner body. So as a practical pursuit at this level, to develop our soul we develop our inner body, an integrated and enduring structure of spiritual energy, a spiritual body within our physical body.

The full development of our inner body typically requires many years of persistent effort. But each step along the way, each effort, brings its own major benefits on many levels from our sense of physical well-being, to our mental and emotional health and happiness, to our increasing appreciation of and effectiveness in life, to our strengthened and deepened relationships both with people and with the spirit, to a concrete, always-available experience of the spirit through our body, to an opportunity to engage, in any moment, in a meaningful action that serves us and our world.

Where to begin? Fortunately, there are practical, verifiable approaches to developing our inner body, approaches that do not depend on some imaginative or qualitative notion of spirituality, but rather on a visceral, directly perceptible sense of our formative inner body. From the very beginning of these practices, that visceral perception guides us surefootedly along the path. When that perception is not there, we know we are not in contact with our inner body. And contact with the substances of the inner body is exactly where we begin.

Sitting quietly, place your attention in your right hand. Let the hand stay relaxed as you hold your attention in it for a few minutes. When you notice that your attention has wandered, simply bring it back to the hand. Your attention is in your hand so that you can have a direct perception of the hand, from inside it. Thinking about the hand or visualizing it only interferes with that direct perception. After a few minutes, notice the difference between your immediate perception of your right hand and your left hand. The right hand may be more alive, more vibrant. In contrast, the left hand seems empty.

This is due to the presence of the sensitive energy in your right hand. The act of holding your attention in the hand has drawn that energy into it. We say that you are *sensing* your right hand and that it is full of the sensitive energy. This is the fundamental practice in developing your inner body: the sensitive energy is the basic substance that will form that part of your soul.

Now move your attention into your right foot and hold it there for a few minutes. Gradually the sensitive energy will begin to collect in your right foot. You will be sensing your right foot. Next sense your left foot and then your left hand.

After some time you will begin to acquire the taste of sensing, so that you can easily recognize its presence or lack thereof. Then you can begin sensing entire limbs. Putting your attention in your right arm and holding your attention there in the whole of your right arm, the sensitive energy will spread throughout the arm. Next, sense your right leg, then your left leg, and then your left arm.

After some weeks or months, as your perception of and facility with the sensitive energy continues to grow, you can shift into sensing both arms or both legs, or all four at once. And then practice sensing your whole body, all four limbs, as well as your torso and head. In sensing your torso, however, just work on a general overall sense of it, rather than trying to sense particular inner organs, so as not to interfere with their automatic functioning.

This practice of sensing maintains its value throughout our path. Our ability to sense evolves as we do and we evolve as our ability to sense does. The completeness, intensity, frequency, and duration of sensing our body offer one way to measure our state and our being. Sensing builds our inner body, builds our soul. As such, it occupies a central place in the pantheon of spiritual practices. Certainly there are other, deeper practices. But an inner body of sensitive energy serves as our platform from which the deeper practices can be much more effective.

For this week, practice being in contact with your physical body and with your formative inner body through sensing. If you have never worked on this before, please try it. If you have practiced sensing, please renew and extend that practice. If you are currently practicing sensing, work to make that practice more complete, stronger, more frequent, and for longer periods.

The practice of sensing is suitable both for formal, seated meditation-type sessions, as well as for use during your daily activities. If you are going for a walk, sense. If you are sitting down relaxing at a meal, with other people, with a book, or with TV, sense. Sensing enhances any experience and can turn our most mundane moments to serving our spiritual evolution. The only caveat concerns dangerous or critical activities, like driving, that require all our attention, so we do not divert attention into sensing in those situations.

In the coming weeks we will address various further aspects of inner body development, which may be represented as:

1. Body Contact
2. Emotion Contact
3. Mind Contact
4. Nourishing
5. Being
6. Inhabiting
7. Persistence

13.2 Emotion Contact
(Inner Body Development: Aspect 2 of 7)

Very often, when in the grip of some strong emotion, or even just the influence of a mild one, we do not realize it. When we get angry, our immediate focus falls to the cause and object of our anger, and we may miss the fact of the anger itself. Same with fear, jealousy, sadness, happiness, and the rest. Emotions shape our inner experience, channeling our thoughts along paths symbiotic with the emotion, directing our attention toward those aspects of our immediate environment relevant to the emotion, and urging us to actions dictated by the emotion. This all happens automatically, without any choosing on our part, as if it were hardwired into our nervous system.

One problem with this lack of emotional awareness for our spiritual work is that some of these emotions drain and waste our inner energies. On the other hand, if we were to succeed in flattening our emotions, our life would become dull indeed. The solution, though not easy, is to bring more consciousness into our emotional life. Enhanced awareness itself changes the tenor and quality of our emotions, generally raising them to be more positive, less self-centered, less draining, and more integrated with our wholeness.

Our inner body, like our physical body, needs its center of emotional awareness. For that, we can simply use our attention to contact our emotional center, similarly to the way we sense for body contact. For contact with our inner body emotional center, we collect and hold our attention in the physical area of our emotions, our chest and upper abdomen between our breasts, our solar plexus and the upper part of our sternum. This awakens the sensitive energy of emotion, which mediates our contact with that center. The sensitive energy takes three forms relating to our body, our emotion, and our mind. Our inner body needs all three, including the sensitive energy of emotion.

Put your attention in the area of your emotions and stay with it. Five effects of this are (1) to make us aware of the physical aspects of our emotions, (2) to make us aware of particular emotions as they arise, (3) to make us aware of our emotions as emotions, (4) to awaken the sensitive energy of emotion, and (5) to keep us in contact with our emotional center even when no particular emotions are apparent.

This last point matters because often our emotional center seems quiescent. That would leave us nothing to be aware of, were we just trying to be aware of our emotions. But instead, we are working to be present in our emotional center regardless of what and whether emotions are there. Without any explicit effort to change our emotions, this sensitive energy contact with our emotional center enhances the quality of our emotions. Emotional center presence sensitizes our emotions to respond more readily and appropriately to the world around us. Suddenly, we are more complete. We are not just chattering mind and unruly emotion: we have a heart.

But on its own, emotional presence tends to evaporate quickly, either into nothing or into some strong emotion. So we always couple it with body contact, with sensing our body. In fact our inner work, to be most fruitful, generally begins with sensing our body, as completely and robustly as we can. Then once we are settled into body contact, we widen our presence to also be in contact with our emotional center. We practice this both in sitting meditation and in daily life, by sensing our whole inner body and feeling our emotional heart. Again, this does not mean that we try to generate a particular emotion, or intentionally change some emotion that is there, nor that any emotion will be there. It simply means sensitive presence in our chest and upper abdomen, in our center of emotion, while also sensing our entire body. We are alert in body and in heart.

For this week, practice sensitive contact with your center of emotion, while sensing as much of your inner body as you can.

13.3 Mind Contact
(Inner Body Development: Aspect 3 of 7)

As with our body and emotions, we typically have at best a fairly shallow awareness of our mind. We identify with our thoughts and are continually carried away with that endless stream. Our thoughts chain off each other and react to or comment on events around us, all by association and by our past conditioning. One brain circuit activates another adjacent one, and on and on. But in itself, our thought stream is not really problematic for our inner work and is often useful, even essential, in our material life.

The problems for our inner life begin when we collapse into identification with our thoughts. Identification occurs when the subject disappears into the object, when the one who is aware becomes totally enthralled by and lost in the content of awareness. We mistakenly believe we are our thoughts, that they define us, that they are the primary instrument representing and expressing the real me. Our personality, which masks who we really are, is to a large extent just the habitual patterns of our thoughts. We also mistakenly believe that thinking and memory are the only significant functions of our mind and mental apparatus. These unexamined beliefs severely limit us.

Our mind and brain are preeminently cognitive instruments. Our mind cognizes or perceives our thoughts and memories. Through that cognitive faculty we can also direct our thoughts and scan our memory, though most of the time we let our thoughts direct themselves — and direct us. Each thought, which we perceive as a kind of inner mental voice or as a mental image, is the firing of some set of brain circuits.

Thoughts may be fueled by the automatic energy, which does not transmit much of our intention. Automatic thoughts just chain and react, without any intention on our part. Beyond that, our thoughts may be fueled by the sensitive energy, which transmits some degree of our volition. Sensitive thinking means being aware of the meaning of our thoughts. It means being able to direct our thoughts, say to do some planning or to consider a problem.

To raise ourselves out of identification with our thoughts, out of just being carried along by our thought stream, we can bring the sensitive energy to bear in our mind. One way toward this is simply to put our attention into our head, sensing our head. Gradually this sensitive energy in our physical head spills over into being the sensitive energy of our mind. Then we can be aware of the meaning of our thoughts, have some ability to direct our thoughts, and not be totally lost in them or at their mercy. Whereas automatic thinking is like being swept along in the stream of our thoughts, sensitive energy contact with our thoughts is like standing still in that stream and noticing our thoughts flowing by. We notice each thought come and go, we notice what each thought means. We no longer quite believe that each and every thought speaks for us or that we are thinking the thought. And in the gaps, the silences between thoughts, we are still there, in sensitive contact with our mind.

As with contact with our emotional center, we find crucial support for contact with our mind through full body sensing. We begin our practice with sensing our body as fully and robustly as possible. Then while maintaining that full body sensation, we extend our awareness into our center of emotion and into our mind. These three aspects of our inner body awareness support each other. Indeed, whole body sensing spills over into our cognitive and emotional centers. If we focus attention solely on our mind, we are soon carried away, captivated by some catchy string of thoughts. But sensing our body helps us stay rooted in the present and see beyond our thoughts to our mind as a center of cognition.

For this week, practice simultaneous contact with your body, emotional center, and mind. Be in touch with all three through the sensitive energy.

13.4 Nourishing
(Inner Body Development: Aspect 4 of 7)

Because our developing inner body is a structure of spiritual energies, a major part of our task concerns those inner energies: collecting them, building them up, and refining them. For that we need to engage in three types of energy work: conserving, ingesting, and transforming.

If the vessel of our soul has major leaks, the energies we receive or transform will rapidly dissipate, leaving us at a continuing low plateau. So we need to plug our energy leaks. This does not require an overly-controlled, austere, or monkish lifestyle. But it does require awareness of our inner energies and moderation of the ways in which we waste those energies. We can measure the level of our inner energies by gauging our ability to practice, to be present, and by judging the amount of sensitive energy in our body — how thoroughly and strongly we are able to sense. From that we notice which of our activities and indulgences cost us the most energy, leave us less able to be present, less able to sense our body. And then we take the steps necessary to mitigate those leaks.

We can frame this issue in terms of the energy leaks in our body, our heart, and our mind. In our body, the kinds of activities that may be wasteful include excessive, unnecessary physical tensions and fidgeting, smoking, overindulgence in food or alcohol, and the use of marijuana and other drugs of abuse. In our heart domain we may find that strong bouts of the afflictive emotions, like anger, jealousy, envy, and greed, burn our energies and leave us flat. For our mind, we may find that overindulgence in strongly-held opinions and in daydreaming wastes our energies. Of course these are just examples, not an exhaustive list of all the many ways we can and do waste our inner energies.

We are not attempting to establish a fixed and universal code of morality in the ordinary sense. Rather, we take a pragmatic approach of moderating our activities so as to conserve the energies we need for our inner work. Furthermore, the particular set of activities and indulgences that waste the most energy varies from person to person. Something that flattens my inner life may not be at all harmful for you. So we each need to see for ourselves how we waste our energies and how to conserve them, always using the measure of our ability to practice, to be present, to sense. If something makes us less able to sense, less able to be present, then we need to moderate or even refrain from it altogether. For example, we need to avoid excessive use of alcohol, but completely abandon the use of recreational drugs, such as marijuana.

Having fewer leaks in our vessel is not enough, however. We also need more energy, much more than we produce in the normal course of life. Our inner energies are dynamic, not static. So the action of accumulating energies is not like putting wine into a bottle and keeping it there. Rather we seek to increase the flow of inner energies through our being. With fewer leaks and increased flow, we have more energy available for our inner work, which includes building our inner body. We work toward a condition in which our perception of our inner body, our energy body, is stronger and more vivid than our perception of our physical body.

So how do we proceed? How do we obtain this increased energy flow? Fortunately, we are surrounded by a sea of spiritual energies, available for our use. We need, however, to refine our perceptions to be able to recognize and contact those energies and to develop the ability to deal with them, to draw them into us and make them part of our being, part of our soul.

One of the primary, classical ways to do this is through energy breathing. The air around us is a reservoir of spiritual energies. Normally when we inhale, those energies enter us with the air and then flow right back out when we exhale. Energy breathing entails focusing our attention onto the air as we breathe it. This act of attention, coupled with the intention to draw that energy into us, separates the energy from the air and allows it to enter our inner body. This is the essence of the yoga practice of pranayama, drawing the prana energy from the air. Similar practices can be found in Sufism and Taoism.

Crucially, though, energy breathing must be conscious to be effective. To become able to recognize this action, our perceptions and attention need to be refined by meditative practice. If we do not perceive the energies from the air entering and staying in us, then they are not. Energy breathing does not happen by itself, without our knowing it, nor is it a matter of imagination. The perception needs to be vivid, of energies flowing into us as we draw them from the air. No changes to our physical pattern of breathing are needed. Physically we breathe normally. The difference lies in our attention and intention, in our inner action while we breathe.

Another approach to increasing our energy supply involves opening to higher energies. The classical way toward that lies through deep meditation and contemplative prayer.

Deep meditation touches levels beyond the stillness. Contemplative prayer does not concern petitioning the Higher, but rather directly approaching and opening to the Sacred. Both allow the grace of higher energies to flow vividly down into us, building, strengthening, and refining our inner body.

An interaction takes place between the sensitive energies and the higher energies. Each supports the other. The sensitive energies can give us a stable platform from which to address the higher. And the higher energies act on the sensitive energies, producing more energy and refining it.

There is also a very important middle layer of energies, the conscious energy, which we will address in the next, or fifth, aspect of Inner Body Development. Resting in consciousness allows a certain transformation of energies to occur in us. Transforming energies into the substance of our soul also depends on presence, on intentionally inhabiting our inner body. We turn to that in the sixth aspect of Inner Body Development. From all this, we can see that no single practice can be as effective as a well-balanced set of complementary practices for developing our soul, our inner body.

For this week, look for the leaks in your personal energy vessel and also practice drawing in or opening to more energy.

13.5 Being
(Inner Body Development: Aspect 5 of 7)

In the process of developing our inner body, we include an opportunity for the various energies engaged to settle, mix, and blend, to form a new substance in us. For that we relax. In particular, we practice deep meditative relaxation, into the space behind our thoughts and senses, letting go into the inner peace of consciousness, just being. We can practice this resting in awareness not only in meditation, but also during our ordinary daily activities. We open to being the screen on which all the contents of our experience, inner and outer, are displayed. The ramifications of this practice of just being, of being in consciousness, are far-reaching. In that vast and timeless inner space, we find freedom, we find ourselves, and we find our connection with others, our essential sameness.

The freedom of being in consciousness confers great peace and contentment, a quiet joy unlike any other. In just being, we reside in such spaciousness that there is room for everything to be as it is, for all our identifications to evaporate. Our life flows easily. Our inner constraints fall away and we have no need to impose our will, to shape our experience. Nor are we carried away in the stream of thoughts, emotions, and sensory experience. We are free. This state does not preclude us from being active, from acting and responding, even vigorously, as necessary and as we choose. But behind our activity, we reside in the ocean of peace, of being.

With the falling away of our inner constraints, our true self emerges. The peaceful ease of consciousness allows our ingrained modes of behavior, our reactive emotions, and our knee-jerk thinking to dissolve into the background. We just are. No longer bound by the patterns of our personality, we can finally be ourselves, without pretense, without fear, without conditioning, and without our mask. Our senses, fully alive, continually stream into our consciousness, whose function is cognition. We see and we know what goes on, within and without.

Soon enough, we see that this cognitive consciousness, so intimate and personal, does not belong to us. We see that consciousness is more than personal and has no boundaries. We see that our neighbor, that all of us share the same consciousness. The tent of consciousness embodies a profound unity among us, the sameness that we are. In just being, we transcend ourselves to be all. There is no difference between your consciousness and my consciousness. Indeed the possessives of "your" and "my" do not really apply to the all-pervasive consciousness that we all participate in.

We would do well indeed to attain a condition in which we could live our life in consciousness, in the fullness of being. However, we also remember that this state of consciousness is not the ultimate. There are still deeper levels beyond it. We want to live in consciousness, resting in awareness, without being attached to that state, without being seduced by its pleasures. Happiness comes as an important byproduct of rightly conducted spiritual practice. But happiness is not the goal of the path: service is. And one major way of serving life and the sacred consists of our spiritual practice itself, through the transformation of energies, purification of will, kindness, and prayer.

Consciousness is right here with us, in us. But nearly all the time our thoughts and sensory experience mask consciousness, distracting us from it. The conscious energy in our mind manifests as our cognitive faculty. In consciousness, we can be aware of our thoughts as thoughts. We can see the process of our thinking, its ebb and flow. In consciousness, we cognize or know directly, without the intermediary of our thoughts, without our thoughts necessarily explaining or commenting, without our thoughts intervening or inserting themselves between us and what we see. In consciousness, we just see, we get what is going on. Thoughts may occur, but as passing clouds in a huge blue sky. The big sky of consciousness is not compromised by our thoughts. We see through and beyond them. Being in the conscious energy in our mind is like being the streambed, banks, and valley surrounding the stream of our thoughts. The thoughts may continue flowing, but they are only a minor part of our presence.

Continuing along this line, attention to our mind can open us to conscious presence in our mind, to the cognitive stillness behind our thoughts. And that cognitive presence can merge with our body presence and heart presence to give us the fully human and complete presence.

For this week, practice resting in awareness, practice just being.

13.6 Inhabiting
(Inner Body Development: Aspect 6 of 7)

Once we make contact with our inner energies and nourish our inner body by drawing and absorbing more energy into us, we face the challenge of entropy: left to themselves, those energies will surely dissipate. In response, we engage a power outside the realm of energies, our will. We inhabit our body by inhabiting our energy body. In so doing, our will extends into the energies and stabilizes them by its presence, by our presence.

Presence depends on energies, but its core feature, its core, is us, our I, our will-to-be and to-do. Perhaps the simplest approach to presence consists in putting and holding our attention into our body, our whole body, and in particular into the inner energies, the sensitive energies, in our body, mind, and heart. But even this act of attention does not fully capture what is meant by inhabiting, which calls for more than attention.

When we give attention to something, we may have the feeling or attitude that I am here and I send my attention out from me to that something, and thereby my attention connects me with that something. By contrast, inhabiting means expanding my I, my Self, to include all of what I am inhabiting. In the present case, this means extending my I into my entire inner body so that I live in the whole of it, I participate in my energy body. Rather than just send my attention out into my body, while I remain in my head, I expand to be in my whole body. My will-to-be fills my whole body and finds an affinity with the sensitive energy in my body. They mutually stabilize each other. The will and the energy make a whole.

Tension can arise in the act of holding of our attention fixed on something. With inhabiting, however, we relax that tension and let ourselves move from the constricted inner space we usually occupy into the whole of our inner body, into the whole of our physical body, mind, and heart.

To keep this up for more than a fleeting moment, we evoke a continuous intention to inhabit our whole inner body and act from that intention. We stay here in our inner body, relaxed and present. And we maintain enough inner force to be here. We sustain our will-to-be, which flows like a constant breeze throughout our inner domain.

Rather than just being in a random part of my body, usually my head, by inhabiting my entire body, my inner body, I am here and whole in the fullness of presence. And slowly, slowly, but very significantly, this stabilizing of my inner energies by being in them turns them into the spiritual flesh of my nascent inner body. This is partially due to the fact that the act of inhabiting brings a higher energy, the conscious energy, into the mix with the sensitive energies of our inner body. Presence serves as a container for our inner energies, so that they can settle, blend with each other, and transform.

The practice of inhabiting our inner body need not be separate from our life. It gives us an inner life, paralleling and eventually merging with our outer life. So if we are awake to our inner energies, even to a small degree, we can practice maintaining that, while at the same time giving attention to our usual life interests, demands, and attractions. Indeed, we bring our full presence into whatever we do in life. And this presence is concrete, not just a passing idea or whim, not just being in consciousness, which evaporates so quickly unless rooted in our body, in the readily perceptible and sustainable sensitive energy in our body, in our energy body.

Be here in your physical body and also in your sensitive energy inner body, which enhances your perception of your physical body. We occupy both our bodies, which are co-located, one inside the other, one a refined version of the other.

For this week, practice fully inhabiting your physical body and your inner body.

13.7 Persistence
(Inner Body Development: Aspect 7 of 7)

The secret ingredient of progress on the spiritual path is persistence, simple, dogged persistence in the practices of the path. Yes, other qualities and conditions matter, but overshadowing them all is the determination to keep going, come what may. A steady, daily persistence allows our inner work to build on itself. Our energy and determination from one day's practice carry over to the next, so that each day our baseline, our starting point can be slightly higher than the day before or, at the very least, not much lower.

We naturally have ups and downs in the quality and quantity of inner work we are able to come to on any given day. Many factors conspire to produce these ups and downs. Our body may be ill, or just slightly ill, or tired from lack of sleep or overexertion. And that can negatively impact our inner work, pointing up the importance of a physically healthy lifestyle. Our vital energies set the conditions for our ability to practice. A vital and vibrant body can support stronger inner work. Conversely, certain inner work, for example energy breathing, can increase our physical vitality.

Our emotions may be in turmoil due to some unwelcome event in our life. So we need to work toward equanimity and moderation, particularly with the destructive emotions. We can live our life wholeheartedly, without ever letting our emotions overwhelm us or derail our inner work.

Our mind may be obsessed with something that has happened or may happen, or something we want or don't want, or something we disapprove of, and so on. So we practice awareness of our thoughts as thoughts, which mitigates their power over us. Or our mind may fill with doubt about the spiritual path. In response, by faith, we continue our practice, without needing certainty about the outcome or demanding proof of the spiritual reality. This is not blind faith. We are realistic about our position, the level of our experience, and about our need to practice diligently.

All these and many other ups and downs are part of living and part of spiritual practice. What matters is that we keep on, come what may, following a blue-collar ethic of inner work. Then we will inevitably bounce back from the lows. We adopt an attitude of stopping our losses by not allowing our inner work to disappear entirely on any day. We keep watch, so as not to be infected by an attitude or assumption of failure with regard to our inner work.

The less we backslide, the quicker we recover from the lows. We do not give up, even temporarily. Some degree of inner work, some body awareness, for example, or some letting go is always feasible. If we have been practicing sensing regularly and come to a moment when our sensation is weaker than usual, then that weak, partial sensation itself may viscerally call us to strengthen our body awareness. This is persistence under clouds and rain.

But persistence is not only about mitigating the low points, it also concerns pushing forward when we are able to practice. When we can, we persist in deepening and strengthening our presence. We work to fully inhabit our inner body. We engage in practices to raise the quality and quantity of energy in our inner body. We persist in staying in our inner body in this moment, increasing the duration and frequency of our practice. We allow a relaxed inner body presence to become an increasingly continuous condition of our life. We carry on attempting to approach the Divine through deep meditation and contemplative prayer. We explore our inner world to understand it better and enter its unknown but marvelous regions.

When our sitting meditation sessions are strong and deep, we may be tempted to slip into just cruising for the rest of the day. Our inner state may be clear and free and pleasant. There seems to be no pressing reason to practice presence in such times, because we are already where we want to be. Yet those days offer opportunities not to be squandered. Here we follow the old adage: make hay while the sun shines. So we practice presence even when it seems unnecessary. We work to broaden, deepen, and strengthen our presence, even when we already feel good. Our spiritual work is not only to help us in our down moments. We practice at all times because it builds our soul and serves the Sacred. This is persistence in the sun.

Another common limitation is settling for the spiritual station or plateau we currently occupy. We grow accustomed to a certain level of inner work. By level or plateau we mean the amount and quality of our inner work and presence. It tends to vary within a range and we accept that range as part of who and how we are. This is an artificial and self-limiting envelope. When we notice our plateau, we work to raise our practice beyond that level. This is persistence on the plain.

And we are creative in devising methods to remind ourselves to practice presence during our day. Such reminders typically do work for a time, if we take them seriously. But then they lose effectiveness, growing stale as we start ignoring them. So we change reminders as needed. Here is smattering of specific examples of normal daily activities to train ourselves to be present in, one at a time. We practice presence, beginning with sensing and inhabiting our energy body while:

- shaving
- putting on makeup
- brushing our teeth
- dressing
- using a keyboard
- thinking about some particular issue
- awakening from sleep in the morning, while still

in bed
- washing dishes
- cooking
- eating
- exercising
- walking
- shopping
- standing up from a sitting meditation
- going through a doorway
- speaking
- listening
- reading
- watching TV

But most of all, we adopt the straightforward attitude that we want to be present at all times, that our new normal is full presence. Then when we are not fully present, we have some existential discomfort that draws us back into presence.

For this week, persist in developing your inner body.

14.0 The Path of Liberation

14.1 Illusion of self
(Part 1 of 9)

We believe we are whole and we believe we are free: two beliefs that prove false, misleading, and a source of untold angst. Our mind and emotions consist of many moving parts, some appearing infrequently, others persistent and familiar. These parts include all kinds of urges and tendencies, skills and knowledge, styles and patterns of thinking, feeling and interacting, likes and dislikes, attitudes and assumptions, fears and aspirations, strengths and weaknesses, and much more. Taken together, these parts make up what we call our personality, our self, what call me. This is who we believe we are, who we give our name to.

The parts of a car combine to function as one whole, all serving the same overall purpose. When we drive the car, all its components respond in a coordinated fashion. We view the parts of our self, of our mind and emotions, in the same way, as forming one whole like the components of car do. The problem with that commonly held view is that, unlike the parts of a car, the parts of our mind and emotions do not make a whole, do not all serve the same overall purpose. The parts of our personality are like a jumble of unrelated or semi-related small programs inside a computer, each with its own agenda and serving no collective function. These programs vie for run-time in a nearly random fashion; though not quite random, because some are strong patterns of thought and emotion, whether genetically driven or acquired by habit, patterns that get more run-time than our other programs.

Because one or another of our programs is always running, with others waiting, clamoring, in the wings, because the computer, in this case our body, exhibits stability, and because we are so familiar with the more frequently running programs, we believe this is who we are. We believe this set of programs, this personality, this mask, is us. And remarkably, insidiously, that is a self-fulfilling belief, because it moves us to allow our I, our will, to be controlled by whichever program happens to be running. We buy into our personality, our program of the moment, and let it run the show, which it does by usurping the power of will from the true I that we have surrendered to it. Because we have unwittingly given our power over to it, our personality appears to be the source of the power to run our show and thus we believe in it. And that belief enables it to run the show. If this sounds like circular logic, it is, and that is just the point.

This is a messy conundrum.

Messy because our resulting inner life is haphazard, chaotic, and disorganized: anything can happen in us at any time. External events push our buttons, starting up that particular one of our many programs, without any choice on our part. Someone frowns at me and, depending on the circumstances and my programming, anger, hurt, or disappointment start up inside my mind and heart. But because I believe that my programs are me, I interpret this as I am angry, I am hurt, or I am disappointed. And that belief, that interpretation causes my true I to get entangled and I actually become angry, hurt, or disappointed.

The flow of causation, the flow of forces, goes from outside to inside: the external frown kicks off a reacting program in me, and my belief that the program is me puts my I under its influence, so that I am now angry. One name for this process is identification: using the inherent freedom of my I to give my I over to the reaction, using my freedom to become enslaved. This goes on all day long in an unending variety of ways. I abdicate my freedom and am controlled by every thought or emotion that rises to the center of my mind stage.

Of course, this overstates the situation a bit. We have enough sanity not to act on every crazy notion that enters our head or heart. But still we identify with all of it, whether or not we act on some particular. Every pattern or program that shows up, claims to be me, I believe it, and so it truly is me. I become my personality, I become this jumble of programs and patterns, reactions and associations. In Buddhism, this is known as the illusion of self, the major illusion standing between us and enlightenment. In the West, the self-centeredness behind personality is known as the ego, standing between us and the Kingdom of Heaven.

We experience our personality in so many ways: as our closest companion, as ongoing commentary on our life, as planning or rehearsing what we will say or do, as dreaming about what we want, as our views and opinions, as our anger, hurt, suspicions, and jealousies, as our unending stream of thoughts and memories, each triggering another, on and on. All this is so familiar, so private, and so intimate, that we easily and unquestioningly fall into the illusion that this agglomeration is me, this dynamic hodgepodge is who I am.

In the coming weeks, we will examine further aspects of the Path of Liberation:

1. Illusion of self
2. Cracks in the Illusion
3. Peace of Meditation
4. Coexistence
5. Exposing the Illusion
6. Freedom in Presence
7. Be Your Attention
8. I Am
9. Complete Liberation

For this week, please contemplate this notion of the illusion of self, the notion that who you think you are is not who you are, it is only your personality, your mask, and it hides the your real Self. Does this matter? Deeply, for it blocks our potential of becoming our Self, of fulfilling our destiny, of living a full, complete, and wholehearted life.

14.2 Cracks in the Illusion
(The Path of Liberation: Part 2 of 9)

If our self is an illusion, though a very persistent, convincing, and all-pervasive illusion, if freedom lies somewhere beyond that illusion, and if our contact with the spiritual depths is blocked by the illusion, then where is our hope of lifting this first veil? Only by seeing through the illusion, seeing our self for the illusion that it is, again and again, until the moment comes that we are thoroughly, irrevocably convinced, can the illusion be dispelled for good. For that seeing, it is not the illusory self that sees itself, but rather our I that sees, the one in us who really is us, who sees not just mentally, who sees without needing to resort to inner commentary to prove or confirm the seeing, who sees with clarity and directness, whose seeing results in new understanding that becomes part of us.

To see the illusion of self, we focus on its cracks, on the places that the illusion falters, where it fails to live up to its claim to be us, its claim that our personality is who we are. Those cracks appear in various forms, but arise principally from the fact that our so-called self actually consists of many, disparate, uncoordinated, disjoint parts that lack the claimed integration. Each part of our illusory self says "I," claims to be us, and when it takes center stage for even a moment, is us. But then another part, another "i" comes along that either does not know or does not care about the previous "i" and takes us in a different direction altogether. One part wants to smoke tobacco, another part wants to eat three pieces of cake, a third wants to keep our body healthy, and a fourth wants to look slim and trim. Our supposed self is a seething mass of such contradictions. There is no self in any of that, or rather there are many selves, many i's, many conflicting or simply unrelated wills, urges, and agendas.

In advance, I intend to do some particular thing. But when the moment comes, I do something else instead. One self says yes and another says no. I make promises to myself, promises I do not keep. Even worse, I sometimes make promises to others that I fail to keep. The i that makes the promise lacks power over the i that is in control at the moment we would have carried it out. We tend to sweep such occurrences under the rug of unconsciousness. "Oh well, another New Year's resolution down the drain." But that doesn't quite work. It leaves a bad taste, an uncomfortable feeling of disappointment with our self. If we really take it to heart, that disappointment can turn to disillusionment and point us toward the road to liberation.

We believe in our thoughts, we believe we are our thoughts, or at least that our thoughts are a direct expression of us, of I. We think "I", "I will do this," "I will eat that," "I will say this." We believe we are that thought "I" or that it is very close to us. But the practice of watching, noticing our thoughts, shows us that our thoughts think themselves, quite well, with no prodding or help from us. Our thoughts, for the most part, run automatically, by association with some random external event or perception, by association with another thought, or by chaining off some memory. The thought "I" typically has no more substance to it than any other thought; it is just a sound in our mind. Yet our automatic thought processes and patterns form the bulk of our personality, the bulk of the illusion of self. Our thoughts go on and on, and so we believe that is I going on and on. But our I cannot be just an automatic process or set of sounds in our mind. This automatic nature of our thoughts is another crack in the illusion of self.

Our thought machine also occasionally spews up some disgusting thought or image, something totally out of step with our personal values. Our response goes along the lines of "where did that come from?" "That's not what I really think — is it?" Each such event further cracks the illusion; for clearly those thoughts are not who I am, not what I believe to be my coherent self. They are just thoughts, more or less random, without me in them or behind them. You are not your thoughts.

Our emotions also run on automatic. Someone says or does something or something happens and my emotions react of their own accord. Then the thought arises: "I am angry" or "I am sad" or "I am afraid." But it's really the emotion that is emoting, the anger is angry, the sadness is sad, the fear is afraid, all on their own. The emotion affects my thoughts, which toe the line by saying "I am angry" and thereby give cover, perpetuating the illusion by claiming that there is some unified, independent "I" in me that has chosen to be angry. But each reacting emotion creates its own "i." The automatic nature of our emotional reactions is yet another crack in the illusion of self.

Our emotions also affect our body. Strong emotions affect our breathing pattern, our heart rate, our posture, our muscle tensions, and our facial expressions. Our body is thus not in control because it is subject to our emotions, subject to our thoughts by taking actions dictated by thoughts, subject to our intentions and choices. My body is not who I am.

Yet our body also does many things quite well on its own, like breathing, walking, and digesting. This sounds trivial and obvious, but fully absorbing the fact that our body functions without our intentions or choices necessarily driving it, can be a revelation, for we believe our "intention" is responsible for all our actions. Our body and brain together have many skills, necessary to us, like the language skills of speaking and decoding the speech of others. These skills are not who we are; they function on automatic. Our personality subsumes the powers of our body, adding them to the illusion of self. Personality inflates our episodic intentionality into the false notion of an always-on intention, an always-present me or I. But noticing how well our body performs without any intention on our part puts the lie to this aspect of the illusion of self.

The apparent whole of us, our personality, our self, is not what it seems; we are not what we seem to be. For this week, notice what you can of the cracks in your illusion of self.

14.3 Peace of Meditation
(The Path of Liberation: Part 3 of 9)

Within the endless cavalcade of thoughts and emotions streaming through us, we have no room to see these elements of our personality for what they are: disjointed, conflicting, unrelated, and automatically self-generated patterns and objects of awareness, whose aggregate does not form a coherent, independent self, but does form the pseudo-self of our personality. One automatic thought cannot see another thought, much less an emotion. Even when we are sensitive to the meaning of our thoughts, perhaps even exerting some control over our thoughts by pondering some issue, question, or problem, we are not aware thereby of the programmed, habitual nature of the bulk of our thoughts and emotions.

To see our thoughts as thoughts, as self-generating, automatic thoughts, to see our emotions as emotions, as self-generating, visceral responses and reactions to inner and outer events, we need some space, we need a place to see from, a place to gain some perspective on our inner world. That is one of the primary purposes and powers of meditation: to find the spacious inner peace of cognizant stillness, the true consciousness.

That peace affords us a taste of what it might mean to put down the burden our personality imposes on us, the burden of protecting and enhancing our self-image, of taking all our emotional upheavals so seriously, of being at the mercy of every passing whim or thought, of living a second-hand life lost in thought, of being this name of ours that claims to define us. Relaxing more and more deeply, in body, in mind, and in heart, can temporarily relieve of us of all that burden, the yoke of personality: we just sit and be, without having to be anything in particular, without being dragged along by our thoughts, emotions, and self-image.

Meditation shows us the possibility of living in awareness itself, rather than in thoughts and emotions, attitudes and reactions. Relaxing into awareness, into the cognizant substrate beneath our thoughts and emotions, takes us out of that busy stream. From pure awareness, we see our thoughts as just thoughts, our emotions as just emotions, our patterns as just our personality, and we see that none of that is who we are. We let all that come and go, arise and pass away, while we sit unentangled.

But learning to attain that state takes time and a good deal of practice; it takes many sessions on our meditation cushion, bench, or chair. Gradually our mental chatter settles down enough for us to move behind it. We have moments of no thought, of quiet, glittering, blissful peace. With more meditation practice, we learn to enter that peace, that pure awareness, behind thoughts. And we find that the peace of consciousness is always there, but typically obscured from us by our thoughts and emotions, by our attention, our center falling out of that ever-present pure consciousness and into that ongoing mental stream. Continuing to practice meditation, we learn to enter the peace of consciousness even when there are thoughts. Like clouds passing in the sky, thoughts need not obscure our contact with consciousness. We become like the sky, we enter consciousness and the thoughts passing by neither obscure nor obstruct our peace and presence. So we need not and do not try to stop our thoughts, which would only give them more fuel, in any case. We just let them come and go as they will, without dragging us with them. And we rest in awareness itself.

The effects of meditation accumulate; over the years, it gradually builds up our fundamental consciousness, enabling us to go from living at the surface of awareness, in the stream of thoughts, emotions, and sensory perceptions, to living in the cognizant stillness within. This shifts us toward liberation from our personality, toward unburdening ourselves and the people around us from the yoke of our identification with our surface stream. If we are not to live in and as our personality, with all its drama, boredom and the rest, then we need an alternative, we need to live more and more in our depth, in the always-new consciousness, in the here and now. Thoughts, emotions, sensory perceptions, and our personality patterns are in time, passing through the here and now. The path calls us to live in the eternal depth of the here and now, not caught in time. We can still live effectively, even more effectively, in time, with respect for the past, realizable plans and hopes for the future, and appreciation of the present. We see our life in time as our field of action in the material world, but not as our only field of action. We live in depth and our inner actions also acquire significance.

For this week, reinvigorate your practice of meditation, of approaching inner stillness, and see whether it takes you toward freedom, toward unburdening yourself of yourself.

14.4 Coexistence
(The Path of Liberation: Part 4 of 9)

At this stage of the path of liberation, we still spend the bulk of our time living in the illusion of self, in the illusion that our personality is who we are. But at other times we are free of that illusion, living in awareness in the here and now. It's not that, in these freer moments, we have seen through the illusion; rather the illusion has temporarily dropped away as we experience contact with the real world of sensory perceptions. At those times we rise into sensitive contact with what we see and hear, with our body, even with the meaning of our thoughts and the tenor of our emotions. That sensitive contact raises us out of illusory living.

Though in our mind, we hear our thoughts as sounds, we know that such sounds can be spoken, recorded, or heard in others' speech — all external to us. We also know that our thoughts can be written on paper or electronic media, again external to us. This knowledge points us toward recognizing that our thoughts themselves are external to us, are objects passing through our mind. Though we perceive our thoughts with our mind, we, as the perceiver or thinker, are more internal, more subjective than our thoughts, not defined by them. This is seeing our thoughts as thoughts, as mere thoughts. From that, we extrapolate to seeing our emotions as emotions. And we are deeper than both, more inward, as the one who sees or hears or sometimes guides our thoughts, the one who feels our emotions.

And then we fall back into the automatic mode of living, where our thoughts think us, our emotions drive us, where we are utterly identified with our thoughts and emotions, with believing that we are our thoughts and emotions, that we are the pattern of our personality.

Back and forth, up and down, we oscillate between these states of illusion and relative freedom, of identification and some measure of presence. Our life becomes an uneasy and confusing coexistence of these two worlds, these two modes of being. We experience rising intimations of truth amidst the illusion. This is where we begin to realize and feel the true urgency of spiritual practice, of the work of presence, in daily life. We begin to understand what it costs us to be our personality, to live by rote automatism, even though we have not yet fully penetrated the illusion. We begin to know the taste of living ensnared by our personality, a constrained and uncomfortable taste in comparison to living in sensitive contact with our life.

For example, a simple, accidental daydream about someone insulting you, or saying something nasty about you to someone else, starts a whole train of angry thoughts and vindictive, resentful emotions. But your seeing of this process does not have the power at this stage of the path to release you from its grip, so you stay captive to this pattern until it subsides. You know you are caught in this web of mirrors, yet you cannot step out of it. You try coming into awareness of your body and sometimes that helps, but if the emotions are already strong, it is too late, and you stay trapped until they dissipate on their own. Then you come back again to some degree of presence, breathing the fresh air of sensitive contact with your body, mind, and surroundings. And so it goes, up and down, back and forth.

The disturbing contrast between these two modes of our life, between the involuntary mode of identification, constraint, and absence and the intentional mode of relative freedom and presence, no longer blindly acquiescing to the former, but not yet able to enter the latter at will, fuels the fire of our inner work, our need to practice presence and letting go. Our unwillingness, having seen some truth, to go back to the personality-only life, where our presence collapses under our personality, coupled with our inability to stay in the life of presence, where personality serves presence, leaves us bewildered and stranded. Only the forward movement of our personal evolution can free us.

So our need and determination grow and we practice presence more and more. To be specific, at this stage of our path, the practice of presence consists primarily of sensing our body, of body awareness, of awareness of the sensitive energy in our body, on an ongoing basis. Sensing our body spills over into contact with our thoughts and emotions, with the meaning of our thoughts and the tenor of our emotions. Sensing gives us a foothold in the present moment and a way to climb out of identification with our personality. The more we sense, the more we can see our personality in action, how its siren call seduces us into its empty embrace. Sensing is the foundation that enables us to see clearly and vividly, to see our personality for the empty shell that it is.

Stranded between the taste of freedom and our inability to stay free, we constantly renew our inner work. For this week, notice when you are free and notice when you are under your personality, believing it is who you are. Each moment of such seeing adds to the account by which you buy your freedom.

14.5 Exposing the Illusion
(The Path of Liberation: Part 5 of 9)

Eventually we reach a tipping point, where enough moments of directly seeing and accepting the truth about our identification with personality, about its illusory nature, have accumulated and purified our view of ourselves sufficiently to prepare us for that singular moment of particularly clear seeing and letting go, the moment when freedom, permanent freedom, dawns. For the ten thousandth time, we see our thoughts and emotions generating themselves in response to each other or to our body or to some external event, we see how we fall into believing we are these thoughts and emotions, believing we are the patterns of our personality. But this time it all changes, this time we get it. We see it as a mechanism, as a set of learned programs and automatic tendencies. We see it as our mechanism. We see that we are not now and never were that. And this time all the pieces fall into place: the seeing is vivid, effective, permanent, and irrevocable. It changes our understanding and changes who we are. After this moment of unmasking, we are never again fooled into believing in our thoughts and emotions, believing that our personality defines us or is us.

  This is the great transition from achieving intermittent states of seeing how automatic, disjointed, self-generating our personality is, to the permanent station, the new level of being of understanding the illusion, of incorporating that understanding into who we truly are, so that the understanding is now part of us. No longer do we need to try to remember the truth about our personality, for now we are that truth, we have moved beyond that illusion.

  Though this new understanding signals a permanent change in our level of being, our personality does not disappear, nor would we want it to, for it contains all that we have learned, our skills, our patterns of interaction with the world, our knowledge about the world. So associative, automatic thoughts and reactive emotions still arise, and may even catch hold of us temporarily. But soon we notice that and their hold on us diminishes and evaporates. We now truly understand that our personality is not who we are and never again do we surrender ourselves to it. We have debunked and discredited the illusion, and put down a great burden in the process.

This step of permanently exposing the illusion of personality is a kind of inner death, which the Sufis call the *fana'i afal*, the second *fana*: ceasing to be attached to our personality, to the contents of our mind and emotions. In Buddhism, this is the first liberation, the first stage of enlightenment: realizing the emptiness of self, that the contents of our mind and emotions are not a self, that there is no self, no independent self in that.

Prior to this freeing ourselves of ourselves, we may have some fears about it. *What would I be without my personality, without what I have known as me all these years? Without my likes and dislikes, won't life be dull?* In the event, these and similar fears prove unfounded. Our personality does not disappear. Our old familiar habits of thought and emotion remain. Our likes and dislikes stay with us. If we liked chocolate cake before the moment of freedom, we still like chocolate cake afterward, only now we are not driven by those likes and dislikes. We are free to choose. The big difference is just this freedom, the cessation of attachment and identification. *But will I still care about my loved ones when I am no longer attached to them?* Yes indeed, love does not diminish, it even grows, as does our capacity for responsible action. Nothing is lost in this freedom, except the illusion of something that never existed, the illusion that our personality is our self. And in its place, in our further work, we gain our real self.

From here, the next steps on the path of liberation are a matter of consolidating our new-found freedom, putting it on a sound footing, and ultimately moving toward further fanas or stages of enlightenment; this first liberation is not the end of the path, nor at this point of exposing the illusion is the first liberation fully accomplished. After every death, after every fana, there is a resurrection, a *baqa*, a new beginning, a new life. So now we move toward that new life.

Meanwhile, the self may try to reappear in various guises. Consider the following. Before we realize that our personality is not our self, that we have no independent self, we may fear that step, that possibility. When we do discover the truth directly, it seems obvious. And then as we realize its ramifications, that truth seems wonderful and exciting, seems to and actually does open a new chapter of our life. In that excitement and wonder we face the trap of making something of nothing, of considering the situation as having a no-self self, that I am no-self. We make no-self into a thing.

Just as we formerly reified our evanescent collection of patterns of thought and emotion into a personality, and our personality into our self, the discovery of the illusory nature of that supposed self prods us to reify its absence as the no-self, as if we are the no-self. At first the realization of no-self is liberating, but then it can fall into making the "the no-self" into a new self. Instead of becoming a person liberated from self, we fall toward becoming a person who has a "no-self self." We may think "I am free because I have no self," when what we really mean is "I am liberated — and thus wonderful — because I have a no-self self." With time and continued practice, this danger passes.

For this week, notice your personality, your associative thoughts and reactive emotions, notice your perceptions causing reactions, and notice how all of that has a pseudo-life of its own without your initiative or intervention. Notice that your personality is not you and let your attachment to it evaporate.

14.6 Freedom in Presence
(The Path of Liberation: Part 6 of 9)

Having exposed the illusion of self, our former false belief that we are our personality, and having thereby awakened to a measure of freedom, we turn now to consolidating that freedom and living it. In the practice of presence, we find the primary path to living in freedom. Just as presence helps awaken us from the illusion of self and slavery to our personality, it can help us stay free and live without falling back under the illusion. In this article we discuss the energy aspects of presence, while in the next three parts of this inner work series we elaborate its will aspects.

Presence means, in part, full awareness of the here and now, both of external events brought to us by our senses and of inner events such as thoughts, emotions, and body sensations. Three levels of energy are relevant here: automatic, sensitive, and conscious. When we live by the automatic energy, we allow a direct, habit-laden connection between our perceptions and our reactions, between what happens and our inner responses. We are at the mercy of events and the patterns of our personality. Our work on this path of liberation has enabled us to see the truth of this situation, this unsatisfying mode of living, wholly driven by random perceptions and conditioned patterns.

As soon as we intentionally bring the sensitive energy into our perceptions, we start dissolving the automatic connections between what happens and how we react, we start being able to see what happens more objectively and have some freedom of choice in our responses or non-responses. To work with the sensitive energy, we practice sensing our body, first in parts, then the whole, then more often, for longer periods and more strongly. Sensing our body spills over into sensitive awareness of our thoughts and emotions as they occur. Energy breathing offers a way to further increase our store of sensitive energy. And all of this ongoing, practical, blue-collar inner work with the sensitive energy raises us out of the thrall of the automatic mode of living.

To awaken the sensitive energy and organize it into our inner body requires a higher action, that of our attention and its attendant conscious energy. Our will directs our attention, acting through the medium of the conscious energy. So intentionally sensing our body not only draws and keeps the sensitive energy in our body, but also brings the conscious energy to bear. While body sensation may be experienced as granular and particulate, vibrating particles of sensation, the conscious energy is a smooth, continuous, malleable, cognizant field. Sensing our body brings these two types of energies together, gradually blending them into a persistent platform for presence. The sensation seems to be embedded in the conscious energy, stabilizing both in a new form.

But how does presence serve inner freedom? Living in awareness, living in the conscious energy raises us out of identification with our personality, with our thoughts and emotions and our body as me. It does this by ushering us into the halls of inner peace. The cognizant stillness of consciousness, the kind of state we enter in meditation, is available always, even during a busy day. The deeper our practice of meditation, the more we are able to recognize and stay in consciousness in our life beyond the sitting cushion. When our thoughts and emotions and sensory perceptions arise and pass through the vast spaces of consciousness, we see them as they are: a small, fleeting aspect of our total being. Seeing our thoughts, emotions, and personality from that perspective, naturally protects us from identifying with any of that. The work of presence means staying in contact with the cognizant stillness of consciousness, which enables us to not identify with all that goes on. It's a matter of living in the cognizant stillness intentionally, of standing in that cognizant stillness, in the peace of consciousness, in the midst of daily life, even as we speak and act and do what we do.

For this week, practice presence through sensing and living in the cognizant stillness of consciousness. And practice freedom, seeing what you already know to be true: that your thoughts, emotions, and personality patterns are not you.

14.7 Be Your Attention
(The Path of Liberation: Part 7 of 9)

If I am not my personality or my thoughts or my emotions or my body, then who am I? After persistently looking into this question, we come to an answer, though a misleading one: that I am my awareness itself, that I am consciousness. But looking even more carefully, we notice that awareness does not choose or act; it only serves as the screen on which all our perceptions, choices, and actions are projected. I may rest in awareness, but this does not mean that I am awareness. This is a subtle but crucial distinction, crucial because the deeper realms of spirituality increasingly concern will. Consciousness is an energy; will is not. Will is will. Consciousness can seduce us into believing that it is who we are, principally because it is more inward, more central than our body and thus seems to be closer to us, which it is. Now this is not a bad place to be, for to live in and as consciousness does afford us freedom from our personality, our false self.

But consciousness is not the most inward aspect of our totality. The fact that we can direct and focus our consciousness, our awareness, shows that there is something in us deeper than consciousness. We are not our consciousness. To move in depth, we must move beyond it.

One way, perhaps the simplest way, toward discovering who we truly are and becoming ourselves is through the practice of being our attention. We all have attention and depend on it throughout our day, throughout our life. Yet we take for granted and do not notice our attention, because it is so familiar. But attention is a core aspect of who we are, who I am, for attention is a power of our will.

Try this experiment. Focus your eyes, your mind, and your perceptions on some material object close at hand, and hold your focus, your attention there. Ordinarily there is the object and there is you perceiving it. But now, double up on this, by being your attention, by being this channel of attention that focuses your perceptions onto the object. This does not mean being your eyes or your awareness or the object, but rather being this action of focusing, being the focusing. Ride your attention as your attention. Participate in and as attention. Be attention. Be the act of focusing your awareness, in an ongoing way as you hold your attention on a particular sensory object. Rather than letting your attention wander here and there, with you only partially engaged, as is so often the case with us, practice being entirely in your attention and staying with it for some time.

If you can catch hold of this, it can open a new and more vivid experience of living: seeing what you are seeing, hearing what you are hearing, doing what you are doing. You are right there at the receiving edge of your perceptions, the whole of you taking it all in. Your attention may be narrowly focused on a single object — a sound, a sight, a thought, a touch, a fragrance — or your attention may be broad, allowing all of your current surroundings, sensations, thoughts, and emotions to be equally perceived across the whole field of your awareness. Either way, narrow attention or broad, you can practice being your attention, thus raising the perceptive value of whatever comes into your attention and, even more importantly, moving along the path of becoming yourself.

Like learning to ride a bicycle, you learn to be your attention by getting on, peddling a short distance, falling off, and then getting back on. You do that again and again and again, until you get the feel of it. And then a new world opens. You sit in the seat of attention, transforming your ordinary awareness by giving it a presence, a core.

At first this is a subtle and elusive practice, as you experiment with it, trying to discover what it means, trying to find your attention. But later, as your inner perceptions become more refined, the reality of being your attention becomes obvious, as does its centrality in your whole way of life. For this week, please practice being your attention.

14.8 I Am
(The Path of Liberation: Part 8 of 9)

In the practice of being our attention, the question naturally arises: "who is directing my attention?" The answer of course is "I am," that is, if and when our attention is actually being directed, not just being passively attracted or pushed around without any intention on our part. After the fana, the "death" of our attachment to and belief in our personality, the resurrection, the baqa comes as "I Am." Our I is free of the entanglements of personality, of attachment to opinions, judgments, reactions, likes, dislikes, and habits.

But what is this I? Who am I? Who is aware, when we are aware? Who is present, when we are present? Who sees what we see and knows what we know and does what we do? Who chooses and who decides in us? The answer is I. In rising above our personality, above our associative thoughts, reactive emotions, and physical habits, and taking care not to identify with our awareness itself, we are left with our I, our will. This I is the something that can take our rightful place at the center of our being, at the center of initiative, rather than allowing personality or ego to occupy that place. This is the something in us that is free. It is not a thought and not an emotion, but rather our formless will. When it is active, it is a force, our force. When receptive, it is our impulse to open, to accept, to be.

When it is synergic, we connect, worship, and even love. We cannot pin down our I, because it is formless. But we can be our I, we can be the one who perceives, chooses, and acts. We can be the one who directs our attention, moment to moment.

The outer end of our channel of attention opens to the world of sensory inputs. And those sensory inputs can be received and perceived by us, by our I, at the inner end of the channel. That same channel communicates the choices and actions of our I. This is why we need a strong attention, a developed and responsive attention: it enhances our contact with I, enabling I to enter us more completely.

This I Am is not the same I we are so accustomed to in our thoughts and personality. While our I can drive our thoughts and emotions, our I is beyond thought, beyond our ordinary emotions. Freedom means, in part, not having our I driven by our personality, but rather the other way around. The ordinary thought or feeling of I pales in the presence of I. This I Am is not our ego, is not self-centered, in fact it has no center, for it is intimately connected to the Great Center of All, beyond space and time. This is our true I, our true individuality.

Yet we should not regard this as distant from us, as some long-term goal. Our I is already here and now, closer to us than anything else can be. We have only to step forward, as ourselves, to step out of the shadow of our personality, to step away from our self-centered ego, to step into and through the stillness within us. We have only to be I, to say "here I am" with the whole of our self and truly mean it, knowing that the words themselves are at best only pointers.

For this week, be your I. Be the one who directs your attention. Be the one who sees what you see and does what you do. When you walk, be the walker, be the one who is walking, the force behind your walking. Inwardly say "here I am" and mean it. Notice what in you can mean that, what in you can legitimately say it. Say it from yourself, from the whole of yourself. Say I and be I, not the sound or the word or the thought, but the actual I, the sayer.

14.9 Complete Liberation
(The Path of Liberation: Part 9 of 9)

No discussion of liberation would be complete without coming to the Ultimate. At the current stage of human evolution, only rarest of the rare attain the spiritual station of complete liberation. For the rest of us, though, an understanding of this possibility creates a valuable image for us, an image of our own potential perfection, an image that calls to us and guides us along our path.

Having come into ourselves, into our own I, we know that our spiritual work is not nearly complete. The second fana, the death of our attachment to our personality, and the attendant resurrection into I Am must give way to the third fana, which moves us from I Am toward what is put in the Old Testament as "I Am That I Am," a phrase that points to the Divine Will that continually creates, sustains, loves, and endows this universe with freedom.

One indicator reaches us when we notice that, though we are able to be I, we are not able to pin it down, to exhibit it or examine it, because it is always the subjective factor, the one who does the pinning, exhibiting, and examining. We notice that our I is centerless, though it does have force. That no-center quality holds the key to our further evolution, to our perfection, because the higher may enter our centerless center, the higher as more subjective, deeper within us than what we took to be our own I. By leaving the inner end of the channel of attention and will open, first in the sense of looking inward to what is beyond, and then in the sense of allowing the higher to see and hear and act through our channel of will, we allow the sacred to look through us, as us. Closely related to I, is our conscience, the voice of Wisdom, which offers a way forward toward complete liberation. Our I can open to conscience and thereby align us with the higher will.

Our I is our will and it appears to have qualities of independence, if not separateness. Now that deeper illusion of self also must go, the illusion that we exist as an independent being. Even if we are free of the false belief that we are our personality, we still harbor the belief that we are the separate one who experiences our life. This fundamental view is both valid and not valid, depending on the level from which one looks. From the level of I, we are indeed the one who lives and breathes, the one who chooses and acts, the one who does what we do.

Yet, there remains a deeper possibility. Can we, will we, open, surrender our will, our separateness, to the Higher Will? Can we allow the channel of our individual will to widen and transmit the Higher Will? Can we allow the Higher Will to inhabit our individual will? From a distance that sounds frightening and distasteful, as if we were going to be absorbed into the Borg. But the closer we come to that, the clearer we see that our individuality itself will not disappear, but rather become an embodiment of the Higher. This ultimate transformation is not about loss of control: it is about Love and about recognizing what is already true, namely our oneness in the Sacred. The completely liberated person is an individual on the level of individuality, one on the level of oneness, and inwardly free on all levels.

The belief in our ultimate separateness, though, is robustly enshrined in our egoism. On the way toward complete liberation, we must pass through the gate of egoism, the gate of transcending our belief in and acquiescence to that illusion. This self-contained, self-referential, self-inflating bubble must burst. Even our spiritual practice is not immune from its reach. The ego-inflation that attempts to misappropriate, take credit for, and rob us of any real or imagined progress in the spiritual path challenges us all. The saving grace is that true progress does include the ability to see our ego a little more clearly, to listen to our conscience in this regard, and to turn toward real humility in our innate emptiness. This letting go of our ego, our self-centeredness, is the third fana, the third spiritual "death," the death of our attachment to the self-centered view.

Complete liberation entails understanding that though there is indeed someone who lives our life and experiences what we experience and does what we do, that someone is the same one in all of us, not the separate me or I that we assumed it to be, not individualized to us personally. The one will flows through us all. This does not negate our individual I, that great gift entrusted to us at birth and toward the revealing and development of which much of our inner work can fruitfully be applied. It simply and willingly places our I in its true context, as a particle of the Great Will. The one Divine Will flows through all and is the root of all Will, including the I of each and every one of us. That is the source of our freedom. And the free choice is ours alone, a choice made on the level of our individuality, of whether and how much to give ourselves to the path of liberation and finally to union with and service to the Divine Will.

The result matters, much more than personally. The liberated person is free to serve our world in crucial but hidden ways. The most obvious of those concerns the transformation of energies. As we engage in spiritual practices, we gain some understanding, some perception of and facility with various spiritual energies. We even come to recognize that those energies have a positive effect, not only on us, but on the people around us, as we can see, for example, in comparing the power of meditating or worshipping in a group versus alone. The liberated person has access to much higher qualities of spiritual energy, bringing them into this world and benefitting us all.

We distinguish between the loving non-attachment of true liberation and the cold detachment of pseudo-liberation. Complete liberation does not mean an inner or outer divorce from life, though in an effort to attain that station, many have followed a cloistered path. Yet that is not our way. We maintain and even increase our inner and outer engagement and concern with life, while simultaneously following the path of liberation. And the path heals our life, heals all the aberrations resulting from identification with our personality and self-centered egoism, and enables us to love and to bring a creative and effective flair to what we do and how we serve, enables us to be responsible on every level.

For this week, create the image in yourself of your own perfection.

15.0 Obstacles on the Way

If humanity were at a later stage of our evolution, perhaps there would be fewer obstacles on the path of spirituality. No doubt there would still be many challenges, but obstacles? Challenges we need to strengthen our will. Obstacles can slow and even block our progress, derailing us from the path.

Even a person who conscientiously adheres to a moral way of life will face many obstacles preventing him or her from entering the deeper realms of the spirit. So in this approach to dealing with obstacles, we are not referring to moral codes, laws, or the Ten Commandments. We take straightforward morality as a given, as a prerequisite for the spiritual path. Lack of morality raises an insurmountable barrier to the path. Because temptations never stop coming our way, moral self-vigilance remains necessary throughout our lives — necessary, though not sufficient.

That insufficiency of morality leads us to the many other kinds of obstacles that confront us all. The great traditions offer various formulations, for example, the seven deadly sins from Christianity and the five hindrances and the ten fetters from Buddhism. Over the coming weeks, we will take a careful look at and make certain efforts to address nine sets of such obstacles, namely:

1. Sense Desire
2. Aversion
3. Laziness
4. Hurry and Worry
5. Thoughts and Opinions
6. Greed
7. Envy
8. Fault-Finding
9. Ego

When we start looking at our own inner and outer behaviors with a more objective view, we might see such obstacles everywhere and be tempted to despair of ever making significant progress. Fortunately, very fortunately, our spiritual development does not depend on eradicating all, and perhaps not even any, of those obstacles. What is required is that we raise the level of our being, that we raise the level of our modes of perception and action. Climbing to live in higher worlds cuts our attachment to the impediments that plagued us in our ordinary way of living. Spiritual practice is all about that climb. Such a change of station frees us all at once, even from obstacles that we had not particularly addressed. So we are not embarking on a program of self-reform, which might never end, but rather on a path of transformation, integrating those very obstacles into our wholeness, so that our unbecoming impulses reframe themselves to serve rather than to take.

The issue for us now is that the obstacles slow our climbing, like so many weights encumbering us. They draw us out of ourselves and we vanish into attachment in these many ways. Indeed what defines an obstacle is precisely its propensity to collapse our presence, to disturb the peace of our meditation, or to adulterate our prayer by making us feel unclean and unworthy. We measure our life by these criteria, by how things affect our inner work.

Our inner work against or despite particular obstacles generates energy that we can turn toward more and deeper inner work. Choosing to forgo something you want to do or choosing to do something you do not want to do, can produce valuable inner energy. There is on the one side our desire or aversion, and on the other side our choice to go against that desire or aversion. Like positive and negative electric charges held apart, this action sets up a field of energy within us. If the power of the want is matched by the power of the choice to oppose it, that field engenders energy that we sorely need for our further inner work. If the want is strong and the choice is strong, the energy field is also strong. For that reason, people with strong obstacles are not at a disadvantage when it comes to spiritual practice: those very obstacles, if handled well, can help them grow strong, not only in energy but also in will. Their will and their need are called upon to rise to meet the obstacles.

We need subtlety in understanding our spiritual impediments. It is easy to fall into defining as obstacles those aspects of ourselves that we do not like. That not-liking itself, though, is a hindrance, often coming from vanity, and that can lead us into endless programs of self-reform to make ourselves more acceptable to ourselves rather than to remove the difficulties hampering our inner work. This is not to say that our motivations must be pure, because vanity and egoism inevitably insert themselves into so much of what we do and feel. But we do need to observe what actually blocks or diminishes our inner work, our ability to be present, our ability to worship wholeheartedly, our readiness to be kind. Then we focus on what our observations bring to light. Each of us is unique, with our own set of obstacles. Notice also the crucial point that if we do not attempt to practice presence regularly, then we cannot see those processes that would hamper our presence. More inner work leads to more inner work. Less leads to less.

From the outset we also need to understand that overcoming our inner obstacles in no way means divorcing ourselves from parts of ourselves. We honor and respect our whole humanity, our own humanity, including the difficulties in our personal nature. Indeed, the source of all these obstacles can be attributed to their undoubted value in our survival-of-the-fittest path through the eons of evolution. Our spiritual path, though, requires us to live and work with the whole of ourselves, to transform our hindering tendencies to assets, to unify our entire nature in service to the Real. So we are not intending to cut out of ourselves those tendencies that oppose our inner work: we need everything we have. But we are intending to bring all our tendencies, including the entire roiling sea of our contradictory impulses, under one umbrella, under our one unified, individual will.

So we befriend ourselves and work against our obstacles, usually to generate insight and energy, sometimes to make permanent changes, but always to enable ourselves to step along the way toward freedom, unity, and love.

For this week, before we start looking together at specific types of obstacles, please look into your own life to see what particular obstacles hamper your path. Choose one thing or tendency and find a way to work toward freedom with respect to that.

15.1 Sense Desire
(Obstacles on the Way: Part 1 of 9)

Sense desire is built into our genes, for example through the great natural imperatives of our need for food and our need for sex. Our troubles begin when our desires multiply beyond our needs. We are not going to examine here the well-known health benefits of moderation, important as they are. Rather we look to see the effects that overindulged physical appetites and other sense desires have on our inner work.

There is a theory that some of the energy that our body uses in digesting our food is the very same energy we use in our inner work. Of course we have to eat, and eating also produces energy for our inner work. But the idea is that beyond a certain point, eating more than we need diminishes the energy available for our inner work. To verify this for yourself is straightforward, at least in theory. Simply observe, comparing your state before you eat and after you eat. On the occasions when you overeat, compare your ability to practice presence after you've eaten to before you ate, or to your usual ability. Compare on the basis of how long you are able to maintain presence, how frequently you come back to presence, how strong and deep is your presence. Observing in this way will teach you a great deal about how much you need to eat and how the amount and quality of your food affects your state.

Some physical indulgences should be stopped completely or they stop our inner work. Primary among those are drugs of abuse. Even in their milder forms, like marijuana, drugs burn up energies we need for inner work, disharmonize our system, and block our spiritual practice. If we wish to follow the path of liberation and love, we need to stop drug use altogether. Otherwise, all inner efforts are effectively wasted. Similarly, tobacco hampers our inner work by its effects on our energies and our health. In some traditions, one does find smokers who have gone far along the way. But that is exceptional. A healthy body is an important asset on the path, as is accepting responsibility for maintaining the health of our body. So smoking needs to be set aside entirely. Concerning alcohol use, moderation is necessary, though some traditions eliminate it completely. We each need to judge for ourselves, taking care not to fool ourselves regarding the effects of our indulgences.

In the realm of sense desire, we can also look to any overindulgence that distracts us from presence. We face increasingly sophisticated temptations to over-consume electronic media: TV, YouTube, Netflix, web surfing, Facebook, email, Twitter, sports, news, music, iTunes, games, and the many others continually being created and promoted. These things are not a problem in themselves, but become a problem for our path if we lose ourselves in them to the point of diminishing our possibilities for presence. Generally speaking, the form and content of modern mass media are designed to grab us emotionally, to cause us to react, to feel, and to become in a sense addicted to the media. Can we be present in the face of this onslaught? Again, moderation is key. Staying connected in the world of electronic media has become almost a necessity, but can we do so with quality and with presence? For example, can we stay aware of our body even as we watch or read or listen or type in that electronic world?

While we may recognize our overindulgences and know what we should do, sense cravings can be so strong that we cannot moderate or curtail them. You see the cake or the cigarette or the beer. Your pulse and breathing quicken. Your entire awareness collapses onto that object of desire. And though you know that going there will harm you in body or in being, you find your hand reaching for it. What to do?

The strategies are many and we may need to alternate among them or use them in combination. Here are a few. We can imagine that we have already indulged in the craving, satisfied our desire, and now feel the afterglow, or rather aftermath, of having done so. We might choose to shift our attention and redirect the energy flowing into the desire by doing something else, like going for a walk, or bringing our awareness into sensing our body, or practicing awareness of our breathing, or simply relaxing our body, mind, and feelings. We might go for a less harmful substitute: instead of cake, we eat a carrot. We can remind ourselves of our competing non-desire, of our wish to be free with respect to this particular craving. We can remind ourselves that procrastination, putting off the hard choice to tomorrow, next month, or the new year, rarely works, that we need to make the effort this time and every time the urge arises. We can renew our caring about our own well-being, our preference for our long-term benefit over any fleeting satisfaction.

Like furtive roaches, our overindulgent tendencies prefer the dark. Often, the part of us driving an act of overindulgence does not want to be seen by the rest of our being, does not want to be caught red-handed, and is ashamed. For these and other reasons, presence itself is a great antidote to overindulgence. Take the example of over-eating. If we bring presence to our eating, actually tasting each bite of food in full awareness, our eating changes. Presence raises us up from the world, from the style of living, in which gluttony reigns. The light of awareness weakens such tendencies. Furthermore, awareness of the taste of each morsel of food brings us greater satisfaction from the food than does wolfing it down tastelessly. This opens our heart of appreciation and gratitude. We have a better chance of feeling satiated without stuffing ourselves.

This principle of presence also applies to every other type of overindulgence. If you are a smoker, try bringing full self-awareness to the act of smoking. See what smoking actually does to you, what its effects are on your mind and body. Some find smoking relaxing. But at what cost? When you smoke, be fully aware that you are, without a doubt, shortening your life, in an act of slow suicide. Is this really what you want to do? When you smoke, be aware that your lungs do not want to breathe the smoke. Be aware of the justifying, fatalistic thoughts in response to such awareness, of any defeatist attitude that claims it is not possible for you to stop, even if you wanted to give it up. Be aware of not wanting to be aware of the act of smoking. Be present to yourself as you smoke. If this takes the joy out of it, so much the better, for the joy of smoking is the joy of the addicted part of you disregarding the long term cost to the whole of you. If you don't want to stop, then examine your desire to smoke. What in you wants to smoke? What are you ignoring? If you care about yourself, you will do whatever it takes to quit and you won't give up until you have. Perhaps this seems harsh, but it's not nearly as harsh as what smoking does to our body.

Presence helps protect us from overindulgence. If you are present while you watch television or play games or surf the web or drink alcohol, you will have a visceral sense of limits, of when enough is enough. And then you can choose to comply with that intuition, to relax in front of the desire to overindulge and let it go without acting on it.

This world is beautiful, luscious, and sensual. Nothing in the forgoing is intended to imply that we should adopt an ascetic approach, rejecting all pleasures. On the contrary, it is natural and normal to enjoy, thoroughly enjoy, the things of this world. In our path, we are not out to become hermits or live in monastic settings. We want to live a fully spiritual inner life and a fully ordinary outer life in the world, and make it be one holistic and satisfying life. In some ways, this may be harder than rejecting the world to pursue the spirit, because it does call for moderation and non-identification, for not allowing our desires to rule us, yet without removing the opportunities for indulgence. Food, in any case, cannot be eliminated. Moderation is harder than elimination; this middle way requires determination and builds inner strength. And the transformation of sense desire leads us to appreciation and gratitude for this remarkable world we live in, without being consumed by lust for it.

The spiritual path is not all smooth sailing on an ocean of bliss. At times, we need to struggle with our obstacles to reach that ocean, struggle intelligently and lovingly. In that struggle, despite our best intentions, failures inevitably come, backsliding into overindulgence for example. When we do fail, rather than inwardly berating ourselves and heaping guilt on our heads, we fully note what happened and then get up and start again.

For this week, notice when you overindulge your sense desires, be present in those situations, and let go of overindulging.

15.2 Aversion
(Obstacles on the Way: Part 2 of 9)

Just as sense desire is built into our genes, so is aversion. We find certain odors repulsive, indicative of food gone bad, air unsuitable for breathing, or noxious materials. Food that tastes bad may well be bad. We tend to find disorder ugly and symmetry beautiful. Cacophonous and harsh sounds seem to attack our ears. All that and much more are normal and natural ways that aversion enters our experience.

But we let it go too far, overindulging our aversions just as we overindulge our sense desires. The more things we don't like and the more we limit our experience based on that not-liking, the more impoverished is our life. Some believe just the opposite: that happiness comes from doing what we like to do and not doing what we dislike. But a much deeper and lasting satisfaction comes from having the freedom actually to do what we dislike and not do what we like. We assume that we have that freedom, that we freely choose to do what we like and not do what we dislike. But that behavior is predictable, wholly conditioned by our largely fixed store of likes and dislikes. Predictable, conditioned behavior is slavish, not at all free. We are free to do anything we like, but only what we like. If we find ourselves in a situation that forces us to do what we don't want to do, we grumble, get bored, do it half-heartedly, daydream or otherwise try to escape. We kill those moments and with them part of our life, because we are only half-alive in them.

Everyone, without exception, finds it necessary at times to do what they don't want to do or to forgo something they want. Life is full of such compromises. Maturity means, in part, being able to deal with that reality and keep going. Spiritual maturity means, in part, actually accepting to do what we don't want to do or forgo what we want, when necessary, accepting so completely that the situation does not drain our energies. This freedom does not mean getting rid of our likes and dislikes, which is not possible and would in any case flatten and impoverish our life, but rather to be able to do what's needed, when it's need, without regard for our likes and dislikes.

To gain such freedom, we must exercise our will. From time to time, we choose something we do not want to do and do it anyway. Or we choose something we want and give it up. We do that for a definite but limited time period that we select in advance, say for a day, or a week, or a month. Notice that we are not applying this to all our likes and dislikes. For the most part, within the bounds of responsibility and prudence, we continue to enjoy doing what we like to do and avoid doing what we do not want to do. At the same time, however, we build up our ability to do otherwise, to not go with our conditioning, when necessary or when we so choose. That crucial ability is our freedom and it emanates from the strength of our will. That freedom in front of likes and dislikes raises the level of our life, of our experience. Living under the domination of likes and dislikes keeps us mired in a dependent, thin, half-aware mode of experience, where initiative comes from outside us, where we are not ourselves.

Another type of aversion appears in our self-destructive judgments. For example, we reject aspects of our self and our body. That rejection slams us into an inner civil war that does us great harm. Self-rejection undermines the loving self-acceptance that we need to move toward self-integration and wholeness, to stop wasting energy on inner conflict. We mistakenly define ourselves by embracing those of our aspects and qualities that we like and rejecting those we do not like. Freedom and wholeness mean embracing, accepting every bit of ourselves, while realizing that none of it is who I am. That realization is not a matter of rejecting anything, even our aversion, but rather of opening to the sacred. Of course, self-acceptance is fully compatible with efforts of self-improvement, as long as we avoid an inner war of self-rejection.

Other forms of aversion involve our attitudes toward people. In its more extreme manifestations, aversion to people comes as anger, ill-will, spite, desire for revenge, keeping accounts, and schadenfreude. Milder versions include insensitivity to and lack of interest in people, avoidance, shyness, fear of what they will think of us, and fear of exposure or embarrassment. All forms of aversion to people isolate us, again impoverishing our life. Listening, really listening to others is a good antidote to aversion.

Freedom in front of aversion transforms it into strength, into acute perception, into a sense of justice and fairness. When we feel an aversion, be it visceral or mild, for something or someone or some situation, it may be a direct and true assessment, or just a reflection of our conditioned prejudices and antipathies, or a combination of the two. Freedom enables us to see into this, to disambiguate truth from reaction. Without freedom, we are simply subject to the aversion regardless of its value.

For this week, pay attention to your aversions and practice toward freedom from being dominated by them.

15.3 Laziness
(Obstacles on the Way: Part 3 of 9)

Natural cycles of activity and repose shape our lives. So also with our inner work: we cannot always be at a peak of intensity or quality in our practice; we need a balance that includes relaxation and non-effort. The trouble sneaks in when we let that slackness go too far, when we neglect our inner efforts of presence or our outer responsibilities, when we settle for half-hearted efforts or none at all. We call this laziness, or one of its variations: sloth, torpor, negligence, indifference, apathy, despair, or hopelessness. This insidious state undermines our spiritual practice by starving it, by not producing the nourishment that our soul so desperately needs.

Laziness directly reflects the state of our will. If we are low on energy, then it may be right to relax and rebuild. But laziness is not due to lack of energy, it is lack of active will, and thus a serious impediment to our path. One primary way for our I, our individuality to come forward into our life is through presence. Inner laziness stops presence before it can begin. Yes, we can be both present and relaxed; presence does not mean being taut. So inner laziness is not the same as being relaxed: it is the lack of will to be, the lack of will to act, the lack of will to see. For our inner work to progress at all, we need to break through that inner laziness, again and again, until it becomes natural for us to rouse ourselves off our inner sofa and work at presence, not to cruise along in absence.

External laziness, as we well know, has many ramifications for our outer life. If we fail to keep up with our duties and responsibilities, our life falls apart. If we fail to rise to challenges, opportunities, and creative changes, if we take shortcuts even when they shortchange us, if we fail to take practical steps toward our goals, if we fail to have goals and set projects for ourselves, then our life tends to stagnate. That's what laziness does to us outwardly.

External laziness, however, also affects our inner life. Not to fulfill my responsibilities means not to obey my conscience. Irresponsibility thus feeds my egoism, my self-centeredness, my conscience-ignoring tendency. If I feel my connectedness with other people, with the world around me, then I will care enough to pay attention to detail and do what I need to do. If in my egoism I feel separate, then none of the outside world matters, except insofar as it affects the fulfillment of my desires and the avoidance of my aversions.

To prevent laziness from running our life, from keeping us stuck in its mud, we work through it: we just do what we need to do despite any inner or outer lethargy. We train our body, our feelings, our mind, and our attention to move, to act when it's called for, regardless of inner or outer inertia. At our job this may be easy, because our livelihood depends on not being lazy in that context. But in our life outside of our job and in our inner life, we find ourselves thrown back on our own inner resources, on our choices about how to live, what to make of our life, thrown back on our own will to follow through on those choices. That's where the challenge of laziness comes into play. Will my passivity rob me of my potential?

Excuses for laziness come in many forms. One such affects our mind: doubt, the inappropriate demand for certainty. We cannot know in advance the outcome of our efforts, outer or inner. Nor can we know the truth about the higher worlds of the spirit before we ourselves attain to those heights. Doubt takes advantage of these situations to give us reasons not to act, to, in effect, justify our laziness. We think: *since I may not win, I won't really try. Since I don't really know whether God or heaven exist, why bother with all that?* But we do not need certainty to act on what our heart is drawn to, and we need not let doubt contribute to our laziness.

Laziness is a choice, or the abdication of choice. It seems like a dense fog, mental and physical. For this week, notice your own tendency to be lazy, to shirk your outer and inner responsibilities. Some inner challenges evaporate just by seeing them clearly. But to counteract laziness, we need to act. See the extent to which the fog of laziness parts when you do choose to act, when with dogged persistence you intentionally enter presence again and again.

15.4 Hurry and Worry
(Obstacles on the Way: Part 4 of 9)

Hurrying to meet the future destroys the present by pushing it aside. Hurrying, we fall forward toward the future and ignore the present. Worrying about some unwanted future yields an unwanted present full of worry. Worrying chews up the present, in the vain hope that worrying will ward off a feared future. These warped relationships with time, our inner slavery to time, divorce us from the present, both from the time present in which we act and events occur and from the eternal present in which we are conscious. Hurry and worry lead us to abandon the eternal present and thus collapse our experience into the time present. Then hurry and worry so orient us outside the time present that our present moment thins down to nothing. In that condition, the never-ending stream of time can and does push us into the future, our immediate experience continually vanishing. All of that happens when we hurry and when we worry.

So what to do? What if we are late for some appointment or event? Hurrying to it means moving quickly with inner agitation and anxiety. But it is possible to move quickly without hurrying, without feeling rushed and harried. We can move quickly when necessary and still be inwardly relaxed and present, fully present and connected with both the eternal present and the time present. Like other aspects of the spiritual path, this takes practice. First, we need to see how things are with us when we do hurry. If we see that in hurrying we eviscerate our present moment, our only moment, then we can resolve to practice presence and let go of hurrying. For that, we prepare in times we when do not need to move quickly. We practice sensing our body and being present when we can move slowly. Then we practice presence when moving at normal speeds. Then we practice when moving quickly. We learn that our presence need not be limited by what we are doing outwardly. We learn that the speed with which we can accomplish something or get somewhere is not enhanced by hurrying, by feeling rushed and agitated. On the contrary, hurrying leads to mistakes and can slow us down.

What about worry? What if we foresee some unwanted possibility looming in the future? What if we are in the grip of some unwanted situation in the present? Does worrying help? If the unwanted possibility or situation is out of our control, beyond our influence, then how could worrying be useful? If we can influence the current situation or influence whether the unwanted event actually happens, then again worry and anxiety do not help: only taking the appropriate action can help. The worry and anxiety can prevent or hamper us in that action. There is a big difference between preparing for the future and worrying about it, between acting to heal the present and feeling anxious about it. We can be concerned with the kind of future we are creating in the present, without the emotional angst, without the fear, which waste our energies and our time.

Worrying can range from mild and intermittent worries to the chronic and debilitating condition known as generalized anxiety disorder, wherein we need medication and/or psychotherapy to get through it. But on the other side of anxiety, we come to acceptance of the present as it is, coupled with a healthy concern for the future and working toward a better future.

Certainly the future matters. On a large scale, the unfolding of history can be seen as a great process of spiritualization, of evolution. The spiritual practice of "be here now" does not entail ignoring the future, does not argue against planning and preparing for the future. It means being fully present in this moment, while doing what the moment calls for. In the present we create our future. We pursue education, we save, we work toward goals, we train our children, and we lighten our impact on the environment. All these are aimed toward the future and are best accomplished fully present in the now.

Fundamental to counteracting both hurry and worry are relaxing and focusing. Relaxing brings us more into the present, as we let go of hurry and worry. Focusing enables us to act effectively, whether in moving quickly or in changing the future by acting in the present.

As with so many other inner difficulties, presence tends to lift us out of hurry and worry. In presence, we live in contact with the eternal, with timeless consciousness, with the peace of cognizant stillness. In presence, the impulse to hurry and the impulse to worry come to us as perceptions, as information alerting us to situations which may require some action on our part. In presence, we are never lost in hurrying or in worrying, nor do we ignore what they call us to see. In presence, we are free. Yet conversely, hurry and worry destroy presence. With persistent inner work, we can have that choice.

For this week, notice when you hurry or worry. Notice the associated impatience, anxiety, and fear. Notice how you are in those states. Practice accepting, relaxing, being present, focusing, and acting with clarity and decisiveness.

15.5 Thoughts and Opinions
(Obstacles on the Way: Part 5 of 9)

To have created a species with the ability to think is perhaps the crowning achievement of evolution so far. So why do we include thoughts and opinions among the obstacles on the spiritual path? It is not obvious that thinking and holding opinions is an obstacle. Thinking gives us remarkable powers to plan ahead, to solve problems, to weigh options, to analyze situations, to search our memory, to learn, and much, much more. The development, through good education, of our ability to think clearly and logically makes an enormous, positive difference in our life.

The power to think should be prized, respected, and used well. But the latter is the problem. We may think well sometimes, while most of the time our thoughts think us and we float away in the stream of daydreams, self-generated associative thoughts, and aimless imaginings that dissipate our energy. Or our fixed opinions, views, and attitudes control us, demand that we promulgate and defend them, even in some cases at the risk of our very life. As has been said, we become machines for the reproduction of memes, as embodied in our thoughts. All these cases, which we experience so much of the time that we take them as normal, are actually aberrations, misuses of our power of thought.

This situation is revealed to us through our inner work, our practice of presence, meditation, and prayer, which enables to see our thoughts as they are, to see how we collapse into them. Through our inner work, we see that we live in a mental fog of thoughts and opinions, a fog that mesmerizes us into believing that we are our thoughts and opinions. That fog clouds our vision to such an extent that we are unable to be conscious and at peace, unable to be present. And even at those moments when something does break through to remind us of the work of presence, we quickly get sidetracked by yet another passing thought.

This endless stream of thoughts is on the whole not intentional, it is automatic. Thoughts enter our mind along established patterns and in reaction to other thoughts and to events around us. And they take us. We hear our familiar thoughts and we feel, "yep, that's me, that's what I think." So we are fooled into believing that these automatic thoughts are intentional, that they arise from who we are. That is how our thoughts think us.

Sometimes though, we do use our thinking mind by intentionally thinking about some subject, perhaps working out a problem or creating a plan. This requires contact with the meaning of our thoughts, contact that comes with the sensitive energy of thought, as opposed to the automatic energy of programmed thinking. Another example of intentional thinking is in those many forms of silent prayer in which we say the prayer in our thoughts. Intentional thinking, regardless of its content, shifts us out of the automatic mode of our thoughts thinking us and temporarily removes that obstacle to presence.

We can be present while thinking intentionally. The prime way toward that is to involve our body, to be aware of our body while we think. This is the work of sensing, of contact with the sensitive energy in our body. The more we practice sensing, the less we are lost in the stream of automatic thoughts and fixed opinions. The more we practice sensing, the more we are able to see our thoughts as thoughts, as just thoughts. The more we practice sensing, the more we can open to consciousness, to the spacious and cognizant stillness within us. In consciousness, we can see that our thoughts and opinions are not who we are, we can see our thoughts passing like clouds floating through the big sky of our mind. When contemplating, when thinking intentionally in consciousness, we see our thoughts in the context of other relevant thoughts. This can even pass into creative thinking, where having steeped ourselves in a subject and its various possibilities, we set it aside and allow the truly new and spontaneous thought to enter.

As with other thoughts, opinions in themselves do not present any difficulty for our path. The problem arises when we identify with our opinions, when we believe our opinions are central expressions of who we are. Opinions, like likes and dislikes, make life interesting, giving us a position from which to approach life, something to defend, to hold up as our perception of truth. Yet holding too fast to an opinion and defending it at all costs, like being ruled by a like or dislike, actually sacrifices our freedom, collapses our presence into the opinion-driven emotional reaction, into being opinionated. We may live by principles and passions, but opinions do not rise to that level. Opinions can easily change with new information and are an expression of our personality. So we may have our opinions, but to keep them from blocking our path, we do not allow our opinions to have us.

For this week, notice your thoughts and opinions. Notice how you believe in them, how you are mesmerized by them, how you identify with them. See your thoughts and opinions for what they are: just one, superficial component that does not define you.

15.6 Greed
(Obstacles on the Way: Part 6 of 9)

How much is enough? Where is the appropriate line between needs and wants? What do we need? When does external work pass from contributing to society and earning our living to taking more than we should? These questions matter to us both personally and collectively, yet they fall into a gray area of personal judgment. The development of that judgment goes with the development of our contact with conscience, and so plays a central role in our spiritual path. How we live is an expression of who we are.

If we take indiscriminately, take just to take, take just to have, accumulate for the sake of accumulation, that affects our planet, which may already be beyond its carrying capacity, and it affects us spiritually. If greed, the desire to take and have more than we need, causes us to be wasteful, then we are irresponsible toward the Earth. If greed causes us to mistreat or manipulate people, then we are irresponsible toward society. If greed causes us to spend so much of our time and energy pursuing wealth, power, and status that we do not have enough left to pursue our spiritual practice, then we are irresponsible toward our own eternal well-being and toward the spirit. More fundamentally, greed is an expression of self-centered egoism and thus strengthens the barrier between us and the spiritual depths.

Now none of this is meant to advocate an intentionally ascetic lifestyle of poverty, for in many ways that also may be irresponsible. Nor does it mean that we should not go beyond needs to enjoy some of the luxuries afforded us by this amazing, globalized techno-economy. Yet, there is a line where what we do passes to overindulgence, to avarice and greed. Our own conscience can tell us where that line is, if we listen.

One major way to recognize that greed may be at work in us is by noticing our thoughts and emotions when they perseverate around wanting something. Again though, we discriminate between wanting something we need and wanting something we want. The subtleties involved help us develop our discrimination, which helps put us in contact with our I, our unified, individual will.

Greed leads to more greed, not to satisfaction. The hole in our center that greed tries to fill cannot be filled from the outside. So greed can never be satisfied: it always wants more and more and more. Greed clings to externals to fill the emptiness within us, an emptiness that can only be filled from within, not by anything external.

To counteract greed, we open and give. The prime way to let go of greed is to open to the richness of this moment. The greater our presence, the more vivid is our immediate experience. Vivid experience is inherently more satisfying than being half-aware. The impulse of greed is a misplaced response to our emptiness, our lack, our dissatisfaction. Indeed, dissatisfaction and greed mutually reinforce each other. Through our spiritual practice that dissatisfaction with ourselves and our life, instead of devolving into greed, can fuel our need, our desire to practice. Presence raises us out of the unsatisfying mode of experience. So presence makes greed superfluous — and our greed evaporates. In presence we are just here, contented and complete. Acting on greed, taking, satisfies temporarily at best. Spiritual inner work and meaningful external work, both of which give, satisfy in a lasting and more fundamental way. As does generosity, which is a direct antidote to greed.

For this week, notice the extent to which greed operates in you, and the extent to which you act out of greed. Work to be more present and let go of any greed.

15.7 Envy
(Obstacles on the Way: Part 7 of 9)

Envy weakens us. If we look at some quality or object that another person possesses and we wish it were our possession, then we are inherently devaluing ourselves, admitting that in our own eyes we are not good enough. Envy is thus an opposite of self-respect. It is almost tantamount to wanting to be that other person rather than be ourselves. But the set of qualities, talents and shortcomings, assets and liabilities, that we have been given, our individuality, defines our challenge and our responsibility, our sacred duty to make of ourselves what we can, to fulfill our destiny. Another person's destiny is irrelevant, having no bearing on our own. One opposite of envy is self-acceptance, to honor ourselves and our situation as is, to take this as our starting point for our efforts to become more, to transform our being, to do what we need to do.

Now perhaps we admire certain qualities in outstanding people and rightly strive to emulate those qualities, to hold such people up as shining examples of what we might become or achieve. But within that is our willingness to work to develop or earn those qualities or achievements. That does not mean wanting to acquire what the other person has in the cheap way that envy does. If it were morally acceptable, envy would have us steal those qualities or possessions rather than earn them. Envy is a kind of inner theft, in our heart taking or wishing to take what does not belong to us.

Envy's sibling is jealousy, the hyper-awareness of and reaction to a real or imagined threat to our ownership of some thing or to our relationship with a person. Jealousy is self-destructive because it poisons our relationships and makes ownership a burden, sources not of joy but of worry.

The source of envy, as with greed, is our inner lack, the hole at our center that erupts into feelings of inadequacy and self-rejection. That hole can only be filled from within, by the spirit. And a prime road toward that consists of spiritual practice: presence, meditation, and contemplative prayer. So envy turns out to be a misplaced response to that inner need, a response that assumes that by having what someone else has, we can be made whole. But in the end, all externals prove insufficient to that need. Understanding this, in experience, leads to the transformation of envy into wish, into the wish for being.

For this week, notice envy at work in your own inner world. Question its premises and goals. See what's behind it.

15.8 Fault-Finding
(Obstacles on the Way: Part 8 of 9)

We set ourselves up as judge and critic of everyone and everything that we care to pass judgment on, including ourselves and our life situation. People that we do not even know, we judge by their body, their mannerisms, facial expressions, posture, and clothing. We evaluate people, weighing their pluses and minuses, whether they are in any way a threat or a potential ally or friend, whether we like them or need them, whether to ignore them or not. In this utilitarian approach to people, we assign them grades and value as if they were commodities like farm animals. And that leads us to speak ill of others, to slander and gossip about them in a negative way.

Setting aside the dubious morality of this attitude to people and its effect on them, what is the problem with it? As always, we examine the issue from the point of view of our inner work, our spiritual practice. Doing so, we see first that all this fault-finding is a great distraction from presence and, second, that it both comes from and inflates our egoism, our self-importance. These two great strikes against it prompt us to look further into this process of fault-finding. We discover that it is habitual yet unnecessary, and inappropriate for a person of conscience and heart.

Do we really need to judge people? Sometimes we do need to make judgments, to discriminate, for example when we are dealing in a formal way with a person, such as in a business or service relationship. Even then, however, we do not need to find-fault in the inwardly accusatory way, which forgets that they are flesh and blood and consciousness like we are. We can simply apply a discriminating perception to see them as they are, all the while respecting their humanity. In fault-finding we make a value judgment, and a negative one at that. As if the person were worth less in proportion to how much we dislike, or disapprove, or cannot relate to them. In discrimination, which is part of wisdom, we just see the person as they are and leave it at that. But with the great majority of people we encounter, it is not necessary to discriminate, nor judge or note their faults. Letting go of this fault-finding stance relieves us of yet another great burden and obstacle on our path. It opens us to the simple joy of just being with people, without the buffer of our judging, criticizing, devaluing and dehumanizing attitude.

What about finding fault with ourselves or our life situation? What would it be like to feel, to really feel, that you are now living the life of your choice, that you would have it be no other way than how it is now? Of course, we exempt some aspects from this, such as loved ones who have died. Disregarding for the moment those exceptional cases, what would it be like to accept yourself and your life as it is, to be utterly content? What would it be like to give up our complaints, our whining, our self-pity, our self-criticism? We send so much of our energy, our life-blood, down that drain. And just as finding-fault with others separates us from them, not-accepting ourselves or our life as is separates us from our own deeper nature. We get distracted with wallowing in self-hatred or with grand programs to improve ourselves and our life. Again though we can apply an objectively discriminating approach to work to transform our being and to change our life situation, but all the while accepting, respecting, valuing who we are and the situation we are in.

For this week, notice when you find-fault with other people, with yourself, and your life. Notice how this affects those relationships. Practice just being with others and with yourself, without judging.

15.9 Ego
(Obstacles on the Way: Part 9 of 9)

"It's all about me." That is the default, though often hidden, central theme of our lives. Everything that happens, everything that might happen, everything and everyone around us — we evaluate all of that from our self-centered point of view. What do I want? What do I not want? How does it or how will it affect me? How can I use this or that to my advantage? How can I get more, have more? How can I hide from others those things that I do not like about myself? What do they think of me? Are they treating me with respect, with the deference I deserve? Do they love me? Will they be faithful to me? Will they do what I want them to do? How do I look? Do they understand that my view, my opinion in every situation is the one that matters, the one that warrants the most interest? Do they agree with me? Do they understand that I am more important than they are? Do they understand that I don't really need them?

Obviously, the common element in this narrow stream is I, me, and mine. And those all refer to our ego, to what we unquestioningly believe ourselves to be. We spend our lives defending it, refining it, building it, and serving it. But right here we need to ask, "so what?" Why is ego a problem for our spiritual path?

Ego is a spiritual problem in several related ways. It leads us falsely to believe that we are separate from everyone and everything else. It blocks the channel to our true individuality and the deeper realms of the spirit. And it distracts us from reality by constantly presenting itself as who I am, so that I believe in it, defend it, and serve it, this false and illusory god of ego, of me.

The solution is twofold. First, we learn to see the truth that our ego is only an illusion, an empty shell with nothing at its core. Second, we learn to recognize our true I, who is not self-centered like ego and who connects us with each other and with the deeper spirit. However, these are not trivial matters, having layer upon layer of subtlety that can take many years to penetrate. But the path to that does pay enormous dividends along the way.

To see our own ego in action, we begin with noticing our thoughts as thoughts and our emotions as emotions, seeing these for what they are: just thoughts and just emotions. It is through our thoughts and emotions that ego does its mischief. Sitting behind the curtain, like the Wizard of Oz, our ego pulls the levers of thought and emotions, making them all revolve around me, so that we believe they are me, we believe we are our thoughts and emotions, we believe our thoughts and emotions are direct expressions of me, we believe the thought "I" is who we are. Yet taking a step back to see them as they are, we realize that our thoughts primarily run on their own, thinking themselves by automatic associative processes, one thought leading to another, ad nauseum. We realize that our emotions are primarily just automatic reactions to events and usually flow in concert with our automatic thoughts. None of that is who I am, it is all just programming and mechanism.

Taking another step back, to look behind the curtain for our supposed I, ego, we find nothing, we find the space behind the curtain is empty, we find that ego is just an illusion, an assumption based on the complex patterns of our associative thoughts and reactive emotions. Our ego is a pretend self. And that, of course, is why we need to defend it so vigorously, because if we did not the whole house of cards would collapse. And since it is the only house we know, that can be a daunting prospect. Yet this illusion of our ego, out of which flow all the other obstacles to our path, must be exposed, sooner or later.

This is where the second part of the solution enters, our true I, the one in us who sees, the one in us who can act for and from the whole of us, the one in us who is connected with the sacred, with love. We approach this first by being our attention and then by being our intention in action, by being the one in us who sees and acts. This I is very different than ego, because it is not self-centered and self-referential, it is real. Though because our I is will and because will is not material, we cannot put our finger on our I, but we can be I. And that I has an affinity, a direct connection with every other I, which is the source of our innate compassion for each other.

Yet here we are wasting our lives in the familiar and comfortable illusion of ego. Instead of striving for the real and the sacred, we stay half-aware and self-centered. We may awaken accidentally for brief periods, but quickly fall back to our former state. Nevertheless there is hope. For a stable personal reality, we engage in the practices of the spirit, in body awareness, in presence, in meditation, and in prayer. Each moment of practice accumulates to help us see through the illusion of ego and become fully ourselves, become our true I.

For this week, look into your own illusion of ego, your own self-centeredness.

16.0 Living in Presence

We understand the notion of *quality of life* as concerning robust physical health, family and friends, adequate financial and material resources, meaningful work that engages us, and leisure time to use as we please. Important as all that is, it only addresses the quality of our outer life, our material life. The spiritual path and its practices extend the notion of quality of life to include the quality of our inner life. Some may have an excellent quality of outer life and yet experience a chaotic and difficult inner life. Others may have a poor quality of outer life and yet experience a loving, blissful, vivid, peaceful and coherent inner life.

Though we do not claim that the inner should take precedence over the outer, our usual way of life is unbalanced toward the outer, to the point of ignoring the need to work on the inner. In doing so, we leave our inner perceptions and capacities undeveloped and disorganized, preemptively sacrificing our chances for a complete life on the altar of the material, partial life. If we do take up inner work, we find that the two ultimately are connected; our spiritual practice opens us to the one life that embraces both inner and outer.

Occupying the central position within the broad constellation of spiritual practices is the practice of presence. Found in various incarnations in every major spiritual and religious way, the practice of presence has a wide variety of effective approaches, as well as layer upon layer of subtleties. And if we practice presence consistently, it develops in us, in duration, from the short-lived to the long-lasting, in frequency, from the rare to the regular, and in depth, from the senses to the Sacred. Our presence does not develop on its own: it depends directly on the quality and quantity of our intentional efforts.

In the coming weeks, we will explore presence, explore how to live in presence through these seven aspects of its practice:

1. Living in Six Senses
2. Sensing
3. Living with Attention
4. Living in Consciousness
5. Living as I
6. Living in the Sacred Now
7. Living as the Sacred

To prepare, we begin by looking at our lack of presence, how we live largely unaware, driven by our thoughts and emotions, physical needs and impulses. We look to notice the extent to which we are present or not. *Am I aware of myself and my surroundings? Am I here within that awareness? How often is that the case? And for how long?* These questions matter because we often just assume that we are present, even when we are not. One source of that assumption is that when we ask ourselves whether we are present, the very question itself wakes us up and indeed we are present, at least for that brief moment. So whenever we ask, we find a positive answer. From that, we extrapolate to assume we are always present. This we may call the illusion of presence. The problem here is that if we believe we are already present, all or most of the time, then we have no incentive to undertake the actual work of expanding and deepening our presence.

When we do work with specific, concrete practices of presence, our general lack of presence and its various degrees in those moments when we are present become more obvious to us. Nevertheless, we need the motivation to begin our work at those practices. So for this week, please notice when you have been absent. Noticing itself is part of presence, so when you do notice then you are no longer absent. But as you awaken from a period of non-presence, you can notice that you have been absent.

16.1 Living in Six Senses
(Living in Presence: Aspect 1 of 7)

To live in presence is to live in the present moment. And the primary content of the present moment consists of our immediate sensory experience, brought to us by our external senses of sight, hearing, body sense, smell, and taste, plus our inner senses of awareness of thoughts, mental images, and emotions. From the vast amount of sensory information coming to us, we are consciously aware of only a tiny fraction. And sometimes not even that, as when we lose contact with the present moment in thoughts about the past or future.

But if we are in thoughts about past or future, are we not in one sense still in the present, in the sense of being aware of thoughts? After all, thoughts of past or future are all happening in this present moment. Well ... no. To be in the present with regard to thoughts means to be aware of our thoughts as thoughts, as currently happening thoughts. In our typical reverie of past or future, or of any other self-generating, automatic thought-stream, we are not aware of our thoughts per se. We are just swept along by them and not at all here in the present. This lost-in-automatic-thinking is so often our state that we need some ways out of it and back into the present.

A whole genre of such ways revolves around the practice of sensory awareness. Most such practices select one particular sense as a focus, and we also will address one such practice in the next aspect of this inner work series on Living in Presence. But for now, we look to develop a global sense awareness, to living in six senses. Each of our senses presents a remarkably rich and vibrant field. Many people specialize in one or another. Painters, photographers, and other visual artists see the nuances of light and shadow, color and texture, shape, depth and detail that the rest of us miss entirely. So also with the chef and the sommelier for taste, the perfumer for scent and fragrance, the athlete and dancer for body sense, the musician and the blind for hearing.

To practice a more global sense awareness, we can take two or more senses and open to them beyond our usual mode. With the soundscape, we can open to the whole array, the whole symphony of sounds coming to our ears, noticing the sounds we normally tune out, noticing all the various channels and sources of sound coming to us. With the lightscape, we can open our vision to notice more of the color and texture and the rest from across our whole visual field, to see more, to take it all in. With our body, we can open to noticing the many sense impressions coming from all parts of our body, the hot and cold, the wet and dry, the proprioceptive sense of visceral embodiment, the kinesthetic sense of movement, the motion of our breathing, the blinking of our eyes, the mild discomforts. As for taste, we always have some in our mouth, whether we are eating or not. And there is always some scent, even if a neutral one. Finally, we notice our thoughtscape, whether snippets or wholly formed thoughts and images coursing through our mind, and our emotional state, even if neutral at the moment.

All of that, or as much of it as we can manage, we open to, we notice. We drop the filters on our perceptions and let it all in. The world continuously refreshes and we are here, present in this cascade of sense impressions. To be in contact with our six senses, or even just two or three simultaneously, is a mode of presence. Certainly it enriches our life, because in such moments we live more. This is the way of living in all our senses, the way of awakening our ordinary perceptions.

So for this week, please see more and hear more, open to all of your senses. In doing so, you come into the present moment, because whatever you see or hear, touch or feel, smell or taste, is always now and enables you to be here.

16.2 Sensing
(Living in Presence: Aspect 2 of 7)

The practice of sensing offers a unique and powerful approach to presence: it gives us a foundation for awareness. The more we work with sensing, the more stable that foundation becomes. Sensing operates at the interface between our body and our awareness. Because our body is always here and now, body awareness is also always here and now. Intentionally enhancing our body sense keeps us in this moment and opens the door to presence. By sensing we create an organic home that integrates the outer and the inner. Sensing just feels right. One of the big surprises with sensing is that we did not know about it before, because it seems as natural as having a body.

So what is sensing? First, a little about energies. Inner, spiritual energies are fine substances of various quality levels that enable all our inward actions and experiences. Some, like the sensitive energy that fuels the practice of sensing, can be accumulated and organized in us to help form the first part of our soul, our inner body or soul-body. In sensing, we use our will, our attention, intention, and inward action, to awaken and build up the sensitive energy in our body. This energy mediates our contact with our body. We simply put and hold our attention on part of our body.

Start with your right hand. Leaving it relaxed, put and hold your attention in your hand. Keep checking to see that your attention is actually in your physical hand and has not wandered off into thoughts or daydreams or anything else. Thinking about your hand does not help, because then your attention is in your thoughts. Keep your attention in the right hand. Gradually your hand comes to life. Your perception of your hand will change: it becomes more of what it is and you feel that you have a right hand. It may tingle. There may be a subtle vibration in the hand. It may feel warmer or larger or heavier or more substantial. To clarify this, simply notice the difference between your perception of your right hand and your left hand. If you can notice a difference, that is due to the greater presence of sensitive energy in your right hand. Your attention in your hand draws that energy into the hand.

Next you can practice sensing your right foot, then your left foot, then your left hand, then back to your right hand and repeat that pattern. Over time, you can build up your ability to sense your body, you can practice sensing your entire right arm, then right leg, then left leg, then left arm. Continuing to build, sense both arms, then both legs, then all four limbs.

Finally, sense your whole body. Note though, that we do not try to sense our inner organs so as not to interfere with their instinctive functioning. We just have a general sensation of our whole torso, neck and head, added to the sensation of our four limbs. Sensing the whole body can give us a strong experience of wholeness and change our level of presence. Some people quickly come to sensing their whole body. For others it may take many months of practice to get to that stage.

Either way, the important thing is to persist in the practice of sensing: at first in formal, seated meditation, then in slow movement such as walking meditation, and then adding the practice of sensing during your ordinary daily life. Within the latter, of course, we use our common sense and do not divert attention to sensing during critical or dangerous activities like driving a car, chopping vegetables, or performing surgery. But during the rest of the day, sensing certainly can enhance our life.

The body sensation that sensing builds has the great advantage of persisting in time: it does not immediately evaporate if our attention shifts away from sensing. So even when our presence fades, which inevitably does happen, the sensation collected in our body, while we were sensing, has the power to reawaken us, to bring us back to the present moment, because sensation is always now. Though sensing does fade when our attention to it lapses, it does so gradually. The vestiges of sensation tug on us, remind us to bring our attention back to our body, back to sensing, back to presence. Not only that, but sensing is also like depositing money in a savings account: it gradually accumulates in us. Over time, we become able to sense more often, more strongly, more completely, and for longer. And that accumulation pays dividends, such as when sensing spontaneously pops back up into our awareness at moments when we lack presence or any contact with our body. Again, if we willingly go with it, that spontaneous sensing reawakens us to presence, to greater freedom from our identifications and difficult emotions, to the richness of this moment.

For this week, experiment with sensing. Begin its practice if you have never tried it before or deepen it if you have.

16.3 *Living with Attention*
(Living in Presence: Aspect 3 of 7)

Attention connects with the core of who we are. One can truthfully say: "I am my attention." Closer to us than our body, our emotions, or our thoughts, closer even than our sensation or our consciousness, attention is our reality. When we pay attention, we put ourselves right in the middle of the action; as our attention, we focus our cognitive energies, our mind on the object of our attention. Who is focusing? We are. One aspect of will is attention. If we are anything, we are our will. And so we are our attention.

Attention always acts in the present moment; indeed, it defines the present moment. More attention means more presence. Less attention means less presence. No attention means a barren spirit, a flat and fleeting experience that does not enter our memory, a piece of our life, a piece of our precious time that may as well not have happened, for we were not there, we were not anywhere.

We distinguish between active and passive attention. When our attention is drawn by an object, without the need of our continuing intention to keep it there, then we are in a state of passive attention. Examples include watching television or a movie or some spectacle, noticing an attractive person or some object we desire, daydreaming, or any other situation that pulls our attention toward it without any intentional inward action on our part.

Active attention occurs when we choose to pay attention to something or someone, and keep on choosing to hold our attention there. Despite the many distractions of stray thoughts and other sensory impressions, we focus on the chosen object of attention. We can listen to the lecture, we can follow and participate in the conversation, we can keep our eyes on the road when we drive, and so on. The power to do such things is the power of active attention.

There is a third form, receptive attention, which comes into play in listening to people, to nature, or to music, and in deep meditation or prayer. In this, we direct our attention without focusing so tightly and at the same time we open ourselves to the object of our receptivity.

Attention is the essential and versatile tool at the center of all we do. Honing our attention pays continuing dividends both for our outer life and for our inner search. How do we improve our attention? We work primarily on improving our active attention, our ability to focus our awareness and stay focused. The broad pantheon of spiritual practices offers many methods for exercising attention. The practice of sensing is one such method, wherein we focus and hold our attention in our body, in contact with the sensitive energy in our body. In some forms of meditation, we focus our attention on our breath. In one form of mindfulness practice, we keep our attention on whatever sensory impression is at the forefront of our awareness in any given moment. In some forms of prayer, we may focus our attention on the words of the prayer, on the melody of the prayer, on adopting the appropriate emotional stance, or on the One to Whom we pray.

One effective exercise for developing attention is to hold our attention on the breath at our nostrils, to keep attention on the sensations of breath flowing in and out of our nostrils. To help prevent our thoughts from distracting us, we engage them by counting breaths, one count for each exhalation. We count 1 to 10 and then begin again at 1. If we lose the count, we begin again at 1. But the primary focus of attention remains with the breath at the tip of our nose, while we keep the count in the background. Because the focus is so narrowly circumscribed, our attention rapidly strengthens in this form of meditative exercise. We can treat this as a fine preparation for meditation, simply beginning a session of meditation with this exercise, and then dropping the exercise once our attention has fully settled on the breath at the nostrils. We then move on to our chosen meditation practice.

In some ways an even more useful exercise of attention entails holding our attention in contact with our body, as a sitting meditation practice. If you have worked on sensing, as described for example in the previous aspect of this inner work series on Living in Presence, then you have enhanced your facility for intentional body awareness. In this exercise of attention, we intensify that practice of sensing by holding our attention in a part, or preferably the whole, of our body. We stay with it and by our intention we strengthen that ongoing contact for the duration. When we notice that our attention has strayed into thoughts or anything else, we bring it back to our body and reinvigorate our immediate, visceral, ongoing, intentional contact. This builds both our being and our will.

Another excellent exercise of attention is to keep our attention in contact with our bodily sensations as we walk, i.e., to sense our body while walking in the ordinary way. This intentional body sense leads toward presence in the midst of action.

For this week, please practice developing your attention. Whatever the current quality of our attention, we can profitably exercise it further.

16.4 Living in Consciousness
(Living in Presence: Aspect 4 of 7)

We will use the word consciousness in a very different way than its usual meaning of sensory awareness. Instead we view consciousness as the awareness behind sensory awareness, the pure cognition prior to and beneath all sensory content. In meditation, when our thoughts finally slow down, a gap opens between thoughts, a gap of silence and stillness. Yet this silence and stillness is not a void, for we are still here and still aware. That awareness, that cognitive stillness is consciousness, the conscious energy at work in us. As our thoughts subside in meditation, they fragment into a soup whose medium is the cognitive stillness of consciousness. Yet not limited to meditation, consciousness is always here with us, behind our awareness of thoughts and emotions, behind our sensory awareness. It is the perceptive film, the blank slate, the screen on which all our ordinary experience is displayed.

While consciousness is always here with us, we are not typically with it, for it is hidden from us by the very content of our sensory experience. We see the clouds, without realizing that our mind is the sky. Our sensory perceptions form a seamless layer that distracts us from being in our underlying consciousness. But in meditation, sitting quietly, we come to know the stillness underneath all that goes on, our unchanging cognitive faculty that perceives all, yet remains still and silent. We come to know it, to soak in that stillness. We see that cognizant stillness is a substance, the palpable substance of consciousness. And in entering that stillness, we cross the first threshold into the realms of the spirit.

With that comes the important opportunity of learning to be, learning to open to our true consciousness in midst of daily life. The familiarity with stillness gained in quiet meditation can carry over into our life, as an effortless calm, the surface of a deep pool of peace, the peace of stillness, the peace of consciousness, the peace that knows no boundaries, inner or outer. More meditation brings more peace, until it permeates our life, creating an undertone of being.

The peace of meditation can carry over into our life not only as an effortless calm, but also intentionally, yes consciously. Sensation, particularly full-body sensation, provides a foundation for consciousness. And consciousness provides a foundation for presence. While we may feel peace and calmness in our ordinary activities, that does not necessarily bring with it the awareness of awareness that is consciousness. Even after soaking in the stillness of consciousness during meditation, the experience tends to be momentary and fleeting during our day, in activity. We can awaken by intentionally coming back to ourselves, but it quickly evaporates.

That instability of our contact with consciousness can be addressed through the practice of full-body sensation. The wholeness of full-body sensation resonates with the wholeness of consciousness, and brings more stability to our contact with consciousness, giving us the possibility of living in consciousness. Of course other factors enter, principally the stability of our will, our intention and attention. When we lose our immediate intention to stay in the wholeness of body sensation and of consciousness, we fall out of it.

Though its contents continually change, consciousness itself is timeless and unchanging. This is a principal reason why we feel the same over time, why we feel that we are the same person we were as a child or teenager. That sameness we feel over time also extends to other people, for consciousness has no boundaries: it is everywhere. Consciousness is not in us, we are in it, in the vast field of consciousness. We all share the same consciousness, the pure cognition underlying our individual contents. The deeper we go into our own being, the deeper and more intimate is our contact with nature and with people. Indeed, in consciousness the wall between us and them, between inner and outer, begins to dissolve.

For this week, practice whole-body sensation, sensing from the top of your head to the soles of your feet. Let that sense of wholeness extend to the wholeness beneath all your sensory perceptions, to the wholeness and peace of consciousness.

16.5 Living as I
(Living in Presence: Aspect 5 of 7)

In looking for who we are, in trying to discover ourselves, our I, we often labor under the misconception that our I is like everything else in the world, that it can be objectified, looked at, studied and known. If even our consciousness can be known to some extent, then why not our I also? I must be something, so let me find that thing.

But that is just the point: our I is not a thing, not even an energy. Our I is always subjective, the knower and never the known. We cannot isolate or display our I, even to ourselves, for our I is the one who looks, the one who chooses to look, the seer and never the seen.

At first blush, it would seem that there is no problem here. I am the one who does what I do: end of story. If only that were the case. Nearly all of what I do just happens, I don't really do it at all. It is easiest to see this in my automatic associative thoughts and reactive emotions. Clearly I am not intentionally thinking those thoughts, nor intentionally feeling those emotions. They just happen on their own by habit, by conditioning, and by programmed responses to sensory inputs. These thoughts that run through my mind are not typically my doing.

Surprisingly, this habitual, conditioned, programmed way of living extends into our life far beyond just driving our automatic thoughts and emotions. Indeed, most of what we do and say just happens. We learn a task and then do it by program. We let our long-established personality patterns drive our interactions with people. Our intentions in what we do are weak, non-existent, or not active in the moment.

But there is another possibility, another way of living: living as I. We do not need look for our I, as if it were some sacred object hidden in the depths of our soul. We just need to be our I, to be ourselves, and not let our body, heart, and mind drift through life with little or no direction or choice on our part.

You cannot find yourself, but you can be yourself. This is not just a slogan or idea. It is an action, open to us to take. It is an act of will, in a moment, an act that can be renewed, moment-to-moment. The act is to be, to be the one who is you, the one who does what you do, who sees what you see, the one at your very core. Ordinarily, no one is at our core. We leave it empty, by default. But we can choose. We can choose to be, to be our core. We can invoke our will-to-be. It is both simple and profound, but its depth and significance can be hidden from us by that very simplicity. Just be. Just be yourself. Be the one who is reading these words.

Here's one specific approach to this. Inwardly say "I am." Get behind it and say it with meaning. Be the one who is saying it. Say it inwardly, silent and calm, but firm and full-throated, with the whole of yourself. Even though the word "I" is just a thought, you can use it as signal to call forth your actual I, to invest the thinking of the thought with the action of being here, being present, being the thinker, the one who you are, your I.

Try it for a minute or two when you can give it your full attention, perhaps a few times a day. To further strengthen the effort, you can simultaneously sense your body. So then you are the one who is thinking "I am" and sensing. Just be clear that the sensation in your body and thought "I" are not you, not your I. You are the one who is choosing, who is thinking that thought and sensing your body. Gradually this exercise can train you to be yourself, your I, train you to live as I.

This practice of thinking "I am" is only a temporary, training expedient. It is neither necessary nor desirable to go about your whole day thinking "I am." That would only get in the way of living your life, interposing the thought "I" between you, your actual I, and what you do or experience. To be your I, yourself, you do not need to think "I." You can be yourself, your I, without thinking it, because you are not a thought. We just occasionally use the thought "I am" to elicit our sense of I, to reinforce the experience of being I.

When our inner life is in disarray, difficult emotions rampant or persistently vociferous thoughts cascading, that situation can remind us to return to ourselves. If someone, our I, is at home in us, in our core, that brings order to our inner world. This simultaneously relieves the disarray and intensifies our experiencing. We live more. For that moment, we stop drifting. We live. In true presence, we continuously choose to be aware, here and now, to be the one who is aware, the one who is living our life.

For this week, work to increase your ability to live as yourself, as I.

16.6 Living in the Sacred Now
(Living in Presence: Aspect 6 of 7)

Our life consists of innumerable moments, one after another, from our birth to our death. As they occur, each moment is our now, our one and only moment: all prior moments are just traces, future moments just imagination. The only reality is now. Our entire life is only and always this present moment.

Yet we hold the present in such low esteem. We dream of a future that will somehow be better, or fear the future will be worse. We dwell on the past, happily reliving it in our memory or thankful that it's gone. The neutral moments we hardly remember at all. This past and future orientation eviscerates the present, leaving the now an empty and transitory shell. Even what we enjoy now gets tainted by our knowledge that it will pass. And when we are in the present, we allow our awareness to collapse into one small part of it, such as daydreams and thought streams.

To transform this situation, we first need respect, particularly self-respect. Respect for our self certainly includes respect for our life, which in turn means respect for this moment as the one and only place of our life. This is it. We can only live now. As such, in the same way that our life is sacred, this moment is sacred. Whatever our situation in life is, we honor and respect it.

That respect does not preclude working to change whatever we wish to change. But it does mean being here, living our life. If things are distasteful to us, or just sort of ordinary, we tend to ignore them, or inwardly escape them when cannot escape outwardly. This is killing time and killing our life. Not paying attention, not being here in this moment, kills it. It is in a sense suicidal, because we irretrievably lose that part of our life. It slips through our fingers without us even tasting it, half-lived or not lived at all.

At the end of our life, we may wish for more time. And we can have more time, by making more of now. Presence stretches and enlivens this moment, giving it more depth and breadth, expanding its boundaries. The more presence we have, the greater the now, and the greater our life, because our life is always and only now. So the biblical choice offered by God, of life or death, can be seen as the choice of living in presence or in a squandering absence. Can we choose to hold this moment now in such great esteem that we recognize it as sacred and live it fully?

Prayer, of course, brings this sacredness explicitly into focus. Personal, petitionary prayer, contemplative prayer, and communal worship all help reveal the fundamentally sacred quality of this world we inhabit, both inwardly in the deeper, spiritual realms and outwardly in this remarkable, simple, complex and beautiful nature. Life, so fragile individually and so robust collectively, warms us. Each living thing a bearer of complexity beyond imagining, imbued with the distilled and concentrated action of nature's laws, and reflecting, however attenuated, the grandeur and grace of the Creator. So even a simple walk in nature becomes a prayer carrying us into the sacred, opening our awareness to the now and our hearts to the qualities therein. And our respect for all of this grows apace.

"No prayer is complete without presence," according to Rumi. To which we can add: no presence is complete without a sense of the sacred. If our presence is full of awareness but lacks heart, we miss the deeper connections. It is just those connections, between our self and other people, between our self and other animals, between our self and nature, that draw us out of our shell, out of a present moment that we inhabit alone, and into the light of the Sacred Now.

For this week, open to that.

16.7 *Living as the Sacred*
(Living in Presence: Aspect 7 of 7)

Are we alone? We certainly seem to be, at least inwardly. Outwardly, of course, we are surrounded by people, nature, and human-made artifacts. We connect with people face-to-face and by all manner of electronic communications. We may feel lonely, but we are not alone.

Yet inwardly, here I am, quite alone. No one else is inside my mind and my perceptions. No one else directly knows my thoughts and feelings, my hopes and fears, my intentions, my joy, and my pain. At the center of all this is my I, uniquely me, distinct from all others. I am. Though we may be connected with other people, it is a connection of separate nodes of will and experience. Any unity among us is a unity of parts making up a whole, as in a family, a team, an organization, or a nation. If God does exist, then again our relationship is one of subject and monarch, creation and creator, or part and whole.

But the reality is very different. The inner separateness we experience is an illusion of our limited perceptions. A veil in the form of a mirror occupies our depth, so that when we look inward we only see ourselves, like Narcissus seeing his reflection on the water. Can we look beyond our reflection and see the water, see into its depths?

Just as we can extend our attention, our will, into our body, to inhabit the whole of it, so God's will is in the process of extending into this universe to inhabit it, and in particular, to us. In the same way that the various parts of our body, plus our mind and heart, can all be unified by the one will that is our I, so can the universe be unified by the one will that is Divine. But for that, we humans have a particular role to play: dropping our inner separation from the Higher, surrendering our independence so as to enter a more complete individuality attuned to the Sacred.

The analogy between how our will enters our body and the way the Divine Will enters the universe falls short at the crucial step. Every part of our body is necessarily subservient to the whole: there is no wiggle room or freedom on the level of the parts. But to spiritualize this universe, the Divine Will needs, among other things, to enter us. Sometime around our birth we do receive that universal will and its inherent freedom. That makes us free to do as we wish, to live and act however we choose, within the constraints of having a body and living in a society. From the viewpoint of the higher will, the freedom granted us is absolutely necessary if we are to serve the Sacred with intelligence, insight, and initiative. To take up our true destiny, our individually unique role, we need to reopen our connection, our unity with the Divine Will.

The question is: how? First and foremost, we need to be willing to become more than our small self, more than our ego, more even than our I. We need to be willing to hear and respond to the call of the Sacred. Perhaps we engage in the inner work of meditation, presence, and prayer. Presence shows us the one who is present, shows us our I. This I seems to be my source, the place where my attention, intentions, and choices come from, the center of my experiencing and doing.

But to live as the Sacred, requires that we look beyond our I, that we open the back door at the root of ourselves and let the higher flow through us, as us. It's not that I disappear, but rather that the boundaries of my I dissolve, so that I enter a greater whole, so that I am not just myself, but that the All is in me. With that comes Love.

This is the ultimate aim of inner work, but not an aim that we can put off indefinitely. In our deepest prayer work, perhaps toward the end of our meditation, we address this directly. We open that innermost door and make ourselves available again and again. We wish and hope and beg and cajole, asking the Sacred to be us. We go all in, bringing all we have, all we are: our body, heart, and mind, our attention and intention, our will. For those moments, we focus everything. We give ourselves totally, utterly, to this opening, to this asking, again and again.

With that inner opening may come a great rush of high energies. We do not confuse that bliss with the Divine Will. The opening to high energies can become an act of will on our part. Contact with the Divine Will, however, is not something that we can do ourselves: it is an action of that higher will. We can only make ourselves available and hope that our wish is fulfilled. To the extent that we have this wish and to the extent that we act to make ourselves inwardly available to the Sacred, the Sacred already lives in us.

For this week, make yourself available to the Higher.

17.0 Developing Will

Will is at the center of who we are. Will is who we are. I am my will. Both spiritual development and self-development, despite any distinction that might be made between them, entail the development of will. Indeed, everything we do is done by will. Usually we think of will in the active sense, of self-control, of working toward and attaining goals. But there are many natural modes of will: active, receptive, and a synergic combination of those two. And there are aberrant modes driven by self-centeredness, such as self-will and identification.

Because will enters all we do and because its many modes all spring from one will, developing our will provides benefits across all aspects of our life. So we can safely focus most of our will-development efforts on the active self-regulation and goal-setting aspects. Nevertheless, the receptive modes still need their own work, to refine and train our will in opening, equanimity, and letting go.

Will does not operate in a vacuum. To be effective, will must act through the medium of various inner energies, which provide an interface between our will and our functions, such as thoughts and physical actions. That is why our will can seem exhausted at times: the necessary energies get used up. For example, regardless of our best intentions, our ability to maintain a focus of attention is limited in time. Then we need a break to replenish the energies used in attention. But the more we exercise our attention, the greater our access to those energies, and the greater the duration of our powers of attention. And so it is also with other modes of will.

The fundamental way to develop our will involves setting a goal, working toward that goal, and monitoring our progress. Each of these steps requires skill and intelligence.

The first hurdle in setting a goal is to choose wisely. In most cases it should be unambiguous and attainable. Our goal needs to be defined clearly enough to enable us to monitor our progress and our attainment of it. Without that self-feedback we cannot truly exercise our will. Another major issue is the degree of difficulty. The goal or task should be something within our power and the right size. If the task is too big, we will fail. If too easy, it does not exercise our will. Our experimentation with this dimension of difficulty helps us understand our own capacities and limitations, helps us see why we need to develop our will. Also, the goal or task should not depend on any other person. We cannot control other people and making our will exercise contingent on their cooperation or action may well put us on a course toward failure.

We have the further choice of time scale. The goal or task may only be concerned with something immediate and brief: an ad hoc, short-term effort like maintaining self-awareness for the next ten steps while you are walking, maintaining your attention for the remainder of a lecture, or keeping your anger in check while dealing with a difficult person. We also work with goals and tasks lasting a day, a week, or some longer period. The biblical forty days is a typical time-period for more serious undertakings.

Finally, we set the goal and commit ourselves to carry it out. Without this step, it all remains too vague, leaving our will to languish in a kind of limbo. We often have thoughts such as "I'd like to that" or "I should do that." But random intentions do not rise to the level of organized, effective will. For that we need to choose consciously and then agree with ourselves that we will carry out what we have chosen to do. Without that inner assent, that agreement to commit ourselves to a particular course of action, our will is never set on the task. Since no decision has been made, we cannot count on fulfilling it.

After choosing and setting our task or goal, we work to achieve it. We do what we have set out to do. Otherwise we weaken ourselves. Self-confidence comes from knowing that you can set yourself to do something and then actually do it. Not following through with the will exercise, with working toward the goal or doing the task, breaks that self-confidence. So we do our very best to ensure that we do what we have set ourselves to do. Inevitably, though, failures come, usually by overextending ourselves, taking on something beyond our capacity. When that happens, we start over again with something easier, to rebuild our will and our confidence.

With a clear goal or task, we can bring self-awareness to bear on our activities related to it. We can monitor our progress and verify the accomplishment of the task. This self-feedback is an essential factor: it closes the loop and brings wholeness to our consciously-willed actions. This monitoring also allows us to adjust our efforts and get back on course when we stray. Implicit in self-monitoring is the more general self-awareness, which itself organizes our energies and rectifies our actions. Seeing changes what we see. When we see ourselves, we change ourselves for the better, even though the seeing may be uncomfortable.

Sometimes we may choose a goal that is not readily attainable, verifiable, or even clearly defined, but simply establishes a direction of effort, for example, when we commit ourselves to the spiritual path. We may couch that goal in terms of enlightenment or sainthood or stable presence or non-stop devotion. Despite the ambiguity, we know whether and to what degree we engage in the necessary efforts.

At other times, rather than choosing a goal, we may find that a goal has chosen us. We may come to realize that some inner imperative, perhaps coupled with our life circumstances, has fully committed us to a course of action. The decision was a gradual one, coming in increments. Yet here we are, pursuing that direction. Again, our will determines how far and how well we travel that road.

In the coming weeks, if you so choose, we will work on developing our will by exercising it in various ways related to our spiritual path:

1. Habits: Self-Regulation
2. Keeping Our Word
3. Responsibility
4. Attention
5. Frequency of Presence
6. Breadth of Presence
7. Duration of Presence
8. Depth of Meditation and Prayer
9. Equanimity and Non-Judging
10. Purifying Will

For this week, please examine your own will, its strengths and qualities, as well as its shortcomings. Notice the limits of your ability to do what you wish to do.

17.1 Habits: Self-Regulation
(Developing Will: Aspect 1 of 10)

As creatures of habit, we know the profound impact on our lives of our habitual patterns of action, thought, and emotion. To change our life, to evolve, we need, among other things, to change our habits, which is a matter of will. Habits run on momentum and thus require little or no active will. Our will is already embodied in the habit. Indeed, a habit is a kernel of will fixed on a particular pattern. And just as force is necessary to change momentum, will is required to create, change, moderate, or stop a habit.

But before we attempt to change anything, there is the question: which habits are good and which are bad? From the many possible perspectives on that value judgment, we adopt the point of view of spiritual development: which habits hinder our inner work and which promote it? Other viewpoints can be subsumed into that one. For example, the health perspective matters, because we need our body as healthy as possible for as long as possible, to give us the energy and time to develop our soul.

Yet we need to take the question a step further. How do we judge whether a particular habit helps or hinders our spiritual development? From the deeper points of view, like whether the habit strengthens our self-centered egoism, it is not so easy to judge, because ego itself infiltrates that judgment. Instead, we judge the question from more objective grounds. For example, if we meditate regularly, we may be able to discern how certain habits impact our meditation. If we ate or drank alcohol excessively the night before, how does that affect our meditation session the next morning? If we practice presence persistently, how do our various habits affect that? How does the habit of meditating in the morning affect our ability to be present during the day? Are we able to be present while habitually watching television? How does the habit of arguing affect our presence? What about procrastination, our favorite daydreams, physical exercise, habitual postures, our perennial worries and fears? How do all these habit patterns affect our inner work?

By asking ourselves these and many other such questions and actually observing ourselves to gather real data for the answers, we acquire a more accurate understanding of what helps or hinders our spiritual life. Then we are ready to address the challenge of creating, strengthening, changing, moderating, or stopping particular habits, the challenge of regulating our behavior to maximize our spiritual development. But we enter that challenge with a particular value judgment to back us up, a value judgment based on eternal values.

That value judgment places our efforts within the context of our broader goals and wishes and helps us shift out of the grip of destructive habits and into constructive ones. For our spiritual development we want to increase or create habits such as meditating daily, regular prayer, work at presence and kindness, and so on. We want to decrease habits like smoking, excessive alcohol or eating, passive TV watching without presence, racially or otherwise prejudiced thoughts, and so on. These lists are meant to be indicative. We each need to observe and judge for ourselves what is useful and what is harmful in our own life.

And then we act. One key to that action is to work on changing only one habit at a time: being overambitious usually ends in failure. Also, if the habit is a very strong one, we may need help or a strategy: better to start with habits that are easier to change and build up strength of will. For stronger habits, we need to judge whether the coalition of the willing to change is stronger than the coalition of the entrenched, because change of such habits does not come easily. We can expect resistance, persuasive resistance, that little convincing voice of temptation: just this one time or why bother changing this habit, or it's too hard, or I have to have it. But if we can just be, allowing this resistance to be there and pass through us without our acting on it, we have a chance. After all, these are just thoughts and emotions and physical urges. They are not us and they do not speak for us, unless we let them. We do not need to fight them or stop them. We just notice them come and go, while we continue to be, continue on the course we have chosen. And after a time, it gets easier. The habit has changed.

Another aspect of dealing with strong, destructive habits involves the strategy of minimizing resistance. If we raise a strong active intention to change an entrenched habit, that very act raises a strong resistance to that change. Instead we look for a third force, a quieter intention that accomplishes the result, perhaps gradually, but effectively. For example, if we are in the habit of overeating and find that it detracts from our inner work, we might be tempted to go on a diet. But diets notoriously fail in the long run.[7] We might stay on the diet for a while, but eventually, in most cases, we lose that battle. Now if instead of adopting a strictly-defined and overarching new regime for eating, we only try to effect small changes, we may be more successful. Those small changes can slip by our body's resistance to dieting. We might try limiting or stopping eating between meals, we might try reducing our carb intake, limiting or giving up sodas or desserts, being fully aware of the taste and texture of each bite of food, and so on. But we only add one of these at a time, over time, flexibly and not stringently, and let them accumulate gradually, until they build up to eliminate our habit of overeating. In this way we avoid the diet-and-binge cycle.

With a habit like excessive alcohol drinking, we need to assess the strength of its hold on us. If very strong, we may need to go cold turkey, quit drinking completely and permanently, and join Alcoholics Anonymous. If less severe, we can adopt simpler controls. For example, never drinking on two successive days and never drinking more than one normal-sized drink on any given day. For tobacco use, we do whatever we can to stop completely, a difficult proposition given the highly addictive nature of tobacco. We might watch anti-smoking videos to engage our mind and emotions more fully. We might attend a stop-smoking class, look into the pros and cons of using nicotine patches or lozenges or electronic cigarettes, exercise more, chew gum, and immediately start over if we fail — in short, whatever it takes. Tobacco harms our energies and our body and hinders our soul development. Similarly, the use

7   Baumeister, Roy F. and Tierney, John; *Willpower: Rediscovering the Greatest Human Strength*; Penguin Press, 2011. An excellent and practical overview of psychological research into the type of will needed for self-regulation, for control of habits.

of marijuana and other recreational drugs needs to be stopped completely, for they burn up the very energies we need for our inner work and for our soul.

What about the habit of gossiping, when it involves negative judgments about people? How does that affect your inner work, your conscience, your relationships?

For this week, please examine your habits. Work to create a good one or eliminate a bad one.

17.2 Keeping our Word
(Developing Will: Aspect 2 of 10)

When we say we'll do something, be it a commitment to another person or a promise to ourselves, the issue sometimes arises of whether we will follow through or not. When we do not, when we break our word, that unfulfilled commitment clouds our conscience and weighs us down in subtle but important ways. Breaking our promises to others damages trust and weakens our relationships, further isolating us on the island of self-centered egoism. Breaking a promise, whether to ourselves or to others, damages our trust and confidence in ourselves and weakens our will. We cannot escape by refusing to give our word or not making promises, because in many cases that would mean shirking our responsibilities, which has an effect on us and our relationships as deeply problematic as breaking our word.

The old saying that you are only as good as your word has several layers of meaning. The usual view concerns how others see you, the extent to which they trust you, and how they rate your credibility and integrity. But of equal importance, particularly for our spiritual development, is the effect that keeping or breaking our word has on us inwardly.

Integrity not only means incorruptibility, it also means wholeness. Why should those two meanings coexist? When we break our word, we are not whole, our will splinters, one part saying yes to the commitment and another part saying no. To be whole, we need to gather our will into one coherent unity, one that persists through time, so that others can trust us and we can trust ourselves. That gathering process includes keeping our word, every time, forgoing the temptation to let it slide.

If, as will happen, circumstances prevent us from keeping our word, then we do what we can to make amends, to make it right. We do not just turn our back, because the unfulfilled commitment that we leave behind trails us, shadows us, and interferes with us by scrambling our wholeness. The insidious baggage of broken promises haunts us. Even in the depths of meditation or prayer, it blocks our access to the spirit. To come before our Maker, even to aspire to open to the Sacred, we absolutely need wholeness and a clear conscience, for conscience is the channel of will through which that connection flows. Here we have the wonder of the Christian doctrine of forgiveness of sins and the Jewish practice of sincere repentance. These help clear the weeds from our conscience, opening our channel to the Sacred. The more certain we are to keep our word, the more transparent we are to the Sacred.

So it comes down to a question for each us: how important to us is our integrity? Not as some abstract concept of the noble life, but as a defining quality of who we are. If our word has no weight, if we lack integrity, what are we? Can we respect ourselves if we do not keep our word? Self-respect shapes us. Without it we flail. With it, we can respect others. With integrity, we can feel and be worthy of respect.

For this week, notice what you do after you make a promise or agree to do something.

17.3 Responsibility
(Developing Will: Aspect 3 of 10)

The mere fact of living imposes an extensive array of obligations: to ourselves, family, profession, society, nation, and planet. To the extent that we recognize and accept these obligations as obligations, we become responsible. To be responsible is thus primarily a matter of will: the will to understand our obligations and all of their layers, nuances, and ramifications, the will to accept our obligations, and the will to act on them consistently. The transition from adolescence to maturity is just this: becoming responsible. These ongoing and ever-changing tasks of understanding, accepting, and acting also require the will continually to adjust and improve our response to obligations.

The inner faculty that enables us to recognize obligations and prompts us to act on them, we call conscience, a high-resolution instrument of perception. Conscience bubbles up, distilled from vast subconscious processes, and yields an intuition of rightness. If we listen to it and live by it, conscience shows us how to be responsible.

The idea of responsibility carries the baggage of drudgery and boredom. We do it, whatever it is, because we must, because we expect it of ourselves. But even the drudgery of acting responsibly in the small, menial tasks of life, has its satisfactions. Indeed, taking out the garbage may yield truer satisfaction than eating cake. Doing the necessary aligns us with reality. And in that alignment there is rightness and wholeness.

We have spiritual obligations, which are not as easily recognizable as our external obligations. The Sacred needs us, needs our inner work of prayer and presence, needs our creative actions, and needs our talents and our excellence approaching perfection. The Sacred needs the energies we transform through our inner work, the order we bring into the world by responsible action, the evolutionary and revolutionary changes we initiate, and the love we give. To fulfill our individual destiny, our personal potential, is to deserve the gift of free will and justify the hope of our birthright, our inherent connection to the Source of All. The slogan "be all you can be" and the notion of becoming yourself speak to this process of fulfillment. This responsibility spreads across our entire life: to discover, in action and in being, the route toward bringing to life the best of our own unique possibilities. We have many assets and, yes, many constraints and limitations. But these serve as our framework, our opportunity and our challenge for a life of fulfillment. Who am I? Who are you? We answer by doing.

Creative action and spiritual inner work yield deep satisfaction, even pleasure and joy. The work of presence, for example, becomes much more than something we feel we should do, something we think is right for us, something we struggle to remember and do, something that evaporates as soon as an even mildly interesting perception draws our attention. Presence makes life vivid. It brings its own inherent pleasure and joy. The responsibility to practice presence certainly transcends drudgery. And the deeper joys of prayer and opening to the sacred have transcendence built right into them.

Yet we do not pursue responsible actions for the pleasures they bring, for that would quickly turn into its opposite, irresponsibility. We act responsibly because it is the right thing to do. We act responsibly because it aligns us with and prepares us for the Sacred. Nevertheless, satisfaction, joy, and pleasure arise as natural and welcome byproducts of responsible action.

So the inner work of responsibility is to act in accord with conscience, despite the difficulties, despite our impulses to avoid, shirk, and procrastinate. We do this again and again and again, until we have confidence in ourselves, the confidence that we will act like a mensch in every situation.

For this week, notice your temptations to avoid doing the responsible thing.

17.4 Attention
(Developing Will: Aspect 4 of 10)

Directed, sustained attention is the most obvious and immediate power of the will. To learn about will, we can start with studying our own attention. To develop our will, we can start with developing our attention. Vital to most productive activities, attention occupies the center of perception. Without attention, sensory impressions do not impress, they just fly past us. With attention, we can notice what we see and hear and feel and think, so that sensory inputs can become perceptions, can register with us. We can only learn through perceptions. We can only live through perceptions. Attention means we are present to see what we see and hear what we hear, present to live our life.

To study attention we observe its many modes, its absence or presence, and its source, hidden in the recesses of our soul. Active attention focuses our senses, as exemplified by the focus of our eyes when we look at something. But just as our eyes can see without our really seeing, there is more to attention than just focusing our senses. Attention, as an act of will, brings us onto the scene, so that we are there to see what our eyes see. In that way, attention connects us, our I, with our senses to create perceptions.

One very instructive practice is to look for the source of your attention. To look for the source of attention is to look for yourself, for your will. Because we are immaterial, it is not so easy to recognize the source of our attention. It means learning to recognize will, which is neither material nor even an inner energy. It is the user of inner energies, for example, when our attention directs our senses and consciousness. Thus attention is a very direct expression of our I, of who we really are. So one aspect of finding yourself is to find the source of your attention.

The primary way to develop attention is simply to practice paying attention, putting our attention on something and keeping it there. Attention tends to wander, distracted by passing thoughts and other random sensory events. In our ordinary life we can practice by sustaining our attention on tasks we do, on the people we interact with, on what we hear, on what we read, on a subject we want to ponder, and so on. In that way, we couple our outer life and our inner work, we make life into our spiritual path. Such practice strengthens our attention and trains us to direct and hold it.

We can also train our attention for subtlety by many of the methods of inner work. Most forms of meditation require directed attention for at least part of each sitting, usually at the beginning to help our minds settle and focus. Prayer without attention rambles and dissipates ineffectively. With attention, prayer connects.

The various levels of inner energies require more and more refined qualities of attention to access and make use of them. On that hierarchy, we begin with attention to our body, to the sensations of our body, to the sensitive energy in our body. This is fundamental and necessary inner work, throughout the path, to establish our soul on a firm foundation. We put and hold our attention on part of our body, gradually building up to embrace and sustain our whole body sensation in our attention.

To practice attention to our mind, we can think our thoughts intentionally, rather than allowing our thoughts to think us haphazardly. With attention to our mind, we can also open to the silent, cognitive space beneath thoughts, so that we can be here, mentally alert, but without necessarily having any thoughts. Those that do come we allow to pass through unhindered, while we stay here in the deep, cognizant pool of our mind.

To practice attention to our emotions, we place our attention in the area of our chest and solar plexus, though not focusing on any particular inner organs. We notice any feelings there, whether physical sensations or emotions. And we just stay with it. Being here in our center of emotion, even without any particular emotion arising, we are ready to feel appropriately to any situation, ready to respond and live with heart. Furthermore, attention to our center of emotion can brings us to peace, to the high emotion of equanimity, and to love.

The attention that embraces all three, body, mind, and heart, is the essential factor of presence, bringing all of our parts within the purview of our attention, our I.

As the core tool of all spiritual practice, we find many other ways to put attention to use. A primary one concerns energy breathing, attention to the inner energies carried by the air. Using attention and intention, we draw those energies into us to help build our body awareness, our sensation, to help nourish our soul.

For this week, notice your attention, seek its source, and practice sustaining and refining your attention.

17.5 Frequency of Presence
(Developing Will: Aspect 5 of 10)

Before we can approach the question of how often we are present, we need to look at what it means to be present. It does not, for example, mean saying to oneself "I am present," because those words may or may not be true. It does not mean remembering our intention to be present, because we can remember that intention without actually rising to presence and because we can be present without remembering a previously-formed intention to be present.

The core of presence is our I. Are we here to experience what we are experiencing? Are we here doing what we are doing? Ancillary to and supportive of that core presence, we may have various qualities, quantities, patterns and structures of inner energies within our being at any given moment. For example, the sensitive energy in our body can support presence: the stronger and more complete the sensation, the firmer the foundation for presence. But the energy issues have greater bearing on the duration and breadth of presence than on its frequency, which we discuss here. So we will defer the energy questions until we address duration and breadth.

Presence essentially means I am here, now. It is an experience of coming to and being here, of suddenly finding oneself here, alive, of being complete, whole, and grounded. It need not be dramatic. Indeed, our aim in part is to make presence un-dramatic, make it more normal, more usual for us.

To be present is an act of will. The actuality of "I am here, now" manifests our will-to-be. And one major issue for our spiritual path is how often we act on that will-to-be, how often we return to presence during each day.

One approach to training in presence involves setting a daily goal of a certain number of instances of presence and then counting how many times we come to presence that day. This can be partly observational: incrementing the count whenever we notice that we have somehow, without premeditation, risen to presence. The other part is intentional: when we remember our task of presence and our goal, we immediately take that opportunity to return to presence and then increment the count. Note that the count is just a measure, important for the goal-oriented specificity and commitment it enables, but not as important as the act of coming to presence which it records. We begin modestly, setting as our goal an easily achievable number of times in the day that we will be present. Gradually, over a period of weeks or months, we increase the daily number and fill our waking hours with more instances of presence. The counting gives us a way to quantify our inner work, engage our will in fulfilling our daily goal, and make our spiritual path a little more concrete.

One hindrance arises when we happen to remember

our intention at moments that we deem so inconvenient that we ignore the impulse to presence and squander that particular opportunity. This might happen when we are relaxing or being entertained and do not want to disturb our enjoyment. But presence does not decrease our joy; it enhances joy by bringing to the scene the only one who could actually enjoy the experience. It might also happen when we are so fully engaged in what we are doing, for example in a conversation, that it seems we do not have enough spare attention to devote to presence. But while certain types of inner work, particularly those to do with energies, do require spare attention, the core of presence does not, because the I at the center of presence is the local source of our attention. So being present in demanding situations strengthens our attention rather than taking part of it away from our current involvement. In presence we get fully behind what we are doing. The one exception is the caveat that certain life-critical activities, like driving, are not the best place to experiment with or practice inner work.

In the grip of some destructive emotion like anger, if we remember our intention to be present, that intention may be summarily rejected. We are lost in the emotion, our I supplanted by it and powerless before it. Such emotions do not want to be seen, because they weaken in the light of awareness. The I at the core of presence not only acts, but sees. It is the one in us who does see. So naturally anger, jealousy, self-pity and the like do not welcome presence. In such situations of full-bloom identification with an emotion, we just wait for the storm to pass and then get back to the work of presence.

The act of coming to presence is deceptively simple. Hidden behind its simplicity is not complexity but rather profundity. We arrive here in this moment and it seems like no big deal. It's just natural, just us, awake and alive. When we are present and complete in that way, we cannot easily recall or imagine our usual state of non-presence. Similarly, when we are not present, we cannot easily recall or imagine actually being present. The two ways of living do not intermingle. Whichever one we are in seems to be our normal state and seems fine.

This masks the profound difference between presence and non-presence. If I am here, I am truly alive. If I am not here, I am only half-alive. If I am here, I have an opportunity to open yet more deeply and complete the circuit of the Sacred, which can only flow through our I. Our will gets involved, because our will is our I. So a moment of presence is a moment of will, a moment where you can truly say and feel "I am here." Non-presence means an absence of will or a fragmented will.

For this week, practice coming into presence more often. Set and monitor a daily goal of a certain number of instances of presence.

17.6 Breadth of Presence
(Developing Will: Aspect 6 of 10)

While we do find great value in training our attention to focus tightly on one small aspect of experience, we also benefit from a broad reach of attention, from mindfulness of all that our senses bring us. Clearly, presence means being in contact with the full range of our immediate experience, both inner and outer. This broad, open, non-selective, non-filtering mode of awareness can be called bare attention or simply mindfulness. As with any mode of presence, breadth of presence, or mindfulness, is an act of will. We choose to be here in this moment, in touch with all that it offers. Our will directs our sensitive energies into all our senses and awakens us to the conscious energy, which serves as the cognizant umbrella tying it all together.

To get a taste of this, open your visual awareness to include not just the center of focus but also the peripheral, so that you see all that your eyes bring you, your entire visual field. Try the same with your hearing by opening to all the sounds coming into your ears, so that you are listening to the whole auditory field. With your body sense, open to awareness of your entire body at once. With your mind sense, notice the thoughts and fragments of thoughts streaming through your mind. In all these cases, our sensory awareness grows inclusive and broad.

Behind that, the cognizant stillness of consciousness, that boundless, sentient field, provides the versatile, pre-experiential substance that becomes awareness of this and that. Consciousness is the ever-present, all-pervasive, timeless, blank screen on which the ever-changing impressions of our senses appear. We can even become conscious of consciousness itself by opening into it, by recognizing it for what it is, the substrate of experience. One practice that takes us toward consciousness consists of becoming aware of the space around us. Like opening to our entire visual field, opening to the space that surrounds us and permeates us brings a sense of wholeness and even peace. Space just is. Likewise, consciousness just is. Consciousness pervades space and us.

Something in us never changes. That something is consciousness. Although the degree of our contact with it does vary, consciousness is always with us as the essence of experience. We have the same consciousness now that we did as a child. All the intervening events of our life have passed through this consciousness, yet here we are in the same consciousness.

To practice breadth of presence, we cast a wide net across all our senses, inner and outer. We enter that broad river of experience. We are here in contact with all of it, without being taken by any piece of it, without losing our self in attraction to or repulsion from any particular arising element of what we see or hear, think or feel. Not to be taken by anything in our experience requires an ongoing act of will, the will to be and to stay here and now, the will to be and to stay fully aware.

Though we cast a wide net of awareness, we practice breadth of presence, not breadth of awareness. The difference is that we are not only broadly aware, we also here and present in the center of that broad awareness. We do not lose our I in the sea of our senses. First and foremost we remain ourselves; we remain the one who is experiencing all this, the one who is doing what we do. We abide in the whole of our immediate awareness. Will transcends time and space, and so do we, our I. We can inhabit the whole of our experience at once by practicing breadth of presence.

For this week, please explore broadening your awareness and your presence within it.

17.7 Duration of Presence
(Developing Will: Aspect 7 of 10)

Now we turn to the question of the stability of our presence: how long does any given episode of presence last? In actual practice, we find that presence is short-lived — very short. Some thought, in the endless stream passing through our mind, comes along and grabs us and we lose ourselves on a mental tangent, our presence dissolved. Or something we see or hear takes us. The variety of ways we lose presence knows no bounds. What to do? Stability requires three legs and more.

We begin with body awareness. Sensing our body helps enormously in stabilizing our presence in the here and now. Our body is always here and now. If we are aware of our body, intentionally, so that there is an in-this-moment relationship between our I and our body, then we have a place to stand, a place to take a stand against the dissipation of time. Sensing creates the fundamental foundation for presence, particularly when we sense and inhabit our whole body. When we lose presence, sensing calls us back. Built-up sensitive energy in our body tends to persist, even during our absence, and awakens us much sooner than would otherwise be the case.

To body awareness, we add emotion awareness. We simply notice our emotions as emotions. We put attention into our front upper torso, our area of emotion. Even if we are not experiencing any particular emotion, having some presence in our area of emotion brings a feeling tone to our life, adding warmth and stability to our presence.

We also add mental awareness, seeing the thoughts and images passing through our mind, seeing them as thoughts, without being caught by any of them. By inhabiting our mind it becomes our own. Rather than being subject to the vagaries of our mind and its thought-stream, we intentionally step into it and own it. This does not mean stopping our thoughts or directing them all, but it does mean contact with a mental cognizance that both includes and transcends our thoughts.

Being aware of our body, emotion, and mind, and inhabiting all three creates a complete and stable presence. The awareness, the sensitive energy in body, emotion, and mind, makes the stable stool of presence. The inhabiting aspect is our I sitting on that stool. Presence is more than awareness: it requires our I, the one who is aware, the one who perceives, the one who directs our awareness.

Beyond those enabling factors of stable presence, we need to train ourselves to sustain presence, to sustain the will-to-be. We can just relax into the present, into bare attention, but we will find that it dissipates all too soon. So we raise and act on our intention to stay present. Short-term goals can be help. Say you are out for a walk or a jog or a bike ride and you decide to be and stay present. You might choose a landmark that you will soon pass, like a tree or a pole, an intersection or a building. And then you work to maintain your presence until you reach that landmark. Once you reach it, you immediately select the next suitable landmark and stay present until you get there. This type of practice has the great advantage of being concrete and immediate. Other examples of short-term goals of presence include: until the next commercial break in the TV show, until you reach the end of the line you are waiting in, until you finish brushing your teeth, until you finish doing the dishes, until the end of the conversation or the meeting. We use our creativity and intelligence to find such ever-present opportunities and adapt them to support our inner work.

Presence leads to more presence, stability to stability. One result of a period of more intensive, steadier work at presence is that presence becomes more natural, more normal for us. Our body and our being remind us to stay in contact with the here and now. Of course, formal, sitting meditation periods do help create the foundation for presence. Nevertheless, the practice of presence amid the endless demands and distractions of our normal daily activities requires continuing acts of will, the will-to-be, that strengthen us in the fire of life.

For this week, whenever you awaken to the possibility of being present, practice staying present for a longer time.

17.8 Delving Deep
(Developing Will: Aspect 8 of 10)

Developing will not only entails strengthening and unifying our will, but also refining it. One important aspect of refining will consists of extending our abilities to perceive higher energies and higher worlds. The deepening of our inner life both depends on and results in raising the quality and refinement of our perceptions. It is our will that can reach toward the higher realms, that can look to notice what we have never noticed, that can stretch our understanding beyond mental, emotional, or instinctive knowing. We seek the Sacred and seek to serve the Sacred. That seeking is an act of will. The understanding of how to seek well is a developing property of will.

Consciousness is the fundamental background of awareness. All our thoughts, emotions, and other sensory impressions are displayed on the screen of consciousness. To move into direct experience of the cognizant stillness of the conscious energy takes a two-fold act of will. This act revolves around relaxing and letting go, around allowing ourselves to be drawn deeper and letting go of what holds us back. The letting go part we will address in the next aspect of Developing Will. For now, we look into what it means to allow ourselves to be drawn deeper.

We are drawn by what attracts us. Certainly we know this externally: when we see something or someone who attracts us, our attention and energies, if not our actions, flow in that direction. But there is also an inner attractor, the source of true satisfaction. We experience this in our need for meaning, in our desire to act creatively and to serve, in our conscience which prompts us to do the right thing, in our desire to love. All of these manifest the inner attractor, the Sacred, albeit in a veiled, indirect manner.

To open more directly to that inner attractor, we begin by relaxing, by allowing the fog of inner noise to settle and subside. And then, on its own, the conscious energy coalesces in us, and we come to recognize and rest in consciousness, to rest in just seeing, to rest in spacious, pre-sensory awareness itself. Thus the first major step into higher energies, into our inward depths, is the step into consciousness.

We can learn to make that step in formal, sitting meditation, although the experience of consciousness, once we understand and can replicate it, certainly is not limited to meditation sessions. So in our sitting, we relax into silence, into non-doing. We do nothing except see whatever arises in us. We neither try to stop our thoughts nor get lost in them. We just are. And in that just being, we begin to recognize our pure awareness, our pure consciousness itself, the cognizant screen on which our senses, thoughts, and emotions are displayed. We soak in this pre-sensory consciousness, in its stillness, in this spacious sea of awareness. Thoughts may come and go, while we stay in this vast, non-specific awareness. The thoughts pass like small clouds floating through the big sky of consciousness.

As remarkable as the discovery of consciousness is, it

is not the end of the story, not even close. There are two deeper domains beyond consciousness. And the true home of the Sacred inner attractor lies beyond even those. Our inner work sensitizes us to its call, so that the inner attractor becomes for us a beacon guiding our way. For that we add to our meditation practice the work of contemplative, silent prayer, the work of opening to and reaching for what is beyond consciousness. This takes will in the form of sincerity, humility, dedication, and persistent exploration to find the way in. If consciousness surrounds us in every direction, what is the direction beyond consciousness? In asking that question, in that silent prayer, we reach inward, toward and beyond our own root, toward the source of our will. At first we seek blindly. Later we begin to touch it. Then more and more, we find our way into the realm of bliss, the creative light of the Sacred. We learn to enter there at will. After repeated experiences of this, as our understanding grows and our will becomes more refined, we move beyond self-indulgent enjoyment of the bliss and see it as profound nourishment for our soul, a flow of a very high energy. That is the first domain beyond consciousness.

Again, though, the realm of bliss and Sacred light is not the end of the story. We delve deeper still. Only the next domain does not open to us as our own act of will, but only as an act of the higher will. Our role is one of opening, of allowing ourselves to be drawn toward that Sacred inner attractor, of true humility and shedding our self-centeredness, of recognizing that our very core is empty and can only be filled by our true connection with the Divine. Prayer that points toward the highest, such as repeating one of the names of God, can support that disposition. We orient and empty ourselves toward the Highest.

We start where we are and reach deeper. Each level requires a different type of inner work. Along the way, our will grows in understanding, refinement, perception and capability. For this week, delve deeper.

17.9 Equanimity and Non-Judging
(Developing Will: Aspect 9 of 10)

A deep pool of peace lies within us, always there, awaiting our arrival. In quiet meditation, we can practice relaxing into the peace of consciousness, into the spacious stillness that allows everything to be as it is. Soaking in that pool, we learn the feel of it, we learn its eternal, unchanging nature, and most importantly we learn our way back to it, even in the midst of life. The key part of that way is letting go, accepting ourselves, our situation, and the world as they are, not resisting. This is equanimity. This is knowing that in the midst of busyness or stress, even in the midst of pain or grief, the loving, accepting, place of peace is with us, in us. In letting go of our inner resistance, our preferences of one thing against another, we become that peace, that acceptance, that love.

One common objection to the very notion of equanimity is that the world and each of us needs work to be set right, to evolve. If we just accept things as they are neither the world nor we will change or improve. True indeed, as far as that goes. But equanimity does not mean indifference or inaction. In equanimity we care, very much, and we act appropriately to the situation. But we are not identified with ourselves or the situation. We are inwardly free. And with that freedom, our actions can be more effective, more responsive, more responsible. Equanimity is not hampered by destructive emotions. Anger, fear, frustration, envy or any of the rest may be there in us, yet we are free, we do not lose contact with that place of peace, that attitude that embraces the whole catastrophe. Thus equanimity removes the distractions of identification and allows us both to be and to act with vigor.

This involves letting go of our identifications, dissolving the belief that our thoughts, emotions, and sensory impressions are us. When something from the sensory realm grabs us inwardly so that we identify with it, we lose our place in consciousness and fall into our senses. Our thoughts seem to represent us, to be us. Our emotions, like envy, anger and frustration, seem to represent us, to be us. Rather than make a futile attempt to stop or reform our thoughts or emotions, non-identification means letting them be, letting it all be as it is, but not being caught up in the various stories, dramas, and events, in the weather and the traffic. We let go of being caught, we let go of identifying, and we abide in consciousness, in peace and in equanimity. Of course, we can be active as necessary and still stay conscious.

When we dislike some aspect of ourselves, we judge ourselves, often harshly. Such self-criticism splits our inner world, dividing us against ourselves. These inner battles rarely lead to constructive outcomes, but do waste our energy and cause us great emotional angst. The alternative approach of accepting ourselves as we are does not mean agreeing to indulge our shortcomings. Non-judging or accepting ourselves means creating a big tent in us, big enough for all our features to feel at home, big enough for our inner contradictions to coexist without feeling threatened.

This big tent of acceptance, also known as love, allows something deeper to move to the fore, our true I. This is the path to becoming ourselves, whole and complete. In that wholeness and acceptance, our contradictions gradually resolve in supporting our I, our conscience, and finding our true path and calling. Indeed, seeing our many contradictions shows us their limitations. The big tent of acceptance integrates our fractured nature and raises our level of being.

We not only judge ourselves, we also apply harsh judgments against others. Non-judging others means mean adopting an attitude of letting them be as they are. We see a person. Our antipathies, fault-finding, dislikes, envy, jealousy, and disdain raise their endless objections, criticisms, and dismissals toward that person. We cannot readily stop all such inner impulses, so non-judging does not mean getting rid of all that. It does mean coming into a place of equanimity and acceptance of the other person, even in the face of all that critical chatter going on within us. It means not believing or following those calls to judgment. We see the critical impulses arising in our mind and heart and we let them pass. We remain in equanimity, just being there and allowing the other person to just be. We respect that person and their life path enough to let them be. We spread the big tent of acceptance beyond our own inner world to include the whole world.

Non-judging, accepting, non-identifying, letting go — these are all acts of will, sometimes difficult and challenging acts of will with many opposing impulses tugging us in other directions. Whenever we are pulled toward identifying or judging, the choice point arises for us to let it go and just be. And the result of making that choice is equanimity, which in turn makes the next choice a little easier, until we find ourselves living more and more in inner peace. Equanimity can become our set point, our new normal, one aspect of our transformation realized.

For this week, please practice non-judging, acceptance, and equanimity.

17.10 Purifying Will
(Developing Will: Aspect 10 of 10)

Movement along the spiritual path, and especially into its deeper reaches, requires purity of will. Intuitively we know that purity means freedom from egoism, feeling that we are neither more nor less important than others, neither more nor less special, that we are unique as all are unique and ordinary in that uniqueness. The less we feel and think and act from self-centeredness, and the less we believe in our own separateness, the greater the purity of our will. The motivations of the pure-hearted come from a concern with doing the right thing, the responsible, kind, and creative thing, rather than the self-serving action. Because the many-headed hydra of egoism insinuates itself in subtle ways throughout our inner world, we employ both direct and indirect means of purifying ourselves. It is a slow process, but persistence pays.

The indirect methods include discipline, kindness, and conscience. The tricky aspect is that our ego attempts to suborn all our motivations and actions. Ego says: "I will do X as a discipline because disciplined people are better than other people." Ego takes a similar tack with kindness: "See how wonderful I am because I'm so kind." Nevertheless, we need not concern ourselves with combating our egoism or even with seeing it, because ego is very slippery and it uses our full intelligence. Direct combat in that arena typically results in strengthening our ego, because it always switches to the winning side, or rather because it occupies both sides from the very start. So instead of direct combat, we just be ourselves, refrain from worrying about ego, and yet pursue the methods that will free us of it.

The beauty of these indirect methods of discipline, kindness, and conscience is that our ego tires of them and rebels, despite its occasional foray into being the "disciplined one" or the "kind one." Discipline and kindness go against the inherent nature of egoism, which puts itself and its desires first. Discipline toward ourselves and kindness toward others weaken our ego, as does following the promptings of conscience.

By discipline we mean bringing order into our life, but without the taint of self-rejection and self-criticism, which often belong to egoism. "I should be better than that" is a common refrain of self-centeredness. Instead, we accept ourselves as we are, while imposing some self-discipline. The specifics of what disciplines to take on is a very individual choice for each of us to make. Generally, they might involve taming our physical appetites and indulgences, engaging in some regular and useful activity, creating order, carrying out our responsibilities well and fully, and so on. We choose disciplines that are neither so hard that we will fail to follow through, nor so easy as to be meaningless. True confidence comes from trusting ourselves to be able to do what we choose to do. Persistent discipline instills that trust, while developing and purifying our will.

Kindness matters. We aim to treat others with kindness and its close ally respect, always and without exception. At a minimal level, kindness means non-harming and following the Golden Rule of doing to others as you would have them do to you, and not doing to others what you would not want them do to you. Beyond that minimum, we pursue positive acts of kindness, for example, civility, courtesy, and generosity. Because ego *usually* puts itself above all others, the practice of kindness forms an effective part of our purification. The *usually* here refers to those forms of egoism that turn against the self and consider themselves lower than all others. In such cases, self-acceptance is a necessary kindness toward oneself, while also practicing kindness toward others.

Conscience gives us our intuitive sense of right and wrong and is often at odds with our self-centered, egoistic impulses. To the bit of truth that conscience sets before us, ego responds by ignoring it, by sweeping it under the rug of inattention. The result is to weaken our contact with conscience, leaving us at the mercy of our ego. In the way of conscience, we pay careful attention to its promptings and act in accord, doing the right, kind, and responsible thing. The way of conscience is our path to wisdom.

Although ego can and does strike at any time, certain practices tend to raise us directly, though temporarily, out of its reach, namely presence and prayer. In presence, in a state of being conscious and here, ego finds no purchase, no hold. We just are. There is nothing for ego to do in that situation except perhaps drive our thoughts and emotions. But if we are present, our associatively activated thoughts and emotions, the usual domain of ego, do not touch us, do not control us, are not able to convince us that they speak for us, that they are us. We just are. And self-centeredness evaporates in those moments.

This evaporation of ego exposes it as an illusion. There is no actual, separate, substantive me to defend, to center on, to nurture, groom, and build up. Ego is just an aberration of will, blocking the channel of will that flows from the Sacred through us. We believe in our ego and as it turns out that belief is all there is to ego. As there is no actual ego, that belief, though strong and utterly convincing, is completely false. Dispelling the illusion of ego, opens the way to our true I, which, as a unique emanation of the One sacred will, does not put us above or below others in importance. Our I is our conscience, is free, and seeks to serve and connect.

Prayer then is an action of I. Ego has no role to play here and is left behind when we enter prayer. Contemplative prayer, wherein we seek to open ourselves to our connection with the Sacred, with what is greater than us, is anathema to ego, further exposing and weakening our ego. Self-centered thoughts and feelings that arise in our time of prayer are seen as they are, simply the automatic activity of our heart and mind without any intention behind them. We let them come and go as they will, while we reach deeper, well beyond the illusion those automatic thoughts and feelings carry.

For this week, renew your work to purify your will by discipline, kindness, conscience, presence and prayer, as the appropriate opportunities arise.

18.0 Sacred Impulses

Our life is not flat. We have peak moments, experiences

that raise us beyond the ordinary, or better, make the ordinary extraordinary. The deepening of our inner life, by our inner work, raises our basic level, so that we need not seek out unusual peak experiences. Rather we find the tenor of our whole life approaching what was at one time for us a peak experience.

How does this happen? We grow more porous inwardly, more open to the higher worlds beyond our usual automatic mode of cognition and reaction, less prone to distraction, to living solely on the flat surface of life. One excellent way to represent this opening is in terms of the Sacred Impulses. In truth, there is only one great Sacred Impulse, the Divine Will. But as It enters the prism of human experience, It breaks into a full rainbow of colors. Various traditions parse this rainbow in different ways. We shall take the following representation:

1. Wish
2. Hope
3. Faith
4. Acceptance
5. Joy
6. Love
7. Wisdom
8. Participation

These Sacred Impulses belong to a higher world than the one we usually inhabit. But they can come into us, if we are open enough, if we can allow them to well up from deep within. Our role in this is not an active one, though not inactive either. We open to receive the higher. We make an opening in ourselves that has the shape, the flavor of one of the Sacred Impulses, and that opening attracts and welcomes that impulse into us. We open to these qualities that have no peer, that are not corrupted, that carry the purity of the Sacred, that will transform our being if we let them.

The Sacred Impulses have been described as higher

emotions and as sublime or immeasurable qualities. We might also describe them as modes of spiritual action or manifestations of higher will, as the principal way that the Divine Will touches our human experience. These impulses transform us and have the power to change the world, to align us with the Force that creates and sustains this universe. When the Sacred Impulses act in us, through us, they bring an unmistakable taste of rightness, they answer our questions and show us our direction.

Our work with respect to the Sacred Impulses is to open to them, to be willing to be their bearer, to disavow our contradictory and self-centered motivations that block these better angels of our deeper nature, to let go of being enthralled by the contents of our mind so we may connect with the Sacred beyond our mind, beyond our consciousness, and then to respond appropriately. One wonderful aspect of the Sacred Impulses is that they can come to us as we are, although they tend to get garbled or ignored. But the deeper we go, the greater the purity of our heart and intentions, the more clearly and directly we come under the influence of these higher impulses.

In the coming weeks, we will explore the Sacred Impulses, what they are, how they work in us, and how to make room for them within our being. For this week, look at the quality of your own motivations. What drives you? What do you care about?

18.1 Wish
(Sacred Impulses: Facet 1 of 8)

Although our body may be complete, our soul is not. That fundamental incompleteness drives us to find wholeness, to find what we're missing, even if we are only vaguely aware of the lack. We may look in many directions to fill that hole in our center, that core uncertainty, and ultimately find that we are still not satisfied, not complete. Thus begins our thirst for self-perfection, our wish for completion, our recognition that nothing external can fill our fundamental need, that nothing external can build our soul, and that the aim of spiritual inner work is the very transformation that we seek.

As a teenager, I thought that achieving a particular goal I had set for myself would utterly change my life, inwardly and outwardly. In the event, on the evening after that supposedly-momentous achievement, I stood in my home and realized to my shock and surprise that I had not changed, that nothing had really changed. It took several more years before I found spiritual practice and saw that here was something that could lead me toward the transformation I sought.

The Buddha's First Noble Truth points to the unsatisfactory nature of life: not getting what you want, getting what you don't want, the impermanence of everything and everyone in time, our personal imperfections and limitations, and so on. We find something similar in the Christian admonitions regarding evildoing and Hell. Such views form one major source of our motivation, our wish for freedom, for transcending time. We wish to escape, not to be subject to that pervasive dissatisfaction, not to do evil.

The other major source of our motivation is our growing perception of the Sacred, the Great Attractor, and wanting to be closer to That. This wish comes from love of the Divine, from seeing that completion of our soul is the way to the Divine. The many forms of prayer nurture this attraction and increase our wish.

Between these two, between fear of the Lord and the love of the Lord, between the need for freedom and the need for completion, we find a balance that drives our wish for self-perfection, that both pushes and attracts us along the way of the spirit. Without that wish, we have no spiritual life. The stronger, more urgent our wish, the more surely we stay on the path.

God does not do our inner work for us, but does give us

the freedom to live as we choose, at least inwardly. The Sacred Impulse of wish presents us our need, awakens our desire for the Divine. It is up to each of us individually whether and how to respond to that desire, to that need. It is up to us to respond by our inner work. No one can do that for us, not even God, Who may need our work, but only as our own ongoing choice. If God did our work for us, then that would be slavery not freedom, servility not service, subjugation not partnership. It is up to us and wish confronts us with that possibility, presents us with that choice.

Although it is up to us to respond to wish, the intensity of our wish is not entirely our own doing, because wish comes to us, as do all the Sacred Impulses, from a higher world beyond our control and beyond our ordinary perceptions. Responding to wish, by our inner work, can help open that channel. Prayer can help. Wishing for wish can help. Seeing the reality of our position, our life as it is, our limited time, can help. Finding intimations of the Sacred in music, in the arts, and in nature can help. Deep meditation, the practice of presence, and noticing their effects can help. The basic thing is to open to, recognize, and honor our wish to serve, our wish for the Real, our wish to be real, our wish to be.

For this week, notice the strength and depth of your wish and what serves to increase it.

18.2 Hope
(Sacred Impulses: Facet 2 of 8)

The universe is not indifferent. The Sacred Impulse of Hope has been defined as the growing perception that the Divine power, the Force that creates and sustains this universe, is benevolent, not just in a general sense, but personally benevolent to each of us. Hope is our sense that the Creator cares about us, about you and about me.

Obviously, hope connects us with the future. It is hope that allows us to set goals, start projects, and work toward their culmination. It is hope that allows us to marry and have children. Hope gives us the optimistic attitude that, despite the inherent uncertainties, despite the entropic inevitability of decay, dissolution, and breakdown of all that we know, despite all that can go wrong, the future, our own future, will go well, will be good and positive, will bring us further fulfillment.

Yet this is not a matter of trusting in blind luck, for we can make our own luck by our intelligent and determined work. Hope gives us a sense of possibility, of opportunity, which we can meet, not by lazily waiting for our lottery number to come up, but by creatively and persistently working our way toward a better future. Indeed the worst aberration of hope is procrastination, followed closely by gambling, excessive risk-taking — including smoking — and unrealistic expectations about the future. Lotteries are popular because they sell hope.

The future may be broken into several domains. One gives us the determined or almost-determined future that may be predicted with high probability, such as tomorrow's sunrise. Another is the partially determined future, such as the one that is influenced by our choices, some conditioned by habit and circumstance and others free and creative within the bounds of rational action.

The third domain is the unpredictable future. This includes the results of the nearly infinite complexity of the world, from all the interactions among its various parts and inhabitants: the butterfly effect of a wing-flap here causing a hurricane there, the choices made by any and all of the billions of people on this planet, the gyrations of uncontrolled, broad-based markets, and so on. Hope is mainly about this unpredictable future. Because it is inherently uncertain and unpredictable, we sense that it is open to the influence of higher powers as well as to our own concerted and persistent action. Where higher powers can intervene, there is room for Hope.

After Pandora released all the evils from her box, one powerful, countervailing factor remained behind, namely Hope. We open ourselves to Hope and allow Hope to inform our inner world, to affect our choices, to usher us toward our future with confidence. We go forward doing what needs doing, what we can do, and what we choose to do. With Hope in our heart, we try and try again, we practice and practice more, we learn and assimilate new knowledge and skills, and we put all that to good use. Hope is a beacon of the Sacred. When we can hope wholeheartedly for something, without our conscience taking exception to any selfish motivations behind that hope, then Hope does indeed align us with the Sacred.

Whereas wish is about aspirations, hope is about possibilities. Hope perceives that what we seek is actually possible for us. Thus hope reinvigorates our wish and our efforts to actualize what we hope for. If we are ill, we hope to be restored to health, but we also pursue medical care and lifestyle changes as necessary. If we have goal and have hope of achieving it, then we work indefatigably toward it.

In the spiritual path, one way to look at hope is as the impulse that connects us with our possibility of the Sacred entering us. Many things must happen for that, including purification and completion of our soul. Hope keeps us focused on that possibility as a real possibility.

For this week, look at the role of hope in your life.

18.3 Faith
(Sacred Impulses: Facet 3 of 8)

Faith, our willingness to be related to the Divine Power, grows by degrees and comes in different types. Intellectual faith, also known as belief, arises from our need for understanding and meaning. It opens us to a coherent teaching about the Sacred and Its role in the universe. Beliefs bring understanding and order to our inner world, while answering our deeper questions like "Why are we here?" and "What is the purpose of this universe?" Intellectual faith begins in knowing about the Sacred and, if acted on in a practical, soul-developing way, ends in participating in the Sacred.

Emotional faith opens our heart to the One, to the Sacred Attractor, the Great Heart of the World. It arises from our need for belonging, for love, for completion. Our emotions may open to the Sacred under various conditions, including hearing religious or spiritual music, hearing stories from scripture, saints, and the effects of faith on ordinary people, seeing the transcendent quality in nature's beauty, participating in sacred rituals such as formal worship services, and becoming disillusioned with what our material life can offer us. In all these ways and more, our heart may open to the Sacred. Emotional faith, experienced as heartfelt devotion, confidence and trust, begins in our attraction to Sacred and, if acted on in a practical, soul-developing way, ends in union with the Sacred.

Perceptual faith derives from and opens us to direct experiences of the Sacred. It is our response to our actual, perceived relationship with the Sacred. Perceptual faith begins with irregular, unpredictable, and rare episodes of deeper experiences, and, if acted on in a practical, soul-developing way, moves toward regular, at-will access to the higher worlds.

It is only half-true to say that Faith is not enough. Indeed our approach to and connection with the Sacred are enormously accelerated by the depth of our meditation and prayer practice. Practice and Faith intertwine in a positive feedback loop: the more Faith we have the more we practice, and the deeper our practice the stronger our Faith. But even at advanced levels of practice there still there remains a final chasm to cross, and for that Faith is essential. If we have yet to learn the way into the Sacred, then that way is unknown to us. With Faith we can move into the unknown realms within us. Faith gives us the confidence to explore beyond our current envelope of experience, beyond our mind, beyond our self.

Faith reallocates our values, so that we begin to give more importance to the invisible spirit. Without Faith, we have nothing but what we can see and touch and know. This leaves us vulnerable to the inevitable ups and downs of life in the material world. But as soon as we open even a little to Faith, we gain some perspective on life and we begin to value and to seek spiritual well-being as well as material well-being.

Though Faith is willingness to be related to the Sacred, it is only partially our own doing or choice. Faith comes to us as a gift, dependent on our willingness to receive it. It is given at a level beyond our mind and beyond our ordinary awareness of our ability to choose. So although we cannot just decide to have Faith, we can choose to feel and act in accord with it, as it grows in the depths of our soul. The awakening of Faith changes our priorities, diminishes our various identifications, relates us to the Divine, and enriches both our inner life and our approach to living in the world.

For this week, notice your own Faith.

18.4 Acceptance
(Sacred Impulses: Facet 4 of 8)

Thoroughgoing acceptance of the true place of the Higher, the Sacred in our inner world takes us toward the apex of the spiritual life, while the role of acceptance with respect to our inner and outer circumstances is well summarized in the first part of Reinhold Niebuhr's Serenity Prayer:

> *God, Grant me the serenity*
> *to accept the things I cannot change;*
> *the courage to change the things I can;*
> *and the wisdom to know the difference.*

In all three domains, the Higher, the inner, and the outer, acceptance brings peace and serenity. That peace, that equanimity dissolves our dissatisfactions with ourselves and our life. It stops the awful waste of our inner energies, our sensation and consciousness, on a fruitless internal battle aimed at remaking ourselves in our ego's image. Acceptance removes the source of our identifications, attachments, and clinging. We let things be as they are. We let ourselves be as we are. And in that letting go, in that as-is acceptance, in that wholehearted embrace, we find room to work to improve ourselves in the ways that need improving. But that self-improvement occurs in a context of acceptance and a wish to evolve, not a context of rejection. We accept and we aspire.

As with any other aspect of inner work, acceptance operates differently at each level of our inner life. At the lowest level, where we fall into unnecessary desperation, overarching desires, simple identification, getting lost in the outer, being driven by our emotions in an unhealthy, destructive, or self-centered way, acceptance means letting go of those things, being at peace with things as they are.

At the level of our personality, acceptance means not rejecting our body, not rejecting ourselves, forgoing the self-recriminations, the self-hatred, the wishing that I were different and not so very this or that. Such destructive self-rejection comes from self-centeredness, from the notion that I should be better than this, better than them. So to accept oneself utterly deflates our overinflated views of ourselves, our overinflated desires. We give up and just be ourselves. Nevertheless, if we have destructive habits, like smoking tobacco or overeating, we can both accept that habit as our habit and work with determination to change it, to stop smoking, to eat properly. Similarly if we want to achieve something, we can accept that as a goal of ours, accept that we have not yet achieved it, and accept that we need to work hard to achieve it.

At the level of consciousness, acceptance means just

being, non-doing. We let all our sensory and thought and feeling impressions come and go without clinging or identifying. We let it all be as it is. And in that being, we rest in stillness, in awareness itself. The conscious energy gradually collects in us, reintegrating from its dispersed state. And we come to peace and equanimity in the vast hall of cognizant stillness, in the field of consciousness that we all share. Indeed self-acceptance and learning to be enable us to drop our barriers to accepting other people as they are.

At the levels beyond consciousness, acceptance means surrender, opening our innermost being to the Sacred. It is there that we clarify our questions, begin to see the answers, begin to understand the reasons for our inner and outer work, find the Source that fills our heart to overflowing, and begin to see how we might best live our life.

For this week, ask yourself whether you are now or have ever been utterly content. If you have the necessities of life, contentment is not then a matter of having everything you want, because there is no end to wants. Contentment comes from accepting and embracing our situation as it is and, for many of us, would represent a radical transformation of our inner lives.

18.5 Joy
(Sacred Impulses: Facet 5 of 8)

It may be surprising to find joy listed among the Sacred Impulses, but it certainly belongs. We need look no further than nature to see joy deeply embedded in the workings of the world. From playful pups to the songs of birds, animals certainly seem to enjoy being alive. From our natural responses to sunsets, mountains, and shorelines, nature provides us with ample opportunities for joy. So it is not so farfetched to consider that joy also goes well beyond life, into the higher realms, perhaps as far as being fundamental to the whole creation. We share in God's joy.

Joy has levels. At the lowest level, joy is a temporary satisfaction of cravings. We feel we must have that cake. Afterwards, the joy and satisfaction vanish into the endless rounds of craving.

At our ordinary, half-aware level, we look to alleviate boredom with fun or thrills or pleasures, which break through our perceptual filters to bring us into actual contact with our life — again though, temporarily. That joy is short-lived, as the thrill evaporates on the flat expanse of the half-aware life.

At the level of being in contact with our senses, joy arises from many sources, such as appreciation of natural beauty, the arts, music, and humor, anything of high quality, seeing excellence in action, delicious foods tasted fully, making music or dancing, and so on. Although we prefer joy to pain, sadness, suffering, unhappiness, or ennui, we understand that life in time, in the sensory world is necessarily mixed and cannot be all joy. So we take our joy as it comes and we savor it.

At the level of being conscious and fully aware, we rise into a natural, un-caused joy. We are suffused with joy in our awareness itself. Our very presence is joy. Sharing moments with friends and loved ones brings us joy. Taking actions that serve others brings us joy. Being useful, creative, or spontaneous brings us joy. Doing something well brings us joy. Dropping the burdens of egoism, dropping the defense of our pretenses, dropping our clinging, we are released into joy. We even feel empathetic joy in others' joys. Our joy is no longer limited or in any way dependent. We live in joy.

And yet, there is more. At the level of the World of Sacred Light, which we may touch in the deeper reaches of meditation or of contemplative or fervent prayer, joy comes as pure ecstasy and leaves its golden trace on our soul.

What can we do to increase our joy? That is not so straightforward, because in seeking joy we do not find it. It comes as a byproduct of a life well-lived. For example, it requires a clear conscience, which in turn allows us to give ourselves permission to enjoy our life. Spirituality, engagement in serious and important matters, career, family, and so on, do not preclude living in joy. Indeed, one mark of spiritual practice rightly pursued is that it gradually increases our capacity for joy. It is not all effort and self-denial. Joy reorders and rebalances our energies in a positive way, while encouraging us to continue our practice.

For this week, please enjoy your life or see what blocks that joy.

18.6 Love
(Sacred Impulses: Facet 6 of 8)

Love: a word full of so many meanings, so central to our life. Even more than the remarkable and endlessly gratifying experience of being loved, when we love, our life seems full and meaningful. Yet we do not love as much or as well as we might wish; we settle for less than the real thing. But at any moment, we can rise to love those around us. One way to explore love is to look at its various manifestations on our different levels of experiencing.

At the level of obsession and attachment, possessiveness turns too easily into jealousy, hate, and anger. Attachment repels the person to whom we are attached, because they feel the needy and devouring fangs of our clinging. At this level also we can be driven by lust, deriving from the necessary, biological imperative to reproduce. We see the object of our obsession as just that, an object, a cardboard cutout of a person, not an actual living, breathing one. Possessive love leads us into an unsatisfying and destructive abyss. Such "love" destroys itself, either by becoming its own opposite or arousing its opposite in return.

At the somewhat milder level of our ordinary, half-aware life, we are driven to seek what we like. We like others, depending on their compatibility with us and on their attitude toward us. This level of "love" is about the lover, not about the beloved. It depends on the others' actions and how they affect us. This transactional love readily turns into dislike if the other fails to uphold their end of the bargain, a mutual-liking contract. It is shallow and not very resilient to challenges.

At the level of being in contact with our life, kindness and consideration without expectation of reciprocity become possible. We have moments of contact with other people and of true generosity. We appreciate other people and we begin to experience a fellow-feeling, brotherhood and sisterhood. We can be a friend and gracious companion. In intense team situations, we can love our teammates. Even with strangers, we can be warm and courteous. At this level it starts to feel like love and to have a transformative impact on us and our relationships. We become aware that other people are not just animated things, but are alive, just as we are. At this level of kind and considerate love, we radiate a positive influence on our corner of the world.

Now we come to conscious love, which experiences and recognizes the sameness that we share with others. We step beyond the relationship of you and me to the sameness of I and Thou. We see directly that we all share the same consciousness, just as we share the same air. And sharing consciousness erodes the boundaries between us. Our defenses drop. Expectations, demands, and contracts have no place here, but compassion and commitment do. Mutual acceptance and respect come naturally when we live in love, even if only for a moment.

Wonderful indeed, yet there is more. Beyond consciousness, there is the love that reaches to devotion. The lover disappears into love. We move beyond sameness to oneness, beyond I am to We are. And ultimately we discover the Great Heart of the World.

So how do we navigate these levels of love? First, can we see where we are, see the nature of the love we give? Seeing this, we aim to rise to next level. Each of these levels of love corresponds to a level of the spiritual path, to a level of being which we may attain. Thus our inner work has a direct impact on our ability to love. For example, seeing that we are obsessed, we look to relax our obsession. At a higher level, presence brings us into contact with ourselves. Being in contact with ourselves, we can be in contact with others. In contact with others, we are led to practice kindness and civility until they become natural for us. Beyond that, the meditative experience of stillness opens us to consciousness, which opening spills over into our daily life, enabling us to see that consciousness surrounds us, not just individually, but all of us collectively. In that shared consciousness we find a new kind of love. And prayer takes us beyond ourselves toward devotion, toward the unfathomable ocean of Love.

The Russian poet Yevgeny Evtushenko once said: "Everywhere I go people love me, because I love them." And why not? What keeps us from the fullness of love?

18.7 Wisdom
(Sacred Impulses: Facet 7 of 8)

The very name of homo sapiens imputes wisdom to our species. But we know that not all people are wise. Indeed we find few who attain the higher levels of wisdom. Mere book learning, though useful and even necessary, is not enough. Mere longevity and experience are not enough. Intelligence and a high I.Q. bring great advantages, but not necessarily wisdom. Yet we recognize the immeasurable value of wisdom. Looking backward, we see the life mistakes we could have avoided and the opportunities we would not have missed, if we had been wiser in our choices, if we had understood ourselves and other people, if we had had the foresight to realize the long-term implications of our actions, and if we had acted accordingly. Looking forward, we want wisdom to inform our future actions. Wisdom is understanding combined with the ability to choose well. We can explore wisdom by looking at how it operates on the different levels of being.

At the lowest level we have arrogance, a perversion of wisdom. The arrogant assumes the mantle of, among other things, being wiser than everyone else. Such misplaced faith in one's own presumed powers makes normal people flee from us, while the rest get angry or subservient. Believing that you already know, leaves no room for growth, for learning something new, for gaining new insight. The arrogant cannot choose well, for he is driven by his own self-centered illusions and self-oriented positions. Humility is a part of true wisdom.

At the level of half-aware living, wisdom, such as it is, takes the form of an accumulation of experience, raw facts and rote learning — all undigested. The years alone do not make us wise, nor does knowledge equate to wisdom. Major blind spots can persist: areas of our life that we ignore, either intentionally or unknowingly.

Some say that to become wise we must suffer. Suffering, if it is real, like physical pain or emotional grief, does tend to awaken us, to bring us here into this moment, to put us in contact with our life, however briefly. Out of that contact, self-knowledge grows and with it wisdom, for self-knowledge does lead to understanding. But suffering is not the only way to awaken and so is not a necessity for wisdom to grow. Our work at presence, puts us in contact with ourselves and teaches us self-knowledge. Taking the raw material of experience, whether inner or outer, and considering it, contemplating it, and experimenting with it, distills that experience into understanding. Maintaining contact with ourselves and with our life makes us skillful in the ordinary sense. Staying in contact with the practice of a craft, brings the skilled craftsman a portion of wisdom.

At the level of living consciously, the stillness of consciousness and the inner peace it brings set the stage for seeing and conscience. Seeing in this sense means to notice a situation and understand it, its causes and possible outcomes. Consciousness allows this because being in the conscious energy means being aware of the one continuous field of consciousness, which contains everything and everyone. A kind of unity comes, in which we know objects and situations from inside them, not just from their externals. This kind of perception is what we mean by understanding. More than mental words and categories to describe something, we know that thing directly. For example, we can learn a subject from a book and practice, but applying it or teaching it transforms our relationship with it from knowledge to understanding. This true expertise enables us to see. The chess master understands the whole situation almost immediately upon looking at the board.

When we can see the most efficacious path, conscience enables us to choose that way over what may be easier paths. This then is wisdom, the ability to see and to do the right thing in any circumstance without overreacting, under-responding, shirking, backpedaling, or taking a wrong turn. This wisdom is a generalized skill that confers prudence and sound judgment.

Now we come to the source of wisdom. The Book of Proverbs offers the image of wisdom as present at creation and rejoicing before the Lord. This implies that wisdom has depth. One kind of perspective comes from long and varied life experience. Another kind altogether comes from seeing in depth, from opening to levels of being, to the spirit, beyond ordinary experience. This latter perspective carries with it a value system that discounts short-term material advantage and places a premium on life, creativity, and love, on the long-term good and on the spiritual. In touching the higher worlds, we are touched by wisdom.

How can we develop wisdom? Slowly to be sure, nevertheless we can work in that direction. We contemplate life, by noting the results of our and others' actions. We notice our own motivations and tendencies and do not allow all our actions to be driven by the ingrained patterns of our personality. We follow the promptings of our conscience, doing the right thing regardless of whether it is personally pleasant or not. We practice patience. We consider the implications and ramifications of what we do or fail to do. We listen to our intuitions, but check to see if they are correct. We seek to live by eternal values while avoiding fixed positions. We seek to be present and to deepen our presence, because the deeper our state, the closer we are to wisdom.

For this week, increase your wisdom.

18.8 Participation
(Sacred Impulses: Facet 8 of 8)

We well know what it means to participate. But here we will use the word participation in a very particular sense, related to presence and spiritual practice. The key to such participation lies in our own presence, whether we ourselves are engaged in the action, whether "I am doing what I'm doing."

Certainly, we do things all the time. But more often than we might know, *we* are not doing those things; they are just happening through us according to some automatic, ingrained pattern of ours, some pre-programmed set of responses, a recipe for living that does not require our active, cognitive engagement. We just go through the motions. Our body eats without us tasting the food. Our mind spews out thoughts on its own, without us really thinking them. Our body walks and talks on autopilot. Our emotions emote without any intention or direction from us. This is how we live, or rather how we abdicate living. Our parts live us, through a conditioned process of programmed, associative activation of our mind, heart, body, and impulses. For the most part, we are just carried along, as life happens to us.

Yet our life need not be that way. A major thrust of inner work consists of being present to our senses, to our self, engaged in what we do, participating as the one who is living our life. To be engaged in what we do is a choice. Rather than live half-heartedly, we affirm ourselves to be here in the moment, fully here, doing what we are doing.

The first level of participation is simply to be aware of ourselves, our thoughts, emotions, and body, as well as our surroundings, other people, and so on. This is the level of contact, of being in touch. We pay attention to what we are doing. We get feedback from it and we are aware of that feedback. This mode of living certainly improves on the mode of just going through the motions. We have a life.

The second level of participation is when we feel ourselves to be present in what we are doing, when we can feel "I am doing this." Not that we need to say or think those words; it's the immediate experience of engagement, the involvement that counts. We bring the whole of ourselves to this moment, whatever it happens to be. Certain Zen sayings capture this well. From Wu Li: *"Before enlightenment chop wood and carry water. After enlightenment, chop wood and carry water."* And this classic from Ummon: *"If you walk, just walk. If you sit, just sit; but whatever you do, don't wobble."*

Participation is not just a matter of being present while you do something, nor just a matter of paying attention to what you are doing. It is both of those and more. It means engaging all of yourself, body, heart, mind, inner body, and spirit, as one whole unit. Further, it means being the one who is doing what you are doing, inwardly showing up. Inwardly agreeing to do it, choosing to do it, choosing that again and again as you do what you are doing.

So for example, when we read, we are not just eyes and brain reading. We are also our body, our heart, our sensation and our attention, wholly engaged in reading. The same holds for eating, for conversation, for anything we do: we are all in. This is living a full life, moment-to-moment.

What we do matters. But so does how we do it. And participation is the key to fullness. Without it, whatever we do cannot produce our best, cannot really satisfy us. Without it, time and life pass us by. With it, we show up and live our life.

And yet, there is even more. There is a higher level of participation, known as effortless effort, or in Lao Tzu's phrase: doing non-doing. This is flow. We no longer have the feeling that "I am doing this." Nevertheless, it is very different from the automatic, autopilot mode of living where we also lack that feeling. Here we have full awareness and freedom. We are not constrained by our programming. Rather our training and skills serve the action. We ride these moments of perfection; it all just flows. Any effort made is only what is necessary.

This is the music playing the musician, the dancer becoming the dance, the actor becoming the role, the parent playing with the child, the sweeper becoming the sweeping. This is the walker walking, in full awareness, unburdened and free. This is the creative force acting through the artist. It is the athlete in the zone, which is sometimes called being unconscious. But that athlete certainly is conscious, more conscious than usual. In that context, unconscious means the lack of consciousness of a controlling self, while being fully conscious.

We transcend our self in becoming the action, and it can happen even in simple things where our life just flows. Excellence in action becomes its own end, without regard to the ultimate result. Here is Chuang Tzu: "*The mind of a perfect man is like a mirror. It grasps nothing. It expects nothing. It reflects but does not hold. Therefore, the perfect man can act without effort.*" We can enter that perfection temporarily, just as we are.

Knowing about participation and its levels is not enough, although seeing our degree or lack of participation motivates us to engage in its practice. So how do we practice raising our level of participation? To be in the first or contact level, we practice paying attention to what we do, bringing more attention to the action. To move from that toward the second or whole level, we practice presence by being in our body, mind, and heart. We leave distractions aside. Sensing our body, our inner body, is fundamental. Intention matters also. Intending to be here, to do what we are doing with the whole of ourselves and renewing that intention continuously, enlivens our attention and we enter the fullness of engagement. We bring ourselves, our I, to what we are doing.

To move into the third level, flowing participation, we start with the wholeness of the second level and allow ease to enter. We let ourselves and the action flow, without compromising the quality of what we do or diminishing our awareness. We let the action take over. Controlling and adjusting come naturally in dynamic self-response to the changing situation. These are very special moments to be treasured, yet they can come in very ordinary circumstances.

For this week, please practice raising the level of your participation in your life.

19.0 The Path of Purpose

We naturally want our lives to have meaning, to have a purpose. Yet we face the complexity of our modern culture, with its myriad, conflicting demands and opportunities. How can we navigate through our engagements of the day without losing contact with our larger vision? For that matter, do we have a larger vision for our life, something that draws us, that fits our unique nature, that engages our higher potentials, that extends beyond the day or the month?

We know the positive feeling of having or serving a purpose, at least on short time scales. We know the rightness of having a job to do, something to accomplish, a responsibility to fulfill, an opportunity to avail. We know the satisfaction of completing a task or project, of following through.

We take on a task, even something small like washing the dishes or going to the grocer. That task is our purpose for those moments. And because purpose is will, and because we are our will, we become that purpose in carrying out the task. So to understand the role of purpose in our life is to understand ourselves. Our purpose is us. Our purpose creates us, in the moment. When we have a purpose, we become real, we become ourselves, and our life becomes meaningful, through that purpose. This is where the domain of purpose crosses over from our external, material life into our inner life, into our spiritual path.

Two of the significant dimensions of purpose interact: importance and time-scale. Generally, the longer the term, the greater is the purpose. Raising a child offers us a long-term task with great importance. Longer-term projects usually yield larger accomplishments. However, the short-term often is very important. In driving, our attention to the immediate road situation matters greatly. In surgery, the moment-to-moment actions of the surgeon matter greatly. And long-term purposes can only be accomplished through a series of short-term actions in the now.

The scope of a purpose helps determine its importance. Does a purpose affect some small scale task only? Does it affect more of my life? Does it affect my family, my organization and its customers, the larger society, even the Earth? Yet the apparent, external importance of a purpose can mask its inner importance. Both the street sweeper and the surgeon can have fulfilling lives, if they accept the task allotted to them and carry it through with fullness of purpose.

We shape the inner significance of an external task by

the importance we place on it. The more purpose we imbue it with, the more it can feed our soul, provided it accords with our conscience. But to imbue a task with purpose takes more than just trying to think it important. We engage in it with the whole of ourselves, with full attention and intention. Engagement injects importance into our purpose.

Possibilities matter. What can you accomplish? What limitations confront you? What assets and potentials do you bring to the task? If we adopt a purpose beyond our current possibilities, then either we work very hard to meet that challenge or we languish in an imaginary life.

Quality matters. How well do we carry out our purpose? To bring excellence to our actions is itself a high purpose, affecting not only the world around us but also ennobling our inner world.

The spiritual path itself has a very high purpose. To engage in spiritual inner work is to become a bearer of that purpose, to become aligned with the very purpose of the universe. That purpose can inform our life both immediately, moment-to-moment, as we live it and act on it through kindness, presence, meditation, prayer, and the transformation of inner energies, as well as for the long-term, as it is a life-long pursuit that continues to spiral upward. As with all great purposes, the spiritual path is not just about personal gain or personal salvation. For example, as we progress along the path, our practices involve an increasingly refined transformation of energies. Those higher energies contribute crucially to our planet's spiritual ecosystem of energies. To experience an example of this effect, we need look no further than the atmosphere of peace created in the immediate vicinity of people meditating. You can feel it. You can also see its effects on you when you meditate in a group, how much stronger that can be than meditating alone. Our inner work affects our world in direct but subtle ways. This is one of the primary purposes of our spiritual practice. That overarching purpose informs all our inner work: our purpose of being present as we go about our day, our purpose of connecting with the Divine Purpose when we engage in contemplative prayer, and our purpose of entering the peace of meditation.

In the coming weeks, we will look further into various aspects of purpose, particularly as they relate to our inner work:

1. Suffering
2. Necessity
3. Self-Improvement
4. Pleasure
5. Soul
6. Conscience
7. Service
8. Destiny
9. Divine Purpose

For this week, notice the role of purpose in your life. How strongly do you feel it and in what contexts?

19.1 Suffering
(The Path of Purpose: Part 1 of 9)

Suffering! We all, inevitably, experience our share of it, some unavoidable, some self-imposed. Naturally, we want to suffer less. And the suffering of others, especially those close to us, awakens our compassion. In these ways and more, suffering motivates us: its avoidance and alleviation offer us a purpose.

Ranging from mild to severe, the levels of suffering guide our dealings with it. We accept a certain degree of suffering to attain goals that outweigh it, for example exercising and doing chores. While severe suffering drives us toward immediate relief.

Yet we do suffer unnecessarily in unproductive ways, principally through our destructive emotions, such as anger, resentment, jealousy, envy, obsession, indignation and outrage. The Buddha taught that the root causes of suffering are attachment, aversion, and identification. So often we take a bad situation and make it worse by layering unnecessary emotional suffering on top of it. For example, inwardly turning away from physical pain does nothing to alleviate it, but does add the emotional suffering of aversion. We want our life to be all smooth. Yet the inevitable problems throw us off balance and out of our center.

Not getting what we want or being subjected to what we do not want causes us to suffer. Rather than forgo our attachments, our wanting and not wanting, rather than accept life's events as they come, which would minimize this form of suffering, we choose to stay in our obsessions, desires, and attachments and suffer for them.

For example, someone insults me or even just slights me or denies me something I want. My self-image, my dignity is attacked and my emotions react in an unpleasant way. I am disturbed. I am angry. I know that my anger feels awful to me. But I don't care. I want to feel angry, because I believe that feeling angry will not only make the other person suffer too, but will somehow patch up my damaged self-esteem. So I accept to suffer the putative cure of anger to pay for bucking up my self-image. I feel strong. I can be angry. Anger is strong, even if it feels so terrible to be angry. Maybe at some point I see that the anger does not heal the hurt caused by the insult, it just masks the hurt, hiding it behind the hot wave of anger. Maybe at some point I see that my anger is just adding pain on top of pain. And if I see that clearly enough, the seeing frees me from the automatic reaction of anger. And if see even more deeply, the seeing frees me from identification with my self-image, from the automatic reaction of feeling hurt by the insult, and from that kind of suffering altogether. And this leaves me room to respond to insults and other events if and as I so choose, room to change and improve my situation, yet without all the unnecessary angst.

So much of our suffering is self-imposed in that way, by our emotional reactions to our identifications and desires. To minimize such suffering, we can seek freedom, inner freedom. The spiritual path is designed expressly for that. So suffering can motivate us toward inner work, can strengthen our purpose of engaging in spiritual practice, in presence, in meditation, and in prayer.

But some suffering cannot be stopped, like the pain of illness, aging, and the grief of loss. These are unavoidable. Just living in the world of time imposes the suffering of choice: the gate of time only allows one event to happen now, excluding all the others. We are constrained to choose and cannot have or do the unchosen, our possibilities thereby diminished. This is a kind of existential suffering. Again though, even such unavoidable suffering can encourage our inner work and be lightened by it. Spiritual practice helps us accept the unavoidable and can even increase our possibilities by opening new doors of experience and action.

When we see others suffering, we want to help. Our own experiences of suffering enable us to perceive and relate to the suffering of others. Many do what they can to help in direct, material ways, in acts of kindness, generosity, and compassion. These diminish our ego and purify our heart, essential aspects of any spiritual path.

Our inner work raises our level of awareness, including of ourselves. In that way it can expose aspects of ourselves which we were not fully aware of and which we do not want, aspects we are ashamed of. This causes us suffering. But it can be a healing suffering, which burns out our attachment to some of our unbecoming impulses. It can decrease our identification and lower the amount of effort we put into defending our self-image, our ego. We accept the suffering of seeing because we understand its roots in our false self-image.

We can learn from our suffering. It constrains us, guides

us, and teaches us. With unnecessary suffering, we can ask ourselves "why am I suffering?" With unavoidable suffering, we can see how attachment, aversion, and identification cause us to layer on unnecessary emotional suffering; we can learn to accept the unavoidable and thereby diminish the unnecessary. All this gives us a purpose. And despite our suffering, through thick and thin, we do our best to fulfill our responsibilities and continue our inner work.

The Buddha spoke of the end of suffering, a condition attainable through the spiritual path. The more we understand our suffering, the more it urges us along the path. For this week, notice the ways you suffer and how that suffering, or potential suffering, drives your life and impacts your purposes.

19.2 Necessity
(The Path of Purpose: Part 2 of 9)

The various necessities of maintaining our life impose on us a set of purposes that we cannot shirk. Yet within necessity lies opportunity: necessity becomes our teacher. Our wisdom grows in learning to distinguish the truly necessary and in learning to do what we must with efficiency, with quality, and without resentment or grumbling, perhaps even with joy. There is a difference between what we must do, what we want to do, and what we should do. For example, we must wear clothing. But how much clothing do we really need? Is everything in our closet necessary for us or could we get by with less? If we choose to have more clothing than we need, then we cross the line from needs to wants. That's fine. But it's useful to be aware of that line between necessity and desire, because that awareness gives us more choice, more freedom. The same applies to our food: what we eat and how much we eat. It applies to our home, how big, where it's located, how it's furnished, and so on. Seeing the difference between what we need and what we want shows us the choices we are making, choices that, once made, go on by momentum, by forgotten precedent. The necessary and the desired on the life side of the ledger limit our time and resources for other things, for family, and for other goals.

For those on the spiritual path, there can be tension between life's needs and time for formal meditation and prayer, tension arising from the simple fact that our physical body can only do one thing at a time. This recurrent issue of how to spend our time often confronts us with difficult choices, choices through which we develop our contact with wisdom. But when it comes to the inner work of the spiritual path, there is less or even no tension with life activities. It is not an either-or choice, because our inner work takes place in our developing soul and can be done in parallel with external engagements, can even support and enhance what we do externally. The one is in time and the other is in the timeless. As we move in time we can carry the timeless within us.

Presence, for example, is a kind of spiritual multi-tasking that gradually transforms so that there is no division. Instead of two parallel processes of living in time and being present, instead of the multitasking of activity and inner work, our life becomes our practice and we live it with presence. This brings a new dimension of depth and meaning to all we do, enriching the mundane. In presence we are already where we're going: we are here. So in doing the dishes, taking out the garbage, cooking, cleaning, commuting, and laboring — in all that necessarily fills our day — we also seek presence. This marriage of necessity and spirit, of the seen and the unseen, completes our life and makes us whole. Without that, the chores can be empty drudgery. Yes, they are necessary and serve a definite life purpose. But we do not live to eat and sleep and have clothes to wear. Those things enable us to live and participate in a greater purpose. By learning to be at peace with the requirements of life, we leave ourselves open to serving purposes beyond those of caring for our body.

Necessity arising from the fact of our physical body is only one of several types. We also bear moral necessity and spiritual necessity. The first refers to our obligations and responsibilities toward other people, society, and our planet. The second addresses our obligations toward the Sacred. These two define and invite us to purposes that we can more easily ignore than those arising from having a body. However, physical necessity itself cannot provide the opportunities for purpose and fulfillment offered by moral and spiritual necessity. These latter we will address in more detail later in this inner work series on the Path of Purpose.

For this week, please look at how physical necessity shapes your purposes and how much room it leaves for other purposes. What do you need? Can you accept that as it is? How do you go about fulfilling your needs? Is there something you need to do differently? Do the choices you are making correspond to your priorities? Does what you do matter?

19.3 Self-Improvement
(The Path of Purpose: Part 3 of 9)

The huge and bewildering array of systems, techniques, and teachers for self-improvement can make it hard for us to know where to turn to develop our own unique set of talents and potentials, while addressing our unique obstacles and difficulties. One way to begin to make sense of all those approaches is to look at them along the spectrum of functioning, being, and serving, or of which self will be improved, our personality, our character, or our spirit. Does a method help us function better? Does it help us be more? Does it enable us to serve more deeply?

How well we function concerns our body, our heart, and our mind, the remarkable equipment with endless versatility, given to us at birth. To live a full life and raise our chances of entering the spiritual path, we need balanced development; we need to cultivate our body, our emotions, and our mind, in the ordinary sense. We look to develop our social, professional, recreational, and artistic skills, as well as our personal affect (our emotions), personal finances, and our time management. Obviously, education is the primary way of improving our mental functions, but many other activities also contribute, such as knowledge work and interests, social interactions, and games. Social interactions also contribute to our emotional development, as does engaging in the arts, whether as a spectator or, even better, as a participant. We develop our body in many ways, such as proper diet, adequate rest, engaging in sports, exercises and dance, and playing musical instruments.

Our most serious, personality-level obstacles generally arise from our disorganized and chaotic emotional life. If something is wrong with our body we seek medical care. If our emotions pose particular difficulties for leading a normal life, or for pursuing our spiritual practice, we can seek psychotherapy. Many of us have, at times, psychological problems severe enough to hamper or even block our spiritual inner work; we need enough psychological health to open a clear path to the spirit.

Some forms of psychotherapy aim to alleviate the immediate issue. Others look to the roots of the problem and straddle the line between improving our emotional functioning and raising the level of our being. In depth psychotherapy, such as Jungian analysis, the client and analyst work together to open channels of communication with the unconscious, often through dream imagery, and to repair and reintegrate our conditioned, unconscious mind. In doing so, the therapy aims at wholeness and at contact with the unconditioned, with the Self. This process is slow, years or decades, and cannot be rushed. Many are drawn to it and benefit enormously.

The spiritual path, which also is slow, has, in part, similar effects, though employing a quite different approach.

The methods of the path enable our awareness to grow in all dimensions. That includes more awareness of ourselves, of what drives us, and through that a process of repair and reintegration of our psyche takes place naturally. In part, this comes from extending our conscious awareness into what was once unconscious, as the practices of meditation and presence widen the embrace of our awareness and enhance our ability to see deeply. For some time, what we see is mostly content: the conflicting and conflicted drives and urges within us. Simply by seeing all this without judgment, with clear-eyed compassion for ourselves, by allowing ourselves to be as we are, our many inner wounds begin to heal.

As all of that begins to settle, our efforts of self-improvement cross from improving our functioning to raising the level of our being. We find a measure of inner peace and become able to be in that spacious, peaceful consciousness itself. And in the practice of presence from that place of consciousness, we come into our Self, we become our I.

Methods of enhancing our body awareness can play an important role in self-development, even beyond the level of functioning well. Yoga and Tai Chi, for example, straddle the line between functioning and being; they train us to be in contact with our body, in terms of external posture and of movement, thus improving the functioning of our body. We also learn to be aware of our body from within; we learn to be in our body. A powerful and direct method for this consists of the work on sensing our body, our inner body. Sensing does not depend on any particular set of postures or movements: it can be practiced in almost any situation.

Sensing also supports the primary methods for increasing our being, namely the practices of presence and meditation. The more we enter into the way of being, the more we wish to enter it. We see our limited time passing and realize that we cannot put off our inner work for later. We see that raising the level of our being leads us into a more joyous, meaningful, and complete life. At some moments, we have the direct experience that we are, that we exist in a timeless fashion. We come into the vast and peaceful hall of consciousness. When such moments recede, they leave a taste, they leave us moving more and more into the immediate practice of presence, into the experience of here I am. This is self-improvement in a deeper sense.

Service puts our functioning and our being to positive use for purposes beyond our own welfare. We may engage in outward forms of service, from simple kindness and courtesy toward the people around us, to helping charitable, environmental, or humanitarian organizations. There are also unrecognized but important forms of inner service. For example, in meditation and contemplative prayer we transform inner energies, making more refined spiritual energies available in this world. Those energies raise the level of awareness and help us and others move beyond self-centeredness in the small sense to serving the greater Self that includes all of life. So in practicing the deeper methods of the spiritual path, we not only serve our own well-being, but also the well-being of all those with whom we share this life, this planet.

Our ego seeks self-improvement for self-centered, even selfish reasons, yet we do not reject that motivation; we use it to embark on and reinforce our lifelong quest to raise our level in the ways that matter to us. Ultimately the skills and abilities we develop can be put into serving a higher purpose than our own self-centeredness. We become ourselves. However, we should not expect perfection as the end result of our efforts of self-improvement, for perfection cannot come in that way: it comes from deep within, from our spirit.

For this week, notice the ways you engage in improving yourself, in directing your own evolution. Notice also what approaches may be missing or need to change.

19.4 Pleasure
(The Path of Purpose: Part 4 of 9)

We are wired to seek pleasure, to get the right neurochemicals produced in our brain. So our biology imposes on us the purpose of seeking pleasure. The endless variety of ways we do that can be categorized into physical, psychological, and spiritual pleasures. To better understand pleasure, we first look at its counterpart, joy.

What are the differences between pleasure and joy? Clearly, there's a difference in duration, with pleasures being short-lived, while joy lasts, even to the point of creating an undercurrent of joy that stays with us at all times. Part of this is due to their causal differences. Pleasures arise from some stimulus to our senses. When the stimulus ends, so does the pleasure. We enjoy the cake as long as we're tasting it, the sunset as long as we're seeing it, the fragrance as long as we smell it. But when the stimulus goes on for too long or too often, we get saturated with it or habituated to it and the pleasure wanes: too much cake too often and we lose interest.

Joy, by contrast, is uncaused. When our heart, our mind, and our conscience are clear enough, joy arises naturally. We meet life with a predisposition to joy. Pleasure depends on what our senses bring us; joy does not. Pleasure is in time; joy is in eternity.

One way that joy comes to us is as a byproduct of spiritual practice rightly pursued. Although deep meditation can be sublimely pleasurable, our purposes matter. If we meditate for the pleasure it brings us, then we will have that pleasure. But we will miss the broader purposes it serves and the deeper realms it can open. So in meditation we learn to allow the pleasure, to welcome it even, but without chasing it. We seek to go ever deeper and, as we do, the pleasure also increases. But we do not let it mask the deeper realms it arises from; we do not let the pleasure deflect our quest.

The practice of presence also brings pleasure, for it makes us alive, awake, and alert to our senses. It makes our ordinary moments extraordinary, even the simple and unexpected pleasure of being in our body. Again though, in practicing presence, pleasure is a byproduct, not our purpose, which concerns developing our soul and serving the spirit.

Our purposes reflect our will. If we practice for ourselves, our will limits itself to our own small domain, our pleasure seeking. Ultimately this proves to be an inadequate motivation to sustain our spiritual work over the long term. But if we practice to serve and to raise the level of our being so that we can serve more effectively, layer upon layer can open to us. The deeper levels of the spirit are all about will. So our intentions, including why we do what we do, shape our spiritual work directly.

We know that many of our physical pleasures are healthy and many are not. We know that some healthy pleasures overindulged cross into unhealthiness. Yet some of us too often allow ourselves to indulge in unhealthy pleasures or overindulge in otherwise healthy ones. So we look to develop a more mature approach to living, wherein we relish our pleasures, yet we do not allow them to run our life. As in all things, we seek moderation and balance in our pleasures. Delicious food, for example, is meant to be savored and enjoyed. And that savoring itself can help enable us to stop eating when we've had enough. We enjoy our pleasures and then we let them go. Moderation not only offers us a more pleasurable life, but also diminishes the negative consequences for society of our collective overconsumption.

Psychological pleasures include appreciation of relationships with people and with animals, ideas, humor, drama and adventure in real life or in the movies, novels and poems, fantasies and daydreams, engaging in creative acts, and more. As with other pleasures, balance is needed and overindulgence leads to negative effects. For example, we can be so caught up in daydreams of winning the lottery that we neglect the practical steps necessary to actually change our financial situation. We can be so busy watching people relate to each other on TV that it interferes with our taking the time to relate to people in reality. We can be so devoted to one set of ideas that we lose interest in what others are doing or, worse, we take offense at anyone who disagrees with us. And of course, there are many forms of unhealthy psychological pleasures, such as gossip, schadenfreude, the satisfaction of greed or acquisitiveness, self-aggrandizing power, and accepting flattery or subservience.

For this week, please look at the role of pleasure in your life. Are there any imbalances, overindulgences, or unhealthy habits that you need to address?

19.5 Soul
(The Path of Purpose: Part 5 of 9)

Do we have a soul? Or not? For that matter, what is soul? Would we even know if we had one? To answer these questions, we seem to be stuck in the position of either believing or disbelieving what others have told us or what we can find in books, because we cannot see the answers for ourselves. Yet such beliefs or un-beliefs leave us unsatisfied and uncertain. Thinking about these questions does not help much either, because, if there is soul, it might be beyond thought, logic, or ordinary perception.

There is however, like Pascal's wager on the existence of God, a prudent path forward. We can take as a working hypothesis that we have a soul, but that it needs developing, it needs work. We could be wrong about that in two ways. Either there is no such thing as soul or we have a perfect one already. Even if there is no such thing as soul, we still find empirically that spiritual practice makes our life better in many ways. As to whether we already have a perfect soul — it seems doubtful because we do not feel perfect. And if our soul is already perfect, then we are not in touch with it. Either way, the prudent path is to take up inner work wholeheartedly and see where it leads. Perhaps it will teach us about our soul directly, through our own experience. Perhaps it will develop our soul and/or our contact with it. And almost assuredly, if we persist, it will bring us a more satisfying life.

Balanced inner work leads to balanced development. One aspect of any complete spiritual path is purification, of our egoic self-centeredness. We come toward that through seeing ourselves clearly, through acting in accord with conscience, and through our growing attraction to the Sacred as our inner work progresses. We cannot attack our egoism directly, because our ego is a chameleon and joins the attack on itself, so it can claim our spirituality for itself, like thinking "I am more spiritually developed than he is." So we use the indirect approaches of seeing, conscience, and attraction to the Sacred, to help us past egoism, to help us set ourselves aside, to help us make our ego irrelevant. Conscience will be the focus of the next part of the Path of Purpose series. Seeing ourselves depends on self-awareness and the willingness to look without bias, without flinching, and without judgment. That willingness arises from the realization that self-centered egoism blocks our spiritual path and that seeing weakens our egoism. Some of the deepest nourishment for and activity of our soul can only come through the channel that our ego occupies, the channel of our will. Witness Christ's *"Blessed are the pure in heart, for they shall see God."* Self-centered egoism, an aberration of will, usurps the place of our I, blocking the connection between our will and the Divine Will. Again from Christ, "… *not my will, but thine* …" Purification from egoism opens that channel, opens our attraction to the Sacred, and is thus a self-reinforcing, positive-feedback process.

Another key aspect of balanced development of soul

concerns our energies. Self-awareness grows with the quantity, quality, and organization of our inner energies. Our inner work of sensing, presence, meditation, and prayer, if pursued intelligently, persistently, and with a keen eye toward exploration and learning, has a profound effect on our spiritual energies. We need to explore and to learn, because the world of the soul, our inner world, is largely unknown to us. We can learn methods from other people. But to grow in wisdom and understanding requires us to see for ourselves, directly. Methods help us see. So again we come back to the classic approaches of sensing, presence, meditation, and prayer. These have both short-term and long-term benefits. Just as our body feels better from a healthy meal, exercise, or a good night's sleep, so our soul feels better when we engage in the actual practices of the spiritual path. It feels nourished, present, peaceful, and clean, ready to meet the challenges and opportunities of life with wisdom and with heart.

The practices of inner work open a new dimension to our life, open us to a new life, an inner life. Our inner world is not separate from our outer world, but is a side of our reality that we neglect. When we work to establish ourselves in presence, to stabilize our presence, we are working to stabilize, to form our soul. When we can feel "I am here," with presence in our body, our mind, our heart, our senses, and our Self, we are residing in our soul. When we sense our body, our energy body, completely and robustly, we are in our inner body, or outward part of our soul. In contemplative prayer, we strengthen the highest part of our Soul, our unified and purified will that connects us with the Divine Will. The deeper we go, the more unified and purified we are. This soul work, then, can be one of the central purposes of our life.

For this week, examine your attitudes toward your own soul. Notice what you can about your soul and its varying states. Work to develop your soul.

19.6 Conscience
(The Path of Purpose: Part 6 of 9)

We all know the sacred feeling of remorse of conscience: when we've done the wrong thing or neglected to do the right thing, we feel an uncomfortable pang in our core. That feeling is sacred because of its source and because if we pay attention to it and resolve not to arouse it again, ever, it can purify us of our self-centered egoism. That resolve to follow our conscience turns remorse from a feeling we experience after a misdeed to a future-oriented intuition of a potential misdeed. Conscience obeyed can thus guide our choices to avoid remorse. Notice that this is not about burying remorse. On the contrary if we have it, we need to feel it and reflect on what we've done or not done to arouse it.

No, what we're after is to open to our intuitions of conscience about the choices in front of us, not just those behind us. If we take on a personal moral imperative to obey our conscience, it can override those of our egoistic impulses that would have us act against conscience. Thus conscience can weaken the hold that our ego has on us. Freedom from ego does not mean not having one; ego is a self-referential, self-oriented pattern in our will that persists, perhaps until we die. But it is a pattern or set of patterns with nothing substantial at its core. That insubstantiality allows us the possibility of giving up the burden of ego. Freedom from ego means freedom in front of ego, it means seeing our self-centeredness as self-centeredness whenever it arises and not allowing it to control our choices and attitudes. Obeying our conscience will often go against our ego, prompting its protests, and unmasking it for what it is, so that we can see it and step out of our bondage to it.

The notion of freedom from ego raises the question of who is it that is free. To begin with, our conscience is free.

And as it turns out, conscience is part of our I, our higher Self. So it comes down to following my conscience so that I can be free, or ignoring it and living the small life of an ego. When we work to live by conscience and we experience some nasty thought or impulse that, if acted on, would go against our conscience, we notice that thought or impulse more clearly, we see it. And we know that this nastiness is not who I am, this is not what I would do. That knowing, that seeing in the light of conscience, shows us that the thoughts and impulses that form the patterns of our egoism are not who we are. Each time this happens, we gain a little more freedom from our small self, we come more into our I. Our thoughts and emotional reactions are not us; they are just thoughts and just emotions.

We can distinguish between the emotion of guilt and the sacred feeling of remorse, between Freudian superego and conscience. Guilt and superego are learned responses, imposed or impressed on us from outside. For example, when someone wants you to do something and you refuse, you might feel guilty. If you have not promised to do whatever it is, if you do not have some commitment to do it, and if there is no genuine need behind the request, then your refusal does not arouse conscience. But the difficulty of refusing someone might make you feel guilty. It is a fairly low level emotional reaction and does not cut to our core as does remorse.

Conscience is objective. Take, for example, the Golden Rule of doing unto others what you would have them do unto you, and not doing unto others what you would not have them do unto you. This is objective morality based in the reality of oneness and love. Conscience and remorse guide us along objectively moral paths.

Our connection with conscience can benefit us beyond serving as our moral compass. It can also help us discriminate between alternatives to see the better choices, even when the choices do not involve moral issues of right and wrong. In such cases, instead of calling it conscience, we call it wisdom. They both come from a connection with and openness to our deepest nature. In the same way that we learn to pay attention to the still, small voice of conscience, we learn to be aware of our intuitive wisdom.

We can be a person of conscience, someone who is trusted to do the right thing. For this week, listen for your conscience. Adopt the purpose of honoring your Self by doing the right thing.

19.7 Service
(The Path of Purpose: Part 7 of 9)

> *If I am not for myself, then who will be for me?*
> *And if I am only for myself, then what am I?*
> *And if not now, when?*
> Hillel

Some make it their life purpose to serve others or our planet. We respect them for that, knowing its inherent rightness as well as the purity of motivation behind it. But service is not only for the devoted few; it is an element of all our lives and a central function of the spiritual path. To earn our living, we provide some service to society, something society values. To have a happy home life, we serve our family. Through our generosity we serve those in need. Through simple acts of kindness and courtesy, we serve the people within our present moment. Our role in outward service is to do it well, to be intelligent, effective, and compassionate, to pay attention and learn how to serve better. We know the satisfaction it brings us when we do something useful for someone, something that matters even in a small way. We serve others to fill their need and our own. When someone does us a kindness, it predisposes us to pay it forward in another act of kindness. These ever-expanding circles of kindness raise the tenor of our world.

But there is also an inward service, one which we typically do not recognize as service. Through our spiritual inner work we serve ourselves, our society, our planet, and the Sacred. This radical notion sounds nice in theory, but can we have any direct perception that our spiritual practice affects anything or anyone beyond ourselves? Certainly it affects us; otherwise we would likely not have gone into it. But does it affect others?

When we meditate in a group, we see that our meditation is stronger, deeper, or more profound than when we practice alone. So if the group affects us, then our own meditation must be affecting others. The same holds for communal worship. How much more vibrant is our prayer when in a community of prayer! What we bring to that community affects it. When we are around someone who carries an inner peace, we feel more at peace ourselves. So if our inner work brings us peace, we carry that to the people around us. When we are with someone who exudes the joy of life, it rubs off on us. So if our inner work brings us joy, it spills over to others. When we are with someone who is calm, alert, and awake, we tend to wake up as well. Likewise, our own presence helps others be more present. All this adds up to show us that our spiritual practice is an act of service.

And it goes well beyond these localized benefits. Through our practice we gain perception of and facility with inner energies, spiritual energies. For example, by practicing sensing, or contact with our inner body, and by energy breathing we work with the sensitive energy; we have a direct perception of it. In silent meditation and in true presence, when our mind and heart settle, we come into the cognizant stillness of consciousness, the conscious energy that surrounds us all and always. And there are higher energies beyond those, for example in deep prayer when we are flooded with the light of the Sacred. Our inner work transforms energies, raising their level by generating higher energies from lower ones, and opening us to receive energies directly from a higher world. Associated with this is the notion that this planet, in its atmosphere and otherwise, has a pool or reservoir of spiritual energies. Just as we each have our own collection of energies in our nascent soul, so does the Earth in its nascent soul. And just as the state of our being, our very experience, is a function of the quality, quantity, and degree of organization of our personal supply of energies, so it is with the Earth as a whole. By our inner work, we contribute directly to the Earth's complement of energies, to its soul. In our own small but significant way, our spiritual practice affects the level of society, of our civilization, as a whole. We need the Earth and the Earth needs our inner work.

We know that the life on this Earth forms a complex ecosystem, based on the exchange and transformation of the material and energies of life. This ecosystem also has an inner dimension. The ongoing exchange and transformations of spiritual energies form a spiritual ecosystem. Whether or not we are aware of it, we all live in that spiritual ecosystem, we all take from it and give to it. The quality of what we give to it depends on our inner life. If we live in an inner chaos, in continual identification, self-centeredness, unawareness, and autopilot habits, we give little but a fairly low grade of energy, with a neutral or even negative impact. If we engage in spiritual practice, in meditation, presence, and prayer, we produce a higher quality of energies for the Earth's spiritual ecosystem.

The transformation of energies is not the only way we serve that ecosystem: our will, our actions, our attitudes make a difference. We affect the people around us not only by the quality of our energy, but clearly also by what we do. So in meditating together, it is not only the atmosphere of conscious energy that has an impact, but also our inner attitude of keeping to that particular practice. Our presence affects others, not only because of the sensitive and conscious energies we engage, but also by our will, our will-to-be, by the fact that I am here. Prayer is primarily an act of will, dependent as it is on the purity of our motivation. The person-to-person atmosphere of peace or joy is due to an attitude of will.

Service is one aspect of spirituality, perhaps the central one. Outward service, with its expanding circles of kindness, matters dearly. On the inside, seeing that our inner work serves purposes beyond the personal gives us a sound basis for its practice. In the inevitable ups and downs of a long-term pursuit of the spiritual path, the realization that our inner practices serve society as well as ourselves adds that extra bit of non-self-centered motivation that we need. Regarding our inner work as service allows us to enter its high and noble purpose and stay with it.

For this week, look at service as the purpose of your outward acts of kindness and your inner acts of spiritual practice.

19.8 Destiny
(The Path of Purpose: Part 8 of 9)

> *... I have set before you life and death...*
> *So choose life in order that you may live...*
> Deuteronomy 30:19

When we see an infant, we feel the child's almost limitless possibilities. At the beginning of life, everything is open to us. But many of those possibilities vanish with time. Can we live in such a way as to open new possibilities? We want to fill our life with meaning, to live our life fully, and to be ourselves. To what extent is that up to us?

Similar to fate, the notion of predestination claims that God has foreordained all that will happen, including all that will happen to us personally. But it seems obvious that we have free will and that our choices matter, otherwise life loses much of its meaning. If our destiny has something to do with God's plan for us, then surely our talents, understanding, and choices play key roles. We are given this body and we make our choices, but the imponderables, the unpredictable events of life also shape us. Together, our genes, our circumstances, and our choices determine our possibilities.

Surely God's plan for us embodies our highest possibilities. We have the central role in fulfilling that plan, in attaining our own unique destiny: to overcome our limitations, the box of fate, to understand our destiny, the most meaningful and fulfilling path of life for us, and to make the choices and efforts necessary to walk that path. In so doing we enter a kind of conversation with our destiny. What actually becomes of us is not predetermined; what we do matters and uncertainties accompany us at every step. We can never be fully certain what our destiny is. There can be no certainty of the ultimate outcome of our choices. But the closer we come to making the right choices, the more we align ourselves with our destiny, with God's will for us.

Given that our highest possibilities are multifold, our choices can create our destiny, our vision of our best role in life, of what we can become and do. That vision may lack detail, may be no more than an intuition or drive in a particular direction. Yet if we hold to that vision and allow it to evolve, it can guide us toward the future that is meant for us.

And we can fail to achieve that destiny, fail to actualize our highest potential. That uncertainty, that possibility of failure makes life interesting, gives meaning and urgency to our choices, and makes us responsible. Without that risk of failure, we could not evolve; we would be stuck in a dependent state like children. So we do what we can, without demanding assurance of success or some particular result.

Like many other endeavors, the spiritual path is uncertain. It is an exploration of an unknown territory. Yet the path changes our being and enables us to be more ourselves. In becoming more who we are, we inevitably approach our destiny as well. So our inner work can and does help us see and achieve our destiny, even when that destiny does not concern the spiritual path directly. If we are to enter what we envision as our life's work, the practices of the path can help us in that pursuit.

Destiny is not only about a destination, about the future. Rather, it concerns living our highest potential now, today. Of course, we prepare ourselves for our destiny, through education and practice. But that can only happen now. Obviously, we create our future by how we live today. And given time and direction, all of our small efforts, small changes or improvements, can add up to significant results: new skills and abilities, long-term projects completed, relationships cultivated, services rendered, or whatever else may be part of our vision for ourselves. Who we are, our core, does not change, for our I comes into us from above. But we can gain experience, skills, and inner freedom. As our destiny unfolds and the vision grows clearer, we become more committed to it, we come to see the possible as attainable, and the attainable as doable today.

For this week, contemplate the direction of your life. Where are you going? What do you envision for your life? Is what you are doing of value in itself? Is it leading toward what you envision? Imagine yourself at the end of your life, looking back. What would you want your life to have been? What would you want to have become? Are you taking the steps to realize that vision?

19.9 The Divine Purpose
(The Path of Purpose: Part 9 of 9)

The question of whether the Divine Purpose exists is tantamount to asking whether God exists, though "exists" is the wrong verb, because something that exists does so in time. God is not and could not be contained in time, although the Divine Purpose does, in part, manifest in time, if only in a veiled way, like Adam Smith's invisible hand of market economics.

One of the great and broadly evident lessons of the Old Testament is that God acts in and through some of the events of human history. This is not to say that history always moves in accord with the Great Purpose. Obviously, there are detours and reversals. But generally, the vast sweep of history seems to be unfolding and evolving in accord with what we might imagine to be a high purpose. A prime example is the increasing value we place on human rights. Technological advances such as air travel and telecommunications are allowing much greater connectedness among people. Technology is making us all better informed, with more information readily available, which is leading us to be more discriminating, less suggestible, more individual. As medical, hygiene, and nutritional advances give us longer lifespans, we have more time to consider what our life is for, consider how best to use our time. Living solely for one's own self-centered purposes gets old. Longer lives mean looking for what we can give, what we can offer for the greater good. Surely that tends to align us with a higher purpose.

And then, of course, there is the role of spiritual practice: meditation, prayer, presence, kindness, and letting go. All spiritual practice transforms spiritual energies, which serves our own personal welfare, the growth of our being and individuality, and serves the Sacred. The more we become ourselves, the closer we are to the Divine Purpose. Prayer directly addresses that reality, but not as a relationship, because relationship implies separate entities. In pursuing the Divine Purpose, there ultimately is no separation: we seek to embody That in the way we live, in who we are.

Can we know that Purpose? We can imagine God as a mountain of purpose, as the Will that, among other things, creates and sustains this vast universe at every moment. We may be personally and directly touched by that Purpose in a moment of grace and know it thereby. But that does not mean knowing It in a way that can be put into words or even concepts. How does one know a mountain, especially if it is a mountain of intelligence, power, love, and purpose? Up close and personal, It is overwhelming, infinite in comparison to us. Am I worthy to know that mountain? Am I pure enough? Am I strong enough? Perhaps the answer is no, for now at least. Yet we have hope: we hew to our inner work and pursue our highest destiny.

The Divine Purpose, with its vast scope of endless time and boundless space, far transcends our human capacities for understanding. So we cannot know the Divine Purpose in Its objective fullness. But we can participate in It. This does not mean seeking marching orders delivered to us by some inner voice, which is too easily corrupted or coopted by our self-centeredness. The Divine Purpose is much more subtle than that and is not like orders propagating down through an army. We are created to be unique and independent sources of initiative, serving the Good as we understand it. So though we may ask God what to do in a given situation, the answer best comes from our own deeper nature, our lifeline to the Sacred.

As our inner work progresses, our understanding of the Good comes closer to Truth. As the Divine Purpose extends Itself out into the expanding universe, we can be the leading edge of that vast process of spiritualization. The Divine Purpose can work in and through us, to the extent we are willing participants. This does not mean surrendering our individuality, only reuniting ourselves with what we have never truly been separated from. Uniqueness is the nature of the Sacred and we remain individually unique. Indeed, the deeper we enter our inner work, the more individual, the more unique, the more ourselves we become.

Is the Divine Purpose so far removed from us as to be inaccessible, even in principle? This is a question of faith and the answer of faith is no: we each can and do have a direct and inalienable connection with that Great Purpose. We each bear within us a seed, a particle, a ray of that Greatness. And by our inner work, by kindness, by devotion, by deep meditation and contemplative prayer, by inner exploration to plumb the depths of our inner world, we seek to uncover, to remove the veils hiding that vibrant mountain of Divine Purpose from us, hiding our true nature descending from and as that Sacred Purpose, hiding our innermost self.

There is a door in our very core. We stand with our back to that door, facing the world. Our attitude is: I am here. I am the source of my actions, of my will. I am who I am. Yet just behind us, that door awaits. We do not see it because we face away from it. But we can turn ourselves and make room for it to open. And when that door does open, onto the ineffable Sacred, we open back into our true Source.

For this week, open that door and stand within the Divine Purpose.

20.0 Spiritual Habits

As creatures of habit, we would do well to manage our lives, in part, by cultivating useful habits and letting go of destructive ones. In this inner work series, we will focus on certain useful habits that we will call spiritual habits. The term spiritual practice itself implies a repeated or regular return to some attitude, action or technique that develops our soul. But a practice is more than just a habit: practicing means being engaged enough to improve, if only slightly, with each repetition. We will use the term spiritual habit to refer to any spiritual practice which has been so deeply ingrained in us, in our manner of living, that we do it regularly and with little resistance.

Positive habits can be difficult to form. It means giving something up, be it some other activity, some desire, or some attitude. It means that, despite distractions and conflicting desires, we make that positive choice again and again, until it becomes second nature for us. Once a spiritual practice develops into a habit, its very regularity becomes a source of peace, of energy, of hope for us. We trust the practice to lead us in the direction of our evolution. It gives us confidence in our own possibilities, because rather than just thinking or talking or reading about soul and spirit, we start actually doing something about it. It gives more meaning to our life. Then instead of always being faced with our own resistance to the habitual action, we begin to appreciate it, to look forward to it. We know that, at least for those moments, we are doing something necessary, right, and useful, something that gives us satisfaction and makes us a better person, something that makes a contribution.

The key step in establishing a positive habit is to create an effective trigger that will remind us to enter the spiritual action that we seek to make habitual. Such reminders can be of many different types, which leaves ample room for our creativity in developing a trigger that works for us and for the particular spiritual action.

Once we have the trigger, we need to will ourselves into action whenever the reminder occurs. This takes persistence and determination, both of which are enhanced by remembering why we are doing this, by recalling the benefit of that spiritual action.

Sometimes established and effective triggers or reminders lose their potency. The reminder comes and we fail to follow up with the action. In such cases we can either reinvigorate our commitment to keeping that reminder effective, or we can drop it and develop a new one.

Managing these reminders and the practices that they remind us to do is a major part of the art of effective inner work. We pay careful attention to see what works for us, what does not work, and what needs to be changed. How we go about creating spiritual habits depends very much on the practice in question. And to develop all sides of our spiritual nature, we need a balanced variety of such habits. Each of these positive habits reinforces the others. In the coming weeks, we will address the process of entering the path and transforming our lives by making the following categories of spiritual practice habitual:

1. Meditation
2. Prayer
3. Presence
4. Letting Go
5. Kindness
6. Integrity
7. Inner Exploration

It is a mistake to equate habits with unawareness, with auto-pilot living. While it is true that habits, by definition, operate by automatically eliciting our response to a cue, that response itself need not lack awareness or intention. We may have the habit of brushing our teeth, but we could brush them consciously. All spiritual habits depend on full awareness in the habitual action; otherwise they are empty, like praying without contact with the meaning of the prayer or without an attitude of devotion.

For this week, please notice your own spiritual habits, how regular you are about them, what needs strengthening, and what needs changing.

20.1 The Habit of Meditation
(Spiritual Habits: Part 1 of 7)

If we were to form only one spiritual habit, we would do well to make meditation that habit. The profound benefits of a daily meditation practice occur on multiple levels and accumulate over time. The perceptible benefits include peace, kindness, and joy in our heart, clarity and agility in our mind, understanding our patterns and reactions of thought and emotion, improved understanding of our body and its needs through direct, visceral, inner contact with it, improved ability to focus on tasks, more vivid perceptions in all our senses, improved relationships, the growing substantiality of our soul, moments of utter bliss, and so on.

But perhaps the most significant benefit of a regular meditation practice is that it gradually and steadily leads us deeper into the spirit. When we come back into ourselves for a set period every day, we find our inner world opening up. We enter the grand and unexpected hall of consciousness — unexpected because we had no idea that our inner world is so vast. So accustomed are we to being absorbed in the noisy chatter of our minds and the tides of our emotions, that when all that subsides during our periods of sitting meditation, we seem to be left empty-handed, we see nothing of significance left behind. Slowly we begin to realize that what we thought was nothing is in reality the spacious peace of cognizant stillness, the very substance of our fundamental consciousness itself. What a surprise to learn that we live in that, that our mind is that! Not in theory, but in direct, daily experience. And then at times, we may even be touched by the sacred world beyond consciousness. Regular meditation lays the foundation for our spiritual path.

Now it's not all lights and bliss, especially in the earlier stages of our practice. Most of us have much to work through before we begin letting go of our identification with our thoughts and emotions. But dogged persistence works. So an important aspect of developing a regular practice of meditation consists of refraining from judging the quality of our practice. We just sit and do the chosen practice as best we can. Every day we sit for the allotted time, whether it's pleasant, unpleasant, neutral or boring. Indeed, the freedom we gain in learning not to be driven by what we like or don't like is another significant benefit of training our body and mind to meditate. Then there is the meditative freedom from the constant need for stimulation and distraction. By sitting with ourselves, we get to know ourselves, we get comfortable with ourselves, and we start to know what is beyond ourselves, what is beyond all things.

The best time for meditation is at the start of our day, typically in the morning before breakfast. That sets our inner tone for the day and makes an immense difference to our other spiritual efforts during the day, such as presence. Generally, the longer our sitting, the more deeply we can enter into it. Our inner fog, our immersion in the mental chatter, takes time to settle enough so that we can focus on our method of meditation, although we do begin our effort or non-effort as soon as we sit down.

Is there a minimum length of time? No. Any meditation, even a few moments, matters.

Is there a preferred length of time? Yes. But that is an individual matter, which we discover by ourselves through experimenting with longer and shorter sittings. And that preferred length of meditation can change over the years. To make it into an effective habit, we choose a set minimum period of meditation and then sit for at least that long every day. Occasionally, perhaps weekly, we extend ourselves by sitting for longer than usual or by sitting twice in one day. Evening meditation can quickly usher us into a deep and comforting peace.

We are fortunate in the amazing variety of meditation techniques taught through books, retreats, and teachers. We begin by finding one that suits us and staying with it, or several and alternating among them. But particularly at the beginning, we stick to one practice or one set of practices for some years, so that we can enter them deeply and learn from them. Over time, as we change, our practice will change: we may adopt new methods learned from others or adapt our old ones through experimentation.

Creating a positive habit takes effort. We have to make time for it, again and again. We have to choose to do it, again and again. We have to persevere through the ups and downs of our inner meditative experience. But once established, the habit of meditation pays great dividends. Instead of considering it a chore, we come to cherish our periods of meditation. They become a source of joy and solace, a steady, welcoming, and healing space we return to every day. And it's not just about us. In meditation we transform higher energies and thereby become the bearers of a beneficial influence for the society around us.

For this week, begin, renew, deepen, or extend your habit of meditation.

20.2 *The Habit of Prayer*
(Spiritual Habits: Part 2 of 7)

In prayer, at its best, we give our attention, energy, and heart to the Sacred and we receive purity, peace, and love. It's a pretty good deal all the way round. Most significant for our spiritual work is the purifying nature of prayer. It is inevitably humbling truly to attempt to present ourselves before the Divine, to stand before the Infinite One. However we may or may not conceive of the Higher, we know that somehow God far transcends us. We can only relate ourselves to That to the extent we shed our arrogance and self-centeredness, the sure belief that we personally are the important center of the universe. The spiritual person is free, or at least becoming free, of all that.

Regular prayer chips away at egoism. In fact, sincere and regular prayer takes us beyond belief altogether, by bringing us into direct experience, however veiled, of the Sacred and Its precincts. In that inner place, life is very different: not so fragmented and contentious, not so fragile and incomplete.

We come toward this very simply by representing to ourselves, as we pray, that our prayer is addressed, not to nothing, but to some One, the Divine One, Who is present and listening right now, even if beyond our perception. This is the key that keeps our prayer from being a rote, perfunctory, and empty repetition. When we have the feeling that we are standing before the Divine, it sobers us, awakens us, and opens our heart. It helps us understand that we are here for a reason, even if we cannot comprehend that reason. It arouses in us the wish to live rightly, to make the best of our life. It alerts us to the possibility that that best life somehow concerns our inner development, service, and spirituality as much or more than it concerns outward success.

So how do we create, reinvigorate, or extend our regular habits of prayer? We begin with cultivating our faith that there is a Higher Power, that there is much more to reality than science reveals, that this remarkable universe was and is being created. Of course, prayer itself increases our faith by bringing us closer to the Source. But we can also cultivate faith by contemplating this world, its complexity and beauty, our lack of understanding what makes it tick and what decides which possibilities get realized. Is love just some psychological trait that helped us survive the long rigors of evolution? Did this universe just create itself, by accident? Is there no greatness behind the scenes that beckons to us? Who am I really? When I look deeply into myself, do I find nothing? Or chaos? Why are we here? Are all those who follow a religious way just deluded holdovers from a pre-scientific era? Do the enlightened see that nothing is sacred, that everything is sacred, or that there is a Sacred One? Deep questioning awakens faith, because the answers lie beyond our mind, beyond our ordinary perceptions. And prayer is a road toward the answer.

So how should we pray? Usually, the best way is to draw on the liturgy of our childhood religion, or another religion that may have attracted us. Religions are of full of prayers.

We look for those prayers that touch us personally. And if we do not find any, we create our own. The important qualities of the form are that it invite us, that it enable us fully to engage our mind and heart in the prayer, and that it orient us toward the Divine.

Then we look to make it regular. How we do that depends on the nature and length of the prayer: perhaps each morning before we meditate or at the end of our meditation or perhaps each evening, or all three. We can have different prayers for different circumstances. Some prayers may be petitionary in nature, asking for the welfare of our family, neighbors, and our self. Some prayers may be contemplative, looking to open to a certain sacred quality, like love or acceptance, or looking to open ourselves directly to the Divine. Other prayers may be of gratitude, such as at the beginning of a meal or at the safe end of a journey. Some may be the formal, set prayers of a religion, done at certain times of the day or the week or the year, on our own or in a community of prayer. Some may be spoken or chanted, others said inwardly and silently. Still others may have no words.

Some prayers may be episodic or spontaneous, while others are regular and repeated. The latter create a space for the former. To develop that regularity, we choose one prayer and one regular daily time for it. And then we do it. If we persist, soon enough it becomes a habit. We need to monitor that habit, not just the regularity but also the quality. We make sure that we bring the whole of ourselves to the prayer: our heart, mind, body, attention, and intention. The more fully we enter it, the more useful it is.

At first prayer is a one-way conversation, from us to the Divine. At times it can be a celebration in gratitude. More and more, an appreciative joy becomes our attitude toward life. And in contemplative prayer it becomes an intimate participation in the root of world: in that silence we enter the Holy Land. We are meant for that. Prayer is one of the principal factors that give our life completeness.

For this week, invite yourself to pray.

20.3 The Meta-Habit of Presence
(Spiritual Habits: Part 3 of 7)

To be present is to live, truly live. In presence we are awake and alert to all of our senses, our thoughts and emotions, and most importantly we are here ourselves, we are the one receiving all those sensory inputs, the one who knows our thoughts and emotions, the one who does what we do. On the face of it, this appears to describe our ordinary state. But even some rudimentary attempts to be and stay in touch with our sensory perceptions or with our thoughts as thoughts, on an ongoing basis, shows us that we are usually not present or, at best, in partial and limited contact with our life. To see this, try to be aware of your right arm continuously, moment-to-moment for an hour as you go about your day. How about ten minutes? How about one minute? You may see that it is not as easy as it sounds. That's because we live in the habit of non-presence; we allow our ordinary, automatic habits to run our life for us, without our actual participation.

To be clear, presence does not replace our automatic habits: we need all our useful habits. When we tie our shoes, or type on keyboard, or brush our teeth, or walk, or engage any of the myriad small and large skills in our repertoire, we want them to go automatically without us constantly micromanaging. The automatic energy makes our lives efficient and is thus necessary. Presence comes on top of that. We can be present while we tie our shoes. We don't direct every small movement of our fingers as they do their job. We just decide to initiate the shoe-tying routine and let that habit go on its own without our interference. But the crucial difference is that in presence we are here to witness the event, fully here. We can say in complete truth, "I am tying my shoes." We experience this moment of shoe-tying; we live it. By means of the sensitive energy we are in contact with the shoe-tying sensations in our body, particularly in our hands. With the conscious energy, we are aware of ourselves as being here, doing this. Each energy, the automatic, the sensitive, and the conscious, has its place in presence.

This is very different, inwardly, than allowing the shoe-tying to occur while we passively drift along in our automatic, associative thoughts. Such an episode is a non-cognizant void in our non-life. Did we actually live those moments?

To live more fully, we need a new, higher-level habit, a meta-habit: the habit of presence, an intentional, cognizant extension to whatever else we do. Once we have practiced the methods of presence and have some facility with them, we face the challenge of being present more of our time. We want to make it into a habit, but not an ordinary habit that is both triggered and carried out automatically. Yes, we want the triggers, the reminders to be automatic, to be habitual; we want them to remind us to be present. But then the follow through of actually being present can never be automatic, for its very definition implies at least a sensitive contact with our immediate perceptions and preferably also a contextual consciousness of our self as the one who is present. So we work to introduce the habit of presence piecemeal into particular aspects of our life. From those beachheads, from those islands of light, we can expand into more of our life.

One effective approach is to piggy-back presence onto ordinary habitual or automatic actions that require little of us and thus leave ample attention and energy free to engage in presence.

Take the example of walking. Our body knows quite well how to walk and does so with minimal conscious direction from us. We typically set a destination and let our body walk, on automatic, only requiring some minor course corrections along the way. But now, into this walking, we bring presence: first by sensitive contact, by being aware of our body, of the sensations of our body as it walks, without intentionally changing the outward form of our walking. This is fundamental: robust presence is built on the platform of sensitive contact with our body, of sensing our body, whether in walking or in any other activity. Later, once we have come to the point of being able to sense our whole body as we walk, we are naturally led into a more global conscious presence, in which we are the walker, in which we are aware of our surroundings, our body, our thoughts, our emotions, and ourselves — all in the one field of consciousness.

The main point, though, is to train ourselves to sense our body whenever we walk, even just a short distance from one room to another. At first we have to remember to do this; it takes effort. But by repeated practice, the simple act of walking starts to remind us to be present as we walk. And when we notice that reminder, we must be willing to engage in walking-presence immediately. Then presence in walking becomes a meta-habit. This is possible and doable for anyone who persists. And it changes our life because we walk so often.

There are countless ways to create reminders of presence. Besides walking, we could work to be present when answering the phone, or more generally when talking, when eating or drinking, when moving from sitting to standing, when first getting into bed at night, when first awakening in the morning, when brushing our teeth, when dressing, when reading, when watching TV, and so on. You can look into your own life and adapt the meta-habit of presence to how you live. But it's important to establish only one such reminder at a time. Trying too much at once leads to failure; piece by piece though, the reminders build up and enrich our life.

To be in the middle of some habit routine and then add on sensitive awareness of our body, our mind, our heart, and our surroundings, and conscious awareness of ourselves, sounds like and is a challenge in multi-tasking. But with practice, the multiple parts meld into a unified experience: one field of consciousness with one experiencer/doer.

So to develop the meta-habit of presence, we first choose a reminder. Then we notice that reminder. Then, because of its concreteness and because it belongs only to the present moment, we always begin with body awareness and, as we become able to, we expand from there.

For this week, please work on the meta-habit of presence.

20.4 The Habit of Letting Go
(Spiritual Habits: Part 4 of 7)

Letting go is a fundamental practice of every spiritual path. It is unique in its personal intimacy, engaging us at our core. We do not let go with our feet or hands, with our thoughts or emotions, with our personality patterns, nor with our energies. Only we ourselves, our own I, our will, can let go.

But what does letting go mean? We've already addressed the question of who let's go: it is our I. So what do we let go of? In a word: attachments. We say upfront that this does not refer to our attachments to our family and loved ones. And it does not necessarily mean putting something out of our life. It does mean freeing ourselves of our inner slavery, cutting the bonds of indulgence and regret.

Say you have a strong craving for a particular food. For example, maybe you love ice cream to the extent that you eat too much of it, more than is healthy, and perhaps you eat the ice cream with such gluttony that you hardly taste it or enjoy it. This is attachment in action. The ice cream is eating us. The craving is controlling us. With the possible exception of an initial period of complete abstinence, say forty days, to let go of that attachment doesn't necessarily mean not eating ice cream, but could mean doing so with moderation, letting go of the craving to eat more than a modest amount, while savoring what we do eat.

Each act of letting go is a movement from less freedom toward more freedom, from less love toward more love, from small self toward big Self, from taking to giving. Letting go distinguishes in us the higher from the lower, our I from our personality, our conscience from our ego, freedom from identification. When we give in to some craving, it feels like freedom, the freedom to eat ice cream or the freedom to complain. But it's the craving that is free, the craving that has chosen, while we have relinquished our will.

How do we let go? It is a two-fold act of will. First is perception: recognizing an impulse or pattern that we need to let go of. This is crucial. If we don't see it, we cannot let go of it. If we don't see the craving as craving, the anger as anger, the destructive criticism, whether of self or other, as criticism, the complaining as complaining, we will not be in a position to choose to let it go. This is a matter of self-awareness, which we practice by intentionally noticing how things are in us, what leads to what. The practice of presence brings self-awareness, as does meditation.

The question of what constitutes an attachment, what we need to let go of, is personal. It depends on our seeing, our vision, and our wisdom. It depends on listening to our conscience. Generally though, any inner pattern that occurs without our initiating it, or despite our wishing otherwise, or anything we are identified with, is a potential candidate for letting go. When we believe we are the anger, the craving, the criticism — that is identification. We do not want to be under the thumb of our likes and dislikes, our destructive emotions like anger, jealousy, and envy, our physical cravings, our destructive patterns of thought like criticisms, complaints, and arrogance, a slave to our fixed opinions. We want to be free in front of all that. It does not necessarily mean stopping those impulses altogether, which is nearly impossible to do directly. It just means not be driven by them. If we like ice cream, we may continue eating ice cream, with moderation, when we choose to do so, not whenever our craving demands it. We are not seeking an ascetic life, just a free one.

After seeing what to let go of, the second part of letting go is actually to choose to let it go, in a moment of its arising. If we are not willing to make that choice, then we have no chance; we become at best a spectator, as our various impulses live our life for us. But if we truly choose to let go, rather than just wishing we would make that choice, then there are techniques that help. Relaxation is the first key. And the understanding that everything that arises passes away is the second key. Impulses and cravings, anger and criticisms, may seem urgent. But we just relax, physically, emotionally, and mentally, in that moment, and stay relaxed, just being there, doing nothing, neither pushing the impulse away nor taking the action it desires. Soon enough, the impulse, the desire, the craving and the rest will dissipate of their own accord, leaving us free to live, not by our shallow drives, but by our deeper feelings, our true wishes, our principles, our creativity, our uniqueness and our conscience.

Our relationships with people, whether strangers, acquaintances, friends or family, provide a fertile field for letting go. In particular, the practice is to allow oneself to be imposed upon without grumbling or resentment, inner or outer. Each time we do that it deepens that relationship and chips away at our egoism. Trivial everyday examples include the courtesy of holding a door for the next person and yielding to rushed or aggressive drivers. We do the right thing and then perhaps we notice our resentment. Noticing that, we let it go too, and move on.

To form the habit of letting go, like any other habit, we need to cultivate a trigger, a reminder. The reminder to let go is the uncomfortable feeling of being identified, of being caught, of being under the control of some attachment, of not being free. The practice of letting go, helps us acquire the taste of identification, of attachment. Then when we notice that bitter taste, it is our signal to let go. And when we follow through with actually letting go in that instance, we form and strengthen this spiritual habit of freedom.

Rather than attempt to let go of all our attachments, we start with one and build up. Maybe you love to complain and see that you are identified when you do complain and choose to work on letting of complaining. Then whenever you notice that you are about to complain, you check yourself. You turn that energy toward relaxing, physically, mentally, and emotionally in that moment. You let the impulse to complain be there and fade away of its own accord and in its own time. You do this without complaining, outwardly at first, and when you can, you even let go of the thoughts of complaint. You see them and let them be, but you do not buy into them. Those are just thoughts, they are not you.

Mindfulness meditation is an excellent training for letting go. We sit and allow all things to be as they are, without imposing our will to change our inner state. We let the thoughts come and go, as well as the sounds, the sensations, the images, impulses, and emotions. Whatever arises, we let it be and we let it pass on its own. We just sit and be. All these inner events, vying for our attention, gradually settle down when we refuse to engage with them. And it leaves us in the freedom of pure awareness; a freedom that carries over into the natural joy of living.

For this week, cultivate the spiritual habit of letting go.

20.5 The Habit of Kindness
(Spiritual Habits: Part 5 of 7)

Acts of kindness are a natural expression of the Great

Heart of Love, where no distinction exists between self and other. The practice of kindness leads toward love, toward the vision that we are not separate.

We appreciate the person who is habitually kind; we trust, respect, value, and gravitate toward them. There is a purity about them, a selflessness, and other qualities we aspire to. Many years ago, I briefly met a young man, fresh out of seminary, whose eyes and mannerisms conveyed such a perfection of purity, selflessness, and kindness, that I felt a strong sense of shame in his presence, shame at my own imperfections, which led to the questions: can purity and kindness be attained by spiritual inner work and, if so, how?

Kind acts emanate from wholesome attitudes of being. Do we erect and nurture a great inner wall between ourselves and others? In learning to be, just be, that wall grows porous and eventually dissolves. We discover we don't need walls to be ourselves, that in fact we are more ourselves without them. That is how meditation and presence lead toward kindness. Prayer also promotes kindness, for in prayer we address our common Creator. Before that Greatness, we are all the same. And in that sameness is the seed of kindness.

To practice kindness, we first cultivate awareness of how we treat people, both inwardly in our thoughts and judgments, and outwardly in our speech and actions. We notice our interactions with people and the thoughts and emotions driving those interactions. We practice watching this and attempt to see objectively, not only from our own point of view, but how others might see us and how what we do and think affects them. We notice when we are less than kind and we notice the justifications we think up both before and after.

Then opportunities arise for us to treat people as they would want us to treat them, for us to act in their best interest, without betraying our own. We move beyond looking out first for ourselves. Of course, we do this in moderation and reasonably; we do not, for example, give away our home and life savings and thereby impoverish ourselves. For kindness to thrive and become habitual, it must also extend to ourselves. And there are many forms of generosity and charity, not all of which include donating money.

Inner kindness also matters. How do we treat people inwardly, in our thoughts and emotions? Again, we notice how we are inwardly unkind and we look to go beyond this. For that we need to see a little deeper into ourselves, into the source of the particular unkindness. It may be strongly held opinions and points of view that the other person does not share. It may be jealousy or envy. It may be competition. It may be a reaction to their unkindness toward us. We can let go of our attachment to opinions and not insist that others toe the line. We can see that jealousy and envy pollute our hearts and derail us from being ourselves, from confidence in and satisfaction with ourselves. Cooperation and competition are the twin drivers of nature's way of evolution. And competition has its healthy side in spurring us on to do our best. But when our self-centeredness latches onto being the winner, depersonalizing and demonizing our competitors, and putting them out of our heart, then competition passes over into unkindness or worse. And though vengeful unkindness may feel good and justified in the moment, it poisons our heart. To be free inwardly and to move toward love, we need to let go of unkindness and all that drives it.

The basic motivation for kindness is the recognition of our sameness. Our immersion in our thoughts and emotions, in our attitudes and intentions, color, obscure, or even overwhelm our perceptions of other people. Looking beyond all that, when we see another person and ignore our differences, we are left with our sameness. On the surface, we each have our own body and personality, different than anyone else. But there is more. Beneath those differences there is pure awareness, the consciousness that we all share. When you see another person and look beyond your surface differences, you can see that their awareness is the very same as yours — not just similar to yours, but actually the same consciousness, the one consciousness. Even the differences in perspective are on the surface of the fundamental consciousness we share. We look into the sky; regardless of where we look from, it is the same sky.

Going deeper still, beyond consciousness, differences reemerge: we each have our own unique I, distinguished from anyone else's I. To transcend that difference, we recognize that our very uniqueness derives from the nature of the Source of our I, the Sacred, which is the one root of us all. Our will, our freedom, derive from the Divine Will. As children of the same Creator, as particles of the Divine, the extent to which we remember and connect with our Source is the extent to which we honor, respect, and treat with kindness all our fellow children of the Unique.

The result of such seeing is to recognize our sameness with others, that here is a person like I am. Seeing their personhood, we see our own. This person is aware just as I am aware, indeed with the very same basic awareness. This person has hopes and dreams and concerns, just as I have hopes and dreams and concerns. Kindness flows naturally.

From the place of sameness, kindness can become a habit, our normal mode of interacting with our fellow inhabitants of this planet. When we notice an unkind impulse arising in us, we see it and let it pass. When we notice an opportunity to be useful, courteous, or kind, we go with it. Practicing this, our whole way of being moves toward the way of kindness.

For this week, practice kindness. See your own lack of kindness. See your sameness with others. Make kindness a habit and make room in your heart.

20.6 The Habit of Integrity
(Spiritual Habits: Part 6 of 7)

When our will is whole, integral, and always acts in

accord with our conscience, we become a person of integrity. Such people are responsible, honest, keep their word, and live by their principles. Yet integrity does not always come easily, even for them. Integrity can become a habit, but one that requires continual reaffirmation in specific situations both large and small. Temptations abound in this world, testing our integrity. The question that keeps coming back is why bother? Why resist those temptations? As long as it's not illegal, what difference does it make how I act? Can't I cheat just a little? Yet that little may cost a lot.

It turns out that a clear conscience is precious, very precious, especially for anyone who aspires to a spiritual inner life. Once we have established ourselves in the habit of not violating our conscience, the clarity and the inner wholeness it brings become invaluable to us. When our conscience becomes who we are, we act to protect it. We ask ourselves in any situation that pricks our inner sensibilities: what is the right thing to do? If we persist in that questioning and follow through on the responses of our conscience, we establish the habit, wherein integrity breeds more integrity. This makes our commitment to integrity grow stronger and helps us overcome the inevitable moments of weakness.

One difficulty comes as the temptation to cheat in small ways, rationalizing that this minor violation will not affect our integrity. But it does. As the saying goes: God is in the details. Integrity means in part the striving for perfection, even or especially in the details, the small things. Minor temptations have the one advantage that they arise more often than the big ones, and so give us a chance to exercise and reaffirm our integrity.

When we notice ourselves inwardly or outwardly justifying some choice, we can take that as a danger signal. Doing the right thing does not require justification or rationalization, but the contrary does.

If we find ourselves on a downward spiral, falling into patterns of action that lack integrity, we need to find a way to reset. One approach is through self-confession and penance. We take time to take stock of ourselves, to review our actions with as much honesty and objectivity as we can muster, to see clearly our situation. Then we can resolve to break with that behavior and we invest in that resolution by giving up some particular pleasure for a short time. Maybe we skip a meal, or give up chocolate for a day, or forgo watching an episode of our favorite TV program. We give up something simple, not too difficult and not too harsh, but enough to seal the deal. If our wrongdoings have negatively impacted other people, we may also need to make amends and/or apologize.

Without integrity, we sometimes live by conscience and principle, and sometimes not. This split, these divided loyalties, put us at war with ourselves and weaken us. Guilt, for example, is a sign of this, as is the wish to hide. How can others trust us, when we cannot trust ourselves? Lack of integrity puts us at the mercy of whatever impulse gains the upper hand in our chaos of desires. We vacillate with the wind. We lack a stable direction. And we lose ourselves in the process.

If we are not at war with ourselves, we at least do not have that particular obstacle to wholeness. Acting with integrity brings our disparate parts, our conflicting impulses and desires, into the singleness of choice, the singleness of a unifying will, the singleness of I. Instead of our will being splintered among a myriad of impulses and desires, we become whole. We integrate ourselves by harmonizing our inner discord under the umbrella of presence and love.

Each impulse, each desire is a part of us, not an independent actor. We do not give ourselves over to it alone. Succumbing to anger or jealousy, for example, damages us, chews up our inner life. Nor do we ignore such impulses or bury them, because they are a part of us. Instead, our expanding presence, in service to our conscience and expressing our will-to-be, absorbs and integrates all our parts. Love, which must include ourselves, embraces the whole of us and all our parts. We love ourselves enough not to fall into some damaging impulse from one of our parts.

Thus with integrity, we become ourselves. We stand for something: for doing the right thing and being ourselves. Integrity attracts integrity: it is contagious. When we are with a person of integrity, we tend to treat them with integrity. If we know they always keep their word, we want to keep our word to them. And because we are integrating our discordant, contrary parts, we can keep our word.

When it comes to the spiritual life, integrity is an absolute requirement. We cannot fool God, for God, Who gave us the freedom to choose, sees through us. We cannot enter or even touch the deeper realms of the spirit as long as we have a guilty conscience. A confused and contorted conscience makes a confused and contorted self, a barrier to the spirit. This is one of the inner reasons for the religious emphasis on avoiding sin, repenting, and seeking forgiveness. We seek forgiveness to alleviate the burden we carry for our wrongdoings. And going forward, if we build the habit of integrity into our life and become established in it, then our conscience gradually clears up. This leaves us free to approach the Sacred with some degree of the required purity, with an open heart and a selfless mind.

Wholeness, singleness of will is one of the deeper meanings of integrity. It speaks to integrating across the breadth of our impulses, desires, and wishes. Another meaning is inner and outer purity of action, which speaks to integrating in depth, to allowing the Sacred source of our will to affect our choices and manner of living. Out of respect for the higher, we live with integrity, always and without exception. In a very real sense, our integrity is our connection with the Sacred.

For this week, make a habit of integrity.

20.7 The Habit of Exploration
(Spiritual Habits: Part 7 of 7)

    To the early European explorers, the great expanse of the Atlantic ocean hid the unknown at its far shores. In the same way, our inner world remains largely unknown to us and hides the realm of the spirit. We engage in spiritual practices, meditation, presence, and prayer, but we do not really expect to discover anything extraordinary. We may find ourselves more relaxed, less stressed, more energized, more heart-full. But it all remains just an extension of our ordinary experience and at the same level. Our thoughts, emotions, bodily and sense perceptions may change, but all of that still captivates us, still commands our attention and concern as the place of our life. We do not recognize what the experience of a different order of being might be. Even if we read a description of it in a book or if someone tells us about it, we still do not see it, we feel that it does not actually apply to us.

    To penetrate in depth, we need an attitude of investigation and exploration, we need to look deeply with a mind open to new categories of experience, new kinds of perception. For example, we may know about the stillness behind and between our thoughts. Yet we relegate that experience to just a mind that is temporarily blank, and consider it ordinary and uninteresting. That is a mistake, for that blank stillness is much more than a mere absence of thoughts: it is our opening into the ocean of consciousness, it is one portal through which we can explore in depth.

    What is consciousness? What is the substance of our awareness? What is beyond consciousness? What and where is the spiritual reality? What are inner energies? What is presence? Who am I? In what sense and when do I exist? Why are we here? Why is the universe here? What is the purpose of life? Of my life? What can I do? What should I do? Do I have a soul? Do I need to develop a soul? How?

None of these fundamental questions can be fully answered by logic or by science or by any ordinary knowledge, because they all address the realms beyond space and time, the realms beyond the reach of logic, science, and knowledge. To approach such questions we can only delve deep within our own being. An explorer ventures out to discover new worlds, to find what is there, to see the truth. A spiritual explorer ventures inward to discover new worlds and see the truth. That is the opportunity that calls to us.

Each time we meditate or enter contemplative prayer or embark on another episode of presence, we look to cross the boundaries of our ordinary experience. We look to see beyond the envelope we live in. We take an empirical approach to see what is actually there in us. All the great maps of the spiritual reality, all the great philosophies and theologies can provide guidance, but do not in themselves enable us to see. True seeing goes beyond ideas and thoughts. No description can teach us the fragrance of the rose.

We study the teachings and the practices. Then we dive within and see what we see. In our inner work, we try different approaches. We notice what works and what does not. We take what does work and push it further. We try variations, different inner actions and inner postures. We experiment with intensity and focus, with relaxing and opening. We extend in breadth and in depth. We extend in time and in our body space, in duration, frequency, and breadth of presence. We notice what we have not noticed. We question our assumptions regarding what is not possible for us. We extend beyond time to the timeless, beyond form to the formless. If we don't know how, we experiment. Our inner being becomes our laboratory, fully-equipped and ready. We notice conditions and results. We notice how the daily variations in our life-style affect our inner life and our inner work. We cultivate our spiritual intelligence and manage our path.

Wonders await us: worlds of meaning, purpose, and joy beyond conception. Yes, there is much to be said for regular efforts, such as getting ourselves to sit on the meditation cushion every day. Those efforts are necessary. But we also need to push our envelope and explore beyond it.

For this week, look more deeply.

21.0 Presence in Daily Life

If our inner work is to transform our life and our world, it needs to reach as much of our life as we can manage. The impact of the spiritual practice we do on the meditation cushion can be greatly multiplied by our efforts of presence throughout our day. Those efforts always come down to specific moments in specific situations. Every moment presents an opportunity for inner work. Every part of our life counts. Can we open our barren places to the light of our spirit? For example, because so much of life is spent at our job, we cannot afford to leave such a large chunk of our time devoid of presence. Our time is limited and precious. We need to make each day, each hour count. Any moment in which we are not building and perfecting our soul is a moment slipping away from us, irrevocably. One effective response to that gnawing feeling of dissatisfaction that sometimes invades our heart is to redouble our efforts of inner work. Moments of presence are not wasted.

Can we reconcile our inner work with our outer life, with our job and with all our myriad tasks and activities? Obviously, we do not want to allow our inner practice to have a negative impact on our performance at work or anywhere else. But it need not. On the contrary, the two can mutually reinforce each other. Presence does not require us to sit on a cushion in silent meditation. We can practice presence in the midst of our day's activity and even enhance our performance thereby. In any given moment, the more we are present, the more we engage in what we are doing — and vice versa. The more we are present, the more focus, quality, insight, wisdom and persistence we can bring to what we do.

The limits to this are more apparent than real. We don't want our surgeon to be practicing presence by splitting her attention to be aware of her breath while she is operating on us. But if that surgeon is practicing presence by being fully there, fully engaged in what she is doing, then that is certainly compatible with the successful practice of surgery. Indeed, we can surmise that any good surgeon is wholly engaged and present during surgery, whether or not they have ever heard of the concept of presence. This raises the question of what we mean by presence.

Fundamentally, presence means being in contact with whatever is going on in this moment. But there are dimensions of breadth and depth, of more contact or less, of more presence or less. Our body is always in this moment. So presence necessarily includes and is typically rooted in awareness of our body, being in our body, sensing our body, viscerally, organically. It means being aware of our thoughts and our emotions in this moment, including how our emotions affect our body, how our emotions affect our thoughts and vice versa. It means being aware of what our other senses are bringing us, of our environment, the life, the people, the objects around us. Through practice our awareness grows broad enough to include all this at once. But presence is more than awareness.

Our attention can grow to encompass this total moment. That raises the question: who is present? If no one is present, then it is not presence. If your I is present, then the core of presence is there. You have the experience: I am here now. I am aware of all this, I am doing what I am doing. This I is simple and direct, but tends to slip away, to evaporate suddenly and without warning. The practice of presence is at heart the practice of I being here, of exercising the will to be, of being the one who sees what we see and does what we do, the one who directs our attention and makes our choices. Indeed the easiest way to get a handle on who we are, on what our I is, consists of noticing our attention, of being our attention. Our will, our I, directs our attention and is intimately involved in it. By being our attention, by being the root, the source of our attention, we become ourselves, we become I.

To be engaged in what we are doing does not mean getting lost in it or being identified with it. It is a question of whether we are present and doing the activity or whether we are identified and the activity is doing us. When we are present, we are in the flow of the moment, living it. When we are identified, the moment passes without us, because we have lost our I, letting it dissolve into the activity or the thought or the emotion or the experience. The thing we are identified with becomes our self. Identification should not be confused with the much higher state of selflessness, of pure doing, wherein our I takes its place in a greater will.

When we aspire to a spiritual path, it is tempting to compartmentalize our inner life, dividing it between times for inner work and times that are not for inner work, as dictated by outer circumstances. By practicing presence in our daily life, we can break down that wall, reintegrate our inner life with our outer life, so that we do all the things we do while simultaneously building our soul. The path and our life need not be separate. We can live one life, a complete life. We can be whole and here, living our life ongoing. Presence enables that new life, enriching and vivifying our time by adding the timeless.

While life in a monastery has great spiritual advantages, we can practice presence without becoming a monk or a nun, right in this life we now lead. It is available to us all. Our life becomes our path, our practice. Whatever our employment is, we can practice presence. If we don't have a job, or are looking for a job, or our job is to be a student, or to be homemaker, we can practice presence. When we're off the job, we can practice presence.

In this inner work series, we will engage various practical exercises aimed at bringing presence into more of our life, including our life at work. For this week, please look into your day to see what areas of your life particularly lack presence and thus offer an opportunity.

21.1 Waiting Presence
(Presence in Daily Life: Part 1)

Waiting used to be a problem. Standing in line at the grocery, we would fight off the boredom by scanning the tabloids waiting there with us or we would ruminate on our bad luck of getting in the wrong line, coming to the store at the wrong time, or the injustice of it all. But now waiting is an opportunity. We can just grab our smartphone and have an array of things to do while we wait our turn. Despite the improvement in "productivity," this development is in one way unfortunate, because it decreases the possibility of inner productivity while we wait. It does not, however, eliminate that possibility, because we can be present while using a smartphone. It just takes a higher level of effort. Another possibility, though, is not to pick up our smartphone and instead focus exclusively on presence while we wait.

Look more carefully at these interludes, these gaps in time that we call waiting. This is the low-hanging fruit of off-the-cushion inner work. The feeling of incipient boredom can be a potent reminder that we have both the time and the inner resources available to focus on presence, at least at that moment. Waiting can remind us to be here while we wait. That work of presence while waiting, removes the feeling that waiting is wasted time and fills the period with meaning, with vivid life, with something productive and nourishing for our soul.

Sometimes we wait inwardly even when are fully occupied outwardly. This may occur when our outer activity does not require our full attention. Take the example of exercising. Maybe at a particular exercise session we are looking forward to it being over, waiting for it to end. This type of inner waiting is also a good opportunity for presence, because it signals that we have inner resources, attention and cognizant energy, to spare. We can turn that to constructive use by practicing waiting presence right then.

We wait: in line, for our ride, for the bus, the train or the airplane, in the waiting room. We wait for the waiter. We wait for the class or the commute to be over, for the work day or week to end. We wait for a break, for our boat to come in, for the computer to boot up. So much opportunity. So much time ready to be put to constructive use.

We tend to equate waiting with impatience and boredom, twin emotions of rejection, rejecting our life as it is in this moment, and most tellingly, rejecting just being. We want to do something or be entertained, somehow to fill our time, to fill the silence or rush on to the next thing. We rightly abhor wasting our time. But busyness alone does not help; it just masks the more fundamental problem: that we live without presence, that we live without being here to experience our life in the full richness of any moment.

When we wait, we not only have time, ordinary, outer time, to kill as it were; we also and more importantly have inner time. Just as outer time is the framework of action in the physical world, inner time is the framework of action in our inner world. The inner action we seek in this particular mode of spiritual practice is to become and stay present while we wait. Waiting provides the opportunity for that inner action.

When we notice that we are waiting for something, then instead of sinking into boredom or resentment, instead of breaking out the smartphone, instead of scanning the tabloids, we can move into presence, as completely as possible. With practice we become able to enter full presence all at once. Until then, we take a stepwise approach and build up our presence. We start with our body, with awareness of our body, sensing parts and, if we can, the whole of our body. We take time to strengthen that direct, visceral contact with our body, to raise that sensitive energy. To this we add awareness of our emotional state, of what's happening in our chest and solar plexus. To that we add awareness of our thoughts as they come and go. Then we enter the cognizant stillness behind our thoughts, our open, spacious consciousness, whereupon we see that we are not our thoughts or emotions. To all of that we add ourselves: we enter the moment as I. I am here, now. And then we maintain this fullness of presence, as we continue to wait. This is waiting presence.

For this week, don't just wait, be there.

21.2 Entertainment Presence
(Presence in Daily Life: Part 2)

We spend much of our precious time being entertained: by TV, movies, music and concerts, sports, novels, and so on. We consume all these with little thought to the effects on our life and particularly our inner life. Can we bring more value to our time as a spectator?

A primary way we measure the quality of any entertainment is the degree to which it engages us, mentally and emotionally. If it's good, it invites us to surrender to it for the duration. And if it's good, we accept. That is the bargain. We give our mind and heart to the show, the movie, concert, game, or novel and let it play us. For that period we live as that event. Its images form themselves in our minds. Its emotions form themselves in our hearts. The show moves us; it lives us. We allow ourselves to be passive receivers, passive participants. Our life for that time is the show. This we usually consider good entertainment. The drama, the thrill, the suspense, the horror, the righteousness, the anxiety and fear, the romance and humor, the beauty, the reversals, and the breakthroughs: entertainment stimulates us with a wide repertoire of emotion and spectacle. No wonder it can be so addicting. We experience it all in ourselves as our own. Indeed it is our own experience, for those moments. We surrender, putting ourselves into abeyance, and let the show take us, letting it drive our perceptions, feelings, thoughts, and mental images. The entertainment industry has gotten very good at this, keeps getting better, and will continue to become more effective, more immersive, as new techniques and technologies come into use.

So where does this leave us, if we aspire to a spiritual inner life? One answer, that doesn't offer much help, is that there are the rare few works of entertainment, certain great music, a few movies, and others that rather than take us out of ourselves, actually serve to bring us to ourselves, calling us to presence. But those are rare. The great bulk of entertainment takes us away and scripts our time and experience for us.

Another answer is the monkish one of eliminating our TV watching, our movie going, our music listening. Rather than make our life dull, that would enrich it; the ordinary would become more vivid. But the fact is that most of us, including those who yearn for a spiritual inner life, do not aspire to become monks, nuns, or hermits. We seek a path into the spirit, while living an ordinary life in our times. And the ordinary life of these times in the developed world certainly includes consuming entertainment, or rather being intermittently consumed by entertainment.

So the question becomes: can we bring inner work into our periods of entertainment without diminishing our enjoyment of the show? Can we, for example, give our mind and heart over to the show, while keeping some presence in our body? A partial presence to be sure, but presence nevertheless.

Instead of living completely vicariously in the show, instead of the show totally living us, we also live a parallel time, a real time, in the present, in our body. We let our mind be shaped by the images of the show and our heart informed by the emotional tenor of the show, while our body we keep as our own.

Of course, this is much easier said than done. It takes a clear and decisive intention, formed prior to the show and sustained during it. Without that, we very likely will disappear within the first minute and only reemerge sometime after the show ends, with a vague, uneasy feeling that we have somehow lost our time.

It's been a long day. We're tired and just want to zone out in front of the TV. Is there any chance of presence? Well, yes: we can relax into our body and set a simple intention to stay in contact with our body. Presence does not need tension and can even be effortless. But it does need the will to be. Presence may arise accidentally, unbidden, but quickly evaporates without our intention to be here. So in front of the TV, we can relax into a larger awareness that includes both the show and our body. Almost inevitably we soon forget our body and get lost in the show. Our inner work then is to return again and again to that body contact, whenever we notice we have lost it. And at the commercial breaks or at changes of scene or when we turn the page in our novel, we can take the opportunity to reaffirm, to renew our body presence and carry that into the next segment.

While we base our entertainment presence in body sensation, the core of presence as always, is the ongoing experience of "I am here," the direct perception that I am here, watching this show, in touch with my body. The body contact ensures this presence has some reality to it and does not just evaporate nor descend into a fantasy, a pseudo-presence, where we accept a pretense, an assumption of presence, even when there is none. "I am here, in contact with my body and watching the show."

Entertainment is not inherently destructive to our inner life. But there is an opportunity cost to those hours a day we spend in front of the TV or otherwise being entertained, unless we use that very same time to build our soul, through presence. We may even find that the more present we are, the more we enjoy the show. So when we do relax into some entertainment, we can also practice relaxing into our body, into ourselves, into our I.

For this week, be there to enjoy the show.

21.3 Task Presence
(Presence in Daily Life: Part 3)

Our life is full of tasks: tasks we set ourselves, tasks we agree to, and tasks imposed on us by necessity. Some tasks we avoid or shirk, others we relish, and many bore us. Most are mundane, like tying our shoes, doing the dishes, sweeping the floor, or taking out the garbage, and require little cognitive effort from us. Some are complex, like ones we might perform at our job. A few are long, like building a house, writing a novel, or acquiring a college education. But all tasks, simple or complex, boring or interesting, long or short, present an opportunity for inner work.

We might for example set ourselves to bring quality and excellence to the task, which requires careful attentiveness. Or we might set ourselves to persist in a difficult or repetitious task, which requires an ongoing act of will and managing our anti-task emotions. Or we might go for both excellence and persistence, as necessary and appropriate. But the inner work we wish to address here, namely presence, subsumes most other types of task-related inner work: if we are present we are more likely to do the job well and completely.

Tasks have stages, each an opportunity: being there at the start with a vision of the whole process and an intention to stay present for the duration, being present in the middle while monitoring the progress and quality of our work and giving it the appropriate level of effort, and being present in the completion phase, wherein we look to see that it is truly complete, we check that our work has met our original vision for what we would accomplish, and we feel the satisfaction of having done the job, be it large or small. But the key to all of these is being there, being present, being in the whole of ourselves doing the task: being in our mind as we envision, plan, monitor, consider the feedback and adjust, being in our heart as we bring the appropriate feeling tone, being in our body as we carry out the actions of the task, and being ourselves, our I, as in "I am doing this now."

In some ways presence comes more easily in simple tasks, because we have ample unused energy and attention that we can turn to presence while we do the task. But the problem of presence in simple tasks is to stay with it, not to allow the lack of external challenge to lull us into daydreaming, not to allow boredom or any other emotional reaction to seduce us out of our presence, not to allow our outwardly habitual, automatic performance of the task to cause us to be inwardly automatic as well. We stay with the simple pleasure of being there, doing the task, no more and no less. Even though we could leave it entirely to our routine, automatic patterns of mind and body, we do not. We let the automatic patterns do what they need to do. And all the while, we stay with it, we allow the routine action to be done in us, while we remain on the scene, present as the one who knows, sees, senses, and does what we do.

More complex tasks call us to rise to their challenge, rise to presence and stay there. The more complex and variable the task, the more attention, sensitivity, and cognitive effort it requires. These naturally bring us toward presence, toward full multi-level awareness and being there. To perform a complex task we have to put ourselves into it, we cannot just phone it in. This is one way that our outer life feeds and develops our inner life, one way we fulfill the promise of our humanity. We are not the task; the task is not us. But it is what we do.

For this week, our meta-task is to be present, in body, heart, and mind, as ourselves, as our I, in the performance of the tasks that make up such a large part of our life. Be definite about this. Choose one or a few tasks that you do every or most days, and set yourself to be present in them, starting with body awareness, with sensing your body as you do the task.

21.4 Listening Presence
(Presence in Daily Life: Part 4)

Listening implies a more active inner stance than hearing. A wide and rich array of sounds forms the normal soundscape of our life. Listening means paying attention to a particular stream of those sounds. Because hearing is passive, requiring nothing from us other than having functioning ears, listening tends to relapse by default back to hearing. Rather than being there to meet the sounds, actively cognizing our auditory perceptions, we sink toward letting sounds just wash across the shores of hearing, not noticing them unless something calls to our attention.

The act of paying attention arises by having our attention drawn to something, an inherently passive event, or by us intentionally placing our attention on something. If someone is speaking to us, their activity draws our attention and we listen, but passively. To bring presence to this situation, we actively join in the act of paying attention to what they are saying, so that we take it in fully. We are present in body, heart, and mind, so we listen with our body, heart, and mind. In presence we act from and with the whole of ourselves. So in listening presence, we listen from and with the whole of ourselves. In a conversation, we get what the other person or persons are communicating to us, including the emotions behind what they are saying and the body language they are using.

We can be there, present in the conversation, listening to what the other person is saying, noticing our own mental and emotional reactions, noticing our thoughts, our preparation to respond, our urge to interject. Sometimes we stop listening and start paying more attention to planning what we will say. Then the conversation fragments and the level of communication drops. Can we just listen, without considering and formulating what we will say? Can we just listen without looking for our earliest opportunity to speak, to give our view? Can we give the other person space, sound space, to let them speak until they have said what they wish to say? Do we immediately jump in to say what we've been storing up? Or do we wait a moment, letting the other's words settle in us, respecting the other person?

Can we just listen from inner silence, inner presence, in body, heart, and mind?
Can we listen consciously from that inner space that we share with the other person? When it is like that, when we are fully present in ourselves, that presence has its home in inner stillness. The other person's presence has their home in that same inner stillness, that same consciousness. Then listening takes on a very different quality. We listen to the sounds, the words, but we also listen to the person, we inwardly open to and connect with that person. Then we hear more of who they are, even when they are not speaking. We are present with them: I and you here.

Of course, we find many other opportunities to listen, outside of conversations or meetings. We listen to formal lectures, carefully following the ideas presented by the speaker. We listen to music, letting it awaken our heart and our body. We can listen to the ordinary soundscape around us at any moment. Rarely do we find ourselves in a sound-free environment. Artificial sounds surround us and offer an opportunity for presence in listening. We can open to notice the whole soundscape that we rarely notice. It's like an ongoing, mostly artificial, unstructured symphony. Noticing all these sounds widens the reach of our presence, broadens the texture of our life.

The sounds of Nature, though, can connect us with Life and the Elements. We can listen to the insects, birds, and other animals, the wind in the trees, the water rushing in streams, the raindrops falling. Except in its more vigorous manifestations like thunder, we can relax into being ourselves, being part of Nature, through listening with our whole presence. We enter our place as a listener in the soundscape of Nature.

And there is inner listening. We can listen to our thoughts, emotions, and our body. Listening to our inner sounds puts us in context. We are more able to understand that we are not our thoughts, our emotions, or our body.

Between and behind thoughts, between and underneath all sounds, there is stillness, the stillness that is the field of awareness. This is more than silence, more than mere absence of sound. The stillness is palpable, almost viscous. Listening to that stillness itself is a classic and powerful method of meditation.

Lastly, there is the question: who is listening? Naturally, if anyone is listening with my ears, my mind, it is I. I am listening. This is the key difference between hearing and listening. Our body and mind can hear without us being there to take it in. But to listen implies someone is listening. That someone is I.

For this week, practice listening, practice being present in listening, be the listener.

21.5 Speaking Presence
(Presence in Daily Life: Part 5)

To be fully present while speaking is not as easy as it sounds. First, there is the illusion that because words are coming out of my mouth, I must be here, present. I talk, therefore I am. Not so. Usually we are just in one small part of ourselves when we talk, namely our heads, our thoughts. And often even that is at a fairly low level: through lack of any particular intention, we allow the ever-present associations free reign in our mind and let them pour out of our mouth as speech. Sometimes we may not be in ourselves at all: just lost in the situation.

Second, talking is easy, so easy that it goes very well by itself, without our interference, with little intention behind it, and without our presence. We can talk effortlessly, maybe even with charm or wit, all on automatic, on autopilot. It is like drifting along in our automatic, associative thoughts, except these thoughts are voiced out loud.

Third, there is a strong pull toward being identified with ourselves when we talk. This is me. This is my personality. This is my opinion. This is my story. This is who I am. Or so it seems. But it's just my habitual patterns of interaction, of thought, of emotion, drawing on a storehouse of memory to string together some utterance, or a whole series of utterances, usually coherently. Nevertheless we speak so often and so much, and what we say and how we say it matters enough, that despite its difficulty, speaking is an important area for our inner work, for the work of presence: to be fully present as we speak.

To help us overcome the difficulties of being present in speaking, we can use various strategies. One involves preparing our intention prior to speaking. If you see that you are about to enter a conversation, even one as brief as saying hello, you can take that as your cue to come into presence. Then when you do speak, your inner preparation gives you a greater chance to stay present as you begin speaking. Or if you find yourself in the middle of a conversation, listening to the other person speaking, listening in presence, knowing that soon you will speak, then that listening presence, if you intend it to, can carry over into speaking presence when it's your moment to speak.

Phone presence may be a little easier than presence in in-person conversation, because on the phone fewer of our senses are engaged and it takes less attention. Plus we have the advantage of a clear signal that a phone conversation is about to begin. Either the phone is ringing or we are initiating the call. In either case, we can set ourselves to use that signal as our opportunity to enter presence and stay present when we speak. When the phone rings, we first take a moment to come into ourselves, then we answer. When we initiate a call, we take a moment to come into presence before the call connects. And then we work to stay with it and to recover when we notice we have lost it.

It helps to set ourselves to work on specific aspects of speaking presence. Such aspects might include being particularly aware of our tone of voice, actually hearing our voice as we speak. Or being aware of our gestures or our facial expressions as we speak. Such self-awareness in speaking teaches us about ourselves, about our personality, in ways that we might otherwise overlook.

Another aspect of speaking presence is to focus more than usual on how our words are affecting the person we are speaking to. To see from their posture and facial expressions, from their tone of voice and from their words, how they are. This awakens us to considering the other person, to communicating well, to kindness in our speech, to all the nuances of the interaction.

The essence of speaking presence, as with presence in any situation, is to be ourselves, to be fully in our whole body and to be the one who is speaking. Our words are not just forming themselves as they usually do, without our participation, with little intention. In speaking presence, we are there, behind our words, the author of what we say. In speaking presence, I am speaking. We speak from ourselves. We mean what we say.

And we do this in such a way that it is not noticeable to others that we are doing something different. Speaking presence does not mean speaking with intensity or speaking in a slow and ponderous way with emphasis on each word. We speak in a natural, easy way, but inwardly we are there, we are the one who is speaking.

For this week, practice speaking with presence. For most of us this is difficult and requires sustained and persistent intention. What usually happens is that we keep noticing, just after a conversation, that we forgot to bring presence to it, that we were not fully there. Despite finding ourselves forgetting the practice at the very moment we start to talk, we persist, coming back to it again and again at each opportunity. Then a moment comes when we are there speaking, fully there, and the inner difference is remarkable.

21.6 Tool Presence
(Presence in Daily Life: Part 6)

We use an amazing variety of tools to act on this material world. From cars, computers, airplanes and particle accelerators to ovens, pots, blenders and spatulas, the instruments that humanity has created and refined over these many millennia empower us in countless ways and set the parameters of what we can do. But our interest here is not in the tools per se, rather we look to the user of our tools and our relationship with them. Our life, from morning to night, is filled with artifacts with which we accomplish what we wish. And because we are so frequently using one tool or another, we can find in these occasions another valuable opportunity to create reminders for presence. This applies to every tool or useful artifact, from pen and paper, keyboard and mouse, to cooking utensils, brooms, hammers and saws, cars and elevators, light bulbs, umbrellas, phones, gadgets, forks, and on and on.

A part of presence is to know what I am doing, to be in contact what I am doing. Am I aware of myself when I use each of the many tools in my life? Do I know that I am using something or does it happen without my awareness? In many case this is not so easy. For example in wearing glasses, we forget about the glasses and the fact that we are using them to improve our vision.

Do I appreciate the instrumentality of these artifacts, their remarkable qualities and the fact that I could not create them on my own? Gratitude is appropriate toward those who have developed and made these tools and delivered them to me. Do I see why they are built as they are? Do I see the intelligence and artistry embedded in them? Do sense the tool's touch, its texture, heft, and balance, how it feels in my hand? Do I see its shape and proportions?

Do I see how the tool serves as an intermediary, enabling me to act on the world through it? Do I pay attention to how I use the tool, to its effects, to take that feedback to increase my skill with it? Do I use it appropriately, safely and effectively, as it was intended to be used? Do I respect the tool, clean it, maintain it, and return it to its place? Do I notice the quality it embodies?

Our responses to all of these questions reflect who we are, our attitudes to the world, and whether we are here, present, doing these things. Our attitudes and actions flow from whether or not we are here. If we are absent, absent-minded, cruising on autopilot, then any of our habitual attitudes can take center stage at any moment. If we are present, our attitudes and actions flow from something deeper than habit patterns: they flow from us, from our purposes and intentions, from our conscience, from our direct and immediate contact with our surroundings, from our intelligence, creativity, and heart. It's all here when I am here, using this tool to do what needs doing, to serve the situation, to create new possibilities, to bring order to my corner of the world.

In the use of any tool, we have three elements: I, the tool, and the raw material. If in a state of presence, then I am here, with my purposes, intentions, skills and perceptions. Then there is the tool that empowers me with its qualities, its form and function. And finally, the work piece, the raw material to which I apply the tool. Presence in tool use embraces all three.

With presence, practice, and expertise, we may at times approach the perfection that draws us, where we transcend our individualized sense of presence and our skills, and the results flow perfectly and effortlessly. We have many modern examples of athletes or musicians at the peak of their performance. We have the great works of art, in which the artist's transcendence allows him or her to become an instrument of the creative force. All the sweat and sacrifice serve as prelude to that timeless moment. The work just appears as it should, as it could. It comes through us. No longer I, the tool, and the material; the three become one in the perfection of action. Sounds rare and wonderful, but this is possible for any of us, even in the mundane actions of our life. Perfection calls to us, from our workshop, from our kitchen, from our desk.

For this week, practice presence in using tools, in your home, in your job, wherever the opportunity arises.

21.7 Walking Presence
(Presence in Daily Life: Part 7)

That majority of us fortunate enough to be able to walk can make double use of walking to practice presence. In walking presence we are not only going somewhere, we are also already here, in mid-stride. Walking presence begins in our body, with direct awareness of our feet and legs as they move, of the muscles in our legs as they flex and release, of the changing form of our feet as they adapt to each portion of our step and to the contours beneath them, of our arms swinging in coordination with our legs, of the rhythms of our steps, of the effort of going uphill and the relative ease of going down, of the quality of our breathing as it responds to our pace.

All these aspects of body awareness in walking can be enhanced and interwoven by the practice of sensing while we walk. Sensing is body awareness plus. What we add is contact with the sensitive energy in our body. We can best become familiar with sensing in quiet sitting meditation by putting our attention into a hand or foot, an arm or a leg, and holding our attention there. Gradually that part of our body grows more alive and vibrant and we become aware of the energy within it. Through persistent practice we become able to sense our entire body and not just while sitting quietly but also in movement, for example in walking. So as we walk we practice, as continuously as possible, being aware of our body and of the sensitive energy within it. Though this is the essential foundation and in itself can change our state dramatically, there is yet more to walking presence.

We do not walk with blinders on; we need situational awareness, even in the ordinary manner of walking. But with walking presence, we take in the whole scene around us, whatever or whoever is there. Persisting, this leads to a global awareness, an entry into the field of consciousness. Consciousness has no boundaries and through it we open to wholeness, both the whole of ourselves and the whole situation surrounding us. We open to the wonder of being alive, to the beauty of this world, to the freshness of this ever-changing moment, to our mind and our body. Everything, inner and outer, is embedded in this one broad field of consciousness, this holistic continuum underlying all our partial perceptions of this and that. In walking presence, we are alert and alive. And again there is yet more.

We usually treat the event of walking like taking a taxi. We tell the driver — in this case the automatic part of our mind and body — our destination and then we sit back to go along for the ride, daydreaming all the while. Rather than be a heedless passenger when we walk, presence brings us fully into the action, as the one who is walking, as the walker. Presence means doing what we are doing. We see what we see. We hear what we hear. We feel what we feel. And when we walk, we walk. We have the sense that "I am walking, I am taking this step." We become ourselves, walking.

All this may sound complicated, but it is not. The practice of walking presence does build up, layer by layer: from body awareness, to sensing, to consciousness, to I am. In the end, though, it is simple and natural and a joy: just fully here, walking.

Sometimes we walk only a few steps and at other times much further. To be present in walking only a few steps, we need to prepare, to enter presence before we even start. For longer walks, we can use the walk itself to generate and deepen presence as we go. We can set intermediate goals, such as to stay with body awareness until we reach the next corner, tree, or lamppost. Either way, short or long, we walk so often that it presents an important opportunity to insert more presence into our day. And the more we practice walking presence, the more the act of walking itself reminds us to be present: we start walking and spontaneously remember "here I am, walking."

For this week, walk in presence.

21.8 Eating Presence
(Presence in Daily Life: Part 8)

Why is gluttony considered a sin? Does it matter how or how much we eat? Certainly overeating can damage our health. But does that make it a sin? How does it concern our soul? We can explore several layers in these questions.

First, we are given this body of ours and as we mature we also come under the obligation to take care of it. Overeating places the health of our body in jeopardy and is thus irresponsible. Being responsible is fundamental to any religious or spiritual path, because it goes right to the heart of who we are, our will, and to our relationship with the sacred through conscience. Will and conscience, among other things, move us to act responsibly in all matters, including eating.

Second, if we practice presence seriously, we notice that, whenever we eat more than our body needs, it has a negative effect on our ability to be present: our energy somehow gets depleted and our will to be present loses its efficacy. We lose our efficacy. This simple, inverse relationship between overeating and our immediately-subsequent diminished presence can be verified by each of us just by noticing how we are after a too-large meal.

Yet we must eat. We have no choice in whether we will eat or not. But we do have several kinds of choices in how we eat. For example, there is the question of the quality of what we choose to eat: is it nutritious, balanced, and healthful?

Then comes what is for many of us the difficult issue of how much we eat. Yes, of course we enjoy eating. It is natural that we do. And that natural joy in eating often tempts us to overeat, to get greedy about the pleasure of eating. That gluttony comes straight from the grasping nature of our self-centered egoism. It's all about me and what I like. So exercising our will to curb our overeating directly engages our egoism. But ego is slippery and takes both sides of this battle, saying how much better I'll look and feel if I lose weight. So if we approach the issue directly, we start small. Perhaps we cut out one particular mode of overeating: maybe forgoing snacks or desserts or measuring out a particular food we eat. Perhaps we count calories or put other limits on our eating, but very gradually, so that any changes become stable over time.

One indirect approach to limiting overeating, namely presence, also helps us build our soul. The more we taste our food, the more we appreciate it and the less we are driven to overeat. If we do not taste our food fully, we tend to eat extra to make up for it, so that our total satisfaction will be sufficient.

This principle applies to the whole experience of eating and thus gives a central place to presence. Eating less, but with full presence, can be just as, or even more, satisfying than eating a larger amount inattentively. We stay aware of the visceral, bodily act of eating, of bringing the food to our mouth, of its aroma, of biting into it, of chewing, of its taste and texture, and of swallowing. We stay aware of our inner reactions to the food, the liking or the disliking, the wanting, the craving for the next bite, perhaps even the gratitude. We stay aware of our whole body and ourselves, of I am eating. And we do all this while appearing to eat normally, at least to any outside observer.

Something surprising also begins to open when we eat with full presence. Besides the scientifically-known, nutritional components of our food, there are spiritual energies within the food we eat. By eating with presence, we gradually come to be aware that presence unlocks those energies from the food and enables us to absorb them as food for our soul. So when we eat inattentively, we miss this important opportunity.

It helps if we set our intention to eat with presence at the beginning of the meal. A brief prayer of gratitude before the first bite, whether done inwardly for ourselves, or outwardly with our tablemates, can create the tone of presence for the meal. We eat with respect for our food, as our essential lifeline. How we eat is one indicator of the state of our soul.

For this week, please practice eating presence.

21.9 Presence of Mind
(Presence in Daily Life: Part 9)

We believe in our thoughts. We even believe we are our thoughts. But there is a basic, qualitative difference between our thoughts and the thinker of our thoughts, when there is a thinker. Consider the ongoing stream of commentary that flows through your mind, almost continuously. Do you drive those comments? Are you intentionally thinking those thoughts? Or do they simply arise on their own, as pre-conditioned, pre-programmed, habitual, patterned responses to other thoughts and to your experience of the moment? Typically there is no I, no thinker behind our thoughts: they just flow automatically from one to the next to the next. They feed off each other, off our memories, and off what our senses bring us. This stream of thoughts creates the convincing but false illusion that we are thinking them, that they are the embodiment of a person, namely us.

Sometimes we do think intentionally, like when we are considering some problem, planning a course of action, weighing alternatives. In such cases it is right to say with Descartes, I think, therefore I am. The thinker is there.

Usually though, our thoughts think themselves. This would be fine, and is fine, except for the fact that we assume that since we do sometimes think, then all our thoughts are ours and intentional. We assume that we think all our thoughts, that they always speak for us, that they are our inner voice, that we know who we are because we know our thoughts. This is one of our fundamental illusions. Not only are we not our thoughts, but we usually are only vaguely aware of them.

Our brain will go on producing automatic, associative thoughts for the rest of our lives. We cannot stop our thoughts, at least not directly. But we can stop our identification with them, our belief that we are our thoughts. How? Meditation helps. When we sit quietly, not doing anything, we can see our thoughts flowing on their own, without our initiative, without our intention. That stream of thoughts is what our brain does, in the same way that our heart beats, our gut digests, and our lungs breathe. It's automatic, but not always.

A case in point is breathing. We breathe all our lives and our body does so automatically. Yet we can breathe intentionally when we so choose. We can change our breathing pattern for a short time, as in some yoga practices. This is not to advocate yogic or any other change to our breathing patterns, but is just to offer the example of an automatic function that can be non-automatic and intentional when we so choose. So it is with thinking: nearly always automatic, but intentionally directed when we act as the thinker pondering some issue. Seeing all this clearly in quiet meditation begins to liberate us from the tyranny of our thoughts, from identification with them. Just as we are not our breathing, we are also not our thoughts. That is the road toward clarity, toward presence in our mind, toward presence of mind.

There is this cognitive awareness beneath our thoughts. Through that awareness, we are cognizant of our thoughts. But the awareness and the thought are not identical. One is a conscious screen and the other is displayed on that screen. Yet neither the screen nor the thought is who we are. We are the one who sees the screen. Watch your mind intentionally, without trying to change your thoughts. Be the one watching your mind, be yourself, your own I. You are not a thought. Your I is not a thought. Your I is your will, the one in you who sees and chooses and directs your attention, the one who can think intentionally, the one who can be aware of your thoughts.

Presence of mind begins in tuning into the quiet awareness beneath our thoughts. That quiet awareness is not disturbed or hidden by our thoughts. It is always there, awaiting us. It is a place of inner peace, a refuge. We can relax into that stillness behind our thoughts and just be. We relax into the big sky of our mind and let our thoughts come and go of their own accord like passing clouds. We relax into the broad field of conscious awareness and let our thoughts roam at will like cattle on an expansive range, without following, being lost in, or driven by our thoughts. This brings order to our mind. Then, when we need to think about something, we can take the reins of our thinking mind and direct it with clarity. We can cognize, we can see, mentally, what is necessary and appropriate to our immediate situation. This is presence of mind.

The usual definition of presence of mind concerns the ability to see what needs to be done in the midst of sudden crisis demanding immediate action. But we are not going to intentionally create crises in order to practice presence of mind. So instead we practice presence in our mind, in our thoughts and emotions and attitudes, and in the cognizant stillness behind them. We are here in our big mind, but we are not a function of our mind. Rather, we own our mind. When we do not need to think about something intentionally, we let our thoughts go on automatically, giving them a wide berth without interfering with them, and also without falling prey to the illusion that our thoughts are us or even speak for us. Yes, our thoughts are close to us, intimately close. But they are not as close as our I, our will. Our thoughts are external to us; they not who we are.

For this week, please practice presence of mind.

21.10 Presence is Mindfulness Plus
(Presence in Daily Life: Part 10)

Buddhist meditation theory and practice teach us the methods and the value of mindfulness. The classical definition presents mindfulness as calm, impartial, non-judging, in-the-moment awareness and attentiveness to body, emotions, thoughts, other mental activity, and consciousness itself. Mindfulness allows our life to flow in a wonderful way. And it is obviously a major and important spiritual practice. While mindfulness and presence have much in common, there are significant differences. Foremost among those differences is the question of who is mindful or who is present.

In the Buddhist approach, the answer is no one. A central tenet of Buddhism is that the self is illusory. In mindfulness, there is just mindfulness, just that calm, non-grasping, non-judging awareness, with no one behind it. Just mindful. In practice, this experience is liberating, because we drop all the baggage of our self, all the laboriously constructed and carefully defended edifice of our self, our central illusion. There is just the awareness, just the activity of our life. It flows.

In the path of presence, we accept and value the truth of the Buddhist view of mindfulness and self. And we bring more to it. We look to bridge the divide between the Buddha's teaching of no-self and the even more ancient biblical teaching of "I am that I am." The dissolving of the illusion of the self has layers of subtlety, which for our present purposes we divide into four. They do present a progression of depth, but not necessarily a linear progression. On any given day, we may work at several of these levels, depending on our preparation and insight.

At the first layer, in our ordinary, unexamined life prior to any significant inner work, we believe in our self, but what we believe in is an illusion. This self is our personality, trained and shaped since birth to act and think and feel in certain ways, to hold certain attitudes, to interpret new events and our memories in a particular fashion. This self is just a set of psychological patterns, an insubstantial mirage. Yet the mirage is very convincing. We believe in it unquestioningly. We believe this is who we are: this bag of thoughts, emotions, senses, and body held together by our presumed self. It looks like a person, talks like a person, and acts like a person. It must be me. This presumption is so deeply ingrained in us, that we can hardly imagine that it could be false.

At the second layer, our mindfulness, our inner work of seeing, gradually deconstructs the patterns of that presumed self and reveals our personality to be an empty shell. This is the usual interpretation of the Buddha's teaching of no-self. Our inner work enables us to see through the illusion. We see that our thoughts and emotions drive themselves, without any "I" in them. We see that what we took to be our self is just a complex of psychological patterns, memories, tendencies and attitudes, with no core, no central actor, no self. This insight relieves us of our lifelong burden of feeding that insatiable emptiness in our center, the burden of maintaining the illusion of self by painting on curtains around an empty space where we assume that "we" are. Here we pull back those curtains and see the truth: there is no wizard, no I behind them.

At the third layer, we find that there is yet more to this story, that we have will, our I, that in order to truly go beyond self, beyond egoism, we need to come into our will, our I, that we need to become our real Self before we can take the next and ultimate step along the path. So at this level, we have the work of presence, of occupying our consciousness, our mindfulness, of simply and directly being the one who sees what we see, hears what we hear, and does what we do. We become ourselves, our true selves. We form our soul. At this point we have something, something to surrender, something that enables us to surrender into the next layer. That something makes us real. It is our real self, our I, our will.

Yet the Buddha did not mislead us. At the fourth layer, the Buddhist teaching of no-self aligns perfectly with the ultimate teachings of other religions, in that the Self surrenders to the Sacred, becomes subsumed in the Divine. This Union takes us beyond both our ordinary assumed self of the first layer and beyond our true self of the third layer. Here we have the work of contemplative prayer and deep meditation, of purification, of surrender and letting go utterly. It takes us beyond the practice of presence. Yet the work of presence proves invaluable in strengthening our will, our I, so that we are there to turn toward and open to the Divine. Experience comes to a single point in our I, but opens up again beyond our I.

For this week, assess where you are along this path of transformation, from mindfulness to presence and beyond. Practice mindfulness and extend it into the practice of presence. Be.

22.0 Growing a Spiritual Life

Our spiritual life grows like a tree: so slowly as to be imperceptible, yet capable of reaching a great height and strength. Much of a tree's growth is hidden underground and most of our spiritual growth is hidden from us, rooted in the depths beyond our ordinary awareness. The soil for our spiritual growth is our body, heart, and mind as they are when the seed begins to sprout. The seed of our soul comes into us at birth, but lies dormant until awakened, in some cases suddenly and in others gradually. Once awakened, our inner growth can begin.

That awakening rouses the spiritual yearning in our heart. But the awakening is not something we can do intentionally from ourselves. It is not a choice that we make. It happens to us in a uniquely individual manner. Some event or series of events, inner or outer, gives us a taste or a promise of a deeper life and ignites our need for that. What we do with that need is our choice and our responsibility. We can ignore it and leave our spiritual life stillborn, our soul incomplete. Or we can nurture it, even if half-heartedly at first. But the path and our early, halting attempts at inner work have their effects and intensify our need.

The tree works hard, but invisibly, to gather and transform light, water, and nutrients into the substance of its body. Our spiritual inner work is also invisible from the outside, because it takes place within our body, heart, and mind, and feeds our soul. Just as a tree grows toward the sun, our soul grows toward the inner light of the sacred. And the water that enables it all to flow into and through the tree is the heartfelt yearning that keeps us on the path, that keeps us engaged through thick and thin. That yearning informs our will and moves us. The whole process, though, is uncertain: of all the seeds produced few sprout and fewer still attain full maturity. What makes the difference is our own free and repeated choice to practice.

In this series, we will explore the inner work that grows our soul. Many paths offer differing views and different methods. But there is clear commonality among subsets of those paths. We will look at methods that are in some sense shared among several paths and have been developed over centuries or millennia. We also have an eye toward balance in our inner work, so that our practices support each other and the full-spectrum of our wholeness.

It is one thing to know about spiritual practices, quite another thing to develop the ability to do those practices, and yet another to actually do them. If it's suggested to us that we "be conscious" or that we "open to the world of sacred light," we are immediately confronted with a problem. Regardless of any amount of study or theoretical knowledge of practices, levels of energies, or different spiritual realities, we do not really understand what these things mean until we have experienced them for ourselves. So we need to work at the level that we can work. Gradually our ability to do the practices increases. New perceptions and unexpected capacities open to us, if we persevere in the practices that we can do. Once we know and understand a practice, we come to the problem of actually doing it, regularly, in the frequency and duration it calls for. That is why the spiritual path is work, inner work. Though the sacred does help us, only our own actual, long-term inner work can prepare us for that help and make use of it in our spiritual transformation. But the dividends of the work are immeasurable, for ourselves, for the people around us, and for the sacred.

Growing our spiritual life, growing our soul, like any other process, comes in stages. The seed and our need awaken. We learn about some practice. We experiment with it. We get feedback from it and try to improve, to deepen our work with it. It begins to have an effect on our being. Something shifts in us. A new perception or ability opens. We incorporate that in our inner work. The cycle continues and our inner life grows. Time passes and we enter deeper into the timeless, as our inner world opens up. While maintaining our life responsibilities, we dive into our spiritual work. Half-hearted becomes wholehearted. Then we reach a plateau, however pleasant, where nothing much changes for a long time. But we persevere, even redoubling our efforts, because each act of inner work is valuable in its own right. And then a change, a new possibility enters without fanfare. This becomes our new normal, our new plateau. We continue to practice. These cycles continue. And we climb Jacob's ladder. Our life is full. Our heart is full. We serve the sacred.

For this week, notice the difference between knowing about or thinking about a spiritual practice and actually doing it. Thinking about the path is not the same as walking it.

22.1 Meditation
(Growing a Spiritual Life: Part 1)

The benefits of meditation have been laboratory tested in a range of contexts, showing that its practice has positive effects on our body, brain, and emotions. Our interest here, though, lies in its profound effects on our mind, our soul, and our spirit. Those effects accumulate over the years, little by little. Though meditation is only one category of spiritual practices, which together work to transform our life and our soul, meditation is fundamental, paving the way for other forms of inner work.

Of the many methods of meditation, one usually begins with and often returns to the basic one of focusing and sustaining our attention, typically on our breathing, on bodily sensations, on creating some mental image, or on some inwardly repeated sounds or words. For example, while sitting quietly, we might pay attention to the bodily sensations connected with breathing, at our abdomen, our chest, our nostrils and upper lip, or our whole body. We pick one of those locations and stay with that for the duration of the sitting, without intentionally changing our natural rhythms of breathing. To occupy our mind further, we might simultaneously enumerate our breaths, counting each exhalation silently in our thoughts, from one up to ten, and then beginning again at one. When we lose the count, we just start over at one. But the counting is gentle and secondary to the action of keeping our attention on the sensations of breathing. When we lose our attention, we just begin again, without self-criticism, or just noting our self-criticism if it does arise. To think, "I'm not a good meditator" is misplaced and destructive. Bringing our attention immediately back after it wanders, again and again, is itself this first phase of the practice of meditation.

Two of the major benefits of such practice are the training of our attention, in effect strengthening our will, and generating a state of peace, contentment, and calm, free of our ordinary desires and fears. The simple act of sitting still and occupying our mind and attention in a directed way affects us deeply. The state of peace comes from the settling of our energies in meditation, in particular the separation of our conscious and sensitive energies. No longer are we totally taken by what our senses throw at us, including the mental senses that cognize thoughts and emotions. We enter the vast hall of the conscious energy, the underlying continuum of awareness, and against that backdrop each sensory event makes its debut and then fades, while we remain in consciousness.

This training in meditation gradually frees us of the close identification with our thoughts and emotions, with our personality patterns. In that peace, we become able to be, just be. And from being we are able to act, able to act with clarity and efficacy. Rather than just reacting to events, we are able to choose to respond or not, able to take the initiative or not.

Yet the peace of consciousness is not the end of meditation. As our identifications fall away, we may at some point notice that we are still identified, though in a more rarefied way. We are identified with consciousness itself. But consciousness is not who we are, nor is it the highest energy or inner world. So we continue to practice meditation. Now the training of attention may only occupy the first portion of any given sitting, just enough to settle us into that state of focused and attentive peace. Then we begin to let go of that peace itself. We begin to see consciousness as consciousness, not as the unfathomable, ultimate, and all-pervasive substrate of awareness that it appears to be. We live in this medium of consciousness, like fish in water. But there is more to reality. We continue our sitting practice to find that more, to go beyond consciousness itself.

One clue comes by looking toward the source of our attention, toward where it comes from. There in the inner recesses of our will, we find something very different than consciousness: we find ourselves. This proves crucial, for to be fully ourselves is to live fully. To strengthen that true self and live in it is the work of presence. But for deepening our meditation, the question becomes how to go beyond not just consciousness, but beyond our very self. At this point our meditation practice becomes indistinguishable from silent contemplative prayer. The needed action consists of allowing our innermost door to open, asking it to open, opening it from behind it. And it may open just a crack. But that is enough to let the light of the sacred come streaming through. And so it continues.

Whatever our degree of experience or our state when go to sit on the cushion, meditation is an inestimable support for our inner work, for our spiritual life. For this week, examine your practice of meditation with the aim of understanding how you might deepen that practice. Or consider starting or restarting a regular, daily practice, if you are drawn to it.

22.2 Soul Food
(Growing a Spiritual Life: Part 2)

For our inner body, our soul, to grow and function, it needs food, but food of a different nature and quality than our normal three-meals-a-day type of food. A soul body needs soul food. Our physical body takes energy and structural materials from physical food. Our soul needs energy and soul material from its food. To think that this will happen adequately on its own, without our intentional effort and as a mere byproduct of living, is mistaken. Our physical body doesn't eat on its own. We have to earn our food, grow it or pay for it, prepare it, and then eat it — all intentionally. So it is with feeding our soul: it needs to be done intentionally. Much of our inner work concerns just this.

Will and organized inner energies are the two major aspects of our soul. When we focus our attention, we use inner energies. Our will interacts with the conscious energy to direct our awareness, our senses, our sensitive energy. At some point, our attention falters because our energies are temporarily depleted. Our experience of being centered, mindful, aware, largely depends on and fluctuates with the quality and quantity of our inner energies. That experience of being centered, mindful, and aware is a function of our soul and manifests a particular state of our soul.

Before we consider how we feed that, we would do well to look into and plug our energy leaks, to stop wasting our inner energies. It's no use gathering more energy, merely to waste it. Some quantity of inner energies is produced in our body and mind without any particular effort on our part. While that amount is not enough to build a robust soul, it is a base level that we can learn from. We learn by observing our inner state, our ability to pay attention, our centeredness, and calm. What increases that state and what diminishes it? We learn that destructive emotions, obsessive thinking, unnecessary physical tensions, hurrying, fidgeting, overeating, lack of exercise, inadequate sleep, smoking, recreational drug use, and more generally, unhealthy lifestyle choices — all these waste our inner energies. This list is long and not exhaustive. It would be glib to say that we observe, we learn, and we change our ways to stop our leaks. But it is not so easy to change deeply ingrained habits, ruts of energy flows. So we take one thing a time and work on that. We begin with the easier ones and gradually our self-control will improve. Then we can tackle the more difficult problems, like smoking. This is fundamental to our path and needs to be returned to, checked on, periodically throughout our life. We learn to manage our lifestyle to serve our soul.

But then what? How do we feed our soul? How do we enhance the flow of energies into our being? There are different levels, types of inner energies. Each requires its own kind of action. And there is interaction among them. Our inner work gradually opens our perceptions of these energies.

The sensitive energy accumulates in us by the act of paying attention to our body, holding our attention continuously in a part of our body, or in our whole body. This draws the sensitive energy. We perceive it directly, giving us a more vivid experience of our body, like a warmth or a vibration, a fullness, a substantiality. We call this sensing. We practice sensing at first only while in sitting meditation. Later, we become able to sense our body while engaging in the normal activities of life. But it does take practice, sustained, persistent, long-term, repeated practice. And through that practice, we find the sensitive energy coalescing and settling into the form of our body, as the beginning of an inner body, a soul body.

And yet we need more of that sensitive energy. As it happens, we are surrounded by it. The atmosphere, the air we breathe, is full of sensitive energy. But in normal breathing, it comes into us and goes right back out, without our awareness of it. None of sticks. Even the meditative technique of conscious breathing does not change that situation. In breathing consciously, we become aware of the sensations in our body associated with breathing. This does nothing to draw the sensitive energy from the air into our being.

That requires what we may term energy breathing. Rather than attending to our bodily sensations associated with breathing, we pay attention to the air itself. This does not mean changing the normal physical patterns and rhythms of our breathing at all. It does mean using our attention and intention to draw the energy from the air we breathe, as we breathe, and allow that energy to flow throughout our body, if and as it will. We can combine energy breathing with sensing our body to give the incoming energy a place to land and be absorbed. This valuable and remarkable practice can dramatically enhance the flow of sensitive energy into our inner body and its assimilation. It has been known since ancient times, for example as prana by Hindus, and is the reality behind the practice of pranayama. It was also known and practiced by the early Sufis and Taoists. Some people get this almost immediately. Others do not. You might try it for a while, perhaps one period a day for a week. If an unmistakable flow of energy does not occur, just drop it and maybe try it again in a year's time; there are other effective ways to build your soul.

In meditation and in presence we come into awareness of the conscious energy, which also surrounds us, inside and out. This energy is the base of awareness, it is the pure awareness behind all content, behind and between our thoughts, behind our sensory perceptions. It is vast and clear, pure cognizance in a realm of peace. As noted above, when we pay attention our will interacts with the conscious energy to direct our sensitive energies, our sensory and mental perceptions. Our will is who we are. If we sit and just be, being aware moment-to-moment, inside and out, that act of will puts us in the midst of the conscious energy. We relax and open into the wide horizon of consciousness. The more we acquire the taste, the perception of this, the more we can open into it, be in it. We can even come to the point of being able intentionally to draw more of it in, to concentrate consciousness in our own field. This grows our soul.

By intentionally inhabiting our body, being here in our body, in the whole of our body, experiencing it moment-to-moment, we bring the conscious energy into contact with the sensitive energy. We sense our whole body, so that the sensitive energy fills us. Then we inhabit that sensation body, we enter it and stay in it. By doing so, we create a scaffold made of will and conscious energy to give body-shaped structure to our sensitive energy. This sets up an interaction of the conscious and sensitive energies. They help stabilize each other. Our being grows. Our soul is fed.

There are deeper energies still, energies that feed the very roots of our soul. We will address some of that in the next part of this inner work series. For this week, please decrease your energy leaks and feed your soul.

22.3 Prayer
(Growing a Spiritual Life: Part 3)

Why pray? Is prayer only another meditation technique, designed to improve our awareness, our immersion in consciousness? Or is there some higher Reality to Whom we pray? And is that higher Reality a boundless consciousness or something other than that?

Consciousness is a what, an energy. To go deeper we ask who is conscious, whose awareness is it? Consciousness is like a TV screen with a bunch of sensors as input: the camera (our eyes), the microphone (our ears), and so on. But consciousness just reports, presents all that information. To whom does it present? Who decides what part of the screen to look at and what to do about what is seen there? That who is us, our will. We are our will. Will perceives, chooses, decides, and acts, or chooses not to act. What we do, our will does. We are our will. Because we can be aware of consciousness, we are not just consciousness, we are more than that, other than that.

Half of infinity is still infinite. A tenth of something infinite is still infinite. A billionth of something infinite is still infinite. The nature of infinity is not changed by dividing it. The nature of will is not changed by dividing it. The nature of the Divine is not changed by dividing.

We intuitively resonate with the notion of Divine Will, more than with the notion of Divine Consciousness. The Divine acts. The Divine may also see, be conscious, but the Divine is the One Who is conscious, the One Who sees. The Divine is Will.

What about love, Divine Love? To speak of that seems right to us. The Divine loves unconditionally. Love is one thing the Divine does, one thing that the Divine Will does. God may be Love, but is more even than Love. God is Will and that includes the will to love.

There is an infinite greatness, a mountain of creative Force, that makes and sustains this universe in every moment. That Force, that Will flows into every part of this universe.

And a particle of that Will is given to each of us, as our birthright, as our human endowment. Yet a particle of something infinite is still infinite. The Divine Nature is present in us, as our will, with all its freedom and power and infinity, albeit on a different level, a different scale.

Prayer then, is our will reestablishing our connection with the Divine Will. Without that we remain incomplete. That incompleteness feeds the feeling of lack and inadequacy that drives so much of our thoughts and emotions, our attitudes, our wishes and dreams. Our connection with the Divine was never severed, but is buried so deeply under our many attachments to the visible and psychological, that we have effectively lost it. Prayer looks to rectify that, to regain what we seem to be missing at our core, that connection to the Whole, the place where aloneness ends, where narrowness widens, where self-centeredness evaporates.

In prayer we may use words and we may petition for something. In contemplative prayer we may also use words, but the petition, if there is one, primarily addresses the further opening of our relationship with the Divine. This may not be stated in words, but certainly is our intention. Inwardly repeating a sacred phrase or a Divine name helps our focus and orients and elevates us, as does communal worship. At some point in our prayer session, we go beyond the need for focusing and orienting, beyond words, beyond thoughts, even beyond consciousness, beyond our conscious mind. We stand in stillness as if before the Divine, as if the Divine greatness were here with us now, behind and within what we can see and touch.

Entering prayer that way, the shuddering cascades of energy may come to us from the world of sacred light. This feeds us, feeds our soul deeply. It is right for us, even necessary.

Yet the Divine lies well beyond even that world of sacred light. So we take another step into the stillness, into utter peace, and surrender to it. We give ourselves over, begging to be touched by the Unity. Just as we can inhabit our body with our will, we silently ask the Divine to inhabit us, to become us. That infinite, sacred Will of the Creator is there. We ask That to enter our core, to enter who we are, to enter our will, to put us on like a suit of clothing, to be us. We ask in stillness, in non-doing, in allowing, in opening. We ask. And that is our prayer.

This is a process. We start where are and work our way from there. For this week, please deepen your prayer practice.

22.4 Presence
(Growing a Spiritual Life: Part 4)

In growing a spiritual life, we may work at meditation or prayer or doing the right thing, but what about the rest of the day, that vast expanse of time where we enter the stream of life, eating, sleeping, working, cooking, cleaning, shopping, commuting, relaxing, and all the rest? If we leave large gaps between our times of formal spiritual practice, if that practice only occupies a small fraction of our day, our soul growth is limited thereby. Short of entering a monastery, how can we turn more of our day to account, to serve our spirit?

The primary, time-tested answer is presence, fully engaging in whatever we do, but with more, with our body, heart, and mind, with our assembled energies, with our attention, our will, our self. We do this in a relaxed way, not from tension. Yet it usually means being inwardly active, not letting our life live itself, but living it as our self, connecting, immersing in the flow of life, without losing ourselves in it.

If we meditate in the morning, we may have an abundance of inner energy when we get up from the cushion. Without presence, that energy will wane to the vanishing point during our day. By the time we go to bed at night, we have little or nothing left. Yet the practice of presence reverses this process. Instead of losing that precious energy as our day progresses, we gain even more. Presence accelerates our natural production of inner energy and connects us with its sources.

Presence not only helps grow our spiritual life, it is evidence that we have one. The deeper, stronger, and more loving our inner life, the more we are present — and vice versa. To seek the answer to the question who am I, we must be practical, and that practicality consists first and foremost of presence. Without presence, I am not who I really am, I am not fully myself. The core of presence is "I am here," not as the words of that phrase but as the true experience of being myself in this body, in this mind, in these sensory flows, in this moment in time and this place in space.

But presence itself quickly wanes and vanishes. This is

where methods matter, methods for extending and strengthening presence. Though it is necessary to choose to be present, that choice on its own typically has little power. It might be good for 10 seconds and then it's gone. We need something that persists in time. That something is sensing our body. By practicing body awareness in a focused way, so that the sensitive energy accumulates in our body, we build a strong foundation for presence; we create a place to stand in presence.

So if we choose to work in this way, then whenever we remember during our day, we immediately bring our attention to our body, to a hand or a foot, an arm or a leg. We put our attention there and keep it there. Gradually something accumulates: the sensitive energy which gives us a stronger perception of that part of our body. With practice we even become able to sense our whole body.

From that point we work toward a more global awareness that includes not just our body, but also our mind, our thoughts, opinions, attitudes, daydreams, and mental images. This leads us also to become aware of our emotions as emotions. So we have this broad, inclusive awareness intentionally, an awareness that incorporates all our perceptions of body, mind, and heart. Yet we remain anchored in body sensation, because that can persist through time; it is not blown away so easily by a passing thought or distracting perception.

Nevertheless, without the decision to be present, the ongoing choice to be present, and the determination to stay present, methods can only help marginally. It takes both method and choice. Yet the choice to be present naturally leads us back to the question of who is present. To which we answer: I am present. Rather that bouncing among the waves of life and mind, we become ourselves, our I. I am here, now. I am the one who is aware of my body. I am the one who is sensing my body. I am the one who is aware of my mind, my thoughts, my emotions. Yet I am none of those things, neither my body, my mind, or my emotions. I am not my awareness. I am I. I am the one who does what I do.

Our I is a gift from the Creator and is our connection with that Sacred One. So to be ourselves is to grow our spiritual life. Our I is at the center, our center. Yet our I itself has a deeper and sacred source. To assume otherwise is called egoism. This is the difference between being centered and being self-centered. It is not all about me. It is not that my small self is present. Rather, the higher is present through and as me. This is the realm where presence meets prayer. From here, to go deeper into presence is the same as going deeper into prayer, deeper into freedom, deeper into our buoyant soul.

For this week, be more present.

22.5 Conscience
(Growing a Spiritual Life: Part 5)

We can hardly imagine a spiritual person not also being a person of conscience. The two go hand in hand. If being spiritual means, in part, being kind, devoted, peaceful and present then certainly to that list we would add the quality of doing the right thing, not doing the wrong thing, as revealed to us by our conscience. Yet the notion of conscience is very slippery and can easily be twisted to serve either our ego or some group ego we adopt. After all, what is right? Who defines that? If my conscience is personal to me, which it most certainly is, then am I not free to define right and wrong as I wish?

Not exactly. It is a matter of being honest, unblinkingly honest, with ourselves. Let us assume that there is a universal morality, an objective force of justice and compassion that transcends all religions. This is not something that could ever be written down, for it is the eye of truth and compassion that looks afresh at every situation. Justice Potter Stewart said about pornography: though it's hard to define, "I know it when I see it." This is just how conscience works. We know right from wrong when we see it. We feel it, we intuit it directly in our heart and mind. Everyone one of us is endowed with this capacity.

So far so good, but the obvious problem is that we either do not listen for the promptings of conscience or we even actively squelch them, bury them. Further, if we do know what our conscience is telling us in a particular situation — for it's always about the particulars — we may and often do act otherwise, contrary to our own conscience. And what do we gain thereby but a temporary satisfaction of one of our desires? Then we're faced with the same contrary choice to against ourselves, again and again and again, until the voice of our conscience grows so faint that we cease hearing it and it no longer bothers us.

This lack of adherence to conscience is the source of many of our personal and societal problems, on all scales. For example, we take what we can and go for even more, without considering whom we take from and whether our body or our planet can afford our excessive taking.

Yet freedom lies in just the opposite, in listening for and acting on the promptings of our conscience, in doing the right thing every time. Yes, craziness can sneak in through this door, so we notice what our conscience tells us and we test it by the light of day, by the sanity check, the legality check, the compassion check, and the moral norms of our society. If it passes these tests, then maybe it's the real thing. There can be no rule about this; it's a personal judgment and intuition of truth.

We can ask ourselves what is the right thing to do in this situation. But we need to be very, very careful about whether at some subtle level we are shaping or twisting the response to accord with some self-centered motivations. Is the response truly from our conscience, from our better angels, our higher nature? Or does it flow from a back-door egoistic impulse, disguised as purity itself? There is an art to this discrimination, an art we learn through practice. While the vigilance always remains necessary, the wisdom of conscience, if nurtured by respecting it, does grow in us.

Asking ourselves what is the right thing to do, or noticing what our heart tells us in a given situation, is a way of opening ourselves to the perception of that objective force of justice and compassion that is sacred. So conscience is our most intimate and direct channel to the Divine. In striving to become a person of conscience, we strive for that connection.

Obeying our conscience is often not so easy. Conscience tends to be inconvenient: derailing us or depriving us or imposing on us. This is why we call it inner work: it takes effort, determination, self-sincerity, and a readiness to let go of identifying with self-centered motivations. Yet following conscience gives us the great gift of inner peace. Knowing that we have done and will do the right thing, leaves our heart at peace and full of satisfaction.

Conscience may seem to be something other than ourselves, especially when it sets up some inner struggle between two choices. There's me wanting to do option 1 and there's my conscience wanting me to do option 2. Yet the true voice of conscience is our own voice, our own higher nature. We are our conscience. So it comes down to whom we choose to be: our true self or our desire or identification of the moment.

For this week, please be yourself: listen for and follow your conscience.

22.6 Doing and Non-Doing
(Growing a Spiritual Life: Part 6)

"...the Master acts without doing anything..." Lao Tzu

Our lives are full of busyness, always something to do. Yet at times, what we do can reach into the very heart of world, connecting us with the Sacred Will of the universe, what Lao

Tzu called the Tao, what many call God. This does not require us to be sitting on a meditation cushion or kneeling in prayer. It can happen right here in the midst of our life.

We can distinguish three levels along the spectrum of doing and non-doing. The first is pre-programmed reaction. This is the anger or frustration that comes on us in traffic or waiting in a slow line or when someone criticizes us. Yet our brain is so complex that its programmed reactions appear to be freely chosen, as if we decided to get angry. But looking objectively, we can see below the surface, see that these automatic reactions, that our automatic associative thinking, is all done in us, done to us. We do not do those things, they just happen. There is no inner freedom.

The second level is when we are more aware of ourselves, aware of actually being the one who is choosing, the one who is doing what we are doing. We are that one. We are ourselves. We set goals. We make efforts and follow through. We are effective. We are present. There is more freedom. Yet we are limited by being who we are.

Then there is effortless effort, or in Lao Tzu's phrase: doing non-doing. This is flow. This is real doing. We no longer have the feeling that *"I am doing this."* Yet this is not the non-doing of us on autopilot, reacting in unawareness. In real doing we have full awareness and full freedom. We are not subject to our conditioning or even our character. Rather we put our skills to use. The only efforts we make are those that are necessary. We allow these moments of perfection; it all just flows; it all happens through us. We just agree to participate, to be the vehicle of the action, in full presence, in full contact with our situation, with the action, and with ourselves. But we transcend ourselves.

This is the music playing the musician, the dancer becoming the dance, the role playing the actor, the child playing with the parent, the sweeper becoming the sweeping. This is the walker walking, in full awareness, unburdened and free.

This is the creative force acting through the artist. It is the athlete in the zone. It is a lack of consciousness of a controlling self, while being fully conscious.

The action is its own purpose. It may be useful. It may produce something useful — or not. But the action is the thing. It moves through us. We step aside and let it happen. We do not interpose our ego, our self-centeredness, our goal orientation, our wants and desires. We set all that aside and just be. And we let our being open to the doing, the action that acts through us, with our full participation.

In becoming the action, we transcend our self: no doer, no actor. This can happen even in simple things, where our life just flows. We live our life without interfering with it, without damming up the flow. We get out of bed, prepare for the day and do our job. Inwardly at ease, though outwardly strong efforts may be necessary. We make those efforts on the outside, without inner complaint or resentment. We allow what needs doing to be done through us. We do non-doing. This is the life of the Tao. Our whole life can be that way.

By getting out of the way inside ourselves, we leave room for presence, for conscience, for joy, and for love. The action becomes its own end and the ultimate result takes care of itself quite well. Here is Chuang Tzu: *"The mind of a perfect man is like a mirror. It grasps nothing. It expects nothing. It reflects but does not hold. Therefore, the perfect man can act without effort."* We can enter that perfection, just as we are.

These are very special moments to be treasured. Still, they can come in very ordinary circumstances. When we set ourselves, our ego aside, when we give up our misappropriation of the Great Will, it is That which flows: from the inner, creative, loving core of the world, through us, and into action.

If we can make the time for a daily meditation practice, it can ease our way into living in non-doing. In meditation we can practice relaxation of body, equanimity of heart, and the inner stillness which comes from resolving all our various and competing intentions into one: namely, the will to be. And in just being, we stop diverting the will that comes through us; what we do just flows.

For this week, try this with your chores, whether at work or at home. Just do them. Give them what they call for. Leave your complaints and resentments aside. Leave aside wanting to finish and be done with it. Leave aside escaping into your thoughts and daydreams and time-killing. Just do what needs doing, without addition or subtraction. Just do what you are doing. And with the whole of yourself, let it be done through you.

22.7 Love
(Growing a Spiritual Life: Part 7)

"I love you." Collectively, we humans have said those words to each other countless times. The whole mystery of love and of life is contained in that simple statement. But what does it mean? Who am I? Who are you? And what is love? What is that relationship between you and me? Who are we?

If we could know, truly know, who we are, then the phrase "I love you" would not be an assertion, nor would it be a revelation, it would be a simple statement of fact. For those whose vision and understanding penetrate deeply enough, love is just how things are: it is the reality, the fundamental reality, the reality that the rest of us aspire to. To enter the field of love is the goal of the spiritual life.

Here's this from Thomas Merton's *Conjectures of a Guilty Bystander*: "In Louisville, at the corner of Fourth and Walnut, in the center of the shopping district, I was suddenly overwhelmed with the realization that I loved all those people, that they were mine and I theirs, that we could not be alien to one another even though we were total strangers. It was like waking from a dream of separateness...There is no way of telling people that they are all walking around shining like the sun."

Contrast that with our rather jaded view of each other in our day to day dealings. We may view people as objects to be used or as obstacles to be overcome or as inconsequential. But we can learn to see more deeply. We have friends and family and coworkers, people we value, people we respect. Why don't we value and respect everyone? What is the difference? Is there any real difference between those we care about and everyone else?

The Talmud teaches that each person is unique, that the world was created for each individual, and that to save one person is to save a whole world. Within you, you have this remarkably rich life, your personal history, your evolving story, your skills and abilities, your limitations, preferences, style, and potential, your awareness and you. All of it adds up to the unique package that is you. And here comes another person, separated from you by having a separate body, a separate center, a separate inner richness. Yet we share the fact of our uniqueness, our aliveness, our consciousness.

Indeed, the recognition of our shared consciousness is one of the more direct paths toward love. Here I am, at the center of this awareness that is the essence of my life. And there you are, at the center of the awareness that is the essence of your life. Are your awareness and my awareness different? At its most basic level, we have to say no, there is no difference in our awareness itself. There are certainly differences in how we respond to what arises in awareness. And there appears to be a difference in the center of awareness: yours is over there in you and mine is here in me.

But the awareness, the consciousness is a field that we both partake in: one, unbroken continuum. We share in consciousness. And when we look at another person and remember that their consciousness is the same as ours, not just similar, but one field that we are both in, that is a step toward love. We can feel that sameness, we can almost touch it. You are in awareness there inside of you. I am in awareness here inside of me. There are two points of view, but there are not two separate awarenesses. It is the same awareness. This perception profoundly changes our attitude toward other people. The boundaries between us grow porous, the separation more translucent.

Yet love takes us deeper even than the sameness of consciousness. In your center, there is your I, the one in you who sees and is aware and chooses. In my center, there is my I, the one in me who sees and is aware and chooses. You are unique and I am unique. That uniqueness seems to separate us. Here we come toward the mystery of the Singular Uniqueness, the Divine Will. That One plants a seed of itself in each of us. That seed is our unique I and is connected to our sacred Source. In the Source is our deeper oneness: or very will, our freedom comes from There, is an emanation of That. Trace your attention, your will, back into and through your very core. In that direction lies our Source. In that direction lies our oneness, our love.

Maybe that's all nice in theory. But how do we come toward that? One way is to explore inwardly, to trace back our own will into its roots, not in theory, not in our thinking, not in analyzing, but actually in practice. That work can best be approached in deep meditation and contemplative prayer. We trace ourselves back into our roots. And that tracing carries us toward our sacred Source, and toward Love.

For this week, explore love.

22.8 Contemplating the Source through Attention
(Growing a Spiritual Life: Part 8)

Attention is a form of will. The Source of all will, including our own, is the Divine Will. So to contemplate the source of our attention is to contemplate the Source of all. If we were to sit down to direct ourselves toward the Divine, we would be at sea, with no compass, no landmarks, nothing to guide us. Yes, we might have words, thoughts, or emotions, but still, in that inner landscape beyond words, thoughts, and ordinary emotions, we would not know where to turn, what direction take, or even be able to see that there are different directions. It's empty in there, devoid of any recognizable content — no signs, no landmarks, no milestones, no things. Yet the one possibility that does remain, that can show us the way through that void, is our will and in particular our attention.

Consciousness gives a starting point, a platform, but cannot really help because it is not the source; it is the principal substance of the stillness beyond which we seek to travel. Our will, our attention can direct our consciousness. So will and attention are primary, deeper than consciousness. It is right that spiritual practice improves our contact with consciousness, but that is not the ultimate, it is a stepping stone. The real action — love, service, creativity, and such — has to do with will.

So here we are, sitting, relatively quiet inside, and ready to contemplate the source of attention. Now what? We begin, as with many meditation practices, and indeed many of the tasks we face in life, by holding our attention focused on one object. We could focus on a prayer, a mantra, our breath, or a visualization. Those are all good, effective approaches. But another approach is to focus our attention on our whole body. This collects the sensitive energy in our body, which strengthens and then offers an intensifying target and more stable anchor for our attention. We sit with our full attention spread throughout our body and in contact with the sensitive energy there. Then we occupy our attention, we inhabit our body as our attention, as our will. Here I am in my body, whole and complete. We stand in our center, which includes our whole sensation body. Here I am.

Our power of attention is our most intimate quality. Our

I stands at the root of our attention. We direct our attention. Our I directs and chooses what we attend to. We are our attention. I am my attention. So in strengthening our attention, we strengthen our contact with ourselves, we become ourselves, our I. We sit here as I. I inhabit my whole body, my sensation body. I am.

It is tempting to stop there. We feel whole and complete. We feel like ourselves. Life is good.

But there is more. The question arises: where does my I come from, where do I come from? So we look deeper. We look beyond our I. This does not mean somehow sidestepping our I. It means going through and beyond ourselves in depth. It means opening the back door of my I, the innermost side of who I am, relaxing so deeply that I relax my I. In so doing, we let go of the inner cap that blocks the roots of our I. We allow the stream of will flowing from its higher sacred Source to flow through us, through our I, through our attention.

In sitting with attention, as attention, inhabiting our whole body, our attention grows strong. It becomes more obvious, more substantive. It is like a column of force passing right through our center. Its outermost end reaches the objects of attention, our body, our thoughts, our perceptions and so on. Its innermost end is hidden in the recesses of our being. It is toward that hidden innermost end that we search. We trace back along this column of attention. We trace back within ourselves. Our attention, our will, our I, gives us something to follow toward its roots. That direction is not obvious.

The stronger our attention, the stronger we feel ourselves to be here, the more clearly we can see our way within. We open our innermost door and step through, or at least toward its threshold. That is the threshold of the Sacred, of Whom we are each a particle.

For this week, contemplate the Source through your attention.

23.0 Learning to Be

If the pure joy and wonder of infants are any indication, we are born in being. The blank slate of the infant mind presents no obstacle, no distraction from consciousness. But years later, we find ourselves immersed in the daily cares and chores, goals and desires, reactions and dreams, immersed to the point of having lost ourselves, lost our being, lost even the memory of being, and not even knowing what we've lost, nor its profound value.

In one sense, the spiritual path is about regaining that childhood innocence, our original consciousness. But as adults we bring much more, we bring our skills and abilities, our heart, our strength and our power. That power, though, is limited by our misguided identification with ourselves, our ego, our thoughts, and everything that attracts or repels us. We have forgotten who we really are. The practices of the spirit are techniques to help us remember, to help us see through the clutter and return to our self, our true self.

And not only return to something we've lost, but to develop something further, new qualities we never possessed. The ordinary way to look at the long term effect of time on our life is that our possibilities diminish, day by day, that less time left in our life means fewer possibilities open to us. Yet there is the way of inner development that, like studying or saving, increases our possibilities as time passes. And inner development has the major advantage that the possibilities it opens are not in time. Pure being, pure consciousness are not in time; they are in the timeless and do not diminish with the passage of time. In fact, one hallmark of coming back to being is that feeling, that experience of timelessness.

Being concerns energies, inner energies: it is an organic

body whose substance is spiritual energy. For that reason, much of our work on being concerns energy management: conserving, obtaining, and assimilating energies. Our body transforms physical substances into flesh and bone. Through our inner work we transform energies into the substance of our being; they come together, stabilize, and form our being.

Growth of being comes as a total result of all our inner work and our responsible actions in life. It grows under the radar. We do not see it happening, not only because it's so gradual, but also because we do not recognize this most valuable development. Then one day we wake up and understand that we are more, we are more substantial than we used to be. That substantiality is our being, our ableness to be. Awakening to new substantiality also awakens us to the possibility that we could grow much more substantial still.

We can live in time, live in the timeless, or live in both. For the great majority of our life in time, we are completely enthralled by externals, by surface phenomena: we are turned to the outside. In that choppy expanse of time, we are not also in the timeless. That is the difference that being makes: the more being we have, the more we can live in both time and the timeless, the more we can give what is required to our outer life and our inner life, to body and spirit.

In this inner work series, we will look at certain aspects of what prevents our being from growing and what helps us grow. There is a great deal for us to do about our being. Some of what we would do ordinarily, like being responsible, does have a positive impact on our being, while others things we do hold us back. Still other, non-ordinary actions nurture our being directly. This field of endeavor is vast and varied; we will touch on some its highlights.

For this week, ask yourself: what does it mean "to be?" What is being? What is my being? When do I feel my being? When do I feel that I am? Do I ever have the experience of just being?

23.1 Not Judging Oneself: Acceptance
(Learning to Be: Part 1)

One of the most insidious ways that we waste our time and energy is in being overly judgmental against ourselves. This can result from many causes, such as having parents and/or teachers who were too critical, repeatedly failing, receiving insults or taunts, envying what others are or have, or adopting goals too far beyond our reach. We may have "features" that we do not want or lack qualities that we do want. All this can lead us into doubting, rejecting, and even hating ourselves, maybe not all the time, but some of the time, too much of the time. And what we may not notice amid this self-referential circle of doubt is that it's all about ego, all about self-centeredness. "I" should be better than this. "I" don't want to be like that. "I" am a jerk. "I" am not a happy person. "I" am worthless, lame, dumb, fat, and no good. They are better, more important than "I" am. "I" am a loser. "I" am mediocre.

For those with spiritual aspirations, such self-doubt may seem right or even righteous. Isn't the goal of our inner work to become different than we currently are, to be transformed, to be purified, to be complete and whole? That's true enough. But we take this other step and ask: isn't self-criticism and self-rejection necessary for that transformative process? The answer to that one is no. On the contrary, self-acceptance is necessary.

Who or what is it in us that rejects us, or aspects of us? It is ego. Self-referential, self-criticism builds and defends ego. It erects an image of what we think we should be, what we want to be, what we lack: a negative self-image. That image then takes the place of who we truly are. That image is our ego. It is just an image, an emptiness with a strong shell of self-criticism surrounding it. It runs our energies around in a small circle, dissipating them. It is this very self-rejection that pressures us to try to fill our inner emptiness from the outside and that keeps us from being more.

Approaches to spirituality that advocate struggling with our "weaknesses," while perhaps wise in themselves, suffer from the problem that we are too ready to doubt and reject ourselves, too concerned with our personal shortcomings, and so struggle primarily serves to strengthen that type of self-centeredness. This is self-defeating and puts the emphasis of spiritual practice in the wrong place. By contrast, self-acceptance resolves many of those issues, while also bringing us closer to the spirit.

If we can accept ourselves as we are, we put our spiritual work on a sound footing. We stop fighting ourselves and put our efforts where they can useful, like trying to be present and kind, trying to connect with the sacred through prayer, trying to settle into the spiritual depths through meditation. Over time those things can make a positive difference. Beating ourselves up cannot.

Then there is the question of love. It begins at home, with our self. If we do not love our self, how can we love anyone else? If we do not accept and respect our self, how can we accept and respect anyone else? We respect and hold sacred the uniqueness that we are, that we have been given. We are not trying to be someone else.

Self-acceptance allows us to find inner peace, and inner peace is the place where we can just be. It is the place where our being finds its home and grows.

Note, however, that self-acceptance does not mean indulging our destructive desires and destructive emotions. We respect ourselves enough not to smoke, not to overeat, not to get drunk, not to let our anger rule us. The best way to do all that is not to deny these tendencies directly, but rather to affirm something positive in their place. That positive can be presence, being. If we can relax into being, into presence, we have a chance to let go of our destructive urges when they arise, we have a chance not to buy into our self-critical thoughts and emotions when they arise. We see all this come into our heart and mind, we relax and let it pass without acting on it, without believing it. We affirm presence rather than deny self-destruction and self-rejection. We are not running from impurity; we are walking toward purity. We are not trying to get out of the darkness; we are going toward the light.

The flip side of self-criticism is self-aggrandizement, considering oneself to be better or more important than other people. This is just another form of self-judgment and it also serves to build up our ego. Our self-judgment makes us larger or smaller, but in either case it makes us, it creates this illusion of ourselves, an illusion we protect and defend at great cost in increased stress, damaged relationships, and hobbled spiritual development.

For this week, see how you judge and criticize yourself. Practice relaxing that self-judgment and accepting yourself unconditionally. We do not need to judge ourselves one way or another. And in not-judging ourselves we can learn to just be.

23.2 Not Judging Others: Acceptance
(Learning to Be: Part 2)

Once we begin letting go of judging ourselves, we have a chance to begin letting go of judging others. But is that even possible? We seem hardwired by evolution to judge and assess other people. Is this person a threat, a potential competitor, friend, or ally? A potential mate? We may be compelled by our genes and by the exigencies of life to make such necessary evaluations of the people we encounter.

But we go well beyond necessity in how we look at other people. One way is by measuring them against our personal obsessions of the moment. If we are overly concerned about our weight, we see whether they are fatter or thinner than us.

If we are overly concerned by money, we see whether they are richer or poorer. If about popularity, status, looks, or smarts, we see where they rank relative to us. And so on. Our perceptions follow our obsessions.

Even these comparisons are not particularly problematic for our spiritual work, but the next step is. That is where we descend into feelings of envy and jealousy, superiority or inferiority, attraction or repulsion. This pushes us deeper into our illusory ego, and further away from other people.

By judging, we mean something different than assessing or evaluating, something different than a clear-eyed perception of other people, their qualities and deficiencies. In the sense used here, judging means assigning a negative or zero value to particular people, inwardly criticizing and finding fault, consigning them to unimportance, and depersonalizing them.

This seems so ordinary, so commonplace, simply the way we all live. What does it have to do with our being? First, can you imagine a person with real being taking such an attitude toward others? More on that in a moment.

Second, all this judging focuses us on externals and takes us out of ourselves. We focus on what others do or have or what they look like. But what they are escapes us. What we are escapes us. With spiritual practice, with the work of presence, we balance the noticing of externals with remaining at home in our selves, in our being. We rest in the place of seeing and are not taken by what we see.

This whole business of judging others opens an opportunity to notice when and how we do it, or rather when and how it happens in us. We notice how we identify with comparing ourselves with others, how we feel better if we can find fault in someone, especially someone who otherwise surpasses us on some dimension. Yet every instance of judging others diminishes us, weakens our being. It costs us energy. It costs our conscience. It strengthens our ego, our disconnection. It costs our presence. It makes us small.

And it is a lie, a lie that we believe. We cannot see into the depths of other people, the unfathomable value there. If we could, that would be because our being had been purified to the level of love.

But we can practice toward that, just as we are. The practice is to accept other people just as they are. We do not need to judge them. Yes, we might need to assess and discriminate in our dealings with them. Yet even if we must refuse someone in some external way, we can still inwardly accept that person as a person, just as we are persons. We can see them as a person like us, a person with awareness, hopes, and dreams.

One mark of coming into more being is coming into the peace of consciousness, where we can just be. When we can just be, we can let others just be. And then it becomes more obvious that their being and our being are not so different, so separate. The boundaries grow porous. We are here together, just being, just doing what we do. We share this one infinite field of consciousness. In it we live and move and we have our being; they do and we do.

We could just relax and be here with others. We don't need to inwardly harass every passing stranger with our criticism and dismissal. They are and we are. This is enough.

For this week, notice how you judge other people and begin to let it go. That does not mean trying to stop our ingrained habits of thought and perception, which would be fruitless anyhow. It does mean seeing how we criticize and devalue others and not buying into that devaluation, not believing it.

23.3 Beyond Thinking
(Learning to Be: Part 3)

Our thoughts are at once our greatest tool and our velvet prison. We well know the usefulness of our ability to think: planning, learning, weighing options, rehearsing, remembering, creating, solving problems, cogitating, categorizing, conversing, and so on. Without our ability to think, our life would be incredibly impoverished, back to our animal roots. And yet our thoughts constrain us, keeping us on their level, in their circle. It is not a bad place, except when we suffer from anxiety, anger, jealousy, fear, obsession, depression, or some other emotional distress that muddies our thoughts. But even at its best and clearest, our thought-sphere is a very limited place.

Those limitations are not obvious. Our thoughts can soar to the most sublime subjects: the creation of the universe, the nature of the Divine, truth and love. Yet such thoughts still remain just thoughts, just sounds or images in our brain that symbolize something else. The thought of the universe is not the universe. The thought of the creator is not the Creator. And the thought of love is not Love. Thoughts pale to insignificance before the realities to which they refer. Nevertheless, we mistakenly ascribe reality to these thought-symbols themselves and live in thrall to them.

Thoughts are so intimate that they seem to be our true voice, one that no one else hears. *That's me thinking these thoughts.* But the great majority of our thoughts are not intentional. We don't think them. They think themselves: bouncing off each other, pinging our memory bank, lurching to yet another tangent, an endless chain. And this seductive, self-generating stream of thoughts carries us along with it. It lulls us into a kind of inner sleep, wherein we don't have to do anything, we just let our thoughts be who and what we are. This is a poor existence, constrained to a domain of automatic, associative thoughts that take our attention, take us.

To understand this, to believe it, to have any hope of going beyond thought, we need to see our mind situation clearly. In meditation, if we anchor ourselves in body awareness, so that we do not slip away into the stream of thoughts, and if we quietly watch what happens in us, we see our thoughts coming and going on their own, without our directing them. It's like a computer program that jumps from one memory to an associated one, from one notion to another, without any need of outside control.

There is no "I" in our automatic thought stream. The thought "I" is just another thought. The thought "I" that we believe in so deeply is not the reality of who we are, not our will or attention, not our true I. We construct our whole persona around the thought "I." But it is just a thought. We need to see this again and again. We need to become thoroughly steeped in seeing that our thoughts are almost always automatic and are never who we are. Only by becoming completely and directly convinced of this, do we come to the point of being ready to set our thoughts aside, ready to not be taken in by them. Thoughts are just thoughts, nothing more. They have meaning, they are symbols referring to people, objects, events, or abstract concepts, but they are not me or you. Just as spoken language is not the speaker, our thoughts are not the one who sees or thinks them.

Yes, sometimes we do think intentionally. We might consider a problem, make a plan, remember how to do something, and so on. But even then, we are not our thoughts, we are the one who is thinking them. Still, for the most part, no one is thinking them, yet we believe they reflect our intention, our self, even though they just follow a cause-effect, stimulus-response mode of generation. Watch your thoughts. See them in action, until you are ready to step free of them.

Now that does not mean stopping thoughts. In our quieter moments, they may subside temporarily. But we cannot stop them directly and they will be with us for the remainder of our life, just as our breathing and digestion will. No matter. Our spiritual work is to be free in front of them, to move our attention into domains other than thought.

The first of those, as mentioned above, is body awareness, and more generally, sensory awareness other than the cognitive perception of thoughts. Body awareness grounds us in the present, in the concrete reality of our body. Further practice opens us into the energy field, the sensitive energy that enables us to be in contact with our body. This grounding diminishes the hold that our thoughts have on us.

By practicing thought awareness, grounded in our body and watching our thoughts come and go, we begin to see into the gaps between thoughts, into the mind-space around our thoughts. Just beyond and surrounding our thoughts is the silence, the great, welcoming, immediately familiar stillness. Thoughts are in time, define time, while stillness is timeless. Opening to the cognizant stillness within us, we can just be, we can enter our being. This is a new perception for us, the perception of inner spaciousness, of inner stillness, of pure awareness. Our thoughts may continue their ever-changing stream, but we are here, in our being. Thoughts are no obstacle to that. In this state, our thoughts do not take us away from our being. We are like the sky with thought clouds passing by, clouds which cannot affect the immensity of the sky beyond them.

For this week, watch your thoughts. Notice particularly the thought "I." Notice how your thoughts take you for a ride, in which you are passive. Notice the vast stillness of being, the great inner space of your mind, surrounding your thoughts.

23.4 Beyond Desire
(Learning to Be: Part 4)

Our muddled inner life is driven by our desires: we want this and we don't what that. Some desires are superficial and can easily be disregarded. Others are fundamental and deeply ingrained, such as the need for food, clothing, shelter, and security, the need for intimacy, sex, and procreation, the need for friendship and respect, the need to be useful. These desires are not easily disregarded. When one of them is thwarted or threatened, our whole inner world turns desperately and obsessively to resolving the situation.

Most of the time, though, the desires that control us are somewhere in between the superficial and the fundamental. We are happy when they are fulfilled and upset when they are not. This makes our inner life a function of what happens to us and around us. In an automatic, deterministic way our emotions react to events, real or imagined, and sweep us away.

Just as our thought-stream captures us, our emotions do also, but even more powerfully. When we feel an emotion, we are quite sure that is how "I" feel, though typically it is just a preprogrammed reaction with nothing intentional about it, without our true I in it. It is not "I" that wants; it is the want that wants. It is not "I" that am angry; it is the anger that is angry. These things happen in us, to us. They are not our doing. They are not us.

You like one thing, she likes another. You dislike a thing, while he likes it. Our likes and dislikes are predominantly learned behaviors and attitudes that drive our life. The same goes for opinions. We defend our opinions, either secretly in our mind or vociferously out loud. Our likes and dislikes, our opinions and reactions, all seem to be aspects of who we are. But the truth is they are not. We can let go of any of them, even if only temporarily. To do so is instructive and useful to our spiritual work.

We choose a particular like or dislike and set ourselves for a definite time, weeks or months, not to indulge it. This exercise is not about getting rid of our likes or dislikes, which would make life dull indeed. Rather we learn in the process. We learn discipline. We gain confidence. We learn that we are not our likes or dislikes. And more fundamentally, we learn to let go, we gain a measure of freedom. When we can be, just be, we can watch the arising of an impulse of liking or disliking and watch it pass away, without slavishly acting on it. We remain, we are, while all these things pass through us. We just watch and be. We are not slaves to our own conditioning. After the time period is up, we can drop the task and return to acting on that like or dislike, when we so choose, but now with the understanding that we are truly free in front of it. Whereas before we had no choice, because we thought we were that like or dislike, we were lost in it, now we have a free choice, our possibilities increased.

The problem is not our reactive emotions, likes and dislikes, desires and opinions per se. The problem is that we identify with these processes in us. When one of them arises, we believe in it, we collapse into it, we become it, and we lose ourselves in it. We cannot say that I am. Rather, the emotion is, the dislike is, the opinion is, the desire is. We stop living. We stop being.

But it does not have to be that way. The more we work to be free, the more we learn to let go, the more we find equanimity and peace. Beyond our reactive emotions, beyond our thoughts and opinions, beyond our likes and dislikes, beyond our ordinary self, is a realm of consciousness and peace. This is not an emptiness, not a mere lack, although it may appear that way at first, due to our not yet being accustomed to perceive what is there, what is here in us. Equanimity, peace, and consciousness are substantive in their own right, all-pervasive and infinite. We can participate in that, live that. It is here for the taking.

Equanimity is the first of the conscious emotions. It is not indifference. A person with equanimity does care. They can and do act responsively and vigorously as the need arises and as they choose. But they are rooted in their being. They live a life of peace and freedom and, yes, joy. Even in the face of difficulties with regard to fundamental needs, they can act and respond and still live in equanimity, in being. To come to that takes sustained and well-balanced spiritual practice, practice that renders transparent the layers that hide our own being.

Learning not to be driven by our desires is basic and necessary. For that we need meditation, to gain the taste of peace, the work of being aware of our likes and dislikes in the moment they arise so that we can watch them pass by without needing to act on them, and the work of being aware of our opinions as opinions when they arise, so that we are not automatically shunted into believing our opinions are absolute truth.

For this week, practice equanimity. Practice awareness of the things that tend to knock you off center. Practice letting them go. Even when a strong desire, emotion, or opinion comes up, stay yourself. Be.

23.5 The Wish to Be
(Learning to Be: Part 5)

Conscious desires rise beyond those driven by reaction and self-centeredness; we can call them wishes. In particular, there is a type of wish that drives our inner work, a wish that keeps us returning to ourselves, to presence, to the spiritual path. We have a deep-seated longing, a longing for completion, for purification, for meaning, peace, and connection. This sacred longing is part of our human endowment; we all have it. We can call it the wish to be.

This wish is the fundamental fuel of our life; it prods us to action. And not just actions related to inner work and spirituality. It translates into our need to express who we are in the way we live and what we do. Yet this wish to be often devolves into the wish to have, to take, to hold. Because we face outward, it leads us to attempt in vain to fill our inner need with outer things. Nothing and no one that we might have, take, or hold can truly fulfill our wish to be. In the end we are left flat and wanting. Yes, family and friends matter. Meaningful work matters. But still, something more stirs in our heart, a need that cannot be satisfied from the outside.

Not understanding that need, our wish to be, we divert it to other pursuits. It gets crusted over and ignored. And so we go through life with this need in our heart, pretending it isn't there or trying to satisfy it with temporal, material fixes.

But if we look deeply into what we desire, we find at the root of desire this wish to be, this wish to be ourselves, our true selves, to be real, to be here and whole. Being is something that no one can give us and no calamity can take from us. It is the only true security, for it does not belong to time and space. Being is timeless and of a different order than all that surrounds us. And most importantly, being can be earned, it can grow, if we nurture it appropriately. This is precisely where the wish to be derives its great importance. Without the wish to be, we would not practice presence, prayer, meditation, kindness, and all the other aspects of the spiritual path, of growing our being. The stronger and more direct our contact with our fundamental wish, the more we practice and the more we fulfill that wish.

When we engage in life, as we must, should, and do, life takes us. We lose ourselves in the outward action, in the outward perceptions. We are not. The wish to be calls us back to ourselves, back to presence, at the same time as we engage in activity. We can both be and do. Being and doing do not exclude each other. We can be ourselves as we act, as we do all the large and little things we do. Our wish to be calls us not to get lost in doing. We can be in contact with the cognizant stillness, that silent presence that is our true home, as we speak and act and think. But our heartfelt wish to be is the core cause, the enabling factor that makes presence possible. Without it, we never even start, we do not make that first move into presence, we ignore the possibility.

We can feel the wish to be directly. We enter ourselves and feel our longing, here in our center. The deepest longing has no object. We simply long for being, long to be. While we are not, we have no peace. As soon as we enter presence, become ourselves in this moment, we find a measure of peace.

Our longing to be is fulfilled, at least temporarily.

Our wish to be can act as our compass on a moment-to-moment basis. When we are lost in our thoughts, reactions, or activities, that wish reminds us, it gives us a feeling of discomfort, of things not being quite right with us. Our being wants to come forward, to take its place at the center of our life. When we are off that center, out of touch, we know it, even if only at a subconscious level. Yet that out-of-touch-with-ourselves feeling is the needle of our compass, pointing toward our magnetic center. We can follow it back to our inner home.

For this week, practice coming back home to your being, to being yourself, to presence, both in your sitting meditation practice and in your daily life.

23.6 In Body, Mind, and Heart
(Learning to Be: Part 6)

The three flavors of the sensitive energy offer us the foundation on which to build our being. Those flavors correspond to awareness in body, heart, and mind respectively. This energy is a generalized sensor, ready to detect and report to our awareness all kinds of sensory phenomena: internal and external, physical, emotional, and mental. The more of this energy we collect and stabilize, the more vivid our moment-to-moment experience and the stronger our being.

In our body, the sensitive energy manifests as a vibrant plasma that mediates our visceral contact with our body: touch, kinesthetic and proprioceptive senses, pain and pleasure, hot and cold. It also puts us in contact with the other body senses of taste, smell, vision, and hearing. We can work with the sensitive energy in the body by practicing contact with any and, preferably, all of these body senses. But the most straightforward and clearest approach is through contact with our body itself, with arms and legs, torso, neck, and head, feet, hands, fingers and face. We give our attention to our body and through that attention we discover this vibrant, mobile, sensitive substance wherever we place and hold our attention.

Usually we are only vaguely aware of our body. Unless we have some strong sensation, say of pain or pleasure, we have little direct contact with our body. Yes, we are always in our body, but we do not always know it. We don't really feel our arms or legs or face most of the time. So our practice is to put our attention on part or all of our body and hold it there. Gradually we begin to be aware of the sensitive energy in our body. We call this practice sensing. Through sensing we can be in contact our body at any time and with extended, persistent practice, a good deal of the time.

You might ask why, why do this? Is there some reason for sensing, beyond making our bodily experience more vivid? Indeed there are deep reasons. First, sensing lays the foundation for presence, which makes our whole life more vivid. In presence we live more, we are more. And beyond that, sensing lays the foundation for building our soul, the lower part of which we can think of as an inner body made of the sensitive energy, our sensation body. For that, though, much practice is required to accumulate and stabilize our sensation. Put simply, sensing can transform our life, for the better, with many side benefits to its primary benefits of growing our being and moving us along the spiritual path.

Our sensation body needs a mind, a cognitive faculty, also made of the sensitive energy. For that, we work with the sensitive energy in our mind. The method is straightforward: we put our attention into our mind and practice awareness there. The most prevalent content in our mind is, of course, our thoughts. So we pay attention to our thoughts and mental images. The sensitive energy enables us to be in contact with our thoughts, to know their meaning, to notice our thoughts as thoughts. Our usual relationship with our thoughts is to be lost in them, to believe we are our thoughts. Being cognizant of our thoughts, through the sensitive energy, puts us in touch with their meaning, with the fact that they are thoughts, just thoughts, passing through our mind. And this reveals another benefit of sensing our body: if we simultaneously sense our body and cognize our thoughts, the body sensation grounds us in this moment and helps keep us from being swept away by our thoughts, helps give us an inner place to stand, a perspective. With sensation in our body, we can stay aware of our thoughts, stay in our front row seat at the theater of our thoughts.

Then we come to awareness of our cognitive faculty itself, beyond thoughts. We begin to notice gaps between our thoughts. We can be in our mind, in our big mind, and not be lost in our thoughts. They come and go, passing through our mind, while we stay here in this inner mind space.

Our sensation body and mind, need a heart. So we notice our emotions as well. Again, rather than identifying with them, our sensitive contact with our emotions shows our emotions as emotions, as feelings passing through our inner heart space. Just as we can be in sensitive contact with our mind even when there are no thoughts, we can be in sensitive contact with our center of emotions, in our chest and solar plexus, even where there are no obvious or particular emotions occurring. That contact tends to transform our emotional life, freeing us from losing ourselves in the more self-centered egoistic emotions, and opening us to a warmer, more heartful approach to life, to ourselves, and to the people around us.

Working with the sensitive energy in all three, in body, mind, and heart, we gain a broad and stable basis for presence. When one falters, the work on the other two spills over and picks it up by reminding us. And it has the great advantage of accessibility: we can work in this way at any time. For example, once we gain some familiarity with sensing, we find that we can sense during our normal daily activities, without interrupting them, in fact enhancing them. We do not need to be sitting in meditation for a certain period to sense. We can sense anytime, anywhere. It is accessible and verifiable. Once we have the taste of it, sensing is unmistakable. We know if we are sensing and we know whether it is stronger or weaker. This brings our spiritual practice into our daily life in a real, direct, and effective way. It clearly delineates one leading edge of our personal, spiritual journey: how often, for how long, and how strongly can I sense my body today? That clarity of direction proves invaluable.

For this week, work with the sensitive energy in your body, your mind, and your heart.

23.7 Energy Management
(Learning to Be: Part 7)

To be more we need to strengthen our inner being. And work on being is all about working with inner energies. Our will actually does the work, but our energies enable it. The principal energies that can contribute to our being are the sensitive energy, highest of the life energies, and two of the truly spiritual energies, which are not bound by space and time, namely the conscious energy and the creative energy. All of our inner work, all spiritual practices, all meditation, prayer, and inner exercises concern these energies. Though there are even higher energies, they lie well beyond our awareness and understanding, so we need not concern ourselves with them, except by way of prayer. Our work on being does concern contacting, engaging, generating, tapping into, accumulating, and organizing the sensitive, conscious, and creative energies that can form our soul.

In Part 6 of this series (In Body, Mind, and Heart), we delved into working with the sensitive energy in its various forms. The importance of that fundamental work, throughout our spiritual life, cannot be overemphasized. Our ability to sense, the strength, frequency, and duration of our work with sensing during our everyday life, becomes one effective measure of being and shows the status of our inner life. It is a kind of spiritual fuel gauge, a standard which can guide our efforts to regulate our energies.

Some things we might do can be very costly to our inner life because they waste our energies. These may include too much food, too much alcohol, tobacco use, recreational drug use, too little sleep, too much or too little sex, lack of exercise — in short, the usual dimensions of a healthy lifestyle. Except now, our measure is not just our bodily health, but our ability to practice sensing. Destructive emotions like anger, anxiety, jealousy, and the rest also waste our inner energies, in direct proportion to the strength and duration of the emotional storm. Experimentation with, and careful observation of, how we live and how that affects our ability to sense can show us how to manage our lifestyle to maximize our spiritual energies. To change our wasteful habits, we work for awareness, for presence, not against some habit. We work to be aware when a wasteful impulse arises, and to stay aware of it as it passes by, without our needing to act on it. We seek to live in such a way that we can sense more, be more, live more. Indeed, sensing tends to diminish our energy wasting behaviors, both physical and emotional, by bringing us to a less identified state of being.

While minimizing our waste of inner energies is necessary, it is not sufficient to grow our being. Among other things, we also need to increase our intake of spiritual energies. This is a positive feedback process, because as our being grows our access to sources of energies also grows. The most readily accessible source is the air around us: it contains an inexhaustible reservoir of spiritual energy on the level of the sensitive energy. But until we learn and become able to access that energy, it remains just a nice theory.

Energy breathing has been taught and practiced in all the major spiritual traditions, although at times in a disguised form. Perhaps the clearest example comes from the Yoga tradition with its practice of pranayama. Today this is usually taken as a physical exercise of breathing through one nostril or both in a certain pattern. Otherwise the breathing is ordinary. But actually to breathe the prana or energy in the air is a matter of inner breathing, of using our attention and intention to contact and draw the energy from the air. The outward form of one nostril or a breath pattern is unnecessary and can even distract us from the real action required. The inner form is to put our attention into the air as we breathe it in and, with our attention acting as a kind of net, draw the energy into us, draw the vivid, vibrating particles of energy from the air and let them enter our body, our being, where they spread out to join and strengthen our sensitive energy. Visualizing and imagining these shimmering particles entering us with our breath can help get us started, but must not be confused with the actual experience, which is unmistakable. Energy breathing builds our being in a direct way and can be a very important part of our spiritual path. We can try energy breathing during our sitting practice for a week or so and if we still do not have contact with it, we drop it and come back to it later, say in six months or a year, and try again.

There are deeper sources of energy than what comes to us from the air. We will address working with the conscious energy in the next part of this inner work series and with the creative energy in a later part.

For this week, notice what you do that wastes your inner energies by noticing how your actions affect your ability to sense. Try the practice of energy breathing.

23.8 Being Conscious
(Learning to Be: Part 8)

The shortest route toward learning to be conscious is to acquire the taste of it through silent meditation. That is not to say that we will recognize it at first. The main problems are that we do not recognize consciousness for what it is and we believe that we are already conscious. We grow up with that illusion because it is close to being true and even is true, albeit intermittently and briefly. Ordinarily we live on the surface of our senses, including the cognitive sense of our thoughts. Something happens and we react. This is our life on the automatic energy. A step up into the sensitive energy allows us actual contact with our senses, so that we really take in what our sensory perceptions offer in a given moment. That is what we normally call being conscious. But in our terminology, this is being sensitive.

The conscious energy is another step up and a different matter entirely. It gives depth of inner space, perspective, and a sense of our self as the actor in our life. It reveals timelessness to us.

Our situation is like watching a movie at a theater. If the movie is good and engrossing, as our life always is, we lose ourselves in it. There is just the movie: the action, the color, and the sounds. We cease to exist. Our senses, emotions, and thoughts are played by the movie, become a function of the movie. This is how our life is on automatic.

If we become aware of the movie as a movie, of its qualities, we are no longer just being played by the movie. Rather we are in sensitive contact with it.

If we become aware of the whole theater, with its seats and people and large space and images on the screen and sound from the speakers and ourselves sitting in the midst of it all, then this is like being conscious. We come into the contextual depth of experience, of our awareness. We have a sense of wholeness and of ourselves within that wholeness, not separate from it or from anything within awareness. We can even become the actor in our life, rather than a spectator dimly aware of the half-cognized, mental and emotional reactions driving our automatic actions.

In meditation, as our thoughts settle down, gaps open up between them, gaps which are empty of thoughts, zones of no thought. As we look into this, we gradually see that these gaps are more than a mere absence of thoughts. It is like having to wait for our eyes to adjust when going from light into darkness. If we stay with those gaps, stay with active attention in that silence, it reveals a substantive, cognizant stillness that surrounds our thoughts, that fills our mind and more. This is consciousness. It is not just emptiness; it is the cognizant substance of pure awareness, the backdrop of all perceptions.

Consciousness is all-pervasive: here in us all the time. This fools us into believing we are conscious all the time, because if we are asked "are you conscious?" or "are you aware of yourself?" we can respond "Yes" and it's true. For that moment, we are aware of ourselves. Then we quickly sink back to automatic living, staying on the surface, giving no attention to the depth, to the context of awareness: we lose touch with consciousness. We live without contact with consciousness.

But through our inner work and the growth of being that it promotes, we can learn first to recognize consciousness in meditation, then to recognize it in our daily activities, and then to live in it. To live in consciousness is to live in depth, a wholesome and holistic depth that does not obscure the surface. Rather we live on both levels at once; our deep consciousness embraces the whole, both inner and outer. We live in the depth of our being and on the sensory surface of life, enriching both. As we go about our day, thoughts fill our mind. But behind and around those thoughts is the cognizant stillness that is consciousness. We learn to live in that. Our being is quiet and at peace, even when our mind is filled with thoughts, emotions, and perceptions. We learn to be, to be in that depth of awareness, in that peace of stillness. And from that place we can and do act effectively and creatively.

For this week, practice looking into the stillness between and around your thoughts. Open to that stillness. Be in that.

23.9 Affirming Presence
(Learning to Be: Part 9)

There is a qualitative difference between bouncing through our life on autopilot, as we do, and being fully engaged in what we're doing or perceiving in this moment, between letting life happen to us and feeling "I am doing this." This is not just about the big things, the long-term plans and major projects. It applies to the particulars of our life, to each event, to each moment.

So how do we get engaged, get involved? It begins with attention. The secret quality of attention is that it is driven by our will, it is our will. The practice of active attention is the road to coming into our own, our own will, our I. When you pay attention to what you are doing or seeing or touching or thinking, your I is there; it is you who are doing or seeing or touching or thinking. Not paying attention, allowing our attention to be drawn hither and thither, to be distracted easily, with no staying power, indicates that we are not here, that our I has withdrawn beyond our reach. We can learn to affirm our life, our living, our presence.

And we do that first by affirming our attention, by being our attention. It may sound abstract, but the actual practice of it is simple. We just pay attention to what we are doing and/or perceiving and we get fully behind that attention. We are there attending, wholly and completely, simply and directly. If you try this, you may see that you can do it. You may see how it is different than letting your attention just wander wherever it is drawn. We bring our power, the power of our will, our I, into our attention. We become our attention for that moment. Though it is simple, this is not so easy to maintain moment-to-moment over time. To do so, we need to continually renew our attention and our being in it.

Closely related to this is another form of will, namely intention or purpose. We can affirm ourselves, affirm our presence by living with intention, living with purpose. That intention includes the intention to be, the will-to-be, in any given moment, as well as larger scale intentions and purposes that go beyond this moment. But one significant purpose is to be, to be present. Living with intention generally, living with purpose, helps us with that. We can live. We can live as purpose. We can be the bearer of purpose, we can be that purpose. Because our purpose, our intention, is the embodiment of our will, our I, it can be the embodiment of a higher will, which we will address in the next part of this inner work series.

We start with paying attention in more situations and for longer; we sustain it. There are degrees of attention, distinguished primarily by how much we are behind it, into it. There is a big difference between half-hearted attention that only half engages us and wholehearted, unreserved attention that we affirm, that we fully agree to. *Here I am, doing this.* The affirmation of presence is not a thought: it is an act of will. By affirming our attention in this way, we affirm ourselves, we affirm the core of our presence. We take responsibility for our presence in this life, in this moment, responsibility for doing what we are doing, not in an abstract way in our thoughts, but in real way: we are here as the one who is doing what we are doing. We are our attention, our purpose, our intention in this moment. Without us, without someone at home, without our I, we have no presence. With our I, we are present.

Affirming our presence in this way connects us, our I, with what's around us; it connects our inner world with the outer world as one continuum, one great whole. Here we are in the midst of this, our life, our world. For this week, affirm your presence. Be the one who is here, living your life in each moment.

23.10 Affirming the Higher
(Learning to Be: Part 10)

Of the two major components of presence, the far more obvious but still quite subtle one is awareness, particularly the pure awareness of consciousness, which we experience as a substantive, cognizant stillness. The other major component and the true core of presence is us, the one who is present, the one who is aware of our awareness, the experiencer and doer. This is sometimes put in the form of a question, such as who am I? or where does attention come from?

There are three levels of responses to such questions, three levels of who is present. The first is our ordinary I. This is an abstract amalgam of all our learned attitudes, patterns of thought and emotion, physical and emotional needs and desires, skills, memories, and tendencies. Some are mutually reinforcing, while many others conflict. Together they form our personality with its illusion of unity, an illusion created by the fact that at any given moment, only one of these many I's takes center stage and controls what we do. Later another one comes to the fore. The great majority of these many little selves of ours have as their core mission their own satisfaction. In aggregate this forms the illusion that is our ego, centered on this supposed self of ours. But if we look deeply into that self, into who we assume we are, we find nothing there, nothing independent and lasting, no self, which of course is one of the central tenets of Buddhism. It is remarkable to deconstruct our ego, our false I, and find that it simply does not exist and never did. It is just a label with our name on it that we continually build up and defend. But with nothing at its core, this is a futile endeavor and the source of many of our problems. This many-faced, false I is difficult to see directly. Nevertheless, we can gradually work our way beyond it, toward true unity, by the practice of presence.

The second level of who we are concerns our true I, our real unity. This is beyond our thoughts, emotions, and body. This is our will: the will, for example, at the root of our attention. This is the core of our presence, the core that we affirm in presence, as discussed in the previous Part 9 of this inner work series. Having seen through our false I and continuing to look for who we are, we find that one in us who does what we do and sees what we see, the one who lives our life, the one beyond all the myriad thoughts and emotions, beyond all the noise of our personality and false I. Here I am, as myself. If we could be, just be, really be, we would be ourselves, our true I. That is a revolution in our inner world, because instead of being driven by our automatic reactions to what happens to us, the flow of our actions begins with us, with our real self.

Yet even this high, real self, our true I, is limited, in that we believe it to begin in us, to have its origin and center in us. But it both does and does not begin with us. This is the great mystery of the sacred and of will. The third level of who we are concerns the higher will, the sacred will, of which we are part, and which is our source, the source of our will, of who we are. Here we confront a deeper illusion than the illusion of our ordinary I. We have come into ourselves, into our own, into full responsibility, and yet we need to go deeper still. It is not just a matter of connecting with the sacred, of praying as a creature before the Divine. It is more radical than that. It's about becoming the sacred, or more accurately, allowing the sacred to become us, recognizing that the sacred is us, letting our center pass into the center of All. We do not begin in our own inner world. Our true and current origin, our true center, in this very moment, lies in the sacred mountain of purpose, the Divine Will of the Creator. That Will is in us, is us, each and every one of us.

The higher levels of prayer involve opening our very self, letting our innermost self go, letting our deepest notion of our self evaporate in favor of the Great Self of the sacred. The mystery is that it then becomes possible both to be fully ourselves and for the sacred to be fully us. We get out of the way and serve with the full complement of our skills and abilities, including our ability to be present. Only now, when we affirm presence, we are affirming the sacred in us, as us. It is the sacred that is present — and us, both, and with no difference between the two. A thirteenth century kabbalist put it this way: that we seek to elevate ourselves through the power of our intention so that the higher will is clothed in our will, and not only so that our will is clothed in the higher will.[8]

A note of caution is worth putting in here. We are not talking about having the Divine Will manifest to us as a voice or urge telling us what to do. Almost always that inner voice is one of our own, not God's. In our actions we maintain common sense, the golden rule, and adherence to the norms and laws of our society.

What we do want is simply to be, and to open the inner door of our being so as to allow the sacred to be in us, as us. This can also happen when we are doing something, with the whole of ourselves, with full awareness of ourselves and the action, and leaving ourselves as the source of the action out, letting the action flow through us. More on that in the next part of this series.

For this week, practice affirming the higher in your presence, in your being, by opening your innermost door and asking, begging, hoping for the sacred to enter. Allow the higher to affirm you. Allow the higher to affirm Itself in you. This is the road to Love.

---

[8] The Heart and the Fountain: An Anthology of Jewish Mystical Experiences, edited by Joseph Dan (New York: Oxford University Press, 2003), p.119

23.11 Flow
(Learning to Be: Part 11)

We all know and cherish moments, or even whole days, when our life just flows, smoothly and sweetly, when things are fine just as they are. Contrasting those days with our usual ups and downs, we can ask: what makes the difference? At first it might seem that our days of harmony are days without bumps, without big problems coming at us. But we have many days without big problems, yet they do not all flow. So the crux of the difference is not in our environment. The difference is us: do we interfere with the flow? Do we create our own disturbances? Do we get lost in and chewed up by our life?

Well, yes. Some of that is obvious. Take our overwrought emotional reactions of anger, fear, jealousy and the like. Something in our environment strikes us and our emotions react to let us know the event might be significant. What follows is crucial. If we try to push that emotion away, it comes back in full and extended force. If we lock onto it and let our thoughts join the action by going round and round about the emotional event, then we are nurturing that identification and lose our peace. If, however, we are present at the start, remain in presence, take full notice of our emotional reaction as it arises, and stay aware of it without encouraging or rejecting it, then we may find that it quickly subsides and that our life can flow once more, even when we need to take some action in response to whatever instigated this latest emotive storm.

When we talk about being "in the flow," what is it that flows? We are familiar with the notion of the stream of consciousness. But what we really mean by that is the stream of the contents of consciousness. Time marches and brings with it an endless and seamless series of events, of sensory perceptions, thoughts, emotions, and actions. When we are in that stream, we get identified with it and we are no longer in consciousness, just in its contents. In that circumstance, the stream pushes us around. We careen from one thought to another, to an emotional reaction, to a sight or sound, each taking us over for its time. The stream may be flowing through consciousness, but we are not flowing, we are on a jagged path through our day.

To remedy this we need to return to consciousness, to being, to allowing the stream to flow through us, while we stay rooted in the present, in presence, on the conscious banks of the stream. By allowing and accepting life as it is and ourselves as we are, the contents of the stream no longer grab us, no longer push us around. To live in flow does not mean that we are flowing, it means that the stream of life is flowing right through us, without being blocked, dammed up, or ignored by us. For that to happen, we enlarge our inner space.

This requires living in awareness and acceptance, living in time while maintaining contact with the timeless. The roadblocks to living in the flow are like kinks in time. Contact with the timeless, with consciousness and beyond, helps us rise above time, above the kinks. We accept our difficulties and challenges because we live in a place where we can accept them, accept our life, and accept ourselves. That place is the timeless heart of presence.

Acceptance means appreciating our life and being content with our situation. Acceptance does not require us to settle reluctantly for what we don't want, because acceptance does not preclude working to improve our self or our situation. Appreciation and contentment are essential for a happy, flowing life, as is engagement in improving, creating, or serving. Contentment and equanimity cut the cord of desire and leave us free to live in joy.

Flow is our natural state. But our ordinary state is one where we grab onto, push away from, or react to the contents of the stream. We stop the flow thereby. When we can be, just be, the flow goes of its own accord, our life just flows, and we flow through it.

There are also special circumstances that enhance our opportunity for flow. Engaging in creative action, for example in the arts, certainly can be a doorway into flow. These might include artistic painting, dance, making or listening to music, and so on, where the dancer becomes the dance, the musician becomes the music. Here the creative force acts through us; we serve as its instrument. Our ordinary I, our ego, vanishes for those moments, as we let it go and enter the higher stream of the creative.

For this week, look at what blocks the flow of your life: not the external blocks, but the inner attitudes and reactions that block it. These are like clouds passing through our mind and if we follow them and give them energy, they become storms that stop our flow. Let them pass and stop fighting your life. Accept, be present, and live in the flow.

23.12 Being in Love
(Learning to Be: Part 12)

Love is union of the will, a union much deeper than the physical union of sex or the emotional union of attachment. Love asks for nothing in return, not even reciprocity, whereas attachment does ask. If it is union, if it is love, how could we ask something in return from our Self? Attachment competes with love for space in our heart and mind. For that reason, the inner work of love, of becoming able to love, consists of allowing oneself to be imposed upon.

Consider that for a moment. Love, to the extent that it is true, is unselfish, beyond ego. In love, we act toward our loved one in ways that they perceive as positive and beneficial to them. If we are unselfish and not acting from egoistic impulses, then we have transcended our ordinary self, transcended separateness, and love comes naturally. Why then, this formulation that the work of love is allowing oneself to be imposed on? If we are beyond our self in love, then at those moments we have no self that could be imposed upon.

But such moments of purity are rare for us. Our motives are mixed. Yes, we care about our loved one, for and as our loved one. And we naturally care about ourselves. Inevitably, issues arise where the two conflict, where we can either put ourselves first, or put our loved one first, but not both. In love there is no distinction between our self and our loved one. But in our ordinary state, there is. This is where the practice of allowing ourselves to be imposed upon enters the relationship. It is a high and demanding practice that, more directly than other spiritual practices, acts to free us from egoism, which is exactly the condition that enables us to love.

So we take opportunities as they arise to let our self-interest, our self-centeredness, and our attachments to be imposed upon. Yet we do have personal limits we are constrained to honor. We work to push our envelope on this score, work at the edge of what we can bear. But to go beyond that, to try to destroy our envelope, only backfires. We give and give way until it hurts, and then a little more. But we cannot give until we break, for then all giving will cease. So this subtle and demanding work of allowing our self to be imposed upon requires us to understand not only our loved one, but also our self and our current limitations.

Something is asked of us. It is inconvenient or distasteful. We start feeling resentful about this imposition. That is the moment to let go, to allow our self to be imposed on, to acquiesce and do or give what's required. Who am I? Am I the one who looks to myself and refuses the other? Or am I the one who loves, who is in love?

There is a saying that our being is what we can bear, from which we can see that what we cannot bear is due to our attachments, not our being. But there are consequences. If we exhibit attachment and some of the negative manifestations of attachment to another person, then though they may love us, they will respond in kind, with attachment. Our attachment evokes attachment in them, and vice versa in a negative feedback loop, a destructive spiral.

Love is not blind. No one is perfect. Yet everyone has something in them, something we share, that is perfect. That is the source and object of love. Yet love includes the imperfections, whereas attachment reacts against them.

Growth of being comes in growth of freedom in front of attachments. Because we ask for something in return, because we want our love to be reciprocated, because we become angry, resentful, or jealous, should we then assume that we don't love the other person? No. We should not assume that, because we are mixed, we have mixed motivations. We may have love, whereby we care about the other person's welfare as they would for their own and we care for them with no reference to ourselves. Yet at the same time, we also have attachment, wanting something from our loved one. Both coexist in us, but are incompatible. They show us our levels and they show us what to aspire to, what to nurture, and what not to nurture. They show us the direction of love, of the inner work to become more able to love.

Besides this receptive work of letting go of attachments, of allowing our self to be imposed upon, we can proactively work to consider our loved one's needs and desires, to serve our loved one as they would wish to be served. We look for and create opportunities to show our love. We act on them. What does this person want? What does this person need? What would delight this person? How can I provide something toward that?

For this week, explore how to become able to love and how to express love in actions.

24.0 Who Am I?

We love stories, especially the one we tell ourselves, the one in which we are the central character. That story unfolds as a running commentary on our life, a dramatization. We tell it, we listen to it, we make it into a model of ourselves and the world, of reality, and we believe it unquestioningly, until a certain question arises. The question *"Who am I?"* in its various forms, has beset human beings from time immemorial. You would think it would be so easy and obvious, that it would not really arise as a question. But it has and keeps doing so, for good reason. Indeed, some spiritual paths and practices have this question at their center, because it is the key question of our life. How we answer it, or ignore it, determines so much about how we live, because the question addresses our fundamental assumptions about reality, the false assumptions that stop us from seeking the truth.

Consider it. Ask yourself *"Who am I?"* Who am I *really*? Looking within for the answer, we find a muddle. The question reverberates in there, in our mind, as if in an echo chamber. It reverberates because there is nothing to stop it, nothing to hang onto, nothing to resolve it. Every possible solution comes up short, one way or another.

One reason for that: we are all over the place in the transitory I's that claim to be who we are, at least during their brief, though repeated, existence. There is a process we call identification, which some Buddhists call selfing, whereby we passively fall into becoming some aspect of ourselves that is not the real us. When we identify, we create an identity which we assume is us. We become that for those moments, before going on to become the next thing. We can and do identify with almost anything, but usually our body, some emotion, or some thought. We identify with other people, with what they think of us, with how they treat us, with comparing them to us. We identify with the weather, with traffic, with our car, with our bank account, with our plans, with what we have, with what we don't have, with what we do, with what we cannot do, and so on endlessly.

There are two ways to look at identification or selfing. One, taken by Buddhists and some cognitive scientists, is that selfing creates an illusory, temporary I, with nothing behind it, that there is no independent self, that we are just an agglomeration of all the memories and tendencies accumulated haphazardly in the neuronal pathways of our brain. This is a shocking but excellent starting point for pursuing the question of who am I, because it is a true view, as far as it goes. Beyond that however, is the reality of our true I, which, unlike our illusory I's, has no ultimate center. Our true I's penultimate center, though, is in us.

The truth of no self, once seen directly, has the wonderful effect of undermining our false view of who we are, of revealing our identification and selfing, of showing that all these things we believe we are fall far short of the reality. This partial liberation removes a great burden from us and allows us to come more into our own reality. Seeing that we are not what we believed ourselves to be is a prerequisite to becoming what we are. So, much of this inner work series will be devoted to looking at what we are not.

Yet the real story does not end there. We do not end up as an empty void. There is something wonderful within us, something unmanufactured and fundamental, something we can learn to recognize, to be, and to cultivate: namely our real self, our real I.

One way we go wrong with the question of *who am I*, is by transforming it into the seemingly easier question of *what do I really want*? Here the inherent premise leads us astray, because it may well be that our true I does not want anything and is beyond wanting. It is our proliferating temporary I's that want. Indeed, each is built around some type of desire, of which we have an endless, varied, and often conflicting supply. So exploring our wants, be they sacred or profane, selfish or selfless, will not bring us closer to the truth behind the question *who am I*.

Similarly, the version of the question that asks *what should I do*, has the basic problem that as long as I do not know who I am, I cannot know what I should do, except for living a responsible, moral life according to the dictates of conscience and societal norms. So asking what I should do, will not bring us closer to the truth behind the question *who am I*.

And there is a truth behind it. There is an answer to this question *who am I*. But it is not an answer that can be readily formulated in words. It is, however, an answer that we can become. We can be who we truly are. It is at the same time obvious, accessible, and hidden.

In the coming weeks, we will explore the question of *who am I* from several perspectives. For this week, begin as you will. Ask yourself the question, meditate on it, ponder it. But don't accept answers that come as thoughts or concepts, as emotions or perceptions. See where and how the question resonates in you. See what it points to. See who is asking it. Use the question as a means of exploration into yourself. Valid certainty about this is possible. That is what we seek.

24.1 Am I My Body?
(Who Am I? - Part 1)

At some point, not too long after we get out of bed in the morning, we look into a mirror and recognize what we take to be ourselves: "there I am." We see our face, our eyes, our hair: "that's me, still here." From birth we have occupied this body. Though it changes over the years and even on shorter time scales as our cells die and are replaced, we know our body more intimately than anything else. The question is am I my body, or is this body no more and no less than my one and only vehicle for my journey through this life, a life delimited by the duration of this body.

Does the fact that my life depends on my body mean that I am my body? Certainly I feel that I am in my body, yet I do not perceive myself as being my body. I am stuck with my body. I cannot trade it in for another one. But the mere fact that I can conceive such a thing is a clue that I am not my body.

Am I my arm, my leg, my hand? People lose limbs and still remain themselves. Am I my heart? People have heart transplants and still remain themselves. So we are not any of those parts.

But am I my brain? I have some control over my thoughts and emotions. I can direct my attention. I can move my body at will. I can speak and listen, as I choose. So I am not those parts of my brain. What does that leave? Am I the executive function of my brain? Is the perceiver, the chooser, which seems to be who I am, just a part of my brain?

So far no such "I" in the brain appears to have been found by neuroscientists. Some scientists espouse a Buddhist-type philosophy that there is no I, that what appears to us to be our self is just the sum of the parts of our brain. As noted in the introduction to this inner work series, that view has great and important validity, as far as it goes. It exposes the illusion that the self we ordinarily take ourselves to be actually exists independently. But that particular strain of scientific thought promotes another illusion: that each of us is our body and only our body. Nevertheless, we are neither the sum of our body and brain parts, nor are we any particular part of our body or brain.

Imagine someone standing in front of you and asking you: are you here? Clearly, they do not mean is your body here? More likely they mean: is your attention here? And your response to the question, "are you here?" would be to focus your attention on the person asking the question and then to answer affirmatively, "yes, I am here." This shows I am not my body as a whole, nor any of its parts. It shows, in that instance, that I am my attention, or more accurately, that I am the one who directs my attention.

The fact that I have this enormously complex body and brain, with its myriad chemical interactions, its adherence to the laws of nature, and its programmed patterns of memory, thought, and action, does not mean that I am no more than my body. Instead it means that I have been entrusted from birth with this wonderful instrument, my body, that I am to use to live my life. This is our experience, our basic, subjective experience of how things are.

Science has not and cannot show otherwise. Yes, neuroscientists may locate all the various functions of our mind in our brain, including the function of attention. But neuroscience will not find in the brain the I that directs those functions, that directs our attention, that makes our choices, that inhabits and experiences our life, because we are not our brains.

This is no mere philosophical issue, because if I am not my brain, if I am not my body, then the question of who I truly am acquires a new urgency. What am I doing here and why am I doing it? Yes, there are obvious physical and social obligations and responsibilities imposed on us. But much of our time is not occupied with what is absolutely required of us. If I am not my body, then my life need not and should not be only about feeding the needs, impulses, and desires of this body. Perhaps there is something else. Perhaps my I, with which my connection often seems tenuous at best, is actually my conduit to the hidden spiritual layers of reality. If there is a spiritual reality, what else but my I could possibly connect me with it?

Seeing that we are not our body frees us from only being our body. This does not mean neglecting our body; we still depend on it, need it, care for it, nurture it, even respect and honor it. Yet we are not just that. Perhaps our true life does not begin and end with our body. Perhaps our true life is timeless. Perhaps we can turn to developing an eternal body, our soul.

The practice of sensing uses our body as a direct vehicle for our spiritual work. Sensing our body, staying in contact with it, keeps our attention in the here and now, and gradually builds part of our soul, a part that sensing gives a direct hint of, namely a sensation body. Of course there are other spiritual practices at deeper levels that do not directly concern our body, but the practice of sensing builds a necessary and wonderful platform for those deeper practices. The practice of sensing, of being in our body, of inhabiting it through the sensitive energy, keeps us in close contact with our body, while clarifying the fact that we are not our body. This body is an instrument that we use, that we depend on, that we love. But the musician is not the instrument.

For this week, let the practice of sensing help clarify your true relationship with your body.

24.2 Am I My Thoughts?
(Who Am I? - Part 2)

If we were to ask ourselves this question, *am I my thoughts*, we would naturally answer no. We might respond that sometimes I think my thoughts and sometimes thoughts just come on their own, but certainly I am not my thoughts. But then we might look again. In particular, two issues stand out. First, what about the thought "I?" And a second related question: for whom do my thoughts speak?

We think and say "I" countless times each day. Mostly it just slips by with nothing much behind it. But if we stop and consider it in real time as it is arising in our mind or speech, to what does this word, this thought "I," refer? Looking further, we discover that it's fungible, that it depends on the context. If we say *I will do such and such*, we mainly mean that our body will do a certain thing. If we say *I hate that*, we are communicating a particular emotion that predominates at times. If we say *I don't know*, we are indicating something about the state of our mind and its contents. But in none of those cases are we focused on the "I" part of the sentence. We leave the subject I curiously empty so that it can adopt the form of whatever the sentence is about. Instead of I, we have our body, our mind, or our feelings. We become our body, our mind, or our feelings. This is identification, wherein our body, our mind, or our feelings substitute for I; we abdicate our I to become what we are not.

So while it's true that I am not my thoughts, the question becomes am I anything at all or just a fill-in-the-blank zero reputed to be a non-zero? Trying to look objectively at our situation, it seems the latter is the case, at least most of the time. We have an unarticulated belief, an assumption, that whenever we say or think "I" it always refers to the same substantive entity, namely us. But we actually use the word "I" to refer to this or that thing within us and rarely, if ever, to the real thing, if there is a real thing. Is there a real thing, a real "I," who we are?

Setting that aside for the moment, we turn to the other question: for whom do my thoughts speak? Clearly sometimes our thoughts speak for our body, sometimes for our emotions, and sometimes for themselves, but rarely for us. The closest we usually come to having our thoughts speak for us is when we intentionally consider some particular situation by thinking about it, by directing our thoughts and keeping them to that subject. This can be difficult as stray thoughts and perceptions continually intrude, enticing us onto tangents. But we can and do think intentionally, just not as often as we might believe to be the case. The great majority of our thoughts are random, associative, or reactive and do not come from us, from our I. The beauty of recognizing this truth is that it punctures our belief that we are our thoughts.

That is a deeply held conviction for many of us. We have these familiar, complex patterns of thoughts, memories, opinions, ideas, reactions, and attitudes that we feel to be us. If I am not my thoughts, if I am not these patterns that make up my personality, then what, if anything, am I? Who am I? The answer to that is simple and wonderful and even obvious, yet no so easy to discover, because it is obscured by our identification with what we are not, principally with our thoughts, our emotions, and our body. If we can see through those identifications, see that we are not just the sum of all this mind-stuff, we can start to see the truth of who we are, we can start to be more ourselves.

Sitting quietly, inhabiting our body, in contact with our body, we can see our thoughts coming and going more clearly. They arise on their own and pass by on their own. In the quiet it is clear that I am not driving my thoughts, rather, they are driving themselves. In the quiet it is clear that I am not this haphazard, associative, endless stream of thoughts. I sit and watch. The seer is not the seen.

Now I turn to directing my thoughts, say by simply counting from 1 to 10 and then repeating that. I do this intentionally. I count intentionally and slowly. I see that I am driving my thoughts. I see that it is not so different than raising my arm and putting it down. I have some control over my body and I have some control over my thoughts. I am not my body and I am not my thoughts.

My body circulates my blood, digests my food, and breathes the air, all without my participation. It just happens. My thoughts come and go and come and go without my direction. It just happens. I am not my body and I am not my thoughts.

Yet I still believe I am my thoughts. As I go about my day, thoughts come and I believe they speak for me, even when they arise automatically, haphazardly.

For this week, please explore your relationship with

your thoughts.

24.3 Am I My Feelings?
(Who Am I? - Part 3)

Our emotions seduce us. This is how I feel. I am worried. I am angry. I am sad. I am envious. I am jealous. I am resentful. I. I. I.

A strong feeling invades us. Our thoughts follow in its train. The thought *I feel this* comes naturally and we believe it. Our thoughts and feelings conspire, as further thoughts and images accord with the feeling and strengthen it. It leaves us thoroughly convinced that we are this feeling, that this is how I feel, that this is who I am in this moment. And indeed it is who we are in that moment, because we have allowed ourselves to identify with the emotion, to collapse into it, to abdicate our self to the emotion. The emotion takes us and takes control of our inner world.

Yet if we look again, we see conflicting emotions. We are angry, but at the same we do not want to be angry. We are sad, but do not want to be sad. Are we both sides of this? Surely not.

Emotions are our reactions to particular situations. They are perceptions and responses to life. An impression comes to us, either from outside or from inside. The impression triggers a particular emotional circuit in our brain. The emotion gathers steam. Our thoughts add to the flame. Then an inner reaction against the emotion may arise. A battle ensues. All this goes on in us automatically. At best we are spectators. But typically we do not even realize what is happening. It happens right in front of us and still it grabs us before we can see it for what it is, before we can see the contradictions, before we can see how it invades us, how we acquiesce to it. These emotions are not our choice, not our doing. They happen to us by masquerading as our self.

We do not exercise our emotions. We are not taught to exert control over them, except for moderating our acting out on the more extreme emotions. Control over our emotions sounds like it would make us robotic, when in fact it is the lack of control, the lack of seeing our emotions as emotions and as nothing more than that, the lack of seeing that our emotions speak for themselves and not for us, it is this passivity in the face of our emotions that makes us robotic, puts us at the mercy of whatever happens to trigger some emotional circuit in us. We are taught to think intentionally, rationally, at times. We are taught to develop skills with our body. But we are not taught to feel happy or sad or at peace, when we wish to feel one of those ways. That implicitly suggests that we are our emotions. If our emotions get out of hand we are taught that *we* have to settle down, not that we have to settle our emotions down.

Yet by watching from a quiet place in ourselves, we can notice our emotions arise. We can notice what they mean and the sometimes valuable information they carry. We can notice how the emotion colors our thoughts, how it affects our body, creates muscular tensions, changes our breathing, our heart rate, our blood pressure, our facial expressions and posture. If we set ourselves to do so, we can notice our emotions as emotions. We have our body, we have our thoughts, and we have our emotions. And our core, our I, the one who sees what we see, is not any those things. The emotion wanes and we are still here after it's gone. I am not my emotions.

Even in the grip of a strong, destructive emotion, there is a part of us that is free, namely our real self, our I. But that self is weak, or rather our contact with it is weak. Thus our I is unable to deflect the destructive emotion. So it runs its course through us. The more we reside in our real self, in our I, in the one who sees what we see and chooses what we choose, the larger the zone of inner peace grows in us, the zone which our I inhabits.

So our work with emotions is not about controlling all of them. It is about being our self, our real self, the one who perceives our emotions, the one who can expand our zone of peace and awareness and presence to embrace our whole life, including our emotions. Our emotions are a central part of the richness of life. We honor and welcome them. We accept them and do not reject them. Yet we stay ourselves. We do not identify with our emotions, any more than we would identify with our thoughts or our body.

For this week, notice your emotions. See them as emotions. See how they affect your body and thoughts in the moment. See whether your emotions are who you are.

24.4 Am I Consciousness?
(Who Am I? - Part 4)

Consciousness, rightly understood and directly perceived, is one of the major hidden wonders of life. This is not about consciousness of something, but rather consciousness itself. Underneath all our ordinary perceptions, underneath our senses, thoughts and emotions, is a cognizant stillness, pure cognition prior to any specific content. To get a taste of this, sit with your eyes closed in a quiet place. Relax and do nothing except watch. Just maintain a relaxed awareness. No need to try to control or stop your thoughts. No need to try not to hear the sounds that come to you. No need to try not to be aware of your body. Just let your experience be as it is, while you watch the whole show. After a time, your thoughts may slow down of their own accord. Gaps may open between thoughts. Gaps made of silence, of stillness. Settle into that stillness. In there you can taste consciousness. Rest in that.

The more familiar you become with consciousness, the more you acquire that taste, the more you are able to enter the cognitive stillness, the realm behind your thoughts, even during your ordinary activities. Like isolated clouds passing through a blue sky, thoughts and other perceptions do not obscure or hide consciousness from you. You live in it. Into consciousness you can drop the burdens of maintaining and defending you self-centered ego. In consciousness you can just be, you can just be as you truly are, without any pretense, without any mask, without any image to present. And that brings you peace and equanimity, presence and awareness, openness and freedom. What a relief!

Yet even here, the question remains: is this who I am? Am I this consciousness? The answer appears to be yes. What more could there be? This consciousness seems to be, and indeed is, infinite. It has no boundaries. Whenever we come to it, it is always the same, unchanging. It is timeless, with no beginning and no end. That sounds like God. So consciousness seems to possess the right qualities to be the ultimate. And many spiritual teachers tell us exactly that. It is utterly convincing.

Yet... the question remains. And the answer that says that consciousness, this vast cognizant stillness, is the ultimate, is too easy an answer. A formless intuition tells us that there must be more to the spirit than this, something deeper still.

One hint lies in the changeless nature itself of consciousness. Another comes in the fact that once we acquire its taste, we can be aware of consciousness, a self-reflexive awareness. And that leads us to recognize that consciousness is a what, not a who. If I am anything, I am not a what, I am a who. I am the decider, the actor, the perceiver, the agent. Consciousness is in some sense static, while the Ultimate, the Creator must be dynamic. Clearly, I am not static, I am dynamic.

If I can be aware of consciousness, this is not just consciousness being aware of itself. Consciousness is like the movie screen, or the TV, on which all the perceptions of our life appear. It is the screen of our mind. But here I am sitting in the audience, watching those images. I am not the images. I am not the screen. I am the one who is watching that screen. I am the one who is aware. I am not the awareness.

This may sound subtle and abstract, but it turns out to be both crucial and tangible: crucial for our understanding of ourselves and of life, tangible in the reality of our real I. But to come to this distinction, we need first acquire the taste of consciousness and to live in it. We can find ourselves there, and find that we are not our consciousness.

For this week, enter the silence within you. Bask in your consciousness. And ask if you are that.

24.5 I am I
(Who Am I? - Part 5)

And God said unto Moses, I AM THAT I AM [9]

When we enter the vast, silent hall of consciousness, we feel complete and whole. The stillness and the pure awareness form a seamless continuum that embraces everything, including us. It is a form, a vivid and true form, of unity, true on its level, the level of consciousness. But there are higher levels of our spiritual nature. Who we are, our I, comes into us through those higher levels. In consciousness we come closer to ourselves than in the sensitive level of being in contact with our sensory impressions. So consciousness serves as a springboard into our I.

Take the practice of focused attention. For example, focus your attention on your hand. Be your attention. Be the one who is focusing, the one who is aware of your hand. This act of directing your attention works through the medium of consciousness to choose a subset of the massive stream of sensory data and put that subset in the center of awareness. The <u>cognizant stillness</u> of consciousness, unchanging, remains unaf-

9   Exodus 3:14

fected in itself, although it plays a mediating role. Like moving our eyes or scrolling down a page, the act of attention changes which content is displayed on the screen of consciousness.

But notice, this act of attention is prior to consciousness and orthogonal to it. Attention acts through consciousness, but is not directed by consciousness. Rather it comes from a deeper level beyond consciousness, even closer the origin of our I. To get a taste of being our I, we need only to be our attention, to be the source and director of our attention. Consciousness is an energy. Energies do not do things on their own. Someone uses or directs energies, which enable that use. I choose to raise my arm. My I thus directs my energies, which connect my I with my body, and the arm goes up.

Of course it is not always like that. If I am not in my I, if my I is absent, then the automatic patterns of my personality take over to direct what my body says and does, as well as the thoughts in my mind and the emotions in my heart. The whole thing goes on autopilot, with no one directing it and no one experiencing it. This is one meaning of the Buddhist teaching of no self.

Not to be on autopilot means that someone is directing the action and experiencing our experience. That someone can only be our I. So really to be ourselves, we must be the chooser, the decider, the agent of our life in this moment. Be the one who experiences what you are experiencing now, the one who is doing what you are doing now. That one is who you are, your I.

One relevant, simple, yet powerful exercise starts with sensing your body as completely as possible. Holding your attention in your body, inhabit your body. Be the one inhabiting your body. Once you have this contact with your body, inwardly say the words "I am." Say these words with the whole of yourself. Mean what you say. Be there saying them. Be there as the one who is sensing your body, the one who is inhabiting your body. Live the truth in that moment: I am. In this, the phrase "I am" is only a pointer toward the reality of you. The crucial thing is to be the one who is inwardly and intentionally thinking those words in that moment. Get behind them and say them in your mind. Bring your whole self to bear in doing this. There is no trick or secret here. It just brings you, your I, to the forefront. Rather than staying hidden behind the layered patterns of your personality, you come forward, fully into yourself, and you say "I am."

The higher levels of the spirit are not something outside us or beyond us. They are deeper within us, more subjective. Our thoughts and emotions are subjective relative to our body. Our consciousness is subjective relative to our thoughts and emotions. Our individual I is subjective relative to our consciousness. And the higher sacred is subjective relative to our individuality. Each is a step further within, through our core. I am not my body. I am not my thoughts. I am not my emotions. I am not my consciousness. I am my will. I am I.

Although the source of our I lies in the deep, sacred Source of all, we can align ourselves with the Source by putting ourselves in Its stream, the stream that comes right through our core, our I, to the extent we can open to it and be it. Thereby, on our individual level, we become our own source, the agent and doer of our actions, the experiencer of our experience, the will of our will. All the while realizing that our I is a particle of the sacred Source of all, the will of world. This holds true for all of us. Everyone has their own I, their own place in the Source. That is our essential equality, our essential unity. To connect with the sacred, to connect with other people, to connect with ourselves, we become our I.

For this week, practice the reality of "I am." Practice being in yourself as yourself.

25.0 Developing Wisdom

When He appointed the foundations of the earth;
Then I [wisdom] was beside Him...
Playing always before Him
(Proverbs 8: 29-30)

We respect those who are wise and we want to be wise ourselves. But the way there appears haphazard, appears to depend mainly on longevity, though some older people seem wise, while others do not. So the mere passage of the years, perhaps a necessary ingredient of wisdom, does not seem sufficient. How can we develop wisdom ourselves? How can we set ourselves on a course such that, as the years pass, as experience and knowledge accumulate, our own wisdom does indeed grow?

But first, what is wisdom? Difficult to define but easy to recognize, we know it when we see it. Nevertheless, we could say that wisdom is deep understanding coupled with the ability to act effectively from that understanding. Certainly the wise person has sound judgment and can act creatively. Knowledge, experience, and innate intelligence all contribute, but these are not sufficient and perhaps not even necessary to produce wisdom.

One implicit but often overlooked ingredient of wisdom is presence. We cannot understand what is before us if we are not here to take it in, to see it. And we cannot act effectively, if we are not here as the one who acts. Presence puts us here. The more present we are, the more here we are, the more available we are to wisdom. In the silent mind of presence, everything we perceive finds its place. This may be a necessary condition for wisdom, which then takes the next step of connecting our perceptions with our experience and with our foresight, with causes, constraints, ramifications, and goals. All that happens effortlessly, without active pondering or considering. Thus wisdom sees into the heart of the matter at hand. Seeing comes from inner quiet and inner quiet comes from presence.

One part of wisdom surely lies in the realization that this is our life, that what we are doing now, today is our life. So many of us are oriented toward the future. Much of what we do is all about taking us a bit closer to some goal, to some result, to some other day. So what we do today, our life today, takes on the character of a chore, to be gotten through and over with. But this attitude literally kills our time. It is today that we are living. It is the mundane and the chore that we are living. Today is precious. It is our life. Presence makes the mundane magical, makes everything more vivid. In presence we appreciate our life as it is now, even if and as we engage in preparing a better future. Wisdom begins with honoring each moment, mundane or interesting, pleasant or unpleasant. We honor our life, we honor our time, regardless of the particulars.

Presence also promotes wisdom by enabling our experiences to enter more deeply. In presence we tend to take in more of what happens and to be able to remember it later. Thus in presence the experience-base that wisdom can draw upon grows more robustly than if we are not present to our life. Wisdom sits at the junction between the past and the future, open to both.

Another pre-condition for wisdom is to honor it and aspire to it. We doubt that the wise person stops seeking wisdom. At whatever stage of life or wisdom we find ourselves, we look to deepen our wisdom. The extent to which we believe we are wise is the extent to which no further wisdom can grace us.

There are many ways to develop wisdom. In the coming weeks we will explore some of them. For this week, ask yourself what you consider wisdom to be and look at the role that presence plays in wisdom.

25.1 Regret
(Developing Wisdom: Part 1)

If only ...

We all have regrets: regrets about choices that turned out badly, opportunities passed up, mistakes made, misdeeds committed, and times beyond our control when life brought us what we did not want or failed to bring us what we wanted. Regrets can color our approach to life and can even be debilitating. The classic one is to have loved and lost, and then resolved never to love again. Regrets can eat away at us, as we descend into bitterness or its cousins: self-blame, lack of confidence, and even self-loathing. Wisdom, though, knows the limits of regret and does not let regret paralyze us in the present or drain our initiative toward the future. The antidotes for chronic regret are acceptance of and then gratitude for our situation as it is.

Acceptance of our situation as is does not, however, mean giving up on improving it. It does mean letting go of the emotional recoil against what is. That chronic inner rejection, that ongoing regret, does not contribute to healing or remedying the situation: it only exacerbates it by turning us away. So we acknowledge our regrets, face them, adopt the resolve they inspire in us, and then let them go. Failing that, whenever regret casts a continuing pall over our psyche, we can change the inner subject by acknowledging the good things in our life, the good things about ourselves, and by being grateful for all of that. Debilitating regret cannot coexist with gratitude. Whenever we notice such regret arising in our mind and heart, we can let that remind us to turn to gratitude.

Our regrets are useful insofar as we learn from them, learn not to repeat the same mistakes. Regrets can be useful if we let them spur us to action, to improve or to remedy our situation. But really to learn the lessons of regret, we need to experience fully the consequences of our actions, our mistakes and misdeeds, we need to experience fully the events of our life that bring what we do not want or do not bring what we want, and we need to experience fully our actions and situations that do not accord with our principles or goals. To experience fully any of these sources of regret, requires us to be present, unflinchingly present to our life.

So wisdom begins in presence and lets the fire of regret energize our way forward and remind us. In wisdom we do not repeat actions that we know we will regret and we do not allow regret over failures to stop us from trying again, though each time in a little more skillful manner. Whenever we fall, we immediately get up and get moving. Failures and their regrets are inevitable. Yet our response can be free.

For this week, notice your regrets, whether from your distant past or more recent. Notice what you regret. Notice how that regret affects your actions and attitudes. And notice what you need to accept, what you can be grateful for, what you can learn from your regrets, and what constructive course you can adopt in response. Transform the poison of "*if only ...*" into wisdom.

25.2 Self-Management

(Developing Wisdom: Part 2)

When we describe a person as "having it together," we mean just that, we mean that they are inwardly unified. The opposite is when a person "falls apart." The difference between the two states goes well beyond what is readily noticeable by other people; the difference lies deep in the spirit of the person. Certainly, a key part of wisdom is to understand ourselves well enough to manage our inner world to be more often "together" and less often "falling apart."

This notion of falling apart sounds extreme and rare,

like the old idea of a nervous breakdown: a severe, out-of-control, and negative emotional episode. But there are mild forms of falling apart, forms that we live in much of our time.

What is it that falls apart in us? We have our various parts: body, heart, and mind. Often there is little or no relation between these parts of ours. That is the state of having fallen apart. Our mind floats off into daydreams and ruminations. Our emotions react to events. And our body has its own needs and impulses. Each does its own thing. We have no unity in that state, our usual state.

Our inner work offers us two approaches toward unity, toward being inwardly "together." First we have the all-purpose tool of attention. When we pay attention to our body, and particularly to sensing our body, we are relating our self and our body. Attention to our body makes our body "visible" to us, to our presence. Attention serves as the mechanism of that relationship. Similarly, when we turn our attention to our emotions, they become visible and related to our presence. And when we turn our attention to our thoughts, they become visible to our presence. Paying attention to all three of our parts relates them all in our presence. Our presence thus becomes the place of our unity, a unity enabled by and dependent on attention.

The second approach is to enter presence directly, particularly by opening to the consciousness that surrounds us, but typically remains in the background. The cognizant stillness of consciousness, or pure awareness prior to content, has the quality of wholeness and naturally embraces our disparate parts into a unity. Our body, heart, and mind find their home in consciousness. We find our home in consciousness, in the inner peace of consciousness. We come to it most readily in quiet meditation, but with practice it becomes available to us even during a busy day.

Self-management, the ability to direct one's actions along intentional and constructive lines, clearly is part of wisdom. But what does unity or "togetherness" have to do with self-management.

Problems with managing our functions, our body, mind, and heart, stem largely from our lack of direct contact with these our parts and the lack of relationship among them. Presence and consciousness, which is an aspect of presence, brings about the unity that enables our intentions, choices, and decisions to be effective in our functions. Rather than have our bodily addictions and impulses drive our actions, our body takes its place in our presence, in our wholeness and serves its proper role as the basis of presence. Rather than have our emotional reactions apply their dystopian colors to our inner world, our emotions take their place in our presence and serve their proper role in connecting us with people, with life, with the spirit. Rather than have our thoughts, daydreams, and ruminations continually distract our minds, our cognitive functions take their place in our presence and serve their proper role in seeing accurately and deeply into what lies before us in this moment and into the possibilities our future holds.

In the unity of presence, our experiences come into and our actions come from our self, our true self. Self-management is less about managing our self than it is about having a self that can do the managing. Self-management means having such a self with its natural authority over our parts. One way that inner authority matters for our spiritual inner life is that we can then loosen the grip of certain destructive habits, like smoking, alcohol abuse, overeating, anger, complaining, and so forth, habits that destroy the very energies we need for our inner work to thrive.

In wisdom and presence we come into our self, a self that can manage our life constructively, productively, creatively, and with heart. For this week, look at how you manage your actions and your inner world. See what may be lacking. How can you address that? What is the role of presence in living wisely?

25.3 Deep Thinking
(Developing Wisdom: Part 3)

Our functions can operate at different levels, depending on the quality of inner energy at work. This certainly holds true in our mind, in our cognitive function. With the automatic energy our thoughts run by association, one thought leads to another, which in turn leads to yet another, endlessly. Or our thoughts arise as a reflex to some sensory event. We do not control or direct our thoughts. Though we may be fully immersed in, enthralled by our automatic thoughts, the secret voice of our personality, we are not aware of them as thoughts. Instead we are just lost in them. In that automatic state, we are not ourselves, rather our thoughts are us. Automatic thoughts are not intentional. We may let them roam, we may know what they mean, but we are not thinking them. They are thinking us. This is the usual state of our mind.

Sensitive thinking is what we use in school or at work, what we do in addressing an issue or problem that requires some consideration. With the sensitive energy, we are in contact with our thoughts and we are thinking them: our thoughts are intentional. We drive our thoughts along lines we choose. We notice and assess each thought, discarding unpromising avenues, seizing on solutions and new insights, and reverting back to topic when our thoughts stray too far afield.

Sensitive thinking also occurs when we listen carefully to someone speaking. We let their words act on our mind and shape our perception. When we notice our attention straying away from listening, perhaps onto some automatic train of thought initiated by something said to us, we just come right back to listening. We do not particularly need to think. We let the speaker's words be the thoughts of our mind. We just listen. We just open our mind to hear what's being said. We do not need to judge in the moment. We do not need to be inwardly engaged in assessments and rebuttals. We just listen. Without raising defenses or filters, our critical faculty will nevertheless play its role in the background. In the end we may agree or disagree or neither. But in any case, we will have fully taken in what the person said, we will have a better understanding of them or the message they were communicating. This is sensitive listening, the sensitive energy at work in our mind in the act of listening.

With the conscious energy, we can occupy our mind, not by putting some thought or image into it, but by putting ourselves into it. We can be there in the pure cognition, which is prior to and broader than thought. This is the great cognizant stillness, the field of pure awareness that contains all, including our thoughts. Our ordinary thoughts, though they may be occurring, do not interfere, do not touch us when we are conscious. We abide in the context, in the container of all experience. Everything passes through this container. But we are more than all that particular content of our life. In the conscious mind, we may shape the boundaries within which our thoughts play out, but we do not think in the ordinary sense. Rather we see, we address situations, people, and subjects by direct perception, without our thinking mind acting as an intermediary, as a filter, categorizer, commentator, or narrator. We just see things as they are, simply and directly.

This is not as mysterious as it might sound. When you look at a situation or listen to a person, you can let your thoughts come and go, without buying into them. You just abide in looking. In doing so, you see in an unfiltered, unbiased manner. This is true seeing. This is your mind in the conscious energy.

Sensitive listening leads into conscious listening. The difference is that in conscious listening we no longer have a separation between the speaker and the listener. Our consciousness embraces the whole situation. The other person and what they are saying occur within this field of consciousness, which we and they both occupy. Their words act as our thoughts, but our perceptions open into the cognitive stillness which surrounds us and through which thoughts and sounds and everything else pass like small clouds floating by.

The higher the level of energy at work in our mind, the deeper our thought processes, the deeper our insights. We can, for example, sit or walk in contemplation of some theme, issue, or problem. We allow our mind to mull it over, yet we do not fix on a particular solution and we do not direct our thoughts. We let our thoughts come and go as we keep our inner vision on the topic at hand. Gradually our mind quiets down, with fewer thoughts coursing through it. We enter the silence and just see. When thoughts do come, they do not disturb or obscure the silence or the seeing. We let them pass. In this cognizant stillness, insights may come directly, intuitions become more evident. This is deep thinking, beyond ordinary thinking.

Take a question or a subject you care about, one that you want to understand for yourself, one for which you want to come to your own viewpoint. Decide to contemplate that question or subject for a week. Then do so. At times during the week, sit in silent contemplation of the subject. At other times, see how the experiences your life brings you that week impact the question or shed light on the subject. Even if you have definite views on some aspects of the subject, stay open to learning more about the other aspects. A major part of deep thinking is to have an open mind, not to be too fixated on your established opinions. The assumption here is that there is Truth and that by contemplating a specific issue we can come closer to the truth about it, even if that means acknowledging after a week of searching that we know and understand very little about the question we have chosen.

Because so much of our life and experience is bound up with our thoughts, wisdom certainly has a role to play in regard to our thinking. Wisdom sees rather than thinks. In this sense, wisdom operates as consciousness in our mind. For this week, notice the quality of your thought processes. Practice deep thinking through slow consideration, listening to your intuition, and silent contemplation.

25.4 Natural Purity
(Developing Wisdom: Part 4)

As we saw in our study of Deep Thinking, the conscious energy has the hallmark of stillness. That clear, inner stillness, that fully aware inner peace, reveals to us a key quality, namely purity. We are naturally pure. To the extent we can live in inner stillness, we release the bonds of self-centered egoism. When you are in the cognizant stillness of your mind-heart on conscious energy, you understand and see that consciousness has no boundaries, no center, and no divisions. There is no place in consciousness for self-centeredness; it simply does not arise in that open space.

This is not to say that *we* disappear. In consciousness, our individuality, our I, our will, does have its place. Only now we are free of the illusory divisions that twist our will toward egoism. The true connection of our individuality with the sacred, universal spirit comes to the fore, no longer obscured by self-centeredness. I am here. I am the one who is conscious and I am a part, a doing of the All. That inclusiveness, that lack of separateness is our true state and our natural purity. This is not something that we need to create; it is something we can just relax back into by letting go of our singular focus on the surface, for example our focus on all the thoughts that keep going through our mind and the emotional reactions coursing through our heart. Beneath those thoughts and emotions lies the realm of stillness, of consciousness, of peace, and ultimately of love.

We are not outsiders in that place of purity, in the sacred spirit. Our deepest and truest self comes from there, belongs there, is at home there. So it is not a question of going outside our I, or beyond our I. Rather we return to the roots of our I, roots that we share with all people, with all life. Pursuing that return is a worthy undertaking, to which we bring our best, our self, our full engagement. In the wake of entering this purity, we discover that humility and compassion follow naturally.

You might try this meditation. Sit quietly, comfortably, and alertly. Relax. Let your eyes close. Relax your body thoroughly, finding the tensions and letting them go. Relax deeper still by not trying to shape your experience in any way, other than being aware of what is taking place in you in the moment. Just sit.

Let your thoughts go on their own, without getting lost in them. Gradually, if you do not feed them with your reactions, with your interest in their specific content, your thoughts will settle down, slow down of their own accord. You begin to notice gaps between thoughts. Silences between the sounds of your thoughts voicing themselves in your mind, blanks between the mental images.

In these gaps you remain aware. You see that you can be aware of the silence between thoughts. Your awareness of that silence grows. You see that this inner silence exists not only between thoughts, but underneath and around your thoughts. You see that this inner silence has the nature of awareness itself, that it is cognizant, conscious. You see that this inner silence actually is your awareness, your consciousness in its pure state, prior to any content.

At that point you can rest in awareness, in consciousness. In this transition, the invisible background of your mind, consciousness, has come to the foreground. You can be in the pure consciousness that surrounds you, that permeates you, that has no boundaries, that is simply a vast, clear field of awareness itself. You can just be in that. When thoughts come, they float past without disturbing you. You just are, naturally pure.

Wisdom flows from that purity, because without the distractions of self-centeredness, you live your unity with other people and with all life, your choices and actions hold true to the real needs and highest potentials of the moment.

For this week, explore your natural purity.

25.5 Spiritual Efficacy
(Developing Wisdom: Part 5)

> *...work out your own salvation...*
> (Philippians 2:12)

Psychologists define perceived self-efficacy "as people's beliefs about their capabilities to produce designated levels of performance that exercise influence over events that affect their lives."[10] We can define spiritual efficacy in a similar way by inserting the word "inner" before "lives" to make the definition about our inner life. The question of spiritual efficacy matters because many of those who sincerely wish for transformation are not, in their heart of hearts, convinced that it is actually possible for them. Enlightenment and the Sacred seem remote from us. We look for those who know to teach us, to show us the way. But that is not as it would seem.

Teachers can help by instructing us in spiritual practices. They can also help by being examples that ordinary people, no different than us, can enter true spiritual transformation. Teachers can help by easing our way into deeper experiences through the quality of their energy, when we practice in person with them. And teachers can inspire us. All of that is important, useful, perhaps even pivotal in setting our feet on the path. But it masks a fundamental truth: the spiritual path is within us, it cannot be shown, it can only be discovered.

Self-limiting assumptions block our entry to a deeper

---

10   Bandura, Albert. Self-Efficacy. In V.S. Ramachaudran (Ed.), Encyclopedia of Human Behavior, Vol. 4, pp. 71-81. (New York : Academic Press, 1994)

inner life. As long as we believe that we cannot do what's required to be in contact with the sacred on a regular basis, we will not discover what is required. We can profitably look outside ourselves for pointers, but to make the transition, we need to explore within ourselves; we need to bring our own creativity, longing, and determination to look deeply within, to try varying approaches, to build our own experience with and capacity for the spiritual in life. We need to learn to trust ourselves, to listen to our own insights, to pursue and verify them.

What does it mean to come into the great inner silence, the cognizant stillness of consciousness? How do we find and open our inner door to the sacred? Words, formal prayers, and guided meditations can point the way, but only our own action, only our investigation of our private experience, only our own inner experimentation and observation can give us the taste, the understanding, and the ability to enter the spiritual depths.

None of this is meant to downplay the great potential benefits of working with a teacher or a group. It is meant to point up that we each have possibilities for transformation, the realization of which depends to a large extent on our personal efforts, exploration, capacity-building, and understanding. Spiritual efficacy can be shared and enhanced in a group, but it resides in each individual.

Realizing this makes us personally responsible for our spiritual life and empowers us to do the inner work of presence, meditation, prayer, and kindness, with diligence. We do this not because of what we are told, but because we see that each step, each effort does indeed bring us closer to the sacred and to the joy that awaits there. We do this because no one can do it for us. Every day is a new chance, a new beginning. Regardless of how well or poorly our inner work of the previous day went, each morning we begin again. It is solely up to each of us individually to make our efforts of presence and the rest, to enter deeply into the privacy of our being and find our reality there.

Enlightenment cannot be given to us. And there is

no fixed recipe for it. But truly, there is a part of each us that already has its place in the higher world. Our work is to reconnect with that deeper part of ourselves, not with someone else's, but with our own higher self. So we explore within to find our Self. And our growing spiritual efficacy shows us not only that we can, but that we are doing this and will continue to do this. The great I am is who I am: it comes from me. No one can give it to me, because it already is me. Persistent inner work clears away the illusory blockade between my ordinary experience and my true self. I am.

The wisdom we seek cannot be borrowed or acquired: it comes from within. For this week, take stock and build your own spiritual efficacy. It is up to you.

25.6 Asking
(Developing Wisdom: Part 6)

> *Ask, and it shall be given you;*
> *Seek, and ye shall find;*
> *Knock, and it shall be opened unto you.*
> (Matthew 7:7)

To complement the wisdom of spiritual efficacy, we now turn to the wisdom of asking. In any of its forms, by asking we reach beyond our ordinary self with an implicit recognition of our need and a willingness to ask. Asking takes us beyond our opinions. A mind that asks is an open mind. And an open mind is a free mind.

The spiritual path is rightly called a search and its travelers seekers. For most of us, life itself is a search: for love and connection, for happiness and fulfillment, for food, for health, for wealth, for knowledge, for answers, for understanding. To search is to ask. Asking wisely is part of living well.

Sometimes we need physical or material help: times

when we cannot manage on our own. We do what we can, and then we reach out to those near us and ask for their help. We hope such moments are rare, but wisdom recognizes when they do come, sees how best to ask for the help we need, and is willing to do so.

Sometimes we are in a quandary, not knowing what to do, how to choose when pulled in more than one direction. If we ask ourselves what we should do, we may get confusion or we may get our thoughts subtly voicing what our emotions want us to do. If we ask a trusted friend, we may get good advice or at least be able to express and discuss the dilemma, which enables us to frame it well. We wish we had some higher insight that could see into the future and tell us the right choice. But life does not work that way. So we learn by experience, especially from our mistakes. Yet there is more. In a quiet moment we can ask our higher self, we can ask what is deepest in us to guide us. Again, our thoughts may intrude, pretending to be the voice of the higher. So we let them go and wait. Perhaps we sleep on it. Perhaps we live with the quandary for a time, without deciding. Indeed, part of life wisdom is not to make difficult decisions before we must or before we know. And with openness and luck, a moment of inner guidance comes when we just know what to do.

Sometimes we need spiritual help. We may ask a friend or an advisor. Or we may ask God. Heartfelt appeals to the Divine for what we truly need put us in the stream of prayer. Whether or not the help comes, the asking itself works to transform us. It weakens our egoism by breaching its assumed self-sufficiency. If instead, our ego is full of fear or anxiety, self-pity or self-doubt, the act of asking the Sacred for help strengthens what needs strengthening.

What about the spiritual qualities of contentment and letting go? Surely, asking melts away in a contented heart. One just is. Even there though, we find movement. The world beckons, arousing questions of our role in it. The spirit beckons, beyond contentment and non-contentment. The asking continues. *How can I be more awake, more pure? How can I complete my soul? How can I best serve?* Merely entertaining such questions helps empty our cup to make room for new understanding.

In a deeper sense, in a form of prayer, asking aligns us with the Sacred. In the stillness, if we rest quietly, passively, or even receptively, we remain in a static position, waiting. Yet if we actively push, we close an inner door behind us. Asking crosses the middle ground. We ask the Sacred to enter us. We open to the Sacred. This is not purely passive or receptive and it is not purely active. It is a third way, the way of pure asking, the way of sacred asking. We are not asking a question. We are not asking for something. We are adopting an attitude of seeking for the Real in this moment, of opening our innermost door and inviting, begging the Real to enter now. We direct our gaze inward and open from behind ourselves, from beyond what we can see. This is both active and receptive. It is movement in receptivity. It is true asking. It is prayer.

For this week, ask.

25.7 Conscience
(Developing Wisdom: Part 7)

What to do and what not to do? These questions confront us through the details of our life. Ethical principles serve as one guide. For example, the wise person understands the truth of the law of karma, of "as you sow, so shall ye reap." There is no free lunch for unethical or immoral acts. It is just not possible to get away with it. Yes, the consequences may not be immediately apparent, but in every case, *you* know what you have done and *you* know intuitively whether it's right or not. If it's not right, you pay at the very least by burying one of your most valuable possessions a little deeper, namely your conscience.

If God can see with our eyes, then it is not possible to hide what we do. If we sweep our misdeeds under a rug, that rug turns out to be transparent. If we know what we have done, then God can know also. Conscience is God's representative in us. If we honor our conscience and invariably act in accordance with it, it changes our life. For one thing, people can trust us. Perhaps even more importantly, we can trust ourselves. This self-trust profoundly affects our spiritual life, by clearing the channel between our ordinary self and the Sacred. If our ordinary self invariably submits to the promptings of our conscience, then that link to the higher grows strong and new possibilities open to us.

Among those new possibilities is a growing ability to open ourselves to the Sacred, in deep contemplation, in the wordless prayer of connection. That profound opening brings with it intimations and even an influx of the Sacred Light. It transforms our being, creating our soul. But for any of that, purity is a requirement, the purity gained in part by obedience to our conscience.

Beyond questions of ethics and morality, we frequently face issues of responsibility and irresponsibility. Here also, our conscience can guide us toward responsible action. Temptations spring up unexpectedly, not only for wrong acts but for irresponsible acts and the non-action of shirking. Being grounded in conscience, in that circle of inner trust and right action, serves us well when such temptations arise, as they frequently do in both large and small ways.

Conscience only has the power we give it. A mind-heart totally preoccupied with its own automatic thoughts and reactive emotions cannot hear conscience, which gets lost in that inner crowd. Presence puts us in touch with the cognizant stillness of consciousness, of pure awareness. That inner peace allows conscience to make itself known as our intuitive sense of right and wrong. Here we can enter a virtuous circle of positive feedback. The more we listen to and act in accord with conscience, the more inner peace we have, which in turn clarifies our perception of conscience and weakens the many attachments and identifications that turn us away from acting in accord with conscience.

This affects who we are in a fundamental and profoundly positive way. Conscience, along with attention, is one of our major links to our true individuality, to own I. The pretender I's that pop up with every passing thought and whim fade away before our commitment to conscience and our true I. Here I am in the midst of a quandary. Will I do this thing that part of me wants to do, even though in my heart of hearts I know better? Making that hard choice, in the face of desire and identification, is our role in the working of conscience. What do I choose? The road to freedom and the Sacred, or the road to nowhere. Unless I just give up trying, again and again, I am put in front of that choice.

Lastly, conscience goes beyond ethics, morality, and responsibility to show us the way toward quality and excellence. In any domain of our life, can we see whether we have done the job completely? Is it done well, with the appropriate level of care and attention to detail? What are the possibilities for improving what I do? When I am finished with a project, large or small, am I satisfied with what I have put into it and with the result? Presence helps us intuit our conscience, and both together enable us to be here, doing what we do, with quality and excellence.

For this week, notice the decision points, even the minor ones, where temptation pulls us in one direction, while conscience prompts the other way. How would it change you, if you could trust yourself always to follow your conscience? Maybe you already are a moral and responsible person. But if conscience is the representative of the Divine and a link with our true I, it is worth another look at the gray areas.

25.8 Creative Wisdom
(Developing Wisdom: Part 8)

Creativity comes in many forms, across all the activities that engage us. And it always brings more meaning and significance into what we do. Why is that? Why does a creative act, even on a small scale, give us such essential satisfaction? Maybe we find a way to clean our home better or more efficiently. Maybe experimentation enables us to resolve some health issue. Maybe a creative flow enters a session of musical or artistic endeavor. Or maybe we find a new way to do part of our job with greater quality or efficiency. Even the daily chores of creating and maintaining order in our home, in our body, in our society are truly creative. These small scale creative breakthroughs, which we all can and do experience, bring us joy.

But what is it that breaks through? And through what does it break? Our ordinary mind tends to be noisy, flat, random and linear. The creative leap puts together dissimilar, previously unrelated notions and spontaneously melds them into something new, unplanned, and unbidden. A noisy mind that drowns our attention in its associative flow, with thoughts bouncing off each other and off the endless stream of sensory perceptions, has no room for the creative, in several senses. The noisy mind has little interest in creating something new, enthralled as it is with itself. The noisy mind soaks up the attention needed to perceive opportunities for the new. And the noisy mind does not recognize new impulses and their significance. So the creative gets blocked by our noisy mind.

But when the creative does break through, what is it that breaks through? On a blank slate something new can be written. So it comes through a vacuum, through a connection with the stillness beyond our busy mind. That stillness is the condition into which "it" comes. It is an act of will, the creative impulse. It is an action of the spirit, our spirit in concert with the universal spirit.

Yet the vacuum through which the creative acts cannot itself be in a vacuum. Our trained mind, with its skills, knowledge, and perceptions, provides the necessary raw material on which the creative can act. And our interests shape the context. A dream presenting a breakthrough in the fundamental laws of physics would be wasted on anyone not conversant with the state-of-the-art in physics. We would not even recognize the meaning of the dream, much less its significance. The creative vacuum requires a context of skills, knowledge, and interest. So in the midst of all that busyness, we make space for stillness, for the creative to act. It is a very high spiritual energy, the creative energy, that can come into our openness.

In finding our way along the spiritual path, creativity plays an essential role. We begin by building the context of knowledge of spiritual practices, such as various forms of meditation, as well as mind-body-spirit practices like Tai Chi, yoga, Qi Gong, walking meditation, Gurdjieff movements, or chanted prayers. The knowledge of our toolkit of practices gives us experience with how they affect us and shows us the limits of our understanding of the various practices. We also find our interest building up, our thirst for organizing and purifying our inner life, for deepening our experience, for opening our heart. Into this context, the creative appears and points the way forward. The creative impulse prompts us to try different practices in new ways, to try extending the practices we know in new directions, to try different combinations of practices, to cobble together a path that fits us, that develops our soul in all its aspects. All that experimentation, along with impartial observation of the results, leads us further along the path. Even within one practice, say one form of meditation, undertaken steadily, daily for years and years, there is room for the creative impulse to show us how to deepen that same practice.

The spiritual path is creative in another sense as well: our practices create new energy, taking the earth energy of our food and water and air, and generating higher spiritual energies. Indeed, this is one of the primary purposes of the path, of spiritual endeavors generally.

We also cherish the creative action that has no purpose beyond itself: the play of children, the joy of games and sports, of artistic acts of all kinds, of humor. These moments reverberate through our common life, reminding us that creative wisdom is not heavy, it is light: it plays before the Lord.

With all the noise in our mind and all the distractions in our immediate surroundings, we lose touch with the quiet, the vacuum within us and so fail to recognize or to act on the creative impulses that do come to us. For this week, set yourself to notice those impulses, to examine their value, and if so inclined, to act on them.

26.0 Opening our Heart

Love is not a human invention. And it may not even be something created by nature or biological evolution. Yes, we have certain hormonal and other genetic imperatives toward sex, reproduction, and nurturing and protecting our family. And love certainly enters the picture through those means. Yet love itself is not a result of our genes. Rather, the mechanism of sex may be with us for two reasons: its obvious evolutionary advantages and the love it engenders. After all, what is the purpose of evolution? Is it only to create more "successful" species? And what is the definition of that "success?" Is it only about reproducing and earning a living? What is life for?

It may well be that the story of creation and evolution begins with Love, that the very purpose of creation, of the universe, is to serve as a means for the expression of Love. The closer we come to Love, the more valid that view seems to be. Of course we cannot prove which came first, Love or the universe, but most of us can agree that love is at least part of the fundamental meaning of life, if not its very purpose.

So we turn to look at our own heart, our spiritual heart, to see its state, to see our attitudes toward ourselves and others, to see whether love informs those attitudes, and to the extent it does not, to see why not and what we might be able do about that.

We know there's something special about love because it manifests, albeit differently, on every level of being we can experience. On the automatic level, love enters primarily as desire, sex, nurturing, and protecting. On the sensitive level, love appears as the feeling of liking. On the conscious level, love becomes intentional consideration for others' needs and desires. On the level of the creative, sacred light, love comes as the compassion that transcends our personal individuality.

Because our hearts are relatively closed to each other and to ourselves, every major spiritual tradition addresses our heart, and specifically the need to open our heart. Clearly, some people are more open-hearted than others. We admire the open-hearted person and wish to be more like that ourselves. Are we stuck where we are on the spectrum of closed- and open-heartedness? We hope not. We have a certain faith that people can change, that we ourselves can change. We also have fears of changing. Will I still be myself? Will I be used by others? Will I lose my ambition? Will I give away everything I own? In the face of these fears, we again summon faith, the faith that in the transformation toward a more open heart, who I truly am does not change, rather I become liberated to be my Self, liberated from the chains of automatic, half-living and self-centered egoism.

Our self-oriented world-view does seem to have its purpose in our formative years, up into our 20s. It launches us into our life, into society. But like a rocket booster that fails to jettison when no longer needed, egoism becomes a drag on our further journey. Ego cannot love, not even itself, for love accepts and ego does not; it always wants more, demands more. Ego fears the revelation of its own insubstantiality, its own illusory nature. And because of that, our self-centered ego is antithetical to love, because love comes just when our center reverts to openness.

In the coming weeks, we will explore various aspects of open-heartedness and how to move in that direction.

For this week, look at where you are on the spectrum of closed- and open-heartedness. Are your attitudes informed by courtesy, kindness, respect and compassion — or not? See this in how you actually think, feel, and act toward others and toward yourself.

26.1 Transcending Egoism
(Opening Our Heart: Part 1)

We all have an ego and we all need it to survive in this material world. But our ego unnecessarily insinuates itself into every aspect of our life to the detriment of the people around us and to the detriment of our own spiritual nature. We believe our ego is who we are, that we personally are the center of the universe. But it is a pretender, masking and distracting us from our true self.

By definition and by its inherent character, ego is self-referential. Everything and everyone that exists does so by reference to our ego, reference to whether and what, if anything, they can do for us or to us. This self-centered, utilitarian view of the world shapes our life. When ego is kind, it is because it expects or hopes for something in return. Ego gets angry if its plans are thwarted, if its opinions are not accepted, if someone does not show proper respect and even deference. Vanity, self-pity, and greed all come from ego. We want happiness, but our ego misleads us about it. The happiness that we seek through self-centeredness is fleeting at best. Ego happiness does not last, because it always wants more.

Ego is not some external or alien force with power over us. On the contrary, it is who we are when we allow ourselves to believe in it. Its only power is that of a convincing and seamless illusion, of appearing to be who we are. Not in contact with the alternative, with our true self, we fall passively and by default into self-centered egoism, into believing that is who we are.

One effective approach toward loosening the grip of egoism is to loosen the grip that our thoughts have on us. We are not our thoughts. Generally, we do not even think our thoughts: they think themselves. But we believe in them, believe that they speak for us, that they are our inner voice. Yet they do not speak for us, they speak for themselves, and often for our illusory ego. Our thoughts go on and on and on, continually weaving the illusion of ego. We don't have to initiate them, for they initiate themselves. We don't have to think them for they think themselves.

In quiet meditation, we can notice our thoughts arising and passing on their own. We can notice them for what they are: just thoughts. If we can see our thoughts, see them arise without any intention on our part, then it slowly dawns on us that we are not our thoughts.

Sit in meditation. Be aware, be centered in your whole body. Notice whatever perceptions come, including your thoughts. See them come and go. See them as just thoughts. Doing this again and again, as a continuing practice, gradually frees us from our thoughts. This can be a major step toward freeing us from egoism.

If I can see my thoughts as thoughts, then I am not my thoughts. I am the one who sees. I am my true self. This way we can step toward freedom. Our thoughts will not stop, but they no longer own us. We realize that not only do we not need to act on our thoughts, but that they do not represent us, do not necessarily speak for us.

The thought "I" is not who we are, nor does it refer to who we really are. Almost always the thought "I" refers to our ego, to this imputed construct of a self that does not exist. It recurs again and again, convincing us that that this I that is referenced by the thought "I" actually exists, actually is who we are. If we can see through this, see that the thought "I" is just a thought, see that there is nothing substantial that it references, we gain a significant freedom.

Our thoughts and the ego they build form a filter, even a barrier, between us and the world around us. For example, one form of that barrier consists of our harsh thoughts about other people and even about ourselves. Transcending such barriers, we can have hope of connecting. For the purpose of this inner work series on opening our heart, ego's biggest failing is its inability to connect, to connect with other people, with life, with ourselves, and with the Sacred.

The self that can connect, that we become, that we re-enter, after seeing through the illusion of ego is our true self, our I, our will. At first it seems to be the silence, the cognizant stillness behind our thoughts. Going deeper we realize our true I as the one who sees, the one who is cognizant, the one who directs the beam of our attention. That I is real and inherently connected with other people, with all of life, with the Sacred. To open our heart, we need to see through and transcend our ego and become ourselves.

For this week, look at your thoughts, particularly the thought "I." See through this, see beyond it. Who am I, really?

26.2 Love of Self
(Opening Our Heart: Part 2)

Some people hate themselves. That's extreme. The rest

of us, though, tend to be at least mildly dissatisfied with ourselves, wishing some aspects were different. Maybe it's about our body, or about our personality, or our intellectual abilities. While we all have strengths and weaknesses, our attitude toward what we consider to be our weaknesses preoccupies us. This can have positive effects, if it either drives us to work to improve what we are dissatisfied about or if it leads us to have more compassion for other people and their shortcomings.

In any case, we need not reject ourselves, or any part of ourselves. Just the opposite: the more we can accept ourselves as we are, the more joy and freedom we discover. We can work to improve ourselves, while at the same time accepting ourselves fully, loving ourselves. If we do not accept ourselves, we still would not even if we fixed the unacceptable aspects, because our ego would demand yet more perfection. If we do not accept ourselves, we will not accept others. If we do not love ourselves, we will not love others.

How can we come toward self-acceptance? Can we recognize that the one in us who can accept is not the one we wish to change? Our deepest self, our true self, our I, sees clearly, with compassion, and without rejecting. The impulses to reject ourselves come from our ego, from our illusory self that wants to burnish its own image, to look better. One part of our personality wants to change another part. Our thoughts reject some aspect of our body. Our body rejects the impulse-limiting wishes of our thoughts. And our feelings remain torn between wanting to indulge physically, emotionally, or in some daydream and wanting to live in a more disciplined and freer way. But the one in us who sees and has the power to accept is not in our body, thoughts, emotions, or ego. It is our self that we need.

In the spiritual path, the core of all the weaknesses we face is our lack of presence. The conundrum of non-presence is not about our body, it does not emanate from our mind, and it is not a result of our emotions, although all three must contribute to its resolution. This core problem of lack of presence emanates from us, from who we are. This is what we need to change, to come toward. To love ourselves means to love being present, because it is only in presence that we truly and fully exist. There is no self who can love and no self to love when we are not present. And when we are present, love comes naturally, because it has a channel through which to flow, namely our true I, our true self.

In practicing presence, we practice being our self, our true self. The more we practice presence, the more we can be present, the stronger and deeper our presence, and the more love we have, including for ourselves. That heart of acceptance embraces the whole catastrophe that we are, with all our features: the cherished, the ordinary, and the problematic. All those distinctions dissolve in presence, in being. We rise out of our self-blaming mode to cherish the whole of ourselves.

How might that right attitude of loving oneself manifest? We honor and care for our body, giving it what it needs, some of what it wants, and doing what we can to keep it healthy. We honor and care for our emotions, noticing what we are feeling, cultivating healthy relationships, and not allowing the destructive emotions free rein to run amok and damage us. We honor and care for our mind, feeding it the intellectual food and challenges that it wants and needs, and not allowing ourselves to be drawn into the endless stream of automatic thoughts and daydreams. And we honor and care for our self, our true self, by the practice of presence.

For this week, notice when you reject some aspect of yourself. Practice love of self by honoring and caring for your whole self.

26.3 The Crucible of Relationship
(Opening Our Heart: Part 3)

An intimate relationship can be the fiery crucible that enables us to love. In the early days of a new relationship, we live that hormonal glow of wonder and magic. As the newness wanes, however, the warts of ego conflicts inevitably surface. We are each unique: differing in our habits, interests, needs, and desires. Presumably we have some compatibility with our new lover, but not 100%. So the friction begins. In successful relationships the friction is outweighed by growing love and care, and by growing compatibility as we begin to share some of our lover's interests.

But for our spiritual inner work, for opening our hearts, the friction in relationships offers a custom-made opportunity for letting go of exactly those things that coat our heart with an inward facing mirror, so that we primarily see and care about our own habits, interests, needs, and desires. This tempts us to make demands on and find fault with the other person, building up the gulf between us. Yet our love and care want to bridge that gulf, to recognize the personhood of the other as equal to our own. And so we are torn between the higher and lower in us, between self-priorities and a larger Self that can include another person within its span.

So as our relationship deepens, we deepen, and the conflict moves from an outer one to an inner one, from arguments with our lover to the visceral questions of what we can let go of, what we are willing to give to make it work. As we side with love, non-love wanes in us, the self-referential mirror dissolves and we can see the other as a person equal in importance to us. We may even begin to see our partner, despite our many surface differences, as a person the same as us. This sometimes hard work of relationship is spiritual work in a very direct way. Love begins at home.

One method is to resolve to treat our partner with respect, always, both inwardly and outwardly. Never to put them down or treat them as less than our self, outwardly or inwardly. For example, never to inwardly complain, not even while putting on a false smile. This requires an enhanced degree of self-awareness to see our thoughts and emotions. And that sets the stage for us to let go of those destructive, self-centered tendencies, again and again. We respect this being that we are with, even and especially when they act in ways we might not deem worthy of respect. This is our inner work of relationship.

Another method is to consider our partner's interests, needs, and desires by proactively supporting their happiness. The consideration we show to our partner expresses and enhances our love. It can be difficult, though, because so often, to consider them more means to consider ourselves less. We give up something of ourselves in order to act in consideration of them. Of course some people go too far in this direction and wind up neglecting their own interests, needs, and desires to the detriment of the relationship. There is a right balance of considering the other person, even when it is difficult, and considering ourselves when possible and when necessary. Our own love can include both our lover and our self.

There is a quality that we can cultivate, a quality that both expresses our own love and awakens love in others. That quality is harmlessness. Letting go of fault-finding and making demands, acting with respect and consideration, leads naturally to harmlessness. And harmlessness leads to purity of heart. We feel comfortable around a harmless person, confident they will not bite us, verbally, emotionally, or otherwise. We can trust them. We do trust them. We love them.

All of these approaches also apply generally in our interactions with anyone, even with strangers. Frictions with people awaken us to the areas of our own self-centered identification. Consideration and respect become friendliness, generosity, and courtesy. Harmlessness gives way.

The upshot of such inner work is healthy relationships and the purity of heart that enables love. This is where spirituality meets life, in how we treat other people, outwardly and inwardly. For this week, practice consideration, respect, and harmlessness. In so doing, you will cultivate love.

26.4 Love of Nature
(Opening Our Heart: Part 4)

The natural world exerts an elemental attraction on us. Our own body is part of it, made from this Earth. Nature comes into our home in the form of pets, houseplants, sunlight, food, and as the very materials from which our dwelling is formed. As soon as we step outside, even in a densely urban setting, the sky is there, that spreading canopy of grace mirroring our limitless inner world. The songs of birds and frogs, cows and crickets, remind us of our visceral connection with all life. Yet what we see and hear of nature is only the surface of layer upon layer of unfathomed complexity, as told by science to our increasing our wonder. Forests and deserts, farmlands and mountains, oceans and rivers, each with its own ever-changing beauty, give us a feeling of rightness, that this remarkable world of nature embraces, enlivens, delights, inspires, and uplifts us. We feel its boundless freedom and unimaginable beauty awakening the same in us. We are children of this natural world from which we have arisen and in which we live.

Nature can teach us about time scales, from the short life of insects to the eons of galaxies. Stand for a few moments near a large tree and open your being to it. It stands and you stand. The tree has been rooted to its place for decades or even centuries. It stands in eternity. Slow down to the pace of the tree. Though lacking the capacity to move, except through its offspring, the tree lives. Its days come and go, as wind, rain, and drought nurture and assail it, as it cycles through the weeks and the seasons, the cold and the heat, the light and the dark. Yet the tree remains steadfast, sometimes bending, sometimes breaking, but always maintaining its stand in eternity. Be with the tree in the timeless time of seasons and years. Let the tree open your perception of the eternity within.

Nature can teach us to love. While the life of species can be robust, the life of individuals is fragile and fleeting, two qualities that awaken our compassion and love. The very young, of both animals and people, in their newness and purity, beauty and need, draw our hearts to them. Practice allowing your heart to open to animals, starting with the very young animals. For many people, this comes naturally, but for all of us it can be a source of light in our life.

Native peoples have held and still hold nature sacred. This does not necessarily mean that we need to worship nature as we would worship God. But certainly this creation we find ourselves a part of calls us to consider it and treat it as sacred. When we walk in nature we walk in hallowed precincts. In some places this is more obvious than in others. For example, there is an area in the Canyonlands National Park, below the Island in the Sky, nearly encircled by immense rock walls in hues of ochre, forming a natural temple that holds a correspondingly immense silence, a stillness that can lift you into the stillness of the eternal and the Divine.

But even in our own back yard, in our streets and local parks, nature displays its ever-changing beauty, adapting to conditions with the irrepressible force of life finding a way toward growth. Let the force of your own life bring you back to this precious moment, again and again, so that you may live in it. Let that force of life find its way through your heart.

The sun's light reveals nature to us. It illuminates all and stands as a symbol of the Divine beneficence, always giving. Let the outer light of the sun awaken you to the inner light within you. Let that inner sacred light pour forth.

For this week, open your heart to nature.

26.5 Love of Life
(Opening Our Heart: Part 5)

The key to a happy life isn't necessarily finding a way to do what you love, it is to love what you do. We can make room in our life to do some of what we love and consider ourselves fortunate thereby. But necessity, contingency, and service may constrain us to do other things, things we do not love to do. And we do them anyway, because we must or we should or we simply choose to do so.

Yes, sometimes we need to make a change in what we do, but at all times we benefit from learning to love what we are already doing. It begins with accepting our life as it is. We still work to improve it, but all the while we accept it, we do not reject it. But how is that possible, given that we have jobs to do and chores to complete, lines to wait in, difficult people to deal with, aches and pains, sweat and tears? Some of that is distasteful to us and we may wish we could avoid it. Yet there it is, life in its full unavoidable splendor. What to do?

Here our spiritual inner work can profoundly affect our experience of life. The mind of desire, with what it wants and what it does not want, leads us into rejection, into dissatisfaction. Spiritual practice offers many approaches to this: here are several.

First, we practice sensing our body. In sensing we have contact with our body, we become fully embodied. Unless we are in pain, our usual experience of our body is vague and neutral. Enhancing our contact with our body through direct and intentional awareness of it, through sensing, makes it vivid and even pleasurable. Through sensing, we revel in the mere fact of having a body. Through sensing, we love our body. And since our life is synonymous with having a body, through sensing we learn to love our life. During this life, we always have a body and thus always have the opportunity of sensing our body. Living in the sensitive energy, brings more aliveness to life. Through sensing, we can take pleasure in the simple fact of being in our body.

To practice sensing, begin in a quiet situation where you can focus exclusively on your body. Put all your attention in your right hand. Keep your attention there. When you notice that your attention has wandered off into thoughts or anything else, gently bring it back to your right hand. Be aware of the hand directly, from within the hand. Now notice the difference between your experience in this moment of your right hand and your left hand. Your right hand may feel more alive, warmer, more vivid. If so, this is due to the presence of the sensitive energy in your right hand, brought and awakened there by your sustained attention. This is sensing the right hand. With this taste, you can then practice sensing your right foot, left foot, left hand, right arm, right leg, left leg, left arm, all four limbs at once. Then without focusing on particular inner organs so as not to interfere with their instinctive functioning, sense your torso and head, and finally your whole body. This practice of sensing can be carried into your day, so that you sense while you go about your daily activities, except of course during life critical activities, such as driving, where you need all your attention on what you are doing. Sensing enhances your experience of what you are doing. It brings you more in touch with your life. It lifts you toward presence and away from being at the mercy of the reactive thoughts and emotions that obscure your natural joy of living.

Second, we practice presence, based in sensing our body, in visceral body awareness, but also incorporating the full content of consciousness, including awareness of our emotions, our thoughts, and all that our senses bring us of our environment. The core of presence, though, is our I, the direct experience that I am here, that I am aware of this moment, that I am doing what I am doing. Presence brings the innate pleasure of the bare fact that we exist. Here I am. This is not just awareness, mindfulness, but the ongoing recognition that there is someone who is aware, that I am here and aware of all this, that I am one who is aware, the one who does what I do. The more fully we come into our self, the more fully we love life. Our I connects our body, our world, with the deeper spirit within and beyond us. Here I am, in wonder, in joy, and in love.

Third, who or what is it in us that rejects aspects of our life, that blocks our appreciation of our life? We have in us mental and emotional patterns of judging, fault-finding, wanting more. Even in the midst of some wonderful experience, our inner critic stays aloof, sees what could be better, and looks forward to the next thing. In difficult experiences, we tend to fall into depressing or angry feelings, abetted by negative thoughts. What all such emotional and thought patterns have in common is that they refer to me or I: what I want or don't want, how this is affecting me or might affect me. This self-centered attitude is the source of so many of our difficulties, the source of our rejection of aspects of life. It is egoism and is very different than the true I of presence. These self-centered thoughts and emotions refer to me, but that me does not exist. It is the illusion of ego. The I of presence does exist; we can be that I. Seeing all this more and more clearly, as it operates in us, gives us a chance to move toward freedom. Ego may like, but it does not love. With ego, everything starts and ends in this constructed, illusory self. Love, on the other hand, starts beyond us. Love only comes when we allow it to come through us. We relax. See that we are not our thoughts, not our reactive emotions. See that we just are, and allow ourselves to love our life. Here we come back to presence, the enabling practice for just being, for just being in love.

For this week, sense your body and be the one who lives your life, so that you can practice loving your life.

26.6 Love for All
(Opening Our Heart: Part 6)

> *Love your neighbor as yourself.*
> (Matthew 22:39)

Some of us tend to walk around in our own little world, indifferent toward the people we see or meet. Others live in world of rudimentary emotions about people, inwardly reacting in a positive or negative, attraction or repulsion, envying or criticizing, liking or disliking way. But whether indifferent or reactive, our attitude to people is shaped by our habits and hormones, with little or nothing intentional about it. We see or meet someone, indifference or reaction takes over our heart, and we blindly accept that as a given, accept this automatic attitude as right and true and our own, and we let it color our perception of the other person. If we aspire to a spiritual inner life, then we aspire to move beyond indifference and reaction toward love.

There are degrees or levels of love. The automatic and reactive kinds depend on chemistry and preferences, on the likes and dislikes we have acquired. This results in admiration from a distance or in attachment, in wanting to have, to control, to keep the object of such love. With sensitive love we start to care about the other person, with less reference to how they feel about us or what they do for us. Conscious love is altogether different, for we start to recognize our sameness with other people, that their personhood is the same as our personhood, and that we share equally in the great field of consciousness. Ultimately, we aspire to the love that goes beyond sameness to enter unity, to recognition of the One Divine Will, our common and immediate source, from Whom we each have our own unique will.

To train our hearts toward love, we practice kindness,

courtesy, and respect toward all. These are essential. And there is also another effective practice that can help us open our heart toward love: the practice of well-wishing. It takes many forms in the various spiritual traditions, but the kernel of them all is to cultivate a heart-felt, positive, warmth toward others, even without speaking to them or meeting them. Well-wishing can be practiced with perfect strangers. We see other people and we inwardly wish them well, as sincerely and warmly as our heart and mind will allow. Intention matters; the well-wishing needs to have our full intention behind it. We need to mean it. By attempting to do so, we see the elements in us that block or pollute the purity of our well-wishing, we see our closed-heartedness, and we begin to let all that go.

That is the general approach toward well-wishing. There are specific techniques that can help bring us toward true well-wishing. They mostly include an inward affirmation of well-wishing directed toward someone. Here are a few traditional formulations.

May you be happy.
May you be well.
May you be safe.
May you be peaceful and at ease.
(Buddhist loving-kindness practice)

May the long time sun shine upon you,
All love surround you,
And the pure light within you
Guide your way on.
(Traditional Irish Blessing)

May the Lord bless you and protect you.
May the Lord's face shine upon you and be gracious to you.
May the Lord lift up His face to you and grant you peace.
(Jewish Priestly Blessing)

It is not the words, but the warmth of heart and goodness of intention that matter. The words, though, can help guide our heart and intention. Whether with one of these or your own formulation, practice well-wishing toward other people, even with people you do not know and only see from some distance. In close quarters, such as in a conversation, the verbal formulations, repeated inwardly, may actually interfere. So in those cases it is easier simply to warm your heart to the people you are with.

For this week, open your heart in well-wishing toward others.

26.7 Love of the Sacred
(Opening Our Heart: Part 7)

This awesome universe, all of these wonderful forms of life, and the remarkable gift of our own life with our senses, our brains, our consciousness and our ability to move, grasp, and the rest, all of that, if we allow it to, can awaken us to a sense of the Sacred. This sense of the Sacred does not depend on believing in a Creator. The sense of the Sacred is a perception, a heart-felt perception, and as such is close to the tangible reality around us, just like a sense of wonder. Any belief, including belief in a Creator, is a secondary mental construct, changeable and less grounded than a sense of the Sacred. For those who have or have had a direct perception of God or the Creator, or of the Sacred precincts surrounding the Divine, it is no longer just a belief but rather a tangible though ineffable experience.

One way to develop our sense of the Sacred and to open our higher perceptions is through prayer. Though belief is a mental construct, faith is not. Faith bypasses the thin certainty of belief in favor of direct perception. Belief may be dogmatic, but faith is not. Non-dogmatic belief can serve us as a tentative assumption that God exists, an assumption that allows faith to grow. We choose to believe, pending experience, but knowing it is just an assumption. Independent of our logical mind, faith is a perception that connects us with an unseen, unknown, but clearly Sacred reality. Though that perception may be clouded, lacking clarity in itself, it nevertheless transmits to us the Sacred character of what lies behind the perception. We can choose to believe, but faith chooses us. Our role is to allow faith to find its place in us, to welcome it, not to block it, not to disregard it. And the prime way to allow faith to grow is through prayer.

There is a close interaction between faith and prayer. Without faith we would not pray. But less obviously, faith can guide us in deepening our prayer. For the type of prayer whose purpose it is to connect us with the Divine, our major difficulty is not knowing what approach or direction to take. The space of our inner world is a vast territory, largely unknown to us. Somewhere within us is a path, a direction toward the Divine. Where is that? How do we move toward that? In silent, contemplative prayer, what do we do? Where do we go? Here faith as a perception can show us the way. Specifically, and in real time, as we enter this mode of prayer, we notice the response of our spiritual heart, our spiritual intuition, our faith. When it is warming up, we know we are headed in the right direction. When it stays unchanged, we know we are not moving. When it cools, we know we are going in the wrong direction. Thus faith acts as our compass in navigating toward the Sacred through our inner world. It shows us how to open our heart, our being, our soul to the Divine and to the sacred nourishment of the higher energies, how to enter the ultimate realms of prayer.

Faith, then, is the perception of Divine love, both that coming from Above and directed toward each of us, and that returning from us and directed toward the Divine. It is this love that moves us, that draws us into the spiritual journey, that speaks to us, not just in contemplative prayer but from every corner of our life, from nature, and from the people around us. One Will pervades this universe and this love awakens us to our share in that Will.

For this week, let faith guide you toward love.

PRESENCE TO GO

THE RADIANT MOUNTAIN

ABOUT THE AUTHOR

The son of Holocaust survivors, **Joseph Naft** was born in a Displaced Persons' camp in northern Italy in the aftermath of World War II. Recovering from wartime devastation, the family soon immigrated to the United States. That legacy of unspeakable evil engendered Naft's abiding interest in how the seemingly intractable problem of human violence can be resolved.

While childhood experiences of the spiritual depths set the stage for Naft's lifelong pursuit of the sacred, he first learned formal meditation practice in 1970. In 1974-75, he studied Buddhist, Sufi and Christian practices during a year in residence at J. G. Bennett's school of spirituality in England. Subsequently he pursued a range of spiritual practices in Turkey under the guidance of Sufis from the Mevlevi, Helveti, Rifa'i, and Naqshbandi orders. He has also undertaken extensive training in Buddhist meditation. Finally, his Jewish roots remain close to his heart, both the traditional form of Jewish worship as well as meditation methods from Kabbalah.

Through his ongoing spiritual quest, Naft gradually came to see that the ultimate answer to the tragedy of violence must entail a radical change and evolution of the inner life of all humanity. The leading edge of that change lives in those committed to spiritual practice.

Joseph Naft has taught meditation and spiritual practices since 1976. His other books include *Becoming You: Cultivating Spiritual Presence*, *The Sacred Art of Soul Making: Balance and Depth in Spiritual Practice* and two novels, *Agents of Peace* and *Restoring Our Soul*.

www.ingramcontent.com/pod-product-compliance
Lightning Source LLC
Chambersburg PA
CBHW071642160426
43195CB00012B/1333